HUMANISE

How [...] ours[...] change the world

Richard Docwra

Richard Docwra is a writer, coach and consultant aiming to apply his postgraduate academic background in psychology and philosophy to make the world and people's lives better. He's produced books, guides, podcasts and other publications on a wide range of topics. His books include *Life – and how to think about it* and *Modern life – as good as it gets?*, and his articles have appeared in a range of magazines and websites. He is also the host of podcasts 'Humans & Hope', 'The Big Questions with Copson and Docwra' and 'Making the world better'.

Richard also provides consultancy to organisations and movements seeking to change the world for the better. He is the founder and director of social change agency ChangeStar, as well as the not-for-profit organisation Life Squared, which helps people navigate the complexity of life so they can live in a happier, wiser and more meaningful way.

Visit www.richarddocwra.com and www.lifesquared.org.uk for more details and free resources.

By Richard Docwra

Books

Life – and how to think about it

The Life Trap

Modern Life – as good as it gets?

Booklets

Living Well

Manifesto for life

The problem with consumerism

How to be civilised

How to be alone (but not lonely)

How to think about death (and life)

How to achieve less

The story of energy

How to have a better Christmas

The modern life survival guide

The Amazing (how to find peak experience in everyday life)

How to eat and exercise well

How to live ethically

How to find meaning

Podcasts

Humans & Hope

The Big Questions – with Copson and Docwra

Making the world better

For Izzy – and a better future

First published in Great Britain in 2024 by Big Idea Publishing

Big Idea Publishing is a trading name of Docwra Ltd

Registered Office: Lewes House, 32 High Street, Lewes,
E Sussex BN7 2LX

Company Registration Number No. 7793032

All content copyright © Richard Docwra, 2024

www.richarddocwra.com

@RichardDocwra

Design by Richard Slade. Typeset in 10 on 14-point Century Schoolbook

The moral right of the author has been asserted.

All rights reserved. Without limiting the rights under copyright reserved above, no part of this publication may be reproduced, stored or introduced into a retrieval system, or transmitted, in any form or by any means (electronic, mechanical, photocopying, recording or otherwise), without the prior written permission of the copyright owner of this book.

A CIP catalogue record for this book is available from the British Library.

ISBN 978-1-8383396-3-0

eISBN 978-1-8383396-4-7

Contents

Introduction   1

Part 1 – How we think and behave

1. Our thinking has limits   10
2. Our thinking is adapted towards a purpose   16
3. We simplify the world   20
4. We are influenced   45
5. We deceive ourselves   77
6. Five key features of human thinking   88

Part 2 – The challenges we face

Health
7. Why do we lead such unhealthy lifestyles?   98
8. How to tackle the obesity crisis   138

Truth
9. Why do people have inaccurate beliefs?   169
10. How to defend the truth   205

Prejudice
11. Where do prejudice, hate and discrimination come from?   228
12. How to reduce prejudice and hate   258

Violence

13. Where do violence and aggression come from? 303
14. What are we capable of? The case of Battalion 101 303
15. How to reduce human violence 324

Climate Change

16. What is stopping us from addressing climate change? 343
17. How to tackle climate change more effectively 363

Part 3 – How to build a better future

18. Why human beings are struggling 384
19. Why we need scaffolding 403
20. What sort of world should we be seeking? 425
21. A world fit for humans 442

Introduction

'We're screwed'.

Have you ever felt this way about human beings, particularly in the last few years?

People are worried about politics at the moment. Democracy is under threat around the world. Hateful, extremist political ideas and parties are becoming more mainstream and seeing greater success. Millions of people are believing conspiracy theories or forming incorrect views of basic facts about the world. At the same time as all of this, our climate is warming at a speed that is shocking scientists, and we are abjectly failing to address it.

Liberals like me put our heads in our hands and ask what the problem is. Why is one group of people hateful and cruel to another because they look different or believe something different? Why do people vote for politicians who peddle discriminatory ideas and who obviously aren't going to help them? Can't some people discern truth from lies and conspiracy theories? Why are people buying bigger cars than ever[1] when there is increasing evidence all around them that climate change is happening?

We have certain expectations of ourselves as human beings. We think we should be unprejudiced, kind to each other, able to discern truth from lies and unwilling to vote for leaders who espouse intolerant and hateful policies. We think we should be able to take action to tackle global problems like climate change. When we don't meet these expectations, we tend to blame ourselves or particular groups or individuals for not rising to the challenge – often because we think they're either stupid or evil. Human beings are complex creatures, but we seem to be inclined to judge our species – and other members of it – in quite simplistic ways.

This book aims to approach this question from a different angle. Maybe we should stop blaming ourselves – and each other – for our failure to meet our expectations and address our challenges in the way we'd like, and start asking what it is about human beings that makes these things so difficult for us to achieve.

The first part of this book will explore what human beings are really like as creatures, using the latest evidence from psychology and neuroscience. It will argue that most people, including politicians, policy makers and members of the public, have an inaccurate and out-of-date view of how human beings think and behave, based on the assumption that we are rational creatures that just 'think' without many parameters or limitations to our thinking and behaviour. It will examine how we think and behave, and discover that human beings are not exclusively rational, nor 'good' nor 'evil' - we are simply a species of great ape that has evolved with specific traits and capacities in our thinking and behaviour that have both advantages and limitations. These traits can have major consequences for our lives, societies and ability to meet the challenges we face. It will set out a simple 5-point model to summarise our thinking and behavioural tendencies as creatures, describing human beings as LASID – *limited, adapted, simplifying, influenced and deceived*.

Part 2 will explore how we can use this knowledge of human beings to more effectively address some of the challenges we face as a species, including obesity, misinformation and conspiracy theories, prejudice, violence and climate change. It will ask why we struggle to address these challenges and consider how we can set more realistic views and expectations for ourselves, given the creatures we are. It will then show how we can harness our traits of human thinking and behaviour to approach these challenges in more effective ways.

A limited range of global challenges has been selected for discussion in Part 2. There are many other challenges facing human beings, and the same psychological analysis can be applied to these by anyone in academia or civil society who wishes to. Certain challenges, such as climate change, are practical, existential issues, while others represent hopes or aims that have been held for a long time by many humans, such as reducing prejudice and violence. Each chapter in Part 2 is of a reasonable length, because a certain level of detail is needed to understand each topic and explore it adequately. Care has been taken however to strike a balance between including enough detail and keeping the chapters as interesting and readable as possible. Hopefully this balance has been struck successfully, as the insights from each of these issues are fascinating. Despite their level of detail, each chapter in Part 2 can only provide a broad outline of its subject and is simply intended as an introduction to it and how human psychology can help us understand and address it more effectively.

Part 3 of the book will aim to pull together some of the common threads from the insights gained in Part 2, and will initially ask why we are struggling to deal with some of the challenges of the modern world. It will argue that human beings have evolved to think, behave and see the world in particular ways. These LASID traits helped us to survive and flourish in the external and social environments that our ancestors found ourselves in for most of our history, which were hunter-gatherer societies of small tribes. It is only around 12,000 years since human beings began the transition from hunter-gatherer tribes to agricultural societies – a miniscule amount of time in the overall history of our species. Yet the world we live in now, the challenges we face in it, the lives we lead and the expectations we have of ourselves have completely transformed in this relatively short time.

Human beings are adaptable creatures, and this ability to adapt is one of our sources of hope for the future. But the modern environment we have largely built for ourselves has become hostile to human flourishing, given the LASID creatures we are. Part 3 will explore why this is the case, and show how many of the structures, institutions and ideas surrounding us (from the prioritisation of economic growth to the business models of social media platforms that monetise people's attention) have been built either on a faulty, out-of-date idea of what human beings are like, or to serve goals other than enabling humans to flourish. As a result, they can exacerbate our problems and make it harder for us to tackle our challenges (such as stopping the rise in obesity) or meet our expectations of ourselves (such as minimising our tendency towards prejudice).

A core argument of the book is that we need to 'humanise' the societies we live within, including the ideas, structures and institutions that surround us, in order to move towards a global society fit for the LASID creatures we really are – one that prioritises the aim of human flourishing within the natural world we are part of. It will argue that, as LASID creatures, human beings need additional 'scaffolding' round us to protect our mental vulnerabilities and help us behave as the self-determined beings we want to be – for example, by regulating broadcast media channels to protect rather than exploit our vulnerabilities to negative tribalism. This additional scaffolding requires us to challenge a number of our most cherished principles and institutions, including our idea of freedom.

The final chapter of the book will explore the changes we need to make to our structures, institutions and ideas in order to humanise our world. It will include principles such as giving every child a good start in life, extending the content and duration of education, building a more equal society, promoting our cooperative capacities and reducing our tribal instincts, and protecting rather than exploiting our mental vulnerabilities. These principles result in a wide range of practical steps, including banning manipulative advertising and giving everyone the basic material resources they need for a healthy, dignified and self-determined life. Overall, the book argues that we need to build a society that helps human beings to be the best creatures we can be – including protecting our vulnerabilities towards prejudice, hate and untruth, and developing our amazing 'superpower' of cooperation and capacity for peaceful social interaction.

As this book will show, human beings often have different views about how the world should be, and how to achieve their vision of a better world. This book aims to provide as objective a view as possible of the psychological science describing how we think and behave, but when it moves towards setting out recommendations as to what we need to change in the world and how to do this, it is worth keeping my position as the author in mind, perhaps most notably that I am a middle-aged white man with a liberal left political disposition living in the Western world.

The ideas in this book matter. If we don't seek to understand humans better, we will never learn the most important lessons from the most horrific events in history – from genocides to mass starvation. By understanding human beings using the knowledge we have developed in the last 50 years, we can change our world for the better. And we urgently need this insight in the twenty-first century. We face unprecedented existential threats to the whole human race, like climate change, as well as a range of challenges that affect the lives of billions of people, from the rise of misinformation through to continuing mass violence and conflict. The rewards for finding better solutions to these challenges are therefore enormous. Not only could we save millions of lives and a lot of suffering, but we could also tip the balance of the collective human experience into a positive one, where the vast majority of us lead reasonable lives while we have the unique opportunity to do so.

Despite its potential to have a massive impact on the world, it could be argued that psychological science to date has been more concerned with achieving small, detailed fixes to people's behaviour than with analysing the bigger picture of wider society. Its powerful insights have been employed much more by the commercial sector than by groups in politics or civil society trying to seek a better world, and largely to nudge everyday behaviours of individuals. As the British Psychological Society notes[2], if psychology is to change the world it needs to go beyond the useful work it does in people's day-to-day lives and seek to act on a much wider, global stage, looking at the highest level social, political and institutional structures.

This book aims to do exactly this, by applying psychology and other disciplines to the big picture for our species – the human condition and how to build a society in which we can flourish. In tackling this big subject, it aims to build a bridge between academic ideas and the 'real world' of politics, civil society and people's daily lives. It aims to make accessible some of our vital academic knowledge about how people think and behave, both for interested lay readers and practitioners seeking social and political change, so that it can be applied to seek a better world.

If we want to tackle our challenges as a species effectively, we not only need to base our plans on an understanding of the creatures we are, but also be much more ambitious in the changes we are willing to propose. In this book there are some big and bold suggestions for how we could change society and the structures around us. I make no apology for this – as the evidence we have about how human beings think and behave tells us, we need these large-scale solutions if we want to address these challenges. Before we judge these ideas as being too radical or too ambitious, we should ask ourselves whether we really want to deal with these challenges and to make our lives better, or continue to fail to address them and resign ourselves to continued suffering. If we really want to build a world based on human flourishing within the one planet we have, this book offers some effective ways we can do it.

This book can therefore be seen as a thought experiment – an ambitious, wide-ranging and imperfect attempt to look at the big picture and consider what is possible when we apply big thinking from psychology to our global challenges as a species. The recommendations made within the book are broad, simplified and limited in their number for reasons of space, but aim to start a conversation and inspire people in all areas of life – from the public to policy makers – to think more boldly about the human future. It sets out an initial road map that can be followed and built on by others.

We need to challenge our views of ourselves, both as individuals and a species, as well as the societies, institutions and ideas we have built around ourselves. As the book will show, by building a better understanding of how human beings think and behave, we can carve out better lives and a better society – one that's fit for the creatures we really are.

Part 1
How we think and behave

Chapter 1
Our thinking has limits

In brief – As human beings, we don't see and experience our external reality and the world around us 'as it really is'. We only have a partial and particular view of reality, which is determined by our size, location and capabilities as creatures.

What are human beings really like?

Most of us think we can answer this question quite easily, as our day-to-day interactions with other people depend on us having an idea in our heads of how other people think and behave, which we use to inform our own reactions, behaviour and thinking. But is this picture of human beings really accurate?

Also, what about our own thinking and behaviour? Most of us don't think too deeply about how this operates – we just get on with daily life, and our thinking and behaviour just seem to come about naturally. As an individual you may feel that you 'just think' – making decisions for yourself rationally, and then taking action based on these decisions. You may also feel that the way you see the world reflects 'how things are' in reality. These ideas are simply not true. The reality is fascinating, humbling and important for our futures – and this book will explore it. Overall, it is likely that you have an inaccurate view of how human beings think and behave – and you are not alone in this. Most people, including politicians, teachers, health workers and economists, have an inaccurate view of human beings, seeing us as creatures that think in an unfettered, individual and rational way.

It is not surprising that we have this view of people, because it is the received wisdom (or dogma) that we have inherited from the last few hundred years of human thought, beginning with the Enlightenment. This is the period from the 1680s to 1820s in which scientific evidence became the primary way we sought to understand the world, and generated new ideas about human beings, philosophy and politics, including ideas such as individual freedom and the importance of rational thinking. Most of the history of psychology since this point has been dominated by the idea that people are rational, and make decisions by choosing the best option from a range of possibilities[3].

This view is however 300 years out of date. Our understanding of how humans think and behave has moved on a lot since then – particularly over the last century, as terrible events in human history like the Holocaust have challenged us to re-examine human nature and added a real sense of urgency to understand people better. This has spurred a lot of important experimentation in the field of psychology, and our understanding has been further accelerated by technological developments that can now enable us, at least to a certain extent, to 'see the brain thinking'.

The new picture of human beings that researchers have built as a result of this learning is radically different from the out-of-date one held by most people – including those who run our governments, economies and institutions. And, as this book will demonstrate, this difference between our mistaken assumptions about who we are and the actual reality has big implications, including for the expectations we have of ourselves, how we judge other people's behaviour and what a 'good society' that allows people to flourish should look like.

To understand why we have evolved to think and behave as we do, it is essential to understand the environment we have evolved to live within, as the brutal reality of evolution is that every living creature on Earth has developed and changed over time to find the most effective ways of passing on its genes within the environment in which it finds itself. This doesn't mean that we – or any other creatures – have evolved to a pre-determined plan or set of aims; it simply means that we adapt to best suit our environment. In this case, 'environment' does not just mean the characteristics of the physical world around us, but also the external things we encounter in that world – from stimulation such as light and sound, through to the other creatures (including members of our own species) that we encounter in our lives.

The next chapter will look in more detail at the specific environment we have evolved to live in. Before this, it is important to understand the broadest possible idea of what we mean by 'the environment we live in'.

Pause for a moment. Look around you – you can see your environment. This book in front of you, the sun in the sky and the apples in the fruit bowl. You can hear the traffic outside, feel yourself breathing, smell the flowers from the garden and taste the grapes that you're eating. As a result, you may feel that you're experiencing reality 'as it is'. But you're only seeing this environment from a very specific point of view – as a human being. And that is not objective reality.

This point can be quite difficult for human beings to get our heads around. The majority of events and interactions in the universe take place at scales and in dimensions that we don't have the cognitive equipment to see or experience – from large parts of the electromagnetic spectrum through to the subatomic level of particles. We only therefore interact with a tiny proportion of the enormous range of variables in the cosmos. This means we can only end up with an idea of how the universe is *for us*.

In reality then, our viewpoint on our environment is limited. We are looking at the world with blinkers on. This is partly due to our limited sensory equipment and processing power as creatures, partly down to our size and partly due to our situation as creatures viewing things from a single viewpoint and location.

First, consider the capacity of our brains. According to the physicist Michio Kaku, the human brain is the most complicated object in the known universe[4]. Despite this, there are limits to the capacity and processing power of our brains, as well as to the amount of energy that our bodies can gather to power them. This can be illustrated by a brief primer on how our brains work. Everything we think about in the brain, and therefore do as a result, is driven by the binary status of each of our 100 billion brain cells (neurons). Whether a neuron fires or not determines what we think and do – whether it's remembering something, feeling scared of the school bully, deciding to eat a chocolate bar or posting a hateful message on social media. This is a remarkable fact about our existence and experience of life that is almost impossible to believe, until you see the number and variety of neurons we have, the number of connections in the brain, how complex it is, and the length of time over which it has evolved.

Our thinking and behaviour is therefore built from a very simple basic principle in our brain cells ('activate or don't activate'), and we have evolved some incredible ways of using this simple binary process to achieve a lot of complexity and get the most out of the power of our brains. Despite the ingeniousness and beauty of how our brains make the most of this binary process, there are limits to what we can do with it. As a result, thinking is not just a magical process that happens without any boundaries – it takes place within certain physical parameters, and these can limit the power of our brains and what we can achieve with them.

Our senses are also remarkable, but limited. We experience 'reality' as a physical world and with objects, sounds and sensations because this is how our sensory equipment allows us to experience it. If we had different equipment, such as the capacity for echolocation possessed by bats, we'd experience and see it in a different way. This principle of 'you can only experience reality with what you've got' applies to every living creature.

We also occupy a particular position in the world and universe, which contributes to our limited perspective and can make it hard for us to see things beyond our current location. For example, from our perspective, as medium-sized creatures living on the surface of the planet, we believed for many centuries (once we had got round to thinking about these things) that the Earth was flat.

Our experience of things is subjective, but we often forget this. For example, time is relative, but human beings only live for a limited time. If our lives were a great deal longer than they are, we would see the world quite differently. For example, we'd just see a stone as a temporary coming together of particles of sand.

We are also prone to experiencing the world in ways that are quite unusual and feel (to us, as the creatures that experience them) more than just the sum of the parts of the chemical, physical or subatomic reactions that caused them. These phenomena may simply be emergent properties of the creatures we are, but they feel central to our experience of life, including our feeling of having a 'self', our experience of time, and possibly also our sense of consciousness.

These brief examples illustrate the first big idea that should help overturn our common picture of how human beings think. *We do not see reality 'as it is'. We only have a partial view of it – determined by our size, location and capabilities as creatures.* In addition, just because you experience something in a particular way, that doesn't mean that's 'how things are' or 'all there is' in the reality around you. By recognising these points, we can help to avoid mistaken ideas of how we think.

Once we have come to terms with the rather shattering revelation that we don't see reality exactly 'how it is', we can move on to start describing how we actually do see the world, and the way this perception works.

Chapter 2
Our thinking is adapted towards a purpose

In brief – Our ability to think is directed at a specific, restricted set of aims, which ultimately enable us to pass our genes down the line within a specific environment. Our focus on these aims, such as the need to simplify the world, can direct our thinking capabilities away from other aims, including those that we might value within particular cultures or at specific times, such as the social goal of not judging other people before we have got to know them.

Another assumption many of us make is that our brains just think freely, without any parameters, and process whatever information is in front of us in the most effective way possible. But this is simply not the case, and this leads us to our second big idea – *our thinking takes place within specific parameters*.

It might be a good time to turn to a computer analogy to illustrate this. Before doing so, it is worth mentioning that the idea of seeing the mind as a computer has been somewhat discredited over the years, as the comparison fails to convey the extraordinary flexibility and subtleties of the brain. The computer analogy can be problematic when it leads people to think of human beings in the old, traditional way – as rational calculating machines. Computer analogies can however be useful in helping us to picture the brain as a processing unit with finite capacity, which in some ways it is.

The computer analogy can be useful to illustrate the idea that 'we think for a purpose', as it shows us that any information processing unit – whether it's a computer or your brain – needs some sort of operating system in order to function effectively. The term 'operating system' means a structure or set of parameters within which the brain's processing happens, that direct the processing to undertake specific functions or tasks.

For example, if you bought a computer without an operating system, it wouldn't be able to do anything. This is because although it has information processing capacity, it doesn't have any rules or processes to guide what it should be processing. So, by installing an operating system (such as Microsoft Windows) you are focusing and restricting the functions of the computer but at the same time enabling it to actually function by giving it some specific rules and parameters to work within. For example, on a computer these would include booting up, presenting a set of programmes that you can use for specific tasks (from word processing to surfing the web), and presenting these in a language and format that people can use and understand.

Like a computer, human beings need an operating system in order to function, and we have one. In our case, our operating system is incredibly sophisticated, and we're only at the start of understanding how it works in detail. But it appears that it does the following:

- Automatic functions – to keep the body alive and functioning, such as breathing, blood flow, balance and movement.
- Sensory functions – sight, hearing, taste, touch and smell

- Thinking and behavioural functions – this is the area of thinking that we are exploring in this book. It includes decision making – how we make plans and respond to the world, social functions – such as the capacity for speech and how we relate to other human beings, and information processing, such as memory and learning.

So, in reality the thinking and processing conducted by our brains is set up to be directed *at* something – it takes place in order to achieve a specific overall aim, which is to enable us to pass our genes down the line within a specific environment. This is the environment that our tribal, hunter-gatherer ancestors lived in for millions of years, up to around 12,000 years ago when we formed agricultural societies.

The functions that have evolved within our brains to help to serve this aim have to do so within its finite capacity, which means that every functional area has evolved with its own range of 'fixes' to maximise the effectiveness of the core functions to serve our overall aim. This includes the need to simplify the world, make sense of it and identify and respond to any threats to our survival. These aims and the fixes we have evolved to address them will be explored in more detail as the book progresses.

As a necessary consequence of our brain's limited functioning being directed towards particular aims, it is also directed *away from* other aims. This is an important point to acknowledge when we are considering how we think and behave, as these other aims that our thinking *isn't* directed towards could include things we have come to value within the culture and world we live within, such as the desire to seek the truth on an issue rather than go along with majority opinion, or the desire to avoid adopting a prejudiced or judgemental view of other people. It will be seen throughout this book that this can be one of the factors that can make it hard for us to meet some of the challenges we face and expectations that we set ourselves in the modern world. This does not necessarily mean, however, that we are doomed to behave in these ways forever and to fail to meet our modern challenges or expectations.

And, just to repeat, one of the core problems of modern humanity is that most people don't realise that we have these parameters to our thinking, which leads them to assume that we are rational creatures that will always just seek to make the most rational decisions, from pure, cold calculation. It is a mistake that we – as individuals, politicians and decision makers in all walks of life – have continued to make over the last 300 years and which has blighted our lives and societies as a result.

If we can get our heads around the idea that humans function within a particular range of thinking and behavioural parameters, this starts us off on the journey of developing a more accurate picture of how we actually think and behave – and what is possible.

Chapter 3
We simplify the world

In brief – The world we live within is complex, so human brains need to simplify it in order for us to be able to survive in it and make sense of it, and avoid using too much valuable energy doing this. We use several methods to simplify things, including building 'models' of the world in our heads, and employing two levels of thinking – quick, automatic, energy-saving thought processes and more rational, effortful reasoning. These simplifications can lead us to a range of inaccuracies and biases in our thinking, which can have major consequences for our individual lives and societies.

In 2021, physicist Melvyn Vopson attempted an audacious challenge. He wanted to calculate the amount of information contained in the visible universe[5]. He determined that each particle contained around 1.5 bits (units) of information, and therefore that around 6×10^{80} bits of information are stored in all the particles of matter in the observable universe. This is
75,000,000,000,000,000,000,000,000,000,000,000,000,000,000,000,000,000,000,000,000,000,000,000,000,000,000,000,000,000,000,000,000,000,000,000,000,000,000,000,000,000,000,000,000,000,000,000,000,000,000,000,000,000,000,000,000,000,000,000,000,000,000,000,000,000,000,000,000,000 (7.5 octodecillion)

zettabytes – a number that is incomprehensibly larger than the 64.2 zettabytes of information produced in the world during one year (2020)[6].

To put it mildly then, there is a lot of information in the universe. Yet our senses only send *11 million* bits of this information per second to our brains for processing. We are therefore extracting only a minute amount of the information available to us at any given point. In addition, of this 11 million bits of information coming in through the senses, our conscious mind can only process around 50 bits of information per second.

There is therefore simply too much information and complexity available 'out there' at any one moment for our senses to absorb and our brains to make sense of. So, our brains have to help us prioritise what we devote our focus – and our limited processing capacity – to. A third big idea is therefore that even within the limited view of reality that we each have as creatures, *we need to simplify the world in order to deal with it.*

Another reason our brains need to simplify things is that thinking takes up a lot of energy, and our brain is one of the most energy-intensive parts of our body, using 20 percent of all the calories that we burn. We therefore need to use this organ as efficiently as possible, in order to minimise the number of calories we need to consume to keep ourselves functioning. This is because seeking calories can be both energy-intensive and dangerous (or at least, it was when we were hunter-gatherers), and take us away from the key aim of surviving to pass on our genes.

Our brains have evolved several methods of using the information we gain from the external world as efficiently as possible, including building simplified models of reality in our minds and having a two-level approach to processing information. These processes of simplification help us function and survive in the world, but also bring some disadvantages and blind spots, which this chapter will examine, including greater sensitivity to potential losses than potential gains, and a tendency to seek information to confirm our own views rather than seek alternative explanations. The first type of simplification to explore relates to how we perceive the reality we live within.

We build models of the world in our minds

The psychologist Daniel Kahneman argued that the picture of the world we have in our heads is not an exact replica of reality[7]. Not only do we have an incomplete view of reality, given our particular capacities as creatures, as noted earlier, but also our minds are not wired to see reality as it really is. Instead, our brains construct models of the external world in order to simplify and translate the data into a form that is useful to help us survive and achieve our goals.

Professor Bruce Hood takes this further, noting how as part of its simulation of the world, our brain adds missing information and attempts to clarify unclear signals[8]. It also only uses a small sample of everything that's happening around us. So, we have to rely on educated guesses to build our models of reality, given our lack of time, resources and information to build a full and accurate picture, and this can mean we end up with a fairly rough, partial and sometimes inaccurate view of our world.

A good example of this model building is our use of concepts and associations[9]. Our brains aim to represent the world around us by making associations and links between different types of ideas and categories in our minds. The activation of these associations and links is automatic and ongoing[10]. This helps us to build mental models to classify the things we encounter in the world and represent these in our minds, so that we can use information quickly and effectively when we need to. For example, we use concepts to represent a group of related items so we don't have to store information on every individual object in that group. By storing a broader abstract representation of these items – for example, 'plants' – we can understand what we are seeing without having to store the detailed information of whether it is a Venus flytrap or an orchid.

Simply having these classifications and representations does not help us decide how to use them though. We use schemas to do this – structures in our long-term memory that help us process and use information in order to help us navigate the complex world we live in. They help us make sense of events in the world by providing an idea of the rules, objects and behaviours that apply to particular situations. For example, we may have a schema that tells us we need to queue when we are waiting to be served in a shop. If we don't follow this rule, we may not achieve our aim of getting served, as the shopkeeper may ask us to leave if we pushed in. Schemas affect a range of aspects of our thinking, including our ability to recall information. They sometimes operate at an unconscious, automatic level.

Schemas are useful because they help us to minimise the amount of attention (and therefore energy resources) we need to use to get around familiar environments and deal with common situations. They also provide us with acceptable ways to behave within particular contexts and group environments, so that we fit into these groups and societies – something that the next chapter will show is critical to us. Additionally, they enable us to identify dangerous or unusual situations, helping us to boost our chances of survival. So, there are a number of evolutionarily adaptive reasons why we have them.

Schemas can however have consequences that may not be so useful for us, fixing us into patterns of thought and ways of responding to situations that aren't always accurate or helpful. For example, schemas help us understand people's roles within particular contexts, and this may lead us into inaccurate, stereotypical views, such as applying gender roles. Studies have found that children who have been asked to draw a scientist tend to draw men rather than women as part of their stereotypical image of a scientist, because in their minds scientists are associated with being male. Stereotypes like this can have several negative effects: first, they can build biases into our institutions and culture – for example, a study[11] found that the schema of women being inferior musicians stopped conductors from evaluating musician's audition performances accurately. Second, they can also give individuals the belief that they are not cut out for particular roles – for example, by the time they are 6 years old, girls are less likely to believe they are very intelligent and then less likely to engage in activities associated with high intelligence[12]. These factors, and more, show how schemas can restrict and bias our thinking as individuals and societies, which can in turn be evolutionarily maladaptive in the modern world, as they can lead to fewer opportunities and greater danger in life, and overall less potential to lead a successful life – which in evolutionary terms is one in which we pass on our genes.

The aim of this more detailed explanation of concepts and schemas is to emphasise the fact that our perception of the world doesn't get handed to us on a plate – our brains have to develop processes to make sense of things, including building conceptual models that are not the same as the reality we live within.

We use two levels of thinking

Another way in which we simplify the world is in the decisions and judgements we make, and how we approach problem solving – from which house to buy through to how to respond to an insult.

As previously argued, throughout most of the history of psychology, it was thought that human beings make decisions in rational ways – in other words, we consider the range of alternatives available and choose the best one. Research since the 1970s has shown that this is not the case. Many scientists now like to describe the way we think about judgements and decisions as being split into two types of thinking. One of the most popular ways of naming them is 'System 1' and 'System 2', as popularised by psychologist Daniel Kahneman in his classic book *Thinking, fast and slow*[13]. Kahneman's work has massively influenced how we understand human thinking over the last 40 years. It is important to note that these two systems are separated in a conceptual way only – they are not specific, separate parts of the brain, but just a simpler way to describe how we think and behave.

System 1 is classed as quick, automatic, instinctive thinking that is involuntary and where there is little effort made. It uses experience and habit to make choices. When you see a stranger across the road and feel that you don't like the look of them, this is your System 1 thinking at work. System 2 thinking is the more conscious, rational reasoning side of us that makes deliberate choices. It gives attention to thinking activities that require effort, including calculations and regulating the intuitions and impulses of System 1. This thinking is slower and more effortful. So, for the remainder of the book, think of System 1 as 'quick, automatic, energy-saving thinking' and System 2 as 'slow, rational, effortful thinking'. These systems will now be explored in more detail, including how they work and why they work like this. This detail matters as it helps to open up the bigger explanation for why we behave as we do in different situations and the creatures we really are.

System 1 thinking

Our System 1 thinking is constantly switched on and working. It is automatically assessing the environment around us, trying to make sense of the world and to identify and solve any challenges we face to our survival, including dangerous situations. To do this, it is constantly generating impressions, feelings and intentions that provide the basis for the beliefs and decisions we produce with System 2. If its impulses are endorsed by System 2 (whether we are aware of this or not), they turn into actions (which we feel are taken voluntarily), and if its intuitions and intentions are endorsed, they can become beliefs.

We have all experienced the feeling of being able to do many tasks on 'autopilot'. This is just the tip of the iceberg of our System 1 thinking – most of which takes place unconsciously without us knowing it. For example, driving a car along the road is an incredibly complex task, yet we can do that whilst listening to music on the radio or planning the day ahead in our minds. Our automatic System 1 thinking does not just cover motor skills like controlling a car's movements, but all sorts of judgements and decisions we make in our lives, including how we perceive the world, evaluate evidence, what we remember, and how we regard other people.

System 1 thinking has been described by Daniel Kahneman as 'a machine for jumping to conclusions' – its aim is to make speedy judgements in order to make sense of things as quickly as possible. These judgements cover an incredibly wide range of situations – including finding patterns and associations between words, recognising that one object is closer than another and basic assessments such as the ability to discriminate a friend from a potential threat. For example, we have the capacity to evaluate whether a stranger is a threat from a quick glance at their face, in which we make a near-instant assessment of how dominant and how trustworthy they appear[14].

Although System 1 thinking often works effectively, the tools it uses to make these quick, energy-efficient, automatic judgements can bring inaccuracies and biases in our thinking that can lead to important consequences, some of which will be explored shortly, as well as throughout the book.

System 2 thinking

In contrast to our permanently active, energy-efficient System 1 thinking, System 2 thinking allocates attention when it is necessary to mental activities that require effort, such as calculations. It can be seen as the conscious, reasoning part of us that many people would suggest represents how they think[15]. A core function of System 2 thinking is to monitor the thoughts, ideas and actions suggested by System 1, and to regulate or modify these impulses when required. This might include helping us to deal with an unfamiliar challenge or situation, solve a puzzle that requires rational thought and exercise self-control – for example, overcoming our instinct to insult someone when they have been unkind to us.

Psychologist Jonathan Haidt developed a nice metaphor to describe the relationship between the two types of thinking[16] – of the automatic thinking being an elephant, and the rational thinking being a rider sitting on top of that elephant. The elephant, being a powerful creature, makes the basic decisions on where it's going to go, but the rider, although much smaller and less powerful, is able (to some extent) to see where the elephant is going and help steer it in the right direction.

To continue the car analogy where System 1 was in control while driving, our brains will switch to System 2 when the situation changes and demands our conscious attention – for example, if the traffic slows down and we need to brake. In this situation we move our attention away from the music or the planning and towards the more important need to focus it on driving.

The question of how to allocate our attention is an important influence on the way we think. System 2 thinking requires a level of attention, but our attention is a finite resource, as it uses a lot of energy. We can therefore only successfully concentrate on one System 2 activity at a time – so, for example, we can't park our car in a tight space whilst trying to calculate the product of 323 x 34. Our System 2 thinking is also disrupted when our attention is withdrawn.

When we focus attention carefully on a particular System 2 task, this can effectively remove our attention from anything else, making us unaware of other things going on around us. You can find a classic demonstration of this, devised by psychologists Christopher Chabris and Daniel Simons, if you search online for 'selective attention test' and watch the first video by Daniel Simons. Follow the instructions on the screen as the video plays, but try not to look at the explanation in the comments below the video before you watch it!

Another consequence of us diverting our attention (and cognitive energy) to a complex System 2 task is that this leaves us with less capacity to monitor and regulate our System 1 impulses and judgements, which can mean that they are let loose more than they would otherwise be. For example, we are more likely to succumb to temptation – studies have shown that, if people are offered a choice of dessert of healthy fruit salad or unhealthy chocolate cake, they are more likely to select the chocolate cake if they have been told to focus their attention on remembering a 7-digit number. Research has also shown that we are more likely to use sexist language and make selfish choices when we are cognitively busy.

Why we operate between System 1 and System 2

The question of how to allocate our attention is linked to one of the biggest issues in our evolutionary history – why we think the way we do.

As has already been shown, our ability to think has evolved to help us survive in the environment we found ourselves in for most of the period of our species' existence. To do this we need to make sense of the world and solve challenges to our survival, but not only this – we need to do so in a way that is as effective as possible using the physical and mental capacities we have.

Our brains are therefore focused on the need to minimise our mental effort. This helps us to save the valuable and finite supply of energy we have. This principle underlies not only how our System 1 thinking works in practice but also how our Systems 1 and 2 work in combination with each other.

As well as being quick and automatic, System 1 thinking involves relatively little cognitive effort. It is therefore very efficient in terms of the energy it expends, and this is why it pays to have it 'switched on' constantly, as the main part of our mind that is monitoring the world around us. It can however be prone to biases and errors because of the way it is set up to run like this, as will be demonstrated shortly. System 2 thinking is however much more effortful, which in turn requires further energy. It may be more accurate and analytical than System 1, but it wouldn't be feasible to use System 2 all the time, or for it to constantly monitor System 1, because it would use too much energy.

Because System 1 is always 'on' and System 2 can't always be 'on', it can be difficult to prevent all the biases and errors of judgement we might make, so our minds have evolved to be something of a compromise to make best use of the mental capacity we have – we largely use System 1 thinking as it is quick and efficient, and we accept the mistakes and biases it brings because it largely works well and serves us well for daily survival. For example, going back to our ability to identify a friend from a threat with a glance at a stranger's face, this clearly is advantageous to our survival, even if it may be a little inaccurate sometimes. System 2 takes over when things get difficult, but System 1 usually has the final say. Although this usually works well, there are several consequences to this compromise that affect our lives and societies, which will be explored in more detail as the book progresses.

For now, it is useful to recognise the general principle that activities that are demanding for System 2 take up a lot of our mental energy, and this cognitive effort can be unpleasant for us – just think about the strain you feel when concentrating very hard on something complex. As a result, Daniel Kahneman argued that people seek to avoid cognitive effort as much as possible – in other words, we are 'cognitive misers'. This can lead people into placing too much faith in the intuitions and judgements of their System 1 thinking, in order to avoid the challenging cognitive effort of System 2 thinking. This in turn can lead to a range of inaccurate judgements, dubious decisions and poor reasoning. For example, when people believe a conclusion is true, they are likely to believe the arguments given to support it, even if these are spurious[17]. These errors of thinking have consequences in many areas of our lives, and will appear in many of the challenges that will be explored in Part 2.

Many of us tend to think that our decisions, reactions and behaviour are primarily driven by System 2 behaviour, and are rational and considered. One of the great discoveries of psychological science in the twentieth century is that this is not the case, and much more of our behaviour than we think is driven by automatic, System 1 thinking – most of it, in fact.

This makes sense, given the need for us to limit our cognitive effort, which we discussed earlier. If we can find a way to send most of our decision making to the quick, low-effort part of our brains, then this helps us preserve valuable energy. We can use the more energy-intensive, rational side of our brain when we encounter tasks that warrant this additional effort. This suggests that this is worth the compromises we make to the accuracy of some of our judgements and decisions.

It is important to emphasise that this use of System 1 and 2 thinking, and our brain's tendency to seek to simplify things, is a necessity to help us achieve our evolutionary objectives as creatures within the capacities we have. The compromises that have been made to achieve this – in terms of our ability to make judgements, think accurately and behave rationally – should not lead us to impose morally negative labels on ourselves such as 'imperfect', 'bad' or anything else. As we will see later in the book, these negative judgements of human beings arise when we develop other aims and expectations beyond these evolutionary ones – such as global co-operation and non-violence. We can however describe some of these compromises as 'weaknesses' or 'vulnerabilities' when seeking to achieve accuracy in particular tasks – for example, in calculating probabilities. Again, these compromises are here because we didn't need to complete these tasks accurately in the environment we evolved to live within, not because we are somehow faulty creatures.

Our thinking tools and their limitations

Our minds are therefore a compromise between the dominance of quick, automatic System 1 thinking and effortful, energy-intensive System 2 thinking, and this usually works well. There are however several consequences to this compromise that affect our lives and societies. The time- and energy-saving heuristics that bring significant advantages to our survival can have drawbacks that can affect our thinking and behaviour in other areas, including our capacity for decision making.

The next section will explore in more detail how System 1 and 2 thinking work and the potential drawbacks this can have, as well as some of the heuristics and biases that emerge in System 1 thinking. It will only explore an initial selection of these, as others will appear in Part 2 in relation to some of the modern challenges we face.

Some System 1 tools

Our quick, automatic System 1 thinking has some ingenious functionality to help us survive and make sense of the world, but this can also bring potential drawbacks for how we think and behave. Below are some examples of these tools.

Norms and violations[18]

As the brain develops its links and associations between different ideas it has stored, it identifies patterns between them, which build to represent the picture of events in our lives. Associations and ideas we encounter regularly are established as 'norms' in our minds – normal events or occurrences we would expect to see (to be clear, these norms should not be confused with social, cultural or moral norms, which will be discussed later). This helps us to interpret and understand our lives in the present as well as set expectations for the future. Within this, our minds are highly attuned to detecting any violations of normality – whether these are unusual events, words, sights or anything else – and do this incredibly quickly. For example, when participants in an experiment heard the sentence 'Earth revolves around the trouble every year', their brains were found to pick up on the norm violation within two-tenths of a second of the word that didn't fit – 'trouble'[19].

One can imagine how this tool has an evolutionary benefit – as we scan our environment for threats, anything new or unusual that occurs needs to be identified and assessed instantly in order to help us survive and counter any dangers. Our sensitivity to norm violations has other uses, as we have a shared set of norms for categories of information that we encounter, which enables us to communicate about them using a shared understanding of what each thing roughly involves. For example, we know a mouse is typically small and an elephant is large, so we quickly understand the meaning of a joke that involves the two creatures, or are alerted if a norm has been violated with a description of a large mouse or tiny elephant.

Our useful capacity to see patterns and develop norms also has the potential to mislead us – for example, if we develop norms or patterns that are insufficiently detailed to be accurate or lead us to judgemental or stereotypical views – such as claiming that old people are slow drivers. We can be alert to some of the norms that we set ourselves, but many can be unconscious and lead us to prejudices that we are unaware of. These unconscious biases will be explored in more detail in the next chapter.

Priming[20]

The associative network we use to make sense of the world brings another aspect of our thought – the fact that associations between concepts and words can change the way we think, feel and behave in other areas. These are called *priming effects*. For example, if you are given the word 'eat', for a short time you are more likely to complete the partial word 'SO_P' as 'SOUP' than 'SOAP'. These priming effects extend to our actions too. A famous experiment by psychologist John Bargh in 1996 asked students at his university to assemble sentences from a set of five words. For one of these groups, the words related to old age, but didn't explicitly mention this – e.g. 'bald, grey, wrinkle' etc.[21] The participants were then asked to walk down the corridor to complete another task, and without the participants knowing, the experimenters timed how long it took them to complete this walk. They found that the participants who had built words from the selections related to being elderly walked down the corridor considerably more slowly than the others. So, although they were not consciously aware of it, their actions had been primed by some ideas – the *ideomotor effect*.

Priming may have significant consequences for our thinking and behaviour in real life – from the food we choose to eat to how we decide to vote. Minor, barely noticeable tweaks to the context we live within can have significant effects on our thinking and behaviour, which in turn can have big consequences for society. For example, they can influence our voting and the results of elections. In the US state of Arizona in 2000, the levels of public support for policies to increase the funding for schools were much greater when the polling station was located within a school than in another nearby place. These priming effects can also happen unconsciously, and are therefore just one example of how our thinking is influenced by things that we may simply not be aware of.

'What you see is all there is'[22]

Our System 1 thinking aims to build a coherent story, even when information is scarce. So, when we have information available, we make decisions just on the basis of the information we have, rather than asking how we might reach a more accurate answer. This mental tendency is known as 'What you see is all there is' (or, more simply, WYSIATI). For example, if you are told 'John has a fiery temper', and someone asks you whether John is a good person or not, you're likely to judge him based on that one piece of information alone, but if the following additional information was added 'he's also incredibly kind and fun to be around', this extra information would change your judgement again. We therefore don't consider the possibility that crucial information might be missing.

WYSIATI enables us to think quickly, use less energy and make some sense of a complex world with incomplete information. It can however cause a range of biases and weaknesses in our thinking such as over-confidence in our beliefs, even when they are only based on very little information, as our confidence in them is based on the coherence of the story we tell ourselves, not the level or quality of information. These biases in turn can have significant consequences in our lives and society, including in political decisions, our attitudes towards other groups of people and legal matters. For example, a study conducted by Amos Tversky at Stanford University[23] asked participants to consider an alleged episode of intimidation of a union representative by a shop manager. One group heard both sides of the evidence – from the defence and the prosecution – and the other heard just one side. The latter group of participants were also aware that they had heard only one side of the argument. The study found that one-sided evidence had a marked effect on people's judgements, even though they could in principle create an argument in their own heads for the side that they hadn't heard. It also found that the participants who had only heard one side of the argument were more confident of their judgements than those who had heard both.

Causality[24]

We have a capacity from birth to develop impressions of causality – using System 1 thinking. This is not the same as seeing a cause and corresponding effect and putting them together, as this latter reasoning about causality is undertaken by System 2.

This capacity for building impressions of causality was demonstrated by a short animated film made by psychologists Heider and Simmel in 1944, in which a small triangle, large triangle and circle move around the screen. On watching the film, you gain a clear sense of emotion and intention from the movements of the shapes – the large triangle is bullying the smaller one, and the circle is scared of what's happening. All of this is in your mind however – it is simply shapes moving on the screen. Your brain is seeing the shapes as individual agents, and assigning personalities and intentions to their movements. Even infants under one year old can attribute intentions like this, being able to identify bullies and the bullied.

One of the drawbacks of this tendency to attribute causality is that we are inclined to use causal thinking at inappropriate times, when we should be using statistical reasoning instead. For example, someone believing that every time they go out without a coat, it rains – attributing the cause of the rain to the coat rather than atmospheric conditions, and failing to compare the number of times it rains with the number of times they wear their coat. System 1 is unable to do statistical reasoning, but System 2 is, although most people do not receive the training needed to use it properly.

Attitudes and emotions

Our attitudes also help us save cognitive energy, as they mean we don't have to establish from scratch what we feel about something. These can be seen as another form of heuristic. Emotions also affect people's decisions and judgements in a number of ways[25]. They serve as heuristic guides, helping us make complex decisions quicker and with less effort. For example, we use our anticipatory prediction of our future emotional states to guide how we'd feel if we took particular decisions, such as staying with a boyfriend or dumping him. Like other heuristics though, emotions have the potential to lead us away from what might be the most rational or effective decision. For example, we are poor at affective forecasting – guessing how we will feel about something in the future. We tend to overestimate how happy we will feel after positive events such as winning a sporting event or getting married[26], and overestimate how bad we will feel after negative events such as becoming ill or splitting up with a partner[27]. After negative events, we find ways to rationalise what has happened to us and to adapt to the new reality, but we often do not realise this beforehand, or take it into account when anticipating our feelings following future negative events.[28]

One theory suggests that people use their current moods to dictate their judgements and decisions, for example on films or other people, even if they aren't aware of what current mood they are in or how that mood came about. As you can imagine, this can mean that we make some important decisions and behaviours entirely on the basis of temporary, fleeting moods, which may not be the most effective way of living. If people can become more aware of the sources of their moods, they can learn to make their decisions less influenced by their moods.

Heuristics and biases

Daniel Kahneman and his long-term collaborator Amos Tversky discovered that people use a range of mental shortcuts (called heuristics) to help them make decisions quickly and efficiently – essentially enabling us to respond automatically without any real sense of effort. Like the other tools our minds use to simplify the world that have been discussed above, these heuristics can come at a price – bringing biases and inaccuracies in our thinking, including tendencies to favour our existing beliefs, to care more about losses than gains, be overconfident in our predictions, and much more. Although this all happens in all of us at an individual level, it can (and does) lead to consequences at a much broader level.

There are many heuristics in our thinking and too many to cover in this book. An initial selection is set out below, and further examples will be examined in Part 2 when it considers the role they play in developing, exacerbating or solving some of the challenges we face in the modern world.

Anchoring – first, an effect that may be familiar. The *anchoring effect* is our tendency to rely on the first piece of information we receive about a subject in making a judgement about it[29]. We interpret all the new information we receive about this subject through the original frame we built for it. This can happen in a range of situations – for example in our value estimations. When we are trying to work out a value for an unknown quantity but are given a particular value to consider first, we tend to 'anchor' our value judgement around the suggested value. If you are asked whether Henry VIII lived to 81 years old, you will give a higher estimate of his life span than if you'd been asked whether he lived to 42 years old. The anchoring effect can therefore bias our judgements and decisions. This heuristic is often exploited by shops to get us to buy things – a shop will offer an original, higher price alongside a sale price, to anchor our idea of what that item costs, so that the sale price appears to be a bargain.

Mere exposure effect – when we are familiar with something – from people to products to words – we will often tend to favour it more. And even academics are affected by this! A study in 2011[30] found that researchers who were asked to give objective assessments of the contributions made by various academic journals to their fields gave a more favourable review of those they were familiar with. As a result of this *mere exposure effect*, when something is repeated this tends to increase our affection for it. This can be something completely arbitrary, such as a made-up word. For example, another study showed that the more frequently people were exposed to a particular unfamiliar word, the more positively they regarded it, even if they were unaware of its meaning[31].

Why is familiarity so attractive to us? We have a sense of cognitive ease when we are familiar with something and it has proved to be safe in the past. We feel we can let our guard down a little. So repeated exposure to something not only helps us to learn more about our environment and survive within it, enabling us to distinguish things that are safe from those that are not, but also helps us to increase our cognitive ease (and reduce our energy expended) when we identity things that are familiar – and, by association, safe.

One potential drawback of the mere exposure effect is that it can lead to us failing to make the best choices and missing out on learning new information. For example, choosing the most familiar restaurant to us in our town may mean us failing to try out other ones that might be better. Another drawback is that our sense of familiarity can be manipulated by repetition of stimuli. For example, brands spend billions of pounds each year trying to make themselves familiar to us so we will buy them, and techniques such as product placement in films aim to increase their familiarity. In addition, we can be lulled into a false sense of security by repeated exposure to people or things pretending to be safe but which are not – such as in grooming or campaigning by dangerous political figures.

Framing – our choices can be altered and manipulated depending on how information about those choices is represented. Kahneman and Tversky found that, when people are offered the same choice in two different ways, they tend to pick the one that minimises losses rather than maximises benefits. In one study, they presented participants with a choice of two health programmes designed to help save people from a disease that is likely to kill 600 people. Both offered the same outcome but framed it in two different ways. Nearly three-quarters of participants chose the programme that would save 200 people rather than the one in which there was a ⅓ probability that 600 people would be saved and a ⅔ probability that no one would be saved. This effect happens because we tend to worry far more about potential losses than potential gains (*loss aversion*[32]), and it can bias our decision making if choices are presented in terms of losses rather than gains.

Our sensitivity to how information is framed can influence our choices in a range of areas, from the level of risk we are prepared to take in our financial investments through to our choice of political candidates and parties when voting.

Conclusions

This chapter has introduced some of the basic ways that our minds simplify the world in order to make sense of it and help us in our quest to survive in the environment we inhabit and pass on our genes. It has also touched on some of the potentially problematic consequences of these ways of thinking. Naturally, it has only provided a very broad and simple overview and touched on a very limited selection of examples of our ways of simplifying the world, but more will be discussed in Part 2, in relation to some of the major challenges human beings face.

In summary, the System 1 part of our mind is not just a machine for jumping to conclusions – it is also one that can make us over-confident in these conclusions, some of which we arrive at using automatic thinking that is biased or based on an incomplete picture of the world. By contrast, one of the main functions of System 2 thinking is to review and control the judgements and impulses put forward by System 1, enabling some to pass through and express themselves in behaviour, and others to be modified or suppressed[33]. So, the 'rider' of System 2 can bring a certain amount of reflection, rationality and self-awareness to the powerful 'elephant' of System 1.

As you go through some of the examples in this book you may start feeling that it is our System 1 thinking that is the main cause of some of our key biases and misinterpretations of the world. This may be partly true, but System 2 is not just the rational, sensible controller of System 1 thinking – it can also act as an internal 'PR agent' for System 1, by rationalising the automatic decisions we've already made, and making us feel as if we reached these decisions through reasoning. There can be a seductive quality to following our automatic intuitions and it takes effort to engage the rational, System 2 side of our thinking, due to our aim of preserving cognitive energy.

Our minds are therefore incredibly complex and sophisticated, but at the same time consist of a bundle of simplifications and shortcuts which have enabled us to reach this point in our evolutionary history. These simplifications can bring a range of inaccuracies and biases, which can have major consequences for our individual lives and for societies, which will be explored in more detail in Part 2.

It is important to remember though that this book is not claiming that our thinking is 'faulty' because we have these biases – rather, it is attuned to directing a limited thinking capacity to some specific purposes, and this may make it difficult for us to achieve other purposes that we may invent or feel are important in our lives – such as not jumping to conclusions about people who are different from us.

Chapter 4
We are influenced

In brief – some of the biggest differences between the brains of humans and other animals have evolved due to our need to navigate the complexity of relationships and co-operation with other people. Human beings don't think for ourselves anywhere near as much as we believe, because much of our thinking and behaviour is influenced by the presence or views of others. Our 'groupishness' is just one aspect of our overall tendency for our thinking and behaviour to be influenced by the context we are in, and it may be more accurate to see ourselves as 'contextuals' than as individuals.

In 1951 at Swarthmore College in Pennsylvania, USA, social psychologist Solomon Asch conducted a series of experiments that changed our view of humanity.

He presented participants with four lines – one on the left and three on the right. One of the three lines on the right matched with the one on the left. Participants were asked to choose which of the lines on the right matched with the one on the left.

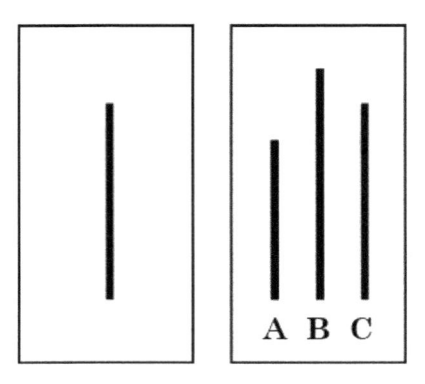

This would appear to be a judgement task that is so easy there is little point in undertaking it. Indeed, when there was no one else present to influence their answer, participants got the answer wrong less than 1% of the time. But when other people were added to the mix, things got interesting. In another experimental group, Asch planted five to seven other participants who were actually confederates with the experimenter, and told them to all provide the same incorrect answer. When they tested participants under these conditions, so that they could hear the (wrong) answers of their peers (the confederates), the participants conformed with the majority to give the wrong answer around a third of the time[34].

The experiments showed that human beings have a tendency to conform in response to social pressure from other people. If this was the case in simple, factual tasks with a seemingly obvious answer, then perhaps the same could happen in other areas of our thinking, such as our beliefs, tastes and moral judgements.

This tendency towards conformity is just one feature of our incredible sensitivity as creatures to the groups and contexts we find ourselves in. This chapter will explore this fascinating area, and show how these social traits have helped us attain some of our greatest achievements as a species, but also represent some of our greatest obstacles to meeting the challenges and expectations we face in the modern world.

To understand why we are like this, we need to go back to our ancestors.

The development of the social brain

Essentially, human minds evolved to function within a specific environment. This is the type of hunter-gatherer society that people lived in for the majority of the lifespan of our species, up to about 12,000 years ago, when we started to live in agricultural societies.

To see the environment we adapted to live within, we need to roll back a few million years. We are the descendants of ape-like creatures who moved from the rainforest to the savannah around six or seven million years ago[35]. Researchers believe that this move from the trees was made out of necessity, in response to tectonic activity in the East African Rift Valley. As large areas of Ethiopia, Kenya and Tanzania were slowly elevated to a higher plateau, this brought changes to the local environment and climate, with rainforests in certain areas drying out and being replaced with savannah.

Our ancestors were well equipped for a life in the trees, but less so the savannah. They were fast and agile in the trees, and able to avoid most predators, but in the savannah they were exposed and vulnerable, and less efficient in moving on two or four legs. Despite the challenges posed by this new environment, it did also offer some opportunities to intelligent creatures whose hands had been freed up from having to swing in trees.

This adaptation process took a few million years and transformed our ancestors as creatures – not just in their physical capacities but also in their thinking and behaviour. Hominid brains have tripled in size over the last 5 million years[36]. At the centre of this growth is a particular area of the brain – the prefrontal cortex. This is the part associated with intelligence and is significantly more developed in human beings than in other primates. We could call this part the 'new mind', which works with, and on top of, the 'old' mind that is shared with our distant ancestors.

This is a useful analogy for our story in this book as the 'new' mind consists of many of the capabilities that we developed to adjust to life in the savannah and flourish as groups of hunter-gatherers.

There are many fascinating details of this transformation that could be discussed here – from our capacity to use tools to our mastery of fire – but many psychologists agree that the fundamental driver of our brain development over this recent period, creating some of the capacity and skills that make humans different from other animals, is the need for social cooperation.

Psychologist William von Hippel notes that chimpanzees – along with bonobos, the species with which we share the closest common ancestry – cooperate with each other in a basic way when they hunt or attack other chimps as a group, but their basic predisposition towards even members of their own group who aren't their family or close friends is essentially competitive[37]. This suggests that our distant ancestors – those that we shared with chimps – on the savannah would probably have scattered when attacked, leaving each individual much more vulnerable. At some point, humans learned to work together to defend ourselves as groups, and this gave each member of those groups a better chance of survival.

One question that has fascinated researchers for years is 'at what point did human ancestors cross the rubicon of separating their abilities from those of other primates?'. Jonathan Haidt argues that this was when our ancestors developed shared intentionality – the ability to share mental representations of the tasks they were trying to do together. This made humans more effective at a massive range of critical tasks, including hunting, defending themselves and raising children. This may have just begun with groups of two or three people who were hunting or foraging together sharing their intentions. As this paid off from an evolutionary perspective, over hundreds of thousands of years the level and type of collaboration increased, as well as the size of the groups in which people were collaborating.

As time went on, human beings reached a point where natural selection began to favour greater levels of group-orientation in people. Those who had greater capacity to feel and communicate group-related emotions, learn and conform to social norms, and behave in line with the rules of social institutions such as religions, did better than those who didn't. Not only this but a new set of social pressures began to emerge on people as individuals, both within and between groups, which they felt compelled to respond to for the sake of their survival and procreation. Within groups, these included the threat of ostracisation for people who didn't conform to group norms. This was a powerful force, because if you lived in a harsh environment with no comforts, it was tantamount to a death sentence to be rejected from your group.

We have carried to the present day an incredible sensitivity towards social isolation – so much so that it can influence our longevity as well as our mental health. For example, a study of over 300,000 people[38] carried out in the US in 2009 found that people who had stronger social relationships had a 50 percent increased likelihood of survival compared to those who did not. This study suggests that social isolation provides as much, if not more, of a mortality risk than some of the best-known health risks in Western societies, including smoking, obesity and alcohol consumption[39]. Social pressures also acted between groups, with those groups that had better internal cooperation able to take territory and other things from less cohesive groups.

As our need for cooperation and social tools developed, our brains grew and developed too. You need a big brain and a great deal of processing power to deal with the complexity of co-operating and living in social groups – including the ability to 'read' other people, use language to communicate, understand social rules, adjust behaviour, think abstractly and plan for the future. Some scientists call this the 'social brain' theory of human development. It was around 500-700,000 years ago that the first creatures with brains a similar size of ours started to appear in Africa and then Europe.

To go back to the two systems of thinking discussed in Chapter 3, it is important to note that the 'social brain' capacities discussed here are not exclusively rational System 2 thinking. Some of our social intuitions are also part of our System 1 functionality. For example, experiments show that babies as young as six months old – way before they develop their capacity for language or reasoning –

watch how people behave towards each other, and show a preference for those who are nice rather than nasty.

'Two minds theory' suggests that the new mind was added to the old mind, and both still exist, working together. They normally work together pretty well, with the new rational side supporting the older automatic side. But the mechanisms of the two can sometimes come into conflict – and we can become aware of this if things start going badly awry. For example, in a compulsive behavioural addiction like eating too much, which we cannot overcome even though we know it's damaging us. It's the old mind keeping a hold over us, sometimes frustrating the aims of the new mind.

To conclude then, the 'big leap' in our minds and our development as creatures was driven by the need to cooperate. This statement comes with a significant caveat, however: we only evolved the capacity for cooperation with some people, those within our groups, and perhaps only in the context of personal relationships. We did not evolve to cooperate between groups, or at least, not all groups[40]. So, there is a limit to our instinct for cooperation, and there are other instincts that may pull us away from each other. The next section will explore how these work together.

The tribal human

Living in their small tribe on the savannah, your ancestors would have faced a range of daily hardships and challenges, including finding enough food to give them and their offspring the calories they needed to survive. An additional challenge that may have reared its head from time to time was the existence of other tribes.

At this time, if you encountered strangers on the savannah, they might have been a threat to you as an individual or your tribe – and this could be for a number of reasons. For example, they, or their tribe, might be competing for the same limited resources as you. How do you know whether to trust them? You have a reasonable sense that you can trust the people in your own tribe because you live and cooperate with them. So, a simple way for our brains to decide whether someone is friendly or a threat – and therefore for us to undertake the all-important task of saving cognitive energy – is to identify whether the other person is part of our tribe or not. And making this decision mattered to our ancestors – it was sometimes a question of life or death. We might have a rather romantic view of what life was like for our ancestors, but, as Steven Pinker points out, in reality it would have been violent and unpredictable, with murder rates higher than in some of the most dangerous cities today[41].

As a result, over millions of years we developed a range of capacities to help us make judgements on whether we can trust people or not, including identifying whether they are familiar or part of our tribe. We also developed capacities to strengthen our affiliation with our own tribe in order to help us succeed, in the event of conflict with other tribes. Research suggests that some of these are universal human traits, common across different human cultures.

We judge others automatically

Whether or not we realise it or want to do so, we make quick, automatic judgements about other people. For example, human beings use faces to help them make many judgements about others – from whether they are trustworthy to who to vote for[42]. Studies show we have the capacity to evaluate whether someone is a friend or an enemy from a single glance at their face, by evaluating how dominant they are (to assess their level of threat) and how trustworthy they are (whether their motives are likely to be friendly or not)[43].

As part of our aim to draw meaning from the world to make sense of it, we also attribute motives to people's behaviour – for example, we may attribute the fact that a stranger was impolite to us to them being an unpleasant person. These attributions can however be inaccurate as we can be biased in our thinking about this – for example, the *fundamental attribution error* is a bias in which we evaluate other people's behaviour in a different and much less forgiving way than we would explain our own, by focusing on personality traits ('Jim isn't walking because he's lazy') rather than situations ('It was too hot for me to walk')[44]. We can see some of these judgemental behaviours as further forms of cognitive shortcut or 'jumping to conclusions' that we use to save mental energy: it is quicker to judge other people in this way than go to the effort of considering the contextual reasons for their behaviour in the same way we do for our own – partly because the latter information is much easier to access for each of us.

We categorise people

We categorise people because we don't have the mental resources or time to conduct a detailed evaluation of every person we encounter. So, our minds are wired to separate people into categories and groups. This is another cognitive shortcut that helps us make judgements and take action quickly on the basis of them – such as 'are people who wear replica football t-shirts likely to be friendly or threatening?'.

In itself, this is a neutral rather than a negative process, helping us make sense of the world, make decisions quicker and reduce our cognitive load. We don't just stereotype people – we use the same process of categorisation to make sense of other stimuli in our world, from sounds to the lengths of lines. We accentuate similarities and differences between groups of things to make sense of them – for example, 'the potatoes in pile 1 are bigger than those in pile 2'[45]. This is known as the *accentuation principle*[46]. We also don't just stereotype people in negative ways; it can be positive and neutral too, such as 'all runners are nice people'. Our stereotypes can sometimes be reasonable guides to the truth – for example, there is evidence to back up the stereotypical idea that men are more violent than women[47]. Like lots of our other shortcuts though, our process of categorising and stereotyping can be a blunt and inaccurate instrument. Not all men are violent.

This process of categorisation can therefore lead us to make poor judgements, both about people and other stimuli, like line lengths. It can also lead us into other errors of judgement – for example, in basic perception. In a study in the US in 2001, white participants were asked to look at pictures of tools or guns, and asked to classify them as quickly as possible. Before they were shown these pictures, however, a picture of a black or white face was quickly shown to them, with researchers explaining that this would indicate that either a tool or a gun would be shown next[48]. Seeing the black faces led participants to identify guns quicker than with white faces, and to mistake tools for guns. These kinds of misjudgement can have potentially tragic consequences, such as increasing the potential for miscarriages of justice, or mistakenly shooting or punishing certain groups, such as black people[49].

If stereotypes are negative, they can lead us into prejudice, where we have negative feelings and beliefs about specific groups of people, and discrimination, in which groups of people are treated unfairly badly based on prejudice. Part 2 will explore these points in greater detail, as they are at the centre of some of our core modern challenges, such as hate, conflict and political extremism.

This process of categorising and stereotyping largely occurs automatically and we may not be consciously aware of it[50]. For example, studies using the implicit association test (IAT) have shown that even white people who believe themselves to be non-racist can actually have an unconscious negative bias towards black people – a phenomenon known as aversive racism. One study[51] primed participants by flashing an image of a black or white face in front of them for a fraction of a second and then asked them to identify whether a word revealed shortly after could be used to describe people. A range of words were presented for participants to respond to from a set of three positive words (good, kind and trustworthy) and three negative words (bad, cruel and untrustworthy). The experiment found that the participants responded faster to the positive words after seeing the image of the white person and faster to the negative words after seeing the black person[52].

We favour members of our own group

We have a bias to favour members of our own groups (known as our 'in-group') more than those in other groups ('out-groups'). Our bias towards our in-group and against others has been shown to reveal itself in a range of ways, including how we choose to distribute resources and how we judge people's characters.

The discussion about groups or tribes here does not just refer to one distinct, fixed family or community that each of us belongs to and lives in, as our ancestors might have done. Each of us can be a member of many groups and tribes at once, including a family, nation, football team, race, religion, political mindset, friendship circle – the list goes on.

In fact, these reactions to group membership occur even when our groups are defined in the most minimal and random way. Psychologist Henri Tajfel had been a prisoner of war during World War II, and wanted to use his research to investigate where prejudice stemmed from. In a series of influential studies conducted in the early 1970s, he found that simply being categorised as a member of a group – however arbitrary and basic the basis of this categorisation was, and whether people knew each other or not – was enough to get people to show competitive behaviour in relation to other groups. This is known as the 'minimal group paradigm'. For example, working with other psychologists[53], Tajfel split a group of British schoolboys into two completely random groups, but told them they had been split on the basis of their preference for one artist – Paul Klee or Vassily Kandinsky. Despite this arbitrary and meaningless reason for splitting the groups, and the schoolboys not knowing who else was in their particular group, when asked to distribute money to other people they favoured the members of their own group to people outside it. Research shows that this tribal instinct is deeply set within us – we can distinguish between in-groups and out-groups from infancy[54].

Favouring members of our in-group and being suspicious of those in out-groups had evolutionary value thousands of years ago in our small tribal groups, but it can present a range of problems for us in a modern world, in which there is less threat from strangers, where different groups of people live together and interact much more and where there is now the expectation that we will treat everyone with equal levels of respect and kindness.

We link our identity to our group membership

Being a member of a group brought a number of benefits to our ancestors beyond some of their more basic aids to survival such as strength in numbers against other hostile parties and better access to food and water. We are still each subject to these same powerful forces today. According to *social identity theory*, groups make an important contribution to our sense of self-esteem[55], as well as reducing our uncertainty about the world around us and how other people will think and behave. People also experience pride through their membership of groups, which becomes an important feature of their own social identity. So, the status and prestige held by a specific group that we belong to (for example, gold credit card holders), will influence our own individual sense of self-esteem and identity[56].

Through this sense of identity, our membership of groups – from sports clubs to political organisations – can affect how we think about ourselves and others, as well as how we behave.

For example, we are constantly being influenced by social norms, which are informal rules and beliefs that govern the behaviours of the groups we belong to[57]. These include the wider norms of our particular society, such as the view in the UK that is polite to queue in order to get served in shops, and the norms of the smaller groups we belong to, such as the belief in a gang that any attack on one of their members must be avenged by death in the other gang.

These norms can have a strong hold over our thinking and behaviour as individuals. For example, evidence shows that when membership of a particular group becomes important to the self-esteem of an individual, they can become depersonalised – in other words, their own sense of identity becomes less important and their thinking, values and behaviour become subsumed in those of the group[58]. In some cases, this might inspire them to acts of great bravery and sacrifice (such as a soldier putting themselves in danger to rescue a colleague), but it is not difficult to imagine how this process can also lead to behaviour within groups that the individuals concerned would not dream of enacting if they were behaving as their own, reflective selves – from football hooliganism to genocidal acts by soldiers. This will be explored in more detail – as well as how our sense of group identity and negativity towards out-groups can be a dangerous cocktail – in several chapters of Part 2.

The social human

We are social creatures. This does not simply mean that we enjoy talking to each other, or that we're inclined to cooperate with each other under certain circumstances, but something much more fundamental, and perhaps surprising: *our minds are attuned to thinking as part of a group – not just as individuals*. This point will now be explored, as well as the major consequences it can have.

We are always comparing ourselves

As individuals we need to feel confident in our attitudes, perceptions and behaviour, and as there is no ultimate objective measure of these, we tend to use the people around us as a reference point to guide our own. We often seek out people who are similar to ourselves in order to validate our attitudes and behaviour, which can result in people basing their self-concept on the groups to which they belong[59]. One possible consequence of this is that we can end up only talking to people who agree with us, and therefore rarely experience alternative views which might lead us to open our minds or challenge our thinking. This contributes to the common modern phenomenon of 'echo chambers' in social media online, which can increase polarisation on political, moral and other issues, and which will be examined in Part 2.

We don't just use comparison with others to learn about ourselves. Psychologist Bill von Hippel[60] argues that, within our tribe, we are in competition with one another for various things, such as people to mate with and roles in which we can contribute to the tribe. Under these circumstances, it is not our individual characteristics or abilities that matter, but how we compare to other people in our tribe. For example, I may only be a moderately attractive person, but if I am more attractive than the other people in my tribe that are seeking a mate at the same time as me, it is only my relative attractiveness that matters. So, we seek to compare ourselves with other people in order to monitor our place within a group and against others.

As an aside, this suggests that some of the behaviours and thinking patterns we have evolved, even within our own cooperative groups, can actually be quite competitive. This should remind us of the overall evolutionary forces driving us as individuals, as although our behaviour within groups often turns out to be cooperative, we are still influenced by individual drives for survival and passing on our genes. So, our cooperativeness is a by-product of our individual survival drives – it has worked out as the best way of achieving our evolutionary aims. From an evolutionary point of view, the idea of cooperation is therefore not the morally positive thing we have often seen it as. It is morally neutral – as is everything else in nature. But it is human beings who ascribe arbitrary moral values to these things.

We are wired to be influenced

We like to think we are autonomous individuals who make decisions for ourselves and are able to fend off the advances of anyone seeking to influence or manipulate us. The reality is that we are highly influenced by other people, whether we are aware of it or not, and whether other people are actually present or not.

We don't just *care* about how we are seen by other people and our social standing in a group or society – we are instinctively, and physiologically, wired to respond to these things. This has a host of profound effects on our thinking and behaviour, including our tendency to conform, our willingness to comply and our response to authority. These tendencies can lead to behaviour that we would not imagine ourselves taking if we had the chance to reflect on our own – and can contribute to acts of horrific cruelty.

Conformity – this can be defined as adapting our behaviour or thinking to match that of other people. It became an important area of psychological study during the twentieth century as psychologists gradually realised that the judgements, behaviours and even perceptions of human beings are hugely influenced by the people and groups around them.

Since Asch's experiments on conformity in relation to judgement, countless studies have shown that conformity occurs with a wide range of variables, including factual judgements, moral judgements, political views and musical tastes[61], as well as in a variety of contexts, both in person and in situations where there are no other people immediately present to represent social pressure – such as online.

In the political arena, it has been known for some time that people tend to conform in their political views with people within their peer group (or in-group). A classic 1960 study of American voters[62] found that people's voting preferences tended to reflect those of the religious, racial and union groups they belonged to. This suggests that social influence can be more important than the power of particular political arguments or people's own convictions. One scholar has argued that political preferences could be seen in a similar way to cultural tastes[63].

Conformity doesn't just happen in the presence of other people. Recent research has shown that moral conformity – where our moral views move towards those of others – can happen online, even with relatively subtle social signals and no other direct social pressure. In one study[64] participants completed an online survey containing a moral scenario (a family deciding to eat their dog after it had died) and were asked to judge how acceptable or condemnable the family's actions were. Participants were split into groups, and each received a slightly different prime with information about other people's moral preferences before they answered the question. This information was presented in the same way as one might see it on social media – for example, '58 people who previously took this survey rated it as morally condemnable'. The study found that people were influenced to conform by these informal prompts, and therefore that people do conform in their moral judgements online, even when there are no other people present and when minimal statistical information is presented about how others responded.

Three main reasons have been cited for our tendency towards conformity. One is informational – that we want to feel our beliefs and perceptions are correct, so we look to other people's views when we are uncertain (for example, when it is an ambiguous situation) or where there is considerable disagreement among people. This can explain some forms of conformity but it can't explain why so many people conformed in the Asch line-length study discussed at the start of this chapter, as there was very little ambiguity in the stimuli it presented – one line was clearly the correct match. To explain this, we can draw upon the second model of influence –

normative conformity. This suggests that people go along with the views of the main group not for reasons of seeking accurate judgements but simply to gain approval, be accepted and avoid alienation from the group.

The two explanations above don't account sufficiently for the influence of group membership on people, so we can look to a third[65], which suggests that members of our in-group are the best source of informational guidance, as they help us to assess what views or judgements are appropriate. We therefore use them for guidance, but as we have drawn this guidance from a very specific, limited range of people, we end up conforming to their norms, and tending to adopt the central position in a range of possible positions adopted by others in order to not stray too far from the group. So, under this explanation, it is the social norms of our group that are making us conform, rather than the presence or pressure we feel from other people. As will be seen in Part 2, a significant amount of our thinking and behaviour is driven by social norms, as these invisible 'rules' can govern many areas of our lives – from how to treat other people to what view to take of particular out-groups. When these rules break down or become more extreme over time (such as under an extremist government), this can therefore bring potentially dangerous consequences, due to changes in people's thinking and behaviour.

In reality, conformity may occur for a mixture of these reasons at different levels, depending on the context. For example, in the Asch experiment, there was little informational conformity but a lot of normative conformity. A study by Deutsch and Gerard (1955) found that there was less conformity in situations where there is less uncertainty and less group pressure, but even in this situation, a significant proportion of people (23%) still conformed[66].

Some studies argue that there is also a strong emotional component to why we conform to the views of in-group members in political contexts, with positive self-conscious emotions such as pride and self-esteem driving us to conform to group norms, and negative self-conscious emotions such as embarrassment and shame moving us away from non-conformity. This conformity functions even when we are alone, due to our capacity to imagine how other people would react to our views and behaviour[67].

Our tendency to conform can therefore bring a range of advantages to us, including helping us to make sense of the world, feel closer to our group and feel a positive sense of self. These advantages come at a considerable cost however, as this tendency towards conformity can bring a range of significant consequences in many areas of our lives – from morality to political issues to personal beliefs. For example, in many cases conformity makes our judgments less reliable[68]. There is an argument that 'swarm intelligence' can be more accurate than the sometimes confused and unreliable judgements of individuals, but studies in moral conformity have shown that this only happens if certain conditions are met, including when people's opinions are independent and unbiased, and when reporting is truthful. These conditions are often not met in our everyday moral discussions, so it is difficult to see many situations in which judgements from conformity are more accurate. Conformity also makes it hard for us to change our minds or think differently, given the social pressures around us. Overall, conformity stops us from 'thinking for ourselves' in anything like the way we think we do.

It could also be argued that some of the biggest problems with conforming behaviour can occur when people are conforming for reasons other than seeking informational accuracy – for example, doing so just to fit in – as our decisions and behaviour in this case have nothing to do with responding to the stimulus or situation itself (for example, whether Donald Trump did make a particular remark), but were simply based on the need to remain part of a group. As Part 2 will demonstrate, these drawbacks of conformity can have a wide range of negative consequences in our lives and society, including fuelling conflict, political polarisation and inaccurate beliefs.

The finding that conformity can take place online even without the presence of other people is particularly important for our lives in the modern world, as it shows how vulnerable we are to influence from social media and other digital forms of communication, even without other people present and with minimal additional information to influence us. The potential consequences of this are big, as our beliefs, our views of reality and even our actions can be pushed, pulled and moulded without us knowing it, or realising that our views are adrift of reality. It also means that those with bad intentions have the potential to gain significant power over us with these tools. These important points will be discussed in more detail in Part 2.

Compliance and obedience – in psychology, the ideas of conformity and compliance are sometimes used interchangeably, but we will consider them separately here, as conformity can occur without any deliberate external pressure, whereas compliance is the question of how people respond to a request or pressure to do something[69]. It can therefore also be associated with the question of whether an individual can be controlled by another person or group of people.

There are many minor ways in which people can be influenced to comply. A common example is *the reciprocity principle*, in which people feel obliged to reciprocate an action if someone has done something for them or given them something. This works based on a common social norm – that we should treat others in the way they treat us. This principle is often used by people trying to sell us things – for example, the window cleaner who starts cleaning our car windows while the traffic is stopped, who gives us a sense of obligation to pay them because they have done something for us (even if it was unrequested).

The world of sales uses a range of compliance techniques like this. Another example is low-balling – in which a sales person offers you an attractive price for something, only to change it once you have agreed to it – for example, saying that the offer has ended, but that you can have the item at the non-sale price. Surprisingly high numbers of people will still take the worse offer, seemingly because they have committed to the purchase in their minds and have been hooked in, making it hard to back out.

The phenomenon of obedience can have far greater consequences than simply making us vulnerable to the tricks of sales people. A classic study on obedience that had profound implications, as well as raising significant ethical questions, was the electric shock experiments carried out by Stanley Milgram at Yale University in 1974[70].

Milgram set up a laboratory scenario, in which teachers (the participants) taught learners (confederates of the experimenters) to learn a set of associated words, purportedly to take part in a study of memory and learning. In reality, the series of experiments was to test the level of compliance shown by the 'teachers' to follow orders, even if it meant taking actions that seemingly caused harm to others. When learners got an answer wrong, it was the teacher's job to administer an electric shock to them, using a shock generator they controlled from an adjoining room, and they were told to administer a progressively stronger electric shock after each mistake a learner made. The level of shocks on the generator in front of the 'teacher' participants went from 'slight shock' up to 'Danger: severe shock' and then to the terrifyingly but ambiguously-labelled 'XXX'. The real test was therefore whether the participant 'teachers' would be willing to give the shocks, and how severe they were willing to make them.

As the experiments progressed and learners got some answers wrong, the participant 'teachers' started to administer the electric shocks, rising to the point where the learners cried out in agony, asking for the experiment to be stopped (all of which was fake – as, in reality, they were given no shock at any point). The participant 'teachers' appeared agitated throughout the process and frequently asked if they could stop, but at these points the experimenter asked them to continue with a range of escalating pre-prepared prompts, from 'please continue' to 'you have no other choice, you must go on'.

You might think that in this sort of situation, where you knew you were volunteering for an experiment, you would not give a shock or would stop as soon as someone seemed to be feeling pain. The stunning results of the study suggest otherwise[71]. In some of the experiments, nearly two-thirds of the participants obeyed all the directions from the experimenter. In one experiment, the majority were willing to give the highest 'XXX'-rated shock to an older man with a heart condition. This study showed that ordinary people can be coerced into obedient behaviours – including those causing great harm – by authority figures and situations that pressurise them into these.

Like compliance, obedience can have some evolutionary benefits – particularly in coordinating and focusing consistent effort among people. A tribe might be wiped out if its fighters continually questioned how they should attack or defend themselves in a battle with another tribe, or starve to death if its hunting team could not agree on how and where to carry out their hunt. Obedience can however blind people's judgements and perceptions, making them obey orders or authority without considering what they are being asked to do or the consequences of this for other people or creatures. Such blind obedience can lead to harmful decisions and behaviour – from medical errors occurring due to nurses' deference to doctors' orders[72] through to playing a significant role in one of the worst atrocities humanity has ever seen.

After the horrors of the Second World War, psychologists such as Milgram sought to understand what could make members of an affluent, seemingly civilised nation like Germany commit such obscene acts as the Holocaust. The willingness to obey orders regardless of their content was a factor in this, for soldiers and the public alike. In 1961, one of the key enablers of the Holocaust, Adolf Eichmann, was tried by a war crimes committee, found guilty and sentenced to death. His defence, as the man in charge of the mass deportation of Jews across Europe to ghettos and concentration camps, was based on the premise that he had simply been 'following orders' and just doing his job. Journalist Hannah Arendt famously described Eichmann's behaviour as 'the banality of evil' in action – how simply following orders in this way can enable terrible acts. Part 2 will look at this issue in more detail.

Persuasion – a final form of influence to note is that of persuasion, in which people try to change the attitudes and behaviours of others. A great deal of research has been carried out in this area from the twentieth century onwards and has been used by advertisers, charities, politicians and others for decades to influence people to buy things, donate money and vote for particular parties, among many other things.

A range of factors can help to increase the persuasiveness of messages, with three core areas identified by the Yale approach, the first popular model of persuasion theory, developed by Carl Hovland and his colleagues at Yale University[73]. These three core areas are: the source (the person who communicates the message), the message itself and the audience (the person or people to whom the message is directed).

The most persuasive messages have a source that is recognised as an expert, is popular and attractive (rather than the opposite), and speaks rapidly rather than slowly, as the former gives an impression of competence. They also carry a message that we think is not deliberately intended to manipulate us, is repeated and has a powerful linguistic style. As has already been shown in Chapter 3, the way a message is framed can also increase its influence – for example, people are more sensitive to losses, so framing a message in terms of potential losses rather than gains can be effective. Sometimes a negative message can be more persuasive than a positive one – for example, a study by Leventhal et al (1967) found that an anti-smoking message that induced a high level of fear in its audience was more effective than a medium-fear one. Sometimes, however, the reverse is true – during the Covid-19 pandemic, a study[74] tested whether people were more likely to respond to negative (high fear) or positive (low fear) messages aiming to persuade them to seek vaccination for the virus. It found that high level fear appeals made people feel their freedom was being threatened, which led them to feel defensive and less inclined to carry out the recommended behaviours. Lower fear appeals generated a more positive response and were a more effective way to persuade people to seek vaccinations. So, context matters when deciding which type of message to use. Messages also tend to be most persuasive when the members of the audience have low rather than high self-esteem, are distracted and are in the 'impressionable years' of early adulthood, in which they are more susceptible to political attitude change than older people[75].

The Yale model provided a useful model to help us start to understand the science of persuasion. Evidence has emerged since the model's development in the 1950s that the process of persuasion is more complex and dependent on a wider range of factors, including social identity.

Conclusions on the tribal and social human

We are therefore wired to be highly sensitive and responsive to other people and their thoughts and behaviour. These automatic, unconscious tendencies range from attributing motives to other people's behaviour through to comparing ourselves with other people. Our attitudes, behaviour and even our perception of basic information about the world are influenced by other people, whether we like it or not. This isn't a criticism of us for being 'weak minded' – it is simply the creatures we have evolved to be.

We have also evolved a sensitivity to the specific tribes we find ourselves in. We have a tendency to cooperate with, and be influenced by, fellow group members but not those of other groups. In fact, some of the traits of thinking and behaviour we have evolved with actually make it harder for us to think positively about, and cooperate with, people from other groups.

We have evolved these traits in thinking and behaviour because they have conferred great benefits to our ancestors over the years. A point that will have become clear from recent pages though is that these tendencies can come with a heavy price, as they also have the potential to stoke division, create prejudice and promote conflict between human beings. They also leave us open to being influenced by other people in ways we would not have thought possible – from simple factual judgements through to behaving in ways that cause others harm. And we are being influenced by other people all the time, through social norms, our sense of social identity and many other factors, even when there is no one actually present to influence us. These points play a significant role in some of the challenges we face in the modern world, such as our desire for people to be less prejudiced, seek truth and live in a peaceful world, and some of these traits will be explored in more detail in Part 2.

It is worth noting at this stage that there are other reasons beyond our tribal tendencies why human beings might come into conflict with each other. For example, we each see the world differently from each other. We have different beliefs and moral ideas, and this has the potential to cause conflict between individuals and groups of people. As Part 2 will also show, these differing causes of tribal thinking and behaviour can interact with, and strengthen, each other.

The fallacy of individual thinking

A critical point to take from this chapter is that our thinking, feelings and behaviour as individuals are driven much more than we think by our responses to other people and our social environment. This reality not only contradicts the view most people have of themselves as rational creatures, but also challenges the very idea that we are individuals at all.

For centuries (since the Enlightenment) in the West we have been brought up to see ourselves – and other people – strictly as individuals. This is broadly the idea that we are independent from other people and each have the chance to think for ourselves and shape our own destinies. Running alongside this is the idea that this personal freedom is sacrosanct and should be treasured – including the freedom to think for ourselves. But what if we aren't as individual as we thought?

The truth is, human beings may be physically separate individual units (as we generally know where our bodies begin and end) but there are many ways in which we are not separate from each other from a mental and behavioural perspective. It is true that we function as individual thinking 'units' using the brain that each of us has, and that we can think individually using this tool. But this brain that drives our thinking and behaviour is highly sensitively tuned to drive our behaviour, feelings, beliefs and even our interpretation of information, in relation to the groups of people around us. This is a critical point, as it runs contrary to many of our assumptions about how people think and behave, and has a big impact on how we deal with some of the real-life challenges and issues that will be covered in Part 2 of this book.

In reality, the power of groups over us is so strong that it can be enlightening not to see ourselves as individual beings with completely independent minds, but as nodes or cells within different groups, that are programmed to respond to, and be activated by, our association with these groups. This could help us gain a richer and more realistic sense of who we are and how we behave. Perhaps we are at the end of 'the age of the individual'.

This is one of the most important points in the book and may also be one of the most difficult for people to accept because of the strength with which we hold the cultural belief of the importance of the individual.

In a culture like ours in which the idea of the individual is revered and protected, we tend to primarily see disadvantages and dangers to the traits in our thinking and behaviour that make us think as part of the crowd rather than individually – for example, our propensity to conform. Yet there are some evolutionary advantages to be gained from responding to, and thinking as part of, the groups around us – such as the potential for more effective collective action. Other cultures exist around the world that have a less individualistic and more communitarian approach to life, including East Asian countries like Japan[76]. In these countries individuals are seen as cells that make up the body of a society, and obtain their sense of meaning not through their individuality but the contribution they make to that society.

This book is not suggesting that we abandon our sense of the value of individual freedom, as this clearly matters a great deal to many people in the West. But these more communitarian countries show that an obsession with the individual is not the only game in town, and suggest it is possible to rethink our individualist dogma and still have good societies and lives. Part 3 of this book will explore how we might use our knowledge of how people think and behave to do this, and outline some of the practical consequences of this in more detail. For example, how can we protect people's freedom to think for themselves if we aren't actually able to think for ourselves in the way we previously believed we could? As the rest of the book will show, there are possible solutions to these tricky questions but they will need us to change the way we structure our ideas, societies and institutions, as well as increase the level of support we give to people to function mentally and behaviourally in society.

Contextuals, not individuals

Groups are just one external factor that can influence how we think. There are others too, including the situations we find ourselves in. An infamous example of this is the prison experiments run by the psychologist Philiip Zimbardo and his team at Stamford University in the 1970s[77]. Zimbardo aimed to explore how people's behaviour can be affected by the institutions around them and the roles they play. He separated volunteer students into two groups – guards and prisoners. Prisoners were 'arrested' and taken to a mock prison that had been set up in a basement corridor of the psychology department at the university, including cells. Guards were provided with uniforms and then asked to do what was needed to interact with and supervise prisoners. They were given minimal instructions on how to do this, and told only to avoid physical punishment or aggression.

The experiment was originally intended to last for two weeks, but it had to be stopped after just six days, as things had got out of control. Some of the guards were behaving in increasingly brutal ways, including intimidating and harassing the prisoners, who themselves became more passive and docile, and some of them had to be removed from the study as they were showing signs of severe emotional problems. All of these participants – both guards and prisoners – were people who had been vetted before taking part to ensure they did not have any previous emotional problems, criminal backgrounds or other major personal issues that would lead them to abnormal behaviour in the experiment. Aside from providing a strong challenge to the value and effects of prisons in society, the study showed the way in which a simple contextual factor like a role or an institution can modify people's behaviour in substantial ways.

When you are in the comfort of your own home reading this book, you may feel certain that you are not capable of behaving like the guards in the experiment, but Zimbardo's argument is that this is simply not true – we are all capable of behaviours that we may not think possible if we are put into certain conditions. Context matters. This is because we are built to respond to the environment and groups around us, and when some of our thinking traits (such as favouring our in-group and negatively perceiving out-groups) are activated in certain contexts, this can have a big effect on our behaviour. As Part 2 will demonstrate, this leads to some uncomfortable truths about the terrible ways in which ordinary people behaved in events such as the Holocaust, and how each of us might also behave in their position.

For these reasons, we should think of human beings as 'contextuals' rather than 'individuals'. We have the capacity to make decisions for ourselves and are self-determined agents to a certain degree, but even in situations where there is no immediate group pressure around us, our thinking and behaviour are still influenced by factors that are often invisible to us, including social norms, social identity and compliance. Because of this, we really are not the closed, self-determined individual agents that we think we are. We need to change our conception of ourselves to accept that we have much more porous boundaries of individuality and agency, which are dependent on our context, including other people and situations.

When we see ourselves in this new way, we can start to consider the range of vulnerabilities we have to certain situations, people and groups (such as those that generate their own warped versions of 'the truth'), accept the fact that we might need support from society and our institutions in order to build contexts for us to live within that activate our positive rather than negative traits and identify the some of the ways we might achieve this. This important principle will be investigated in more detail in Part 3.

Chapter 5
We deceive ourselves

In brief – we do not experience any of these limitations or influences on our thinking in our everyday experiences. We just assume that we make decisions and take action accordingly. This sophisticated self-deception serves several purposes, including making us feel in control of our place in the world. It has several other consequences though, including making it difficult to get people to accept what we really are as creatures, and the related limitations of this thinking.

As we go through life, most of us like to feel we have a sense of personal agency – that we make decisions for ourselves and take action on the basis of rational thought. We also feel that we just see the world as it is and process that information in the most effective way – in other words, we experience thinking as nothing more than 'just thinking', not encumbered by limits, affected by emotions or driven by electro-chemical reactions inside us. The book so far has shown that this is simply not the reality, with our perspectives subject to a range of limitations, biases and influences. So why is our experience of our thinking and behaviour so different from what is actually happening in and to us?

The answer lies within our capacity for self-deception. Human beings are subject to a range of different types of self-deception, each of which can be seen to have evolutionarily adaptive qualities, helping us in different ways – from making us feel in control of our own destinies through to making us feel good about ourselves. This chapter will explore some of these varieties of self-deception, and why they have evolved. It will also consider the potentially troublesome consequences of this capacity for self-deception, including the fact that it makes it harder to convince people that there *is* more complexity behind their mental and behavioural functioning than they experience day-to-day.

Self-deception to provide a focus for ourselves

The first form of self-deception to describe is the basic experience of actually *being* a self.

As I discussed in a previous book, *Life – and how to think about it*[78], we all have a strong sense of what it is like to be a self. I wake up in the morning and I understand there is a 'me 'that is looking around my bedroom, and thinking about the day ahead. This is the same me that feels upset, confident or confused. This goes beyond the physical entity that is 'me' – there is also an experiencing, thinking unit that I, and other people, know as 'me'.

But it has been suggested by psychologists like Bruce Hood[79] that this idea of a single, consistent 'self' that each of us has is actually an illusion conjured up by our brains in order to bring our thoughts and experiences together into a coherent narrative over time, rather than a random set of disparate thoughts. It is speedier and more efficient, Hood argues, to treat other people as individual mental entities rather than disparate collections of memories, motives, and hidden agendas. Treating people as individuals rather than collections helps us optimise our interactions with others.

In reality, our sense of self as individuals therefore consists of the many thoughts, memories, experiences and other information that is stored in our minds. If we stripped away each of these things, the entity you know as 'you' would cease to exist.

This reality does not stop our sense of self from feeling any less real to us. Our brains create the impression of a self, so it is real – for us. Your impression of having a self is backed up by how other people interact and communicate with you, including their assumption that you have a sense of identity and internal sense of yourself, with your memories, views, desires and values.

This 'self illusion' could be seen to have a range of evolutionary benefits beyond how we see, and relate to, other people. As we've seen, it simplifies the world into one cumulative experience rather than a set of disparate sensory and cognitive phenomena. It also gives each of us a coherent, single entity called 'me' that we can prioritise in order to meet our drives, from procreation to aggression, which in turn contributes to our evolutionary development. Many of the other areas of deception we will talk about in this chapter emerge from this initial piece of self-delusion – the sense of a self.

Self-deception to make sense of the world

We also have an over-confidence in what we think we know. This point links to some of the heuristics and biases discussed in Chapter 3 – and the fact that we are not aware that we have these, so we are largely deceived by them. As Daniel Kahneman argued[80], this results in us finding it very difficult to accept just how ignorant we are of the world around us, and how uncertain it is.

For example, the *narrative fallacy* is a type of self-deception that stems from us trying to make sense of the world. We find particular types of stories and explanations compelling – those that are simple, concrete and that suggest a larger role for intentions, talent and mistakes rather than simply luck. We are suckers for stories, as they bring coherence to our view of the world, but they also lead us to construct and believe dubious accounts of the past[81]. This leads to us thinking we understand the past much more accurately than we actually do, and also leads to an over-confidence in our ability to predict the future. This can have an impact on our views of the world and the stories we tell ourselves about the past – for example, holding a particular person responsible for a past negative event when in reality they were not.

Another form of self-deception is *motivated reasoning* – our capacity to deceive ourselves by ignoring information that does not support our views of the world. This is illustrated by a study by American psychologists Peter Ditto and David Lopez[82], in which participants took a saliva test that they were told would identify whether they were likely to develop a serious medical condition later in life. Some were told that if the test strip changed colour it indicated bad news, and others that a colour change meant good news. In reality, the strip was not able to indicate potential illness at all, and never changed colour. The study found that participants waited longer and checked the results of the strip more often when they wanted the strip to change colour (i.e. when colour change indicated a clean bill of future health) than when they didn't (i.e. when colour change indicated future health problems). This wasn't simply a case of participants wanting more information under uncertainty, but actively avoiding information when it was not what they wanted to hear – in other words, selectively gathering information.

This selective gathering of information might enable us to gain the answers we wish to hear sometimes (but not all of the time), but it can give us an inaccurate view of reality and can have significant consequences in daily life. We can see this tendency to select the information that fits our own conclusions in a range of political debates or in issues such as climate change, and it can lead to greater polarisation of viewpoints. For example, research carried out after the 2016 US presidential election showed that the people who consumed the most fake news about Donald Trump were those who already had strong views in the direction of those stories. So they sought out fake news that supported their existing beliefs. This phenomenon may not have persuaded non-Trump supporters to vote for him, but may have hardened the views of those who did already support him, as well as adding to the polarisation of the population – all through the consumption and spreading of information that was false. This issue will be explored in more detail in Part 2, as it clearly has significant implications for our ability to uphold the idea of the truth, as well as our ability to manage hate and extremist political movements.

We also deceive ourselves with illusions of skill – thinking that good outcomes were achieved by skill when they were actually just down to luck. Entire industries have been based on this piece of self-delusion – for example, trading on the stock market. Daniel Kahneman observed that fifty years of research on the success of fund managers suggests that selecting stocks is more similar to rolling dice than to playing poker[83]. Yet we still delude ourselves with this illusion of skill.

Another issue with our minds is that when our ideas or beliefs change, we struggle to remember what we thought before this change occurred. We can therefore underestimate just how surprised we were by past events, often convincing ourselves in retrospect that we knew all along that they were going to happen. This *hindsight bias* can be illustrated by a study in 1972 which asked participants to guess the likelihood of 15 possible outcomes of President Richard Nixon's trip to China and Russia – from the US granting diplomatic recognition to China through to Mao Zedong agreeing to meet with Nixon. Following the visit, participants were asked to remember the probability they had assigned to each outcome. The study found that if an event had actually happened, participants over-estimated the likelihood they had originally assigned to it previously. Conversely, if an event hadn't occurred, they mistakenly recalled that they had previously thought it unlikely. This hindsight bias can lead us to evaluate people's decisions in the wrong way – based on whether the outcome was good or bad (outcome bias) rather than whether they went through the right decision-making process at the time. For example, after 9/11, blaming the CIA for not prioritising a minor lead they received in July 2001 that al-Qaeda might be planning an attack on the US. That this was a priority was only clear after the event itself.

Each of these forms of self-delusion represents an attempt to make sense of the world as well as feel a sense of confidence in our own judgements and identity. They can however create an 'Illusion of understanding' - making us see the world as simpler and more predictable than it actually is[84]. This is indeed an illusion and can cause us problems, as it makes us feel – incorrectly – that we can control the future, and can lead to errors of judgement.

Self-deception to enhance our self esteem

We all want to have a positive sense of ourselves, and feel that we are decent people who act in line with our values. Researchers have suggested this desire to build and maintain levels of self-esteem may be because it gives us a guide as to our levels of social acceptance and belonging, helping us to monitor the likelihood of being socially excluded[85] – a factor, as we have seen, that is critical to us.

We have developed a range of ways of deceiving ourselves in order to maintain this positive view of ourselves, including through social comparison and self-serving biases. For example, the *better-than-average effect* suggests that people describe themselves as above average across most variables of comparison, including intelligence, competence and sensitivity[86]. People with greater levels of self-esteem have also been shown to take greater credit for success and to blame external factors for failures[87]. We also overestimate our positive virtues, are over-optimistic about the future and have an unrealistically high sense of control over events[88]. All of these biases can skew our views of events, ourselves and other people.

Psychologist Leon Festinger suggested that each of us aims to seek a sense of harmony and consistency in our beliefs, attitudes and behaviour, so if there is a situation in which there is a conflict between our behaviour, beliefs or attitudes, this can put us into a state of psychological stress, known as cognitive dissonance. In this situation, we are motivated to try to reduce this dissonance. We might do this by altering our behaviour but might also alter our principles or seek other evidence in order to rationalise our behaviour, especially if the behaviour is in the past and can't be changed. For example, if you believe eating animals is wrong but you eat chicken one night at a restaurant, this behaviour might cause dissonance with the value you hold. But you may attempt to justify it to yourself with 'it was a free-range chicken so it wasn't so bad' or 'there was nothing else to eat' or 'eating red meat is the real problem – chicken is fine to eat'.

We rationalise these things to ourselves, and we sometimes also communicate these rationalisations to other people, who may be more aware than us about our inconsistencies (as we may be about theirs). One consequence of making these rationalisations is that we may not be aware we are doing so, or that we are inconsistent or wrong, and this non-self-aware behaviour could have negative impacts if it is being conducted in a public space – such as causing or escalating conflicts with people in online situations when we won't admit to being wrong or over-reacting. Cognitive dissonance can therefore be seen as a defence mechanism to protect our sense of ourselves as decent, good people.

Immunity to influence

Many of us are aware that there are people out there in the world trying to influence and persuade us, from advertisers to politicians. Most of us however think – incorrectly – that we are less influenced by these mass media messages than other people. This is known as the *third person effect*. This effect can lead to us having an unrealistically high sense of our own 'mental defences' and drastically underestimating our susceptibility to influence. This in turn can make us even more open to manipulation and influence, and can have other further-reaching effects, such as making policy makers feel that the issue of manipulation and influence is less of a problem for human beings than it really is, and therefore preventing any meaningful regulation of potential influences on people, including advertising, political campaigning and many other factors.

Overall – we are built to be deceived

A critical point to take from this chapter is that we are built to be deceived by ourselves.

Some of our most basic forms of self-deception can be classed as 'necessary illusions' for being able to deal with day-to-day existence. In this respect they are similar to other heuristics that were examined in Chapter 3. Among these basic illusions is our general day-to-day ignorance of how we actually think and behave. We assume we 'just think' without knowing any of the details, shortcuts, influences or limitations to our thinking because that is what it feels like to us as we go through our lives. If we spent every minute of daily life continually 'looking under our own bonnet' at how we are thinking, our species would not have survived to the point that we're at, as it would be a massive distraction from more urgent survival needs, and require a lot of energy.

This chapter has explored just a few of the ways in which we deceive ourselves about our motives, behaviour, openness to influence and many other things, each of which sits below this most basic level of self-deception. It has also shown how our capacity for various forms of self-deception has brought us some evolutionary advantages, including enabling us to simplify and make sense of the world, as well as maintain a positive sense of our own identity. Psychologists William von Hippel and Robert Trivers have also suggested that we developed the capacity for self-deception in order to enhance our ability to deceive others – partly because people who are more self-deceived are more effective at persuading others. One evolutionary reason why it might have been important to do this is to win the competition for resources between people. The better we can become at deceiving others, and in hiding this deception, the more resources we can gain access to. Indeed, one study found that around half the acts of deception people carry out daily relate to gaining a resource for themselves[89].

Despite these evolutionary advantages, like the other simplifications and limits we carry in our minds, our capacity for self-deception can bring some significant negative consequences. These include leaving us with inaccurate views of the present, past and future, a vulnerability to manipulation from fake news and an excessive level of confidence in ourselves and the veracity of our own views.

At the broadest level, this capacity for self-delusion essentially leaves us evolutionarily adapted to have an unrealistic view of the creatures we are, and of how we really think and behave. This point is highly relevant to the findings of this book and to getting them heard in wider society – as it shows that it is hard to convince people about how they really do think and behave – whether these are members of the public or political decision makers. And it's even harder to convince people to make changes to society to help us flourish, based on this more realistic picture of human thinking and behaviour.

It is important to be aware of these varieties of self-deception, as they affect how people think and respond to the world around them, and they play a role in some of the challenges that will be explored in Part 2. It is also important to be aware of the general fact that we are often self-deceived, as it can provide us with a greater sense of humility about our judgements and behaviours, as well as opening up a new way to change how we respond to our challenges, and possibly improve our lives and society.

Chapter 6
Five key features of human thinking

In brief – a simple model can help us understand human thinking and behaviour using 5 key characteristics. Our minds are Limited, Adapted, Simplifying, Influenced and Deceived.

For centuries, human beings as a species have generally looked upon themselves as rational individuals with an accurate view of the reality they live in and the capacity to think and behave in the ways they want to. Also, as individuals, most of us don't often challenge our own assumptions of how we think and behave – partly because it takes a lot of effort and knowledge to do so and partly because there seems no reason to, as our experience of life suggests that we just get on with thinking and behaving, and there is not much to look at under the bonnet of our minds.

Part 1 of this book has aimed to shatter these myths and show that, although we are capable of rational thought, our thinking and behaviour takes place within certain parameters and is subject to a range of biases, inaccuracies and influences – many of which we may not have realised were there at all. It has also argued that we are completely different creatures from the ones we thought we were – still remarkable and complex, but more fallible in our judgements, possessing a less accurate view of reality and with our thinking and behaviour much more contingent upon context and other people than our own independent thought.

This new picture of humans also suggests we are much less intellectually robust and self-determined creatures than we thought, and as a result, the contexts that we live within (including our environments, societies, groups, norms, ideas and institutions) are more important than we thought in determining the nature of our thinking and behaviour, and the quality of our lives. Given that we are responsible for constructing many of these contextual factors and their content, it therefore seems to be an urgent priority to make sure we are building them to have positive rather than negative effects on us. This will be the starting point of Part 3.

The outline provided in Part 1 of how and why we think and behave is of course vastly simplified, but it should give us a much more realistic sense of ourselves than most of us have had up to now, and give us a more modest sense of ourselves as another creature on our planet that has evolved its limited set of capacities to achieve a particular set of aims, rather than possessing virtually unlimited intellectual capabilities that make us superior to the other animals that inhabit the earth. It also offers a richer, more nuanced picture of human beings than the rather one-dimensional view of us as simply biased, irrational creatures that some people may have picked up from recent popular psychology books.

We can use a behavioural trick to help us keep in mind the creatures we really are, in the form of a 5-point model to summarise some of the key features of how we think and behave. You can remember it with the acronym LASID – we are Limited, Adapted, Simplifying, Influenced and Deceived.

Limited

We do not see and experience our external reality and the world around us 'as it really is'. We only have a partial and particular view of reality, which is determined by our size, location and capabilities as creatures. Our brains also have limits, which are imposed by the senses we have, the electro-chemical process we use to think and our need to preserve precious energy. We can also experience the world in unusual ways that are more than just the sum of the reactions that caused them – such as the idea of being conscious or having a 'self'.

Adapted

Our thinking is adapted towards specific aims, and away from others. Our ability to think is directed at a specific, restricted set of aims, which ultimately enable us to pass our genes down the line within a specific environment, which is the one our hunter-gatherer ancestors lived in for much of human history, up to around 12,000 years ago. This includes the need to simplify the world, make sense of it and identify and respond to any threats to our survival. A consequence of our brain's focus towards particular aims is that its focus is directed *away from* other aims, such as those that we might value within particular cultures or at specific times – for example, judging everyone we meet in the same way.

Simplifying

We simplify the world, and this can lead to biases and inaccuracies in our thinking and behaviour. The reality of the world we live in is complex, so human brains need to simplify it in order for us to be able to survive in it and make sense of it, and to avoid using too much valuable energy thinking about this. We have a number of ways of doing this, including building 'models' in our minds of the world around us and the things in it, and using two levels of thinking – quick, automatic, energy-saving thought processes and more rational, effortful reasoning. Contrary to what humans have believed over the last 300 years, we tend to think more with the quick, automatic style of thinking than the rational side, as we don't have the capacity or energy to use rational thought all the time. Our use of these types of thinking can bring biases and errors in our judgements and decisions that can have consequences in the real world – from jumping to inaccurate conclusions with little information through to being vulnerable to manipulation when information is framed in particular ways.

Influenced

We do not think or behave as individuals, but in relation to context and other people. Some of the biggest differences between the brains of humans and other animals have evolved due to our need to navigate the complexity of relationships and co-operation with other people. As a result, we human beings don't think for ourselves anywhere near as much as we believe, because much of our thinking and behaviour is influenced by the presence or views of others. Our 'groupishness' is just one aspect of our broader tendency for our thinking and behaviour to be influenced by the context we are in. It may be more accurate to see ourselves as 'contextuals' than as individuals.

Deceived

We are built to deceive ourselves – including about how we think and behave. We are often unaware of the above limitations or influences on our thinking in our everyday experiences. We just assume that we make decisions and take action accordingly. This sophisticated self-deception serves several purposes, including helping us to make sense of the world and to feel in control of our actions. It can also have negative consequences, however, including making it difficult to get people to accept what we really are as creatures, and the consequent limitations of their thinking.

So, what does it mean overall that we are LASID – that we have this collection of traits? *Overall, it means that we are sophisticated creatures with brains built to simplify and simulate our environment, and to enable us to pass on our genes in the particular world we occupied for much of our history, up to 12,000 years ago.*

These evolved thinking and behavioural processes have proved incredibly successful for human beings in many ways, enabling us to build a global population of over 8 billion people and the cooperative abilities to feed this population, produce remarkable feats of learning and scientific ingenuity to improve the lifestyles of many people, and live in relatively peaceful societies for much of the time. But in the modern world we face a number of challenges as individuals and as a species. Some of these relate to our difficulty in fulfilling the expectations and hopes we have of ourselves as a species, such as our desire to minimise prejudice and violence. Other challenges represent existential crises that we are failing to address, such as climate change.

We have seen that each element of our particular mental and behavioural setup as creatures carries some disadvantages and that these can have consequences in our lives and wider societies – so might they be contributing to each of the challenges we're facing? And if so, how?

Part 2 will use our new-found knowledge of human beings to explore some of these challenges facing us in the modern world. In particular it will consider why we are struggling to meet these challenges, and how we can look at them in a more realistic way given the creatures we really are. This may not always result in the most optimistic view of our potential to resolve these challenges, as some may simply be difficult to solve given the creatures we are, and we may emerge with a brutal reality check as to what's possible. It will however explore how we can address each challenge more effectively by using our new knowledge about ourselves and harnessing our unique traits of thinking and behaviour.

Explaining our thinking and behaviour – creature and context

To help us understand why we think and behave as we do within the various challenges explored in Part 2, the 5-point LASID model can be made even clearer, by emphasising the importance of context on our thinking and behaviour. We are so highly attuned to other people and the context we find ourselves in that this can help to explain why we think and behave as we do in certain contexts.

The diagram below shows two things – us, as individual creatures, with our LASID way of thinking and behaving, and the context we find ourselves in. The context includes anything about our environment and relations with other people, from the immediate situation we find ourselves in through to the values that overarch our particular culture. Some simple examples of contextual factors have been included in the model below, and there may be many others.

Part 2 of the book will use this distinction between the creatures we are and the contexts we find ourselves in to understand how we behave in relation to each of the key challenges we face, and suggest some of the solutions open to us in improving our response to them. As will be shown, this model is key to the book – and to building a better future for human beings and our planet.

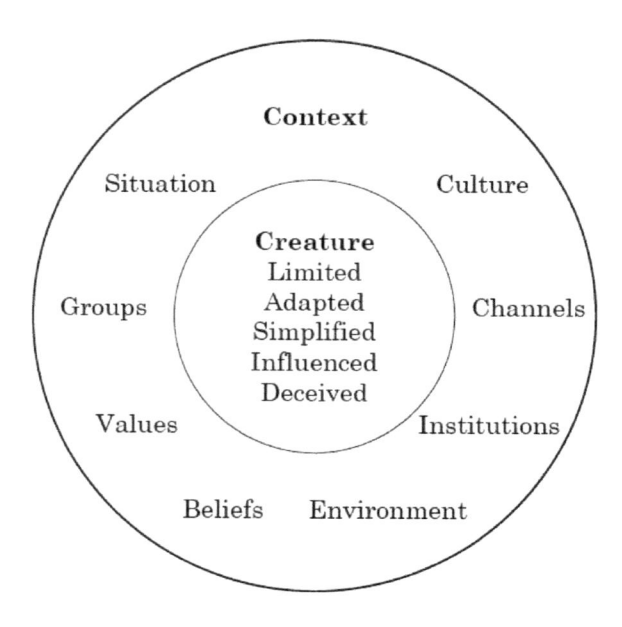

Context
- Situation
- Culture
- Groups
- Channels
- Values
- Institutions
- Beliefs
- Environment

Creature
Limited
Adapted
Simplified
Influenced
Deceived

One final point before Part 2. The book so far has aimed to take an objective view of human beings rather than judging or labelling them. It is meaningless to call human beings good, bad, imperfect, or anything else – we are simply the creatures we are, who have evolved with a particular range of thinking and behavioural processes, sometimes for better and sometimes for worse. Our challenge in building a better world and better lives is to make the best of the creatures we are.

Part 2
The challenges of
the modern world

Health

In brief – we are facing a global obesity epidemic that is killing millions of people every year. We live in a toxic health environment that promotes high calorie foods and sedentary lifestyles, making it difficult for people to eat healthily or lead active lives, given our evolved biological makeup and LASID thinking and behaviour. To tackle the problem of obesity we need to re-engineer our surroundings and society to establish healthy eating and physical exercise as default lifestyle choices.

Chapter 7
Why do we lead such unhealthy lifestyles?

On average, human beings are much healthier and longer-lived than we have ever been. For most of human history, life expectancy was around 25 to 30 years[91]. Between 1950 and 2024, global life expectancy at birth has risen from 47 years to 74[92]. This is an extraordinary human achievement, made possible through a range of technical, economic and cultural developments, including the discovery of effective vaccines, increased access to clean water and sanitation, and improvements in medical diagnosis and treatment[93].

Despite these advances, human beings face a growing global health crisis that is killing millions of people each year and condemning increasing numbers of children to life-long ill health and early death. It is obesity – a chronic disease characterised by an excess of fat deposits that can lead to a number of serious health problems, including an increased risk of heart disease, certain cancers and type 2 diabetes, as well as affecting bone health and reproduction[94]. The World Health Organisation (WHO) defines obesity based on a person's Body Mass Index – their weight in relation to their height. An individual is classed as overweight if they have a BMI greater than or equal to 25 and obese if it is greater than or equal to 30[95]. When someone reaches a BMI of 30, their risk of death has increased by 30 percent[96].

Obesity is a significant contributor to the global rise of non-communicable diseases (NCDs), which are becoming the main form of death and ill-health amongst human beings. The share of global deaths caused by NCDs has grown from 61 percent in 2000 to 74 percent in 2019. And NCDs haven't just caused deaths. They have also affected the quality of people's lives, and were responsible for 63% of global disability-adjusted life-years (DALYs) in 2019, up from 47% in 2000. To put it another way, this is 1.6 billion years of people's lives lost to early death or disability, in one year[97]. Obesity is not only a metabolic risk in its own right that contributes to NCDs, but also contributes to the other metabolic risks, such as raised blood pressure, hyperglycaemia (high blood glucose levels); and hyperlipidaemia (high levels of fat in the blood)[98]. In the United States, obesity is now responsible for more health care costs and chronic illness than smoking[99]. The WHO estimates that the current cost of obesity is just under US$1 trillion per year[100], but if we fail to act on this issue, the global cost of overweight and obesity could reach US$3 trillion by 2030[101] – an amount equivalent to the annual GDP of the United Kingdom[102].

In 2022 2.5 billion adults were classified as overweight or obese – 43 percent of the global adult population. This is a shocking figure and represents a massive rise from 25 percent in 1990 – a period of just 32 years. The proportion of overweight and obese children has also jumped in this period – from 8 percent in 1990 to 20 percent in 2022[103]. Levels of obesity vary around the world according to the diet and culture of each nation – for example, 36.2 percent of adults and 21.4 percent of children and adolescents in the US are obese, whereas comparable figures in Singapore are 6.1 percent for adults and 6.8 percent for children[104]. In recent years, some of the largest levels of growth in obesity have been in regions with previously low levels, including South East Asia (more than doubling from 1.9 percent in 2000 to 4.7 percent in 2019) and the Western Pacific region (again more than doubling from 2.7 percent to 6.4 percent in the same period).

These regional changes in obesity illustrate the main explanation for its overall rise – a new kind of lifestyle, focused on the consumption of calorie-dense foods coupled with a reduction in physical activity[105]. This is essentially the Western diet and lifestyle, which is becoming more popular in countries around the world as they develop economically. These changes have resulted in the tragically contradictory situation in which low-income countries or those in the middle of their economic transition face a double burden of malnutrition[106], with the dual problems of too few calories for some members of the population and too many for others, resulting in a rise in obesity and overweight, and the NCDs that follow them.

This chapter will explore the key drivers behind the rise of obesity – the rise of calorie-rich diets and the reduction in physical activity – and ask what, if anything, we can do to address them, as they represent one of the biggest threats to human life and flourishing in the modern world. It will show the crucial role played by our nature as creatures – our LASID thinking and behaviour and our biological setup in relation to food, as well as the modern environment we live within, including the institutions and communications that surround us. Many of the recommendations made in the next chapter in relation to obesity will also apply to other areas of health such as smoking and alcohol consumption – in particular the importance of changing people's environments so that they are conducive to healthy living, rather than working against it.

This chapter and the next will focus exclusively on how to prevent obesity rather than how to treat it once it has occurred. It could be argued that, up to now, a greater amount of attention has been given to tackling the symptoms and consequences of obesity than its causes. This can be simply demonstrated by the large number and size of charities that exist to tackle issues like heart disease and cancer, and the very few that exist to address the longer-term need to prevent obesity – a core driver of these maladies. It is important to invest a great deal more effort and resource in dealing with the causes of obesity, as prevention is more effective than attempting to treat the symptoms or the disease once it has manifested itself[107]. Dr Kelly Brownell, a nutrition expert, suggests a number of reasons for this. First, enormous numbers of people around the world could benefit from preventing obesity. Second, the disease can begin early in life and have a life-long effect, so early prevention when habits and attitudes are being formed could change an individual's life course. Obesity can also be difficult to treat and reverse in people. No more than 25 percent of people lose weight and maintain the lower weight, sometimes taking several attempts. Treatment is also expensive. Preventative healthcare programmes also have a history of success – for example, mandatory seatbelt laws introduced around the world since the 1970s have reduced the risk of fatal injuries for front-seat car occupants alone by 45 to 50 percent, saving millions of lives[108]. In addition, relying on an obese person to seek help to treat their condition often means that they present themselves to their doctor only when the obesity has led to other chronic conditions such as diabetes, which is much later than it needs to be[109]. So, preventing obesity is much more effective – and cost-effective – than attempting to cure it[110].

Our changing lifestyles

Human beings need energy for our bodies to function and survive, but we need to balance energy input with expenditure. If we expend less energy than we consume, our bodies store the energy as fat and we put on weight. This is the simplest explanation of obesity, but it can be misleading as it suggests that the disease is solely due to overeating or lack of exercise. This can make it tempting to lay the blame exclusively on obese people for their obesity, when this is in fact not the case, with a range of other factors contributing to our propensity to put on weight. For example, people process the energy they get from food in different ways with varying genetics, metabolic rates, exercise levels and other factors dictating how they do this. An obese person may eat considerably less than a lean one, but still put on weight if they do not make use of the energy they have consumed[111].

In addition, not all sources of energy are equal – different foods have different energy densities and our bodies need a range of sources of energy, including fats, proteins and carbohydrates, to build tissue growth (for example, for bones and muscles) and provide the energy for cells to multiply. They also need micronutrients such as particular vitamins and minerals for certain bodily functions to take place – for example, iodine is an essential component of thyroid hormones[112]. So good nutrition for human beings requires a range of foods that contain a particular balance of energy and nutrient sources.

These factors, including the amount and type of energy we consume, the level of exercise we take and even the activation of our genes, can be greatly influenced by the environment that surrounds us. Some of the key environmental factors that affect us will be explored shortly, as well as how our biology and psychology as LASID (limited, adapted, simplifying, influenced and deceived) creatures interact with these factors to influence our behaviours. The key point to note at this stage, however, is that our environment has changed enormously over time.

First, the availability of calories around us has increased and intensified. Food is much easier to obtain than it was for our ancestors – even those of a few hundred years ago. The average number of calories available to (but not necessarily used by) each person per day in the UK in 1270 was 2,203, but by 2018 this had risen to 3,314 – a rise of over 1,000 calories per day[113]. The energy balance of foods has also changed. Since the industrialisation of food production, many foods have been enriched to make them taste better, which results in more energy-dense foods with greater levels of sugar and fat.

There is also a much greater variety of foods available to us than ever before. The globalisation of the food system brings every conceivable food to our doors. The industrialisation of food production has also brought the manufacture and processing of a vast range of new food products, with a complex range of additives, colourings and flavourings that make it harder to understand what we are eating or whether the balance of foods we are consuming is actually good for us. This increase in calorie availability and complexity of food choices has been further turbo-charged by new ways in which food is distributed and marketed, which will be explored later in the chapter.

Whilst the calorie availability in our environment has significantly increased, our levels of physical activity have reduced. In traditional societies, from our hunter-gatherer ancestors to manual agriculturalists, people spent a considerable amount of time and energy on gathering food. As cities and towns built up, only the richest people were able to avoid physical labour. This changed with the advent of the industrial revolution, which brought a range of technological developments that eased the physical burdens across most areas of our lives, including the use of agricultural machinery to process food, cars for transportation and household labour-saving devices such as the washing machine[114].

These developments did not just ease our physical burdens however – they transformed our lives from physically active to sedentary. For many people, work now consists of sitting at a desk for several hours a day. We travel to work using cars rather than walking or cycling. Food is easily available to us with the expenditure of almost no physical effort aside from picking up a mobile phone. These changes have increased our risk of obesity – for example, in China, India and Thailand the rise in childhood obesity has a correlation with the reduction in cycling, walking and other forms of exercise[115]. Our leisure activities have also become much more sedentary – perhaps most notably with the advent of the television. In the UK the average person spends nearly 4.5 hours per day watching TV and video content[116]. The rise of smartphones and computer screens is extending this trend even further, and creating a new set of issues for humankind.

Our physical activity has therefore dropped in every aspect of our lives, including how we work, how we spend our leisure time and how we get from A to B. Physical activity has dropped to worrying levels for a creature that evolved to thrive on it. In the United States, 28 percent of adults undertake no physical activity and 28 percent are not active regularly. Perhaps more shockingly, nearly half of all children take part in no regular physical activity[117].

This lack of physical activity has had a devastating effect on our health, and is one of the top 10 causes of disability and disease in the UK, costing this country alone around £7.4 billion a year[118]. It also plays a key role alongside overeating in driving the rise in obesity. Studies suggest that physical activity can help people to lose weight, but not necessarily to significant levels. One study suggested a total weight loss of around 0.4-2.6kg is achieved through physical exercise[119]. Physical activity has a range of other powerful benefits to human health though, including as an effective tool to help people avoid putting on weight[120], as well as keeping the body physically fit and promoting mental health[121]. Studies show that being fit is related to longer life and lower rates of many of the NCDs, including heart disease, diabetes and stroke[122]. Physical fitness is also important for people who are overweight, as heavier people who are fit have a lower risk of disease than people who are thin but unfit. At the same time, the absence of physical activity is related to poorer health. Less active children have higher blood pressure, and lower levels of 'good' cholesterol – indicators of heart disease[123]. Physical exercise may therefore not represent a 'cure' for obesity on its own, but has an important role to play in preventing it, as well as promoting better general health, better quality of life and greater longevity[124].

In summary then, the number of calories available to us in our environment has significantly increased, whilst our levels of physical activity have reduced. This mix is fuelling our obesity crisis.

Why do we lead such unhealthy lifestyles?

This section will explore some of the key factors that can lead to us living unhealthy lifestyles. It will first examine factors within our biological and LASID makeup as individuals, and then external factors that can influence our thinking and behaviour.

Our traits as individuals

A complex range of factors influence the foods we choose to eat and drink, as well as how much of each we choose to consume. These include our biology, learned behaviours, social norms and other environmental influences. This section will examine some of our characteristics as individual creatures that play a role in the food choices and behaviour that drive obesity, including a range of psychological factors.

    Basic biological factors – our biology can affect our body weight in a number of ways, and interacts with our psychology to do this. It can influence our food preferences, metabolic rate, sense of fullness after eating and ability to lose weight.

    – **Our need for calories** – a fundamental starting point in our relationship with food is that, for human beings to survive, our biology dictates that we need to gain weight or at least maintain the weight we have. To do this, our bodies seek to maintain a positive energy balance, where the calories we consume exceed the calories we expend to obtain them. We are therefore biologically inclined to prefer foods with greater energy density – those high in fat and sugars – above others[125]. If we consume greater energy than we expend, we store this energy for use at a later point – in the form of fat[126].

- **The ecology of our gut** – there has recently been increased interest in the role of the gut environment in our health and diets. For example, the foods we eat appear to affect how we process foods generally due to their impact on the trillions of microorganisms in our guts that help us do this digestive and processing work[127]. A study based at Stamford University in the US found that people who reduced their levels of processed foods (particularly refined grains and sugars) lost a significant amount of weight without needing to worry about calories or portion sizes[128].

- **Pre- and postnatal development** – the main settings that our bodies use to regulate our supply and consumption of energy – including the appetite we have for food, how we burn energy and what we do with any excess energy – are established early in life, some in our developmental stages before birth[129]. The energy system that keeps our bodily engines running evolved, like everything else within human beings, to help us survive and pass on our genes in the environments our hunter-gatherer ancestors inhabited for the vast majority of human history. Our metabolism was designed for a very different environment from the one we inhabit in the modern world[130].

Geneticist James Neel was one of the first theorists to suggest that there was a mismatch between the environments we evolve to live in and those of the modern world. He suggested that our hunter-gatherer ancestors would have experienced periods of either feast or famine, and that we evolved a set of 'thrifty' genes that helped us survive famine, such as those that promote fat storage. In a modern world with a plentiful energy supply, this would lead us to store excess energy as fat, driving diseases such as obesity[131]. This remains a popular theory among some biologists, but evidence in recent decades suggests that it is incorrect, as hunter-gatherers had reasonably good nutrition and suffered relatively little famine, so did not require this 'thrifty' metabolic setup[132].

The idea of an environmental mismatch seems to be correct however, although it is based on the sensitivity of an individual to their environment. As biology Professors Peter Gluckman and Mark Hanson note in their book *Mismatch*, we have the capacity for 'developmental plasticity' in the development of the human foetus, in which the expression of certain genes can be altered in response to environmental signals. In this particular case, the foetus responds to the nutritional signals coming from its mother, as well as the nutritional environment within the womb. This is not of course a conscious process within the foetus, but its response through the activation of certain genes. If the foetus 'forecasts' a nutritionally poor environment, it will activate genes that promote short-term survival rather than long-term flourishing, including reducing muscle bulk, seeking high-fat foods when possible and storing fat to preserve energy when it can.

Our problem in the modern world is that the messages we often send to our foetuses or neonates misinform them about their futures. We indicate a nutritionally poor environment, so the foetus develops a metabolism for short-term survival rather than long-term flourishing, but once they are born they actually live in a calorifically rich environment. This leads to long-term health problems for them later in life such as obesity, insulin resistance and high blood pressure[133]. As an example, research shows that the smaller a baby is at birth, the more likely it will be to develop diabetes or die of heart disease in middle or older age[134]. This is a state of metabolic mismatch.

What could indicate a nutritionally poor environment? First, there is the biological principle of maternal constraint[135] – we have evolved to expect a worse environment than we actually experience within the womb, which gives us a safety cushion of additional energy resources in case we need them. This has become evolutionarily disadvantageous, however, in a world as nutrient-rich as the one we inhabit. There are several other ways a foetus could become misinformed – one is through maternal conditions such as preeclampsia, where fewer nutrients reach the foetus, and another is maternal smoking which also impedes nutrient supply. Mothers-to-be eating unbalanced diets is another factor, either through eating less nutritious foods or through dieting, the latter a common occurrence during pregnancy in many countries due to the belief that it reduces the chances of difficult childbirth. Some of the most important activities in gene expression in the new foetus happen in the first few weeks of pregnancy when a mother might not realise she is pregnant or be monitoring it, as no more than half of women specifically plan when they will conceive[136]. This means that they might not be taking additional measures to improve or support their nutrition, with one study suggesting 50 percent of women were eating what was classed as an 'imprudent' diet around the time of conception[137], and further strengthens the importance of people maintaining good general nutrition throughout life – to give a better life to their children as well.

In summary, a metabolic mismatch in the early development of children is another driver of obesity and NCDs – and one that can be at least partially resolved by better nutrition around the time of the foetus's development.

Psychology and emotions – our interactions with food can be broadly split into three categories – emotional eating, dietary restraint and disinhibition[138]:

- **Emotional eating** – eating food, especially the food we like, releases endorphins (endogenous opioids) in the brain and can make us feel good. Some people, termed emotional eaters, may use food as a way of enhancing their mood when it is low or they are anxious or depressed – for example, eating a bowl of ice cream if feeling upset. Emotional eaters' choices of 'low mood foods' are subjective, but share the same characteristics of being relatively high in sugar or fat, as these properties increase the chances of stimulating the release of opioids in our brains. Emotional eating can bring a number of possible consequences, including compelling individuals to choose more energy-dense foods, overeating, undereating, and generally undermining their usual control of their food choices[139]. It can also become a coping mechanism that makes people avoid dealing with their core emotional issues.

- **Dietary restraint** – this type of behaviour is an attempt to deliberately restrict or control one's calorie intake in order to stop weight gain and promote a certain image. At its extreme is anorexia nervosa but it exists on a spectrum which most of us occupy when we attempt to regulate our food intake in response to environmental conditions – including social factors, such as how we want other people to perceive us[140].
- **Disinhibition** – when we are distracted from our food or the amount we are consuming, this can lead to us eating more than we normally would. For example, watching television while eating can take our attentional resources away from monitoring how much we have consumed and whether we are full[141]. Alcohol consumption is another disinhibitor, as it has been shown to reduce our attentional resources and our ability to control our intake of food, which leads to overconsumption[142]. Other examples of disinhibition include impulsive eating, in which people eat without thinking, as well as emotional eating outlined earlier, in which the emotion itself is the disinhibitor. A final form of disinhibition

to mention, and one that is highly relevant to some of our modern obesity problems, is external eating. This is the tendency to become disinhibited in one's eating in response to environmental cues to eat – something that most of us do – for example, eating more if there is plentiful food available or if there are immediate sensory cues to eat in the surrounding environment.

Learning – the development of eating behaviours in human beings starts before birth, and is a complex process. Infants and children learn food preferences and behaviours from a range of sources, including particular experiences, associations, sibling behaviour and parenting styles. For example, social learning theory suggests that children learn from observing and modelling (copying) the behaviour of others, particularly those close to them who they want to emulate. Parental behaviour and food preferences can therefore influence children, and modelling positive food behaviours alongside positive reinforcement (such as praising good behaviour) can make it more likely that children will adopt this behaviour[143]. Parenting style can also affect children's eating behaviours, with permissive parents (those who set no behavioural boundaries and indulge their children) gaining the worst long-term outcomes for children, potentially making them less mature and responsible[144], and too focused on the pursuit of pleasure when making their food choices[145].

Social environment – as LASID creatures, our social environment also influences how we feel about food, as well as our food choices and behaviour. The groups we belong to can influence our choices of what foods are acceptable and how much of them to eat, as we feel social pressure to conform to the norms of these groups[146]. Examples of this could include a group of liberal middle-class parents wanting to avoid taking their children to eat at a fast food outlet, a religion banning the consumption of particular types of food, or a cultural norm to eat steak in a US farming state like Texas. Foods can induce stereotypical thinking, such as the possible negative attitudes towards working class people eating in fast food restaurants that might form part of the views of the liberal middle-class group above.

Social identity can also play a role in our eating habits, with the desire to be seen in a particular light by others influencing not only the food we eat but also our portion sizes. For example, a study in 2007[147] found that both men and women who eat in the presence of familiar eating companions eat more than those dining with unfamiliar co-eaters. This may have been driven by a concern about how they wished to be seen by the less familiar people and therefore how they presented themselves and their behaviour. It also found that women sought to copy the amount their co-diners were eating, whereas all-male groups differed in their intake. The authors of the study suggested that the matching of eating behaviours could be aiming to foster group cohesion, whereas their differentiation could be linked to a male desire for distinctiveness, as reflected by other studies[148][149]. The desire to manage other people's impressions of us can affect our eating behaviour in other ways – for example, in attempting to display a body image that is favourable to one's social and cultural group.

Heuristics and biases – our choices about food, and indeed about anything else, can be influenced by some of the heuristics and biases in human thinking that were discussed in Part 1. This can make it more difficult for us to make effective, balanced decisions on issues such as which food products to choose. For example, if nutritional information is presented in a complex way, most people are likely to try to save cognitive energy and make a quick (and possibly inaccurate) judgement based on a brief look at the information. This also means we are highly vulnerable to communications – whether advertising, packaging, or anything else – that deliberately seek to manipulate us into buying and consuming particular products by exploiting these traits in our thinking. For example, if a product such as a yoghurt is labelled as 'low fat', our propensity for *what you see is all there is* (WYSIATI) thinking (see page 36) could lead us to mistakenly think it is healthy, and not look for further details indicating it has high levels of sugar. The *mere exposure effect* (see page 41) is used by advertisers to build our loyalty to particular brands through repeated exposure to them through advertising and the media. *Framing* (see page 42) can be used to manipulate a vast array of nutritional information, such as claims that one variety of biscuit is healthier than another, which might be based on one variable alone (such as it having slightly lower levels sugar) but where the product is still unhealthy, despite the favourable comparison.

There are countless other examples of how our traits of thinking and behaviour can make us vulnerable to making poor food choices and being manipulated by those who would want to do so. As the 'context' section below will show, there are plenty of powerful people and companies who want to do this in the food industry.

Summary of individual factors – our thinking and behaviour relating to food and eating is highly complex, driven by a mixture of biological drives, learning, instincts, emotions and thinking, but can be simplified down to the idea that we are naturally attracted towards high calorie foods. This makes us eat more, and higher levels of calories, when we are surrounded by an environment that has high availability of these foods, and strong promotion of them. As will now be shown, the latter is a good description of the modern world.

The context we live within

As LASID creatures, our thinking and behaviour are strongly influenced by the context we live within, from the groups we belong to through to our immediate surroundings. This context dependence is illustrated well by the problem of obesity. Research suggests that up to 40 percent of fluctuation in body weight can be attributed to genetic factors, leaving 60 percent or more down to our environment[150]. How do we know the environment is the major cause of this obesity epidemic? The speed of the rise in obesity levels means that it can't be our genes or shifts in our biology. A report by Harvard University School of Public Health notes that changes in our genetic makeup are unlikely to have caused the fast rise in obesity around the world over the last 40 years, as the gene pool across a population remains relatively stable for many generations[151]. Scientists and the WHO agree it is due to changes in our environment[152] – which we can see from countries in transition, where obesity rates grow as lifestyles become more westernised and modern. One study analysed the weights of 247 people who had moved from the Punjab in India to London, and compared them with 117 of their siblings who stayed in India. The group in London had body weights that were 19 percent higher than the one remaining in India – as well as higher cholesterol and blood pressure[153].

Research suggests that most people intend to eat healthily[154]. But we live in an environment where we are surrounded by influences and structures that tend to steer our food decisions towards unhealthy options. These influences make it difficult for people to maintain a healthy diet[155]. This section will examine some of the contextual factors that influence our thinking and behaviour on food and physical exercise, and that in combination create a health environment that many scientists describe as 'obesogenic' or 'toxic'.

Parenting and social pressure – it has already been shown how parental behaviour in pre-and post-natal stages affects our propensity for obesity later in life, and how many parents-to-be are not paying enough attention to the nutrition they give themselves – and, by association, their developing children – in prenatal stages. Once a baby is born, poor nutrition can continue to send signals to the child's biology to expect a calorie-poor later environment, meaning that when it does receive calories it will put on fat rapidly[156]. Equally, overnutrition, such as when babies are fed cow's milk rather than human milk, can lead to obesity[157].

Leading health institutions recommend that infants should be exclusively breastfed for the first 6 months of their lives. In the US in 2019, a report suggested that around 63 percent of infants were exclusively breastfed around the time of birth, but that this dropped to just under 25 percent by 6 months. The US Surgeon General cites a key reason for this being a lack of paid maternity leave for mothers, particularly those employed on lower incomes, which forces them to return to work earlier than they wish or than is optimal for their infant's health.

As a child develops, it and its parents face a barrage of influences encouraging it to eat unhealthily, many of which will be explored shortly, including advertising through a range of channels, and poor nutrition at school. It also faces a lack of physical activity. Parents still have a role to play themselves in providing nutritious food, an active home environment and modelling positive behaviour, but their own diets have become poorer and their activity levels have declined[158]. This results in a toxic food environment and poor parental models for some children, and, as one might expect, studies show that the diets and exercise patterns of parents predict the likelihood of a child being overweight.

Our lifestyles – food lifestyles at home have changed over recent decades. Convenience food was virtually unheard of before the Second World War, after which technology, social change and economic growth led to a desire for greater convenience and less time spent in household tasks including cooking. Our consumption of convenience foods – often including higher quantities of fat and sugar – has risen significantly over the years and this growth is projected to continue[159].

We also eat out much more than we did a few decades ago. The first McDonald's fast food restaurant opened in the UK in 1974, and the chain now has more than 1,450 outlets across this nation alone[160], and more than 36,000 around the world[161]. Where eating out was once considered an occasional luxury, it is now a regular activity for many people; for example, on a typical day, more than 40 percent of adults in the US eat in a restaurant[162]. A study in China showed that more than 85 percent of respondents ate out once or more each week. The same research found a correlation between more eating out and less intake of fruit and vegetables[163]. A study of the top five fast food restaurants in the US found that their meals contained levels of calories and fat that exceeded dietary recommendations, and lower levels of fibre[164].

Our search for convenience has taken a further step. In the UK there has been a significant rise in the consumption of takeaway food, which rose by 50 percent between the start of the Covid-19 pandemic and early 2022, a trend that the Institute for Fiscal Studies suggests is likely to be long-term rather than a temporary blip due to the pandemic. The rise of takeaways, particularly through delivery services that can be ordered in minutes via the mobile phone, suggests that people are eating more high calorie food but with even less physical effort expended than driving to the supermarket – a toxic mix for their health.

These changes have combined to increase the number of calories people are likely to consume in a week, in comparison to those they would consume if just cooking and eating at home. Along with this calorie-increasing shift in our food lifestyles, we have seen changes in how we spend our leisure time. Televisions only started to become affordable to the general public after the Second World War, and by 2019, 95 percent of households in the UK had a TV set[165]. Watching television now occupies a significant amount of the leisure time of many people, including infants and young children[166]. The average US adult spends over 4 hours watching TV each day[167]. Numerous studies have shown that time spent watching television is linked with obesity and consumption of unhealthy food in countries around the world, including Australia, Spain and the US[168]. Our lifestyles have therefore become richer in calories yet more sedate.

Our local environments – the areas in which we live set up a template for our behaviours. For example, if someone lives in a neighbourhood with poor public transport and where it feels unsafe to walk alone, they are less likely to undertake physical activity there. Our local infrastructures are still geared up to car use rather than public transport, walking and cycling – and our habits follow. In the US, a quarter of all journeys are less than a mile long, but 75 percent of these are taken by car[169]. The demise of our high streets and lack of integrated public transport mean that people drive to out-of-town supermarkets rather than visiting local shops. There are insufficient cycle paths and many people (particularly women) feel uncomfortable walking on the streets after dark.

These trends are often exacerbated by poverty. People who have less money tend to live in less safe neighbourhoods, with poorer facilities for physical activity or shopping. There is also an inequitable supply of healthy food. Supermarkets are much more common in wealthy areas[170], and a study in Australia found that people living in poorer areas are exposed to fast food outlets 2.5 times more than those living in other areas[171]. Living in these 'food deserts' has been linked with poorer quality diets and increased risk of becoming overweight[172].

Poverty also reduces opportunities for exercise. One study in the US showed that people with lower incomes were less likely to meet recommended exercise levels than wealthier people, and reported having fewer places available for exercise than those with more income[173]. Aside from living in neighbourhoods that feel less safe and promote less walking and cycling, sports activities and facilities can also be unaffordable for people with lower incomes. The price of going to the gym, joining a football club or simply going for a swim can be out of the reach of many people. Tackling the inequalities in accessing healthy lifestyles is therefore one of the priorities in preventing obesity.

Institutions – the official structures and organisations that surround us in our lives shape and constrain our thinking and behaviour in relation to food and physical activity in significant ways. Below are some examples of key institutions and some of their impacts:

- **Schools** – although they are supposed to be the institutions we entrust to nurture and care for our most precious family members, schools can exacerbate the high-calorie, low-exercise environments we want to protect our children from. First, school lunches are a key source of nutrition for children, and for some children from lower income families, the most important source in their day. It is therefore depressing to read the evidence from a study by Imperial College London in 2022 which found that 64 percent of the calories in school meals are from ultra-processed foods, including ultra-processed bread, puddings, snacks and high sugar drinks, which increase the risk of obesity[174]. Packed lunches were found to contain even more calories from highly processed foods than school meals[175]. Second, children in many schools around the world are exposed to a barrage of advertising and other influences from junk food manufacturers within their school day. This varies considerably between countries, with children in schools within the UK for example exposed to much less advertising and commercial pressure than those in the US. This exposure can take many forms, including unhealthy food in vending machines, sponsorship of educational materials and direct advertising of junk food. For example, educational materials in the US can be hijacked by food companies, with *Skittles Math Riddles* and the *Hershey Milk Chocolate Bar Fractions Book* just a couple of examples[176].

There is little rebalancing in favour of healthy eating in response to all this promotion of unhealthy food, as there is insufficient education about food and health in schools – from understanding the types and amounts of food that human beings need through to the practicalities of how to adopt and maintain healthy food habits, as well as how to respond to the manifold pressures in a child's environment to eat unhealthy food.

Coupled with the poor food environment in school is an inadequate exercise environment. Only 37 percent of secondary school children in the UK walk to school[177], and in general, when they get there, they do not do enough physical activity. Regularity of physical education (PE) lessons will vary by school, but if a child is only having two PE lessons a week, this constitutes very little exercise, as a typical gym class will only keep a child aerobically active for 3.5 minutes[178]. And if children don't get physical activity in classes, they are very unlikely to do it in other school time[179]. Alongside their sedentary lives at home, it therefore seems incredibly unlikely that most children in the UK will reach the National Health Service's guidelines of at least 60 minutes of moderate or vigorous physical activity daily each week[180].

- **Health care** – health services in countries around the world are at the sharp end of the obesity epidemic, tasked with treating the manifold impacts of our calorie-rich and activity lifestyles on our health. It is therefore surprising to find retail spaces within hospitals and other health settings in the UK being let out to fast food outlets such as Burger King, and many of the shops in these spaces selling largely unhealthy food. This not only encourages visitors to eat poor quality food and buy it for patients, but also sends confusing signals to the public as to which foods are healthy and which are harmful. Studies show that fast food outlets within hospitals can influence people to think that this food is healthier than it actually is[181].

- **Workplaces** – since the Industrial Revolution, work has become a much more sedentary activity for most human beings. We sit for 7 or 8 hours a day in our office or at home – a practice that is known to be bad for the human body in several ways, impeding blood flow, contributing to back pain and making us sedentary[182]. Even when people meet their daily recommended targets of minimum exercise by exercising before or after work, research suggests they may still be in greater danger of obesity, heart disease and diabetes, as their impeded blood flow from prolonged sitting increases the risk of these diseases[183]. We therefore need to be moving at regular intervals throughout the day to keep healthy.

The busy and pressurised nature of modern work, fuelled by the imperatives of greater profit and productivity, reduces people's willingness to take adequate breaks or be away from their desks. It also leads to a choice of grabbing food 'on the go' rather than a nutritious meal, which can increase our amounts of unhealthy foods and snacks. Time is therefore an important resource we have lost that could help us counter obesity.

Food availability and pricing – we have an abundance of calories in the modern world. But the problem lies in the fact that healthy foods are not easily available and affordable for everyone, whereas unhealthy, energy dense foods are. Below are some key contributors to this situation:

- **Types of food** – over recent decades there has been a big change in the types of food available to human beings to eat within a 'Western' diet. For example, our consumption of fast food has grown at a rapid rate. Spending on fast food in the US in the year 2000 was 18 times that in 1970[184]. Children in the US now consume more of their calories from fast food than they do from school food[185]. Fast food generally contains more fat and sugar and fewer nutrients than other meals. So, the energy density of our food has increased, but its nutrient density has dropped, with many food products offering us 'empty calories' with little nutritional benefit. Alongside the ubiquity of fast food is the rise of ultra-processed foods – those that contain at least one ingredient you wouldn't usually find in a kitchen, plus other ingredients not found in home cooking such as preservatives, artificial colours and flavourings. These foods, such as ice cream, ham and crisps, form a large proportion of many people's diets. They often contain higher levels of fat, salt and sugar than other foods, and their level of processing can also reduce the benefits we get from their ingredients. For these reasons, ultra-processed foods present a range of health risks beyond obesity. For example, the World Health Organisation reports that one 50 gram portion a day of processed meat (such as sausages, ham or hot dogs) increases the chances of colorectal cancer by 18%[186].

Another notable food development affecting obesity rates is the rise of snacking. Snacks are responsible for an increasing proportion of our daily calorie intake – representing nearly a quarter of the calories we consume each day. A study in the US showed that not only has the amount of snacking increased since the 1970s, but also the energy density of snacks (both food and drink)[187]. A significant increase has taken place in the consumption of salty snacks, crisps and nuts, as well as a small reduction in the consumption of fruit, dairy products and desserts[188].

- **Cost of food** – healthy, nutrient-dense foods are more expensive than unhealthy, calorie-dense ones[189]. People with lower socioeconomic status (SES) have been shown to consume more energy-dense diets than more affluent people, and food pricing and affordability have been shown to be one of the reasons for this, alongside ease of access to energy-dense foods[190]. Alongside these basic price differences, the food industry provides perverse economic incentives to consumers, which tend to drive the promotion of unhealthy rather than nutritious foods. For example, a 'Meal Deal' in a fast food outlet will buy you a burger, fries and soft drink for less than it costs to buy these items separately, thereby incentivising greater consumption of calories. This only represents value if you were going to purchase all three items anyway, but in most cases it simply represents being persuaded to eat more. This is exacerbated by the practice of upscaling food options, in which food retailers attempt to encourage consumers to 'go large' by offering a tempting financial value incentive to add even more calories to their meal.

- **Portion sizes** – since the 1970s food portion sizes have increased, both for food eaten away from home and food eaten at home[191]. For example, soft drinks have increased by over 50 percent, from 13.1 to 19.9 fl oz (resulting in 49 extra calories) and hamburgers by over 20 percent, from 5.7 to 7.0 oz (by 97 additional calories)[192]. A 'grab bag' of crisps is roughly equivalent to two standard packs, but is now treated as normal portion size by many people. Larger portions are seen as a demonstration of value for money, so food retailers have an economic incentive to provide them, and consumers are keen to seek this value for money. Human beings find it hard to identify what constitutes a serving of food – a study in a weight loss programme found a 64 percent error on average in estimating the quantity of foods and a 53 percent error in estimating calories. Studies also show that, when people are served more food, they eat more[193], and that people are bad at compensating for overeating in an earlier meal at a later one. These factors combined mean that additional portion sizes contribute to the rise in human calorific consumption[194].

Food packaging and labelling – the way food is packaged and labelled plays an important role in its appeal to us, as well as the decisions we make about whether to eat it and how much of it to eat. In the modern world it has become an aspect of marketing – another means of trying to persuade us to buy and eat the food rather than informing us about its content and nutritional value.

The design of packaging includes several factors that can influence us, including the presence of a recognisable brand, the appeal of the particular product to its target audience, and the information about the product that the packaging chooses to highlight. Branding can include characters or logos that make products more familiar and attractive to people (especially children), such as Tony the Tiger on Frosties, and Ronald McDonald. A study of Australian children aged 9 to 10 found that more than half believe that Ronald McDonald knows best what they should eat[195].

Despite the presence of mandatory food labelling requirements in some countries, food companies can present information about a product's nutritional value in a skewed way that casts a positive light on their product but misleads consumers, making it harder for them to make good food choices. For example, in today's world where many people are trying to eat healthily, foods are presented as being healthy when they are not, or where there are much healthier, simpler alternatives available. Take breakfast cereal bars for instance, which are marketed as a quick alternative to breakfast when one is 'on the go'. Their packaging implies that they are healthy, containing terms such as 'Nutri-Grain' and 'wholesome ingredients'[196]. But research by UK consumer watchdog Which? revealed that some of these bars contain 'staggering' levels of sugar[197]. For example, Kellogg's Nutri-Grain Breakfast Bakes Choc Chip bars contain 37 percent sugar – more than a high-sugar cereal like Crunchy Nut Cornflakes[196].

Mandatory food labelling information varies by country. The UK's food labelling regulations were retained from EU law after Brexit. They state that nutritional information must be provided on the back of the packet of most pre-packed foods[198], and set out in a particular format that is easy for the consumer to read, including the amount of certain nutrients (including fat and sugar) per 100g[199]. This is a useful initiative and provides a consistent and clear way for consumers to compare the nutritional value products. Due to our desire for cognitive ease however, many people will not consult this information on the back of a packet in detail, and will look at summarised information on the front instead. Nutritional labelling on the front of food packaging is not mandatory however, and despite the implementation of voluntary 'traffic light' schemes indicating the level of calories, fat, saturated fat, sugar and salt in the product (green signalling low levels, yellow moderate and red indicating high levels)[200], this information is not always consistent and can be manipulated by manufacturers to give the impression of a healthier product. The independent UK consumer company Which? notes that companies use differing portion sizes[201] – with some manufacturers, such as Dorset Cereals, reducing the recommended portion sizes for their products in order to give the impression that their sugar content is shrinking[202]. Which? argues that this has resulted in 'chaos' in food labelling standards and can confuse consumers and can mislead them into poor food choices and selecting unhealthy products[203].

Food marketing – the channels and techniques used to promote food go way beyond the packaging and labelling of individual items. We are surrounded by advertising and other messages from food companies and sellers aiming to influence us to buy their products and eat more – regardless of the health dangers of consuming their products.

- **Advertising** – food advertising is everywhere – online, on TV, in magazines, newspapers and many other channels. Just as one example, in the United States 8.5 to 10 minutes of every hour an individual spends watching TV is focused on adverts, many of which are for food[204].

    Advertising works – watching television promotes increased consumption[205]. Unfortunately, it also increases our risk of obesity and poor health. Children who watch ads for foods high in sugar choose more sugary foods, whether these are advertised or not[206]. Several pieces of research show a link between time watching television and factors such as greater calorie intake and what products children ask their parents to buy[207]. A UK survey by YouGov in 2018 found that the probability of obesity in young people was more than doubled when they reported seeing junk food advertising each day, compared with when they did not recall seeing any such adverts in the previous month[208]. This trend applied across advertising on television, billboards and social media. Research suggests that exposing children to food advertising increases the amount of food they consume, regardless of whether it is relevant to the brand being advertised or not. This is because children don't recognise the brand as a distinct product, and the advertisement for a particular chocolate bar therefore elicits a desire for chocolate bars generally[209].

Advertising can change people's eating behaviours in other ways – for example, a study by the Wall Street Journal found that the most important factor influencing people's decisions between food items is their branding[210]. Brands can become entrenched in people's minds, with other brands not considered, even though they may be of an equal quality and significantly cheaper – for example, supermarket own-brand cereals are often less than half the cost of major brands, yet major brands outsell them many times over[211]. This results in people spending a portion of their valuable food budget on something essentially worthless that could be spent on buying healthier foods.

As a demonstration of the effectiveness of food advertising, in 2022, the food industry in the US spent a total of 7.5 billion dollars on advertising – with restaurants spending an additional 9 billion dollars[212].

Food marketing extends way beyond traditional advertising, however. Television and film characters have become connected with food products, as these have been found to boost sales, often to children. For example, Disney has partnered with food companies on many occasions, including featuring Toy Story character Buzz Lightyear in McDonald's Happy Meals[213], and Beauty and the Beast on

Kellog's Corn Flakes packs[214]. These partnerships may appear to be benign, but they create associations between food products and characters that children love, which can influence them into wanting the unhealthy food product. Adults are not immune to this tactic either, with companies like Pepsi and Coca Cola sponsoring major sporting events such as the football World Cup, or partnering with sporting heroes like Lionel Messi, and creating a potentially confusing and damaging halo effect between healthy sport and their high sugar food products. Product placement is also rife in films and television series, with the subtle (and not-so-subtle) placement of products within entertainment content in order to capitalise on the *mere exposure* effect (to build people's familiarity, and therefore positive feelings, towards brands) or to associate them with attractive characters – such as the regular appearance of beer brand Heineken in James Bond films.

    We generally see marketing as persuasion, and persuasion as benign – at its worst, a salesman who puts his foot in the door and talks for ages – but something we can easily reject. Manipulation differs from persuasion in that it seeks to change someone's thinking and behaviour in ways that target their vulnerabilities – and in this way, can be seen as less acceptable.

    Given what we now know about human beings being LASID creatures in our thinking and behaviour, we can see that many of the influencing techniques used today – including some of those traditionally classed as 'persuasion', can actually be classed as manipulation. For example, at its most basic level, advertising could tell you what a product is and how much it costs, so that you can decide whether to buy it. This is not how advertising works in the modern world however. Advertising uses behavioural science to understand the target audience's needs and motivations, and looks to create new needs and wants within people to convince them to buy products. This is manipulation of people for profit.

Advertisers may argue that advertising helps people to make choices about products available to them. However, as we are LASID creatures, advertising can convince us to eat more, to desire things that we didn't want before (such as extra calories) and to make unhealthy food choices. In short, advertising exploits our vulnerabilities as LASID creatures in order for companies (whether selling food or any other product) to make money out of us. This seems a particularly shameful treatment of other human beings with regard to food, as it is knowingly selling us food that will make us unhealthy and ill – simply to make greater profits.

If this sounds like a rather cynical view, consider how food companies target children with junk food ads in the US, or how 82 percent of billboard advertisements are located in the poorest parts of England and Wales, pushing greater consumption at the most vulnerable people[215]. And, just to complete the food connection, the top 5 spenders on advertising in the UK between 2021-23 included Coca Cola, McDonald's and Kentucky Fried Chicken[216].

- **Role of the mass media** – the media sources surrounding us send confusing and conflicting messages about what is desirable in our relationship with food. They promote a thin body image as the epitome of beauty, making those who don't have this physique feel inadequate, whilst filling the airwaves, newsprint and screens with advertising and promotion of junk food products that will make people obese.

- **Persuasion in the supermarket** – the attempts to influence our food choices and behaviour outlined so far are already overwhelming. But they are not the whole story. When we get to the point of purchasing food, we are subject to another set of commercially-led influences to encourage us to eat more, and consume the products food companies want us to, which more often than not consist of unhealthy foods. Manipulation of the shopping experience has long been known to provide a powerful way to influence people's food buying behaviours. For example, piping the smell of baking bread into the bakery section of a supermarket to stimulate people's sense of smell, or changing the architecture of our journey through the supermarket so that the products that the food companies want us to see are most visible to us, through tactics such as increased shelf space, promotional displays, or presenting products as we walk into the shop. A study of a sample branch of each of the top five supermarket chains in the UK found that 70 percent of all food and beverage products placed in prominent locations were those that made a significant contribution to children's sugar and calorie intake[217].

    Another major influence on our food choices beyond the promotion of products is the range of products within supermarkets. Quite simply, we don't need most of the food that's displayed on the shelves of our supermarkets. In addition, most of it isn't all that good for us. It is there because it sells and makes a profit, which is the core aim of food companies and supermarkets alike, rather than to provide us with nutritious food. If our main aim when buying food is to feed ourselves and our families with nutritious, tasty food then we only need a fairly small proportion of the food products on offer in the shops. These are the basic, individual foods that form the building blocks of our diet – for example, fruit, vegetables, fish, milk and pulses. They are the foods that in the past might have been sold by dedicated individual shops such as greengrocers, butchers and bakers. The proliferation of other products such as convenience foods and the rise of supermarkets in the last 70 years has made it much harder for us to see which food we should be eating. It's distracted us from many of the healthy 'building block' foods, and led us towards other 'composite' foods that are backed by massive marketing budgets.

The food industry – the food industry is the biggest commercial sector in the world, with a revenue of over 9 trillion dollars in 2024[218]. Like any other industry, its aim is to maximise the returns it gives to its shareholders. This can create a conflict of interests when trying to balance this priority with the need to produce healthy, nutritious food. In fact, it could be argued that the aim of the food industry is *not* actually to produce healthy, nutritious food – merely food that is safe to eat, which sells in high volumes and produces as much profit as possible.

The food industry is also incredibly competitive. This is because there is a limit to the number of calories each of us can each consume – even if we are overeating. There is however an overabundance of food supplied by the industry (certainly in the USA whose food supply produces a daily average of 3,900 calories per person – nearly double the required intake for women), so there is massive competition within the industry for the relatively limited number of calories we can each consume. This leads to the industry producing a vast range of products designed to appeal to people so that they will sell more than the other products on the shelves. Food companies work hard to come up with new products and to make their products more appealing in terms of their colour, taste and texture. This often means more salt, sugar and fat, given that there is a general preference among human beings for energy dense foods. Not only is there heavy competition within the food industry to provide the calories we consume, but also to 'expand the market' by getting people to eat *more* – to consume more calories, more often in our daily lives. This is another driver of the growth in food portion sizes over the last 20 years.

The food industry doesn't just aim to influence our eating choices via advertising, even though this is the most immediately visible channel. It also spends millions each year lobbying politicians and other bodies to maintain legislation that is as sympathetic to its commercial interests as possible.

Due to its size, the food industry has a great deal of power[219]. For example, in her book *Food Politics*, former nutrition policy advisor to the US government Marion Nestle describes how food companies in the US have influenced the government's food guidelines over the years to water down their advice about avoiding particular foods –

even though there is clear evidence that they are less healthy. This contributes to common misleading dietary propaganda such as the suggestion that there are no good or bad foods and that all foods can be part of healthy diets, as long as we eat a balanced diet[220].

The industry does not simply influence dietary guidelines – it also intervenes in food regulation and policy. To take a UK example, in 1994, the Committee on Medical Aspects of Food published a report for the UK Government which looked at the relationship between salt intake and blood pressure. It recommended that salt intake should be reduced gradually from 9g/day to 6g/day. The Chief Medical Officer at the time refused to endorse this recommendation after the food industry had threatened to withdraw funds to the Conservative Party[221].

Conclusions

We have a number of biological and psychological tendencies as LASID creatures that can influence us to eat more calories than we need. But the core driver of the rise in obesity rates lies in the food environment that surrounds us, which has changed over a few decades into one that our eating behaviours have not evolved to deal with, and which experts have described as 'toxic' from a nutritional perspective[222].

Not only have high calorie foods become cheaper, more plentiful and more convenient than their healthy alternatives, but they are being promoted to us using techniques that exploit our vulnerabilities as LASID creatures and supplied to us through the institutions that are supposed to help us look after our health, including schools and health care providers. In the modern world we are therefore battling against our environment in an effort to live healthier lives, rather than adjusting it to support us in doing this. We have to turn this around as a matter of urgency, as millions of people are dying and suffering needlessly because of this situation, and we are wasting billions of dollars a year dealing with the symptoms of NCDs when we should be tackling the cause – obesity.

Why are we failing to tackle this situation? A range of factors is involved, including the drive for profit by the food industry, economic and political incentives, an unwillingness to tackle inequality properly, and the assumption that it is people's own fault that they become obese. Being LASID creatures with our particular biological makeup, we now know that this latter assumption is incorrect, and that people should not be blamed for obesity, especially when they live in such a toxic nutritional environment. The onus is on us to transform our society to create a healthy food environment for everyone – young and old, rich and poor – because doing so will benefit us all – in longevity, health, and economic terms.

What can we expect to achieve?

What are our chances of addressing the obesity crisis? We need to be realistic – the issue is a global one, encompassing geopolitics, land use, major industries and a range of well-established assumptions about food and lifestyles that will be difficult to challenge and turn around. Solving it requires global cooperation, significant changes in both local and global systems, as well as acceptance of the idea that human health needs to be a global priority above the need to make money.

So, the jury is out on this one. Significant steps to improve the health of some countries are starting to be taken, and in the UK we are seeing important health milestones like the decision in 2024 to ban smoking completely for anyone born after 1st January 2009, although this legislation was abandoned in advance of a General Election[223]. There is a lot further to go in the battle against obesity though, with many of the ideas in this chapter still not mainstream knowledge or thinking, and a wide range of powerful economic and commercial interests likely to be working against the level of reforms needed.

If we take this issue down to its most basic level however, we can see that it is simply a matter of enabling human beings to live healthier and longer lives by eating nutritious food and taking physical exercise. There are more than enough calories available to feed every human being on this planet. The modern environment we live in however is currently biased in favour of unhealthy diets. We are effectively killing 33 million people a year and harming millions of others, including our own children, through a situation we can change – our health environment.

When the challenge is articulated like this, it is clearly an absurd and tragic situation, and one that is within our power to change. We therefore have to have hope that we can address it. The next chapter explores how we can do this.

Chapter 8
How to tackle the obesity crisis

A range of steps can be taken to address the behavioural causes of obesity, including factors we can change in managing our own health behaviours as individuals through to ways we can change the context around us to support us in living healthier lives. The steps outlined in this chapter are built from a range of sources, including the World Health Organisation (WHO), the US Center for Disease Control and Prevention and academic papers, as well as the evidence presented in the chapter so far. The international community is clearly taking this issue seriously, with initiatives such as the WHO Acceleration plan to stop obesity[224], which contains some useful, evidence-based steps to tackle obesity in order to reach the UN's Sustainable Development Goal to reduce premature mortality from NCDs by one third by 2030. The steps recommended in many of these plans lack a certain level of ambition however, so the recommendations in this chapter suggest ways of addressing this challenge as effectively as possible rather than within perceived parameters such as constraints of political will.

Like the WHO Acceleration plan, the suggestions below include economic, structural and regulatory steps to build healthier food environments, as well as those that promote lifestyles with greater levels of ongoing physical activity. They also include the cultural and political changes required to achieve the transformation in health behaviour we need.

Building individual capacities

The first area to consider is steps that can be taken to enhance the capacities of individuals to make better choices about food and exercise and to manage the toxic food environment they find themselves in.

Improve people's health literacy – human beings are not born with the skills to navigate a food environment as complex as the one we live within, so we cannot expect people to develop these skills across the population if they are not provided to everyone from an early age. It is not just food literacy that is required however – it is a broader set of skills and knowledge relating to looking after one's health more generally. Below are some core aspects of this essential set of skills for a healthy population, each of which needs to be presented in a simple, accessible and intuitive way in order for people to take them on board:
- **Human health** – knowledge of basic human biology in relation to health, including the nutrients and energy we need, the exercise we need and the basic things that can promote or damage our health (including calorie-dense processed food, smoking and alcohol). Understanding the importance of good nutrition and exercise for our long-term health.
- **Food literacy** – understanding the range of foods around us in the world and their value or threat to our health, the food we need to consume, how much to eat, how to simply calculate portion sizes, and when in the day to eat.

- **Managing our relationship with food** – understanding when we may be inclined to eat (including emotional eating), how to be self-disciplined and how to establish good food habits. For example, understanding the power of disinhibition – not eating while watching TV, and having healthy rather than unhealthy snacks available when you come back from a night out drinking.
- **Physical activity** – including the need for exercise, how much exercise we need, how to find exercise you enjoy, and how to build exercise into your daily life.

Teaching critical thinking skills – as has been outlined already, we are surrounded by a complex range of external sources of messages and information in the modern world, many of which can influence our thinking and behaviour, and some of which are designed to do so, often not for our benefit but for other motives such as profit or power. We need to help people to understand how these external sources function and how human beings react to them as LASID creatures. We also need to equip people with the skills and tools to live self-determined lives as far as possible, including defending themselves against unwanted manipulation, for example from advertising or social pressure to conform.

Teaching mental techniques to encourage healthy eating – there is the potential to use non-manipulative techniques to encourage people to eat healthier food. For example, *self-affirmation theory* suggests that people want to maintain a feeling of being competent and morally worthy, and can respond defensively if something threatens this, such as healthy eating messages that suggest they are making the wrong food choices. Self-affirmation is a tool that has been shown to encourage people to respond positively rather than defensively to these messages by building up a sense of the individual's self-worth and competence before delivering the health message. This technique has led to an increase in fruit and vegetable consumption in people[225] and has the potential to drive better health behaviours. It is particularly useful as it can take place online, meaning it can be cheap to implement and applied to large numbers of people, including groups that are most at risk of not eating the right things – such as those with low socioeconomic status (SES)[226].

Changing our context

Even though some of us know we're living unhealthily, we still do it. This is in part because we have evolved as creatures to seek calories and prefer high-calorie food, and also because we face a lot of external pressure from actors in our environment (including advertisers, food manufacturers and the institutions around us) to eat unhealthy foods – and these external forces exert a strong influence upon us as LASID creatures.

It is therefore valid to ask people to take greater personal responsibility for living healthier lives, and to equip them with the knowledge and skills to do it. Some recommendations for this are provided below. But this is nowhere near enough when their environment is weighted so far against healthy living. Some of the most important recommendations in this chapter therefore focus on changing the structures, institutions and ideas around us in our environment to tip their balance away from promoting unhealthy foods, and much more towards promoting healthy foods, as well as providing the infrastructure and incentives to make our lifestyles more physically active, both at work and at home. Below are a number of steps we can take to adjust our environment if we are serious about addressing the obesity epidemic, as well as the other diseases caused by our inactivity and food consumption.

Help children get a good start – evidence shows that the early years of a child's life, both before and after its birth, are a critical time in shaping its life course in a range of factors, including its health. We therefore need to divert more resources and support to helping parents create a healthy and nurturing environment in a child's early years. Below is a limited selection of ideas to achieve this:

- **Promote breastfeeding** – many studies from around the world show lower rates of obesity in breastfed children than those weaned on infant formula. This is in part because it helps the child's biology to predict the future food environment better than alternative milk options[227], but may also be explained by the fact that it is the child rather than the feeder who decides how much they will consume in breastfeeding, and that breastfed children are more willing to try varied foods than others, which may help to establish a liking of fruit and vegetables[228]. Promoting breastfeeding therefore makes an important contribution to reducing obesity. Paid maternity leave should also be expanded to ensure that a larger proportion of new mothers are able to breastfeed their children at least up to the 6 months recommended by leading healthcare institutions, such as the American Academy of Pediatrics (AAP)[229].

- **Promote better foetal and infant health** – support should be given to parents and prospective parents to make good nutritional decisions for themselves and their children, including when they are planning a family but may not know they are pregnant. This step could change the health and life course of those children, by averting the conditions of mismatch for the preborn child discussed earlier in this chapter. This support could be given in the form of nutritional information and training targeted at young couples or people planning a family, and should include content to make people aware of the importance of good parental nutrition habits for their own health and that of their children – both before and after they are born.

Draw a clear line between nutritious food and other food – we need to be clearer within our cultures and politics as to what constitutes nutritious food and what constitutes unhealthy food.

There is a common line of thinking in the food and dietary sector that no individual food is good or bad – there are plenty of foods that can become unhealthy if consumed too much, but which are reasonable if part of a balanced diet. Objectively, this may seem a reasonable viewpoint, but it is incredibly unhelpful when applied to public health communications, as it implies that no types of food should be singled out for regulation – a tactic often used by promoters of unhealthy food to misleadingly promote its place in a healthy diet and stifle attempts to improve food policies[230]. The facts are simple – people need to eat more fruit, vegetables and foods containing the mix of nutrients they need for a healthy life, and fewer high-sugar, high-fat and ultra processed foods. So, from a public health perspective, some foods *are* better than others, and it needs to be made clear that people's diets need to shift towards nutritious foods and away from those that provide empty calories. We need society-wide agreement among politicians, the public and other actors on this point.

This process could be assisted by a simple naming convention – drawing a distinction between 'food' as a general concept (i.e. a set of calories we can consume) and *nutritious* food. Evidence shows that human beings need nutritious food rather than just 'food' to stay healthy and live longer lives – and this important distinction should be made clear to both the public and policy makers. Government and public health policy should be directed at promoting nutritious food, not just 'food'.

Policy makers also need to build public awareness of the foods we know to be unhealthy, based on scientific knowledge – and this list of foods may change and become more nuanced over time. For example, we are learning that the biology of our guts is critical to our health and how we process nutrition, and that certain types of food (such as spinach, seeds and broccoli) contribute to a healthy gut environment and others (such as highly processed foods) can damage it[231]. The problem is, the level of the obesity epidemic suggests that many people are finding it difficult to find this balance. Some of the other recommendations in this chapter set out how we can adjust the conditions around people to help them in this balancing process, including improving food labelling and improving people's health literacy.

Provide every human being with the conditions needed for good health – the modern health environment is particularly toxic for people with low incomes and in marginalised groups[232], and if we are serious about tackling our health crises, including, but not limited to obesity, we need to address this. In the case of obesity, we need to correct the imbalance in health outcomes caused by poverty and inequality, in relation to food and exercise. Below are a couple of initial broad steps to take – and many of the other recommendations in this chapter will help to address this issue:

- **Make access to nutritious food – not just any food – a right of every human being**. This follows from the earlier point about the difference between healthy and unhealthy foods. In some countries, poorer people do not have enough access to the calories they need. Increasingly in westernised countries, poorer people have access to calories but the wrong type – unhealthy foods with high sugar and fat content. We need to establish the principle that everyone should have access to a level of nutritious food that keeps them healthy. This is a significant step, which would not only save public money and protect the health of future generations but is in itself a moral imperative of justice and fairness, where we stop deliberately targeting vulnerable people with life-threatening products for financial gain and instead support the health of our fellow humans. Delivering this overall principle would involve a range of steps outlined in this chapter, including giving people the resources they need for a healthy life (see below), stopping the food industry from targeting poorer people and locations with junk food and boosting people's health literacy.

- **Give people access to the basic resources they need for a healthy life** – research shows that healthy diets are often too expensive for people with less money[233]. Prices of healthy food should be lowered in relation to unhealthy food, and this point is explored later, but this is not enough. An inequality of other resources makes obesity more likely for poorer people, including a lack of cooking facilities, fuel for cooking and the time needed to cook healthy food from scratch. It is therefore critical to give everyone the basic resources they need to eat nutritious food, and one way to achieve this is through giving everyone a Universal Basic Income (UBI) – a regular (often monthly) allowance of money that is paid to every citizen unconditionally. This small but significant amount (a scheme in Spain gave £900 per month, for example) would give everyone the foundations on which to build healthy, safe and dignified lives for themselves and their families. It could not only make nutritious diets affordable but also alleviate the conditions that prevent people from eating well, such as having to work several low paid jobs that allow little remaining time to cook a decent meal. Pilot schemes of UBI in countries such as Finland and Spain have demonstrated great potential for it to reduce poverty as well as health inequality[234]. UBI could be a massive step towards a safer, healthier world for human beings.

Improve health choices in local neighbourhoods – our local areas are the environments in which we shop, walk, socialise and play in most regularly, and the facilities and services they provide therefore have a significant influence on the food we eat and physical activity we take. We can take steps to make our local neighbourhoods places that will mould our behaviour in healthier ways. For example, we can provide incentives for establishing supermarkets and shops selling healthy food in all areas – and particularly those areas that have poor access to healthy food. Restrictions could be placed on the number of fast food restaurants allowed in a particular area, as recommended by a range of studies in the US[235]. We can encourage local store owners to sell a larger range of healthy foods, perhaps by providing economic incentives to do this. We can also create 'fast food buffer zones' around schools in order to limit the availability of unhealthy foods nearby.

Improvements can be made to the local exercise infrastructure surrounding people too. Introducing lower speed limits and car-free streets in built-up areas as well as better cycle paths and footpaths will discourage car use and make walking and cycling safer and more attractive to people. Increased community policing and crime prevention measures can make local areas feel safer for exercise. We can improve access to public transport to encourage more people to walk to places and leave their cars at home – and also ensure the public transport serves local shops and sports centres well, so that people have easy access to these facilities. Establishing more community infrastructure – including local shops, community centres and dental surgeries – will encourage people to walk to their local services rather than jump in their cars to out-of-town supermarkets. We can also establish more facilities to promote physical exercise – not just gyms and sports centres, but free services that people can use in their daily lives, such as parks, nature trails, outdoor fitness equipment and games. As previously noted, it is critical to ensure that these facilities and infrastructure are distributed equitably among socioeconomic groups and locations. Agreements could be negotiated with schools, colleges and other bodies to provide public use of their recreational assets to increase the opportunities available for exercise[236].

Improve health choices in institutions – not only can we improve the infrastructure of our local neighbourhoods to promote rather than prevent healthier eating and more physical activity – we can do the same in our institutions. Below is a small selection of examples of how this could be done.

- **Education** – overall, we need to ensure that the education system prioritises the task of building the physical health of its pupils, as this is the fundamental building block of a flourishing life, and research also shows that it is linked with better academic performance[237]. So, promoting and providing healthy eating and physical exercise should become key aims of schools. This can be implemented in a number of ways, aside from the health literacy education outlined earlier. These include:
    - **Set clear and high nutritional standards for all school meals** plus any 'competitive foods' available outside school lunches, including snack machines. Include clear, consistent nutritional labelling on all meals and teach children how to evaluate this information as part of their health literacy education.
    - **Provide free or low-cost healthy snacks,** such as fruit and vegetables, daily for all children[238].

- o **Prevent any advertising or commercial partnerships with food manufacturers** in schools.
- o **Enable more walking and cycling to school** – not simply encouraging children to take physical activity to get to school but making it easier for them to do it, including setting up walking and bike trains for pupils to travel together, suggesting pleasant routes into school and providing safety equipment such as lights if children need them.
- o **Teach children to enjoy exercise, nature and the outdoors**, and help them to appreciate them as life-long joys and promoters of mental and physical health, rather than simply activities that need to be done.
- o **Introduce more time for physical activity** – including more PE lessons each week and a daily communal physical activity, such as walking or running a 'daily mile'. As part of their PE programme, give children more opportunities to find the physical activity that they enjoy – not just a limited range of competitive sports. Also, where possible, encourage schools to keep their sports facilities open late so that pupils can use them after the end of the school day[239].
- **Health care** – our health care systems are massive and complex infrastructures, so the recommendations for this area below can only be limited and illustrative.

- o **Make healthy eating a more prominent part of health care** – our health system is generally reactive – it is there for us when things go wrong – but it could be re-focused to also have an active, preventative arm, including ongoing programmes to help people live healthily (from eating to exercise) and monitor their progress in doing this.
- o **Make health institutions 'walk the talk' with healthy eating** – for example, close down junk food franchises within hospitals. Serve and promote only healthy food within health institutions instead.
- o **Build nutrition into healthcare strategies** – one group of senior health and nutrition academics recommends a number of measures to address nutrition within health care itself, including multidisciplinary lifestyle programmes to tackle certain chronic diseases such as diabetes, and making fruit and vegetables available on prescription for certain medical conditions[240].
- o **Set high food procurement standards** – governments are one of the largest buyers of food in a nation, so they should set high nutritional procurement standards for the health service and all other state-run institutions[241].
- **Workplaces** – a central aim of workplaces, as with schools, should be to promote the health of their people, as this is their most crucial resource and doing so also helps to increase productivity[242]. Below are some basic steps on how this could be achieved:

- **Create a healthy food environment** – establish a set of clear and high-level nutritional standards for food procurement, including providing healthy lunches and snacks and removing unhealthy options.
- **Provide, and promote participation in, workplace wellness programmes** – these are schemes that provide employees with initial health checks and personalised ongoing support to build healthier lives, including improving their nutrition and increasing their physical activity. Evidence suggests these programmes can not only improve the health of staff but also increase productivity and reduce costs. One analysis from the US suggests that every $1 spent on workplace wellness programmes yields a reduction of $3.27 in medical costs and $2.73 in reduced absenteeism[243].
- **Create a healthy physical environment** – encourage and subsidise walking and cycling to work. Experiment with new ways of working that encourage greater physical activity, particularly for sedentary office workers. This might include giving people regular breaks in which they need to get up from their chair and walk around, offering 'walking meetings' (both in and outdoors) rather than those stuck in meeting rooms and providing mandatory lunch breaks, as well as opportunities for lunchtime exercise, including walks and sport. Employers could also subsidise physical activity, such as gym or sports club membership.

- Ensure that these changes are modelled by senior management and that cultures are established in which healthy lives are seen as part of good work performance and part of the employer's duty of care to the employee. Employers have a vested interest in reducing obesity in their staff, as it can increase the number of employee sick days and reduce morale and productivity[244] [245].
- **Public facilities** – ensure that healthy foods are promoted and more available in public facilities controlled by the state and local councils, including parks and libraries. Aside from offering healthier options, this helps to normalise the choice of healthy food against other options.

Change the balance in food marketing – we need to remove or weaken the external factors that seek to influence people into buying and eating unhealthy food. As has been shown, human beings are biologically inclined to prefer calorie-dense foods, and as LASID creatures, are also psychologically inclined to be vulnerable to external manipulation. Most of the agents that seek to exploit this vulnerability – including the food industry – are simply looking to do so for profit, despite the widespread death and suffering this causes. Removing or weakening these manipulative external influences therefore serves several purposes – as a moral imperative to protect human beings from exploitation of their vulnerabilities as creatures, to stop the preventable harms to millions caused by obesity, and to encourage commercial agents to redirect their profit motives towards securing behaviours that will aid rather than harm human health and flourishing. Steps that can be taken in this area include:

- **Ban manipulative advertising** – many writers and campaigners on the subject of obesity recommend banning junk food advertising to children, but this is not enough. Using the latest psychological knowledge of human beings as LASID creatures (as set out in Part 1 of this book), we can see that everyone – young or old – is susceptible to the power of advertising. It exploits our thinking traits as LASID creatures in order to make us do things that we might not do if we were in a context where we could think about it rationally, and these are often things that are bad for our health, well-being and the planet.

    A key step in setting up structures around human beings to protect them, help them flourish and make good decisions as LASID creatures is to ban all forms of manipulative advertising – from the food industry and beyond. It is easier to describe what isn't manipulative than what is. What isn't manipulative (or, is at least far less manipulative) is an advertisement promoting a product that provides a brief factual description of it, possibly with a picture of the product on its own and without any further information, claims or context that could lead consumers to imply anything about its properties (including how it will make them feel or look) or the context it can be consumed in or who it can be consumed by (including its consumption by people we admire). We are therefore left with promotional information shorn of much (but not all) of its ability to instil further wants and needs in us – for example, 'Granny Smith

Apples – £1.60', with a picture of the apples alongside. Aside from this step, all advertising for unhealthy food should be banned, as well as all advertising to children, as they are particularly vulnerable to manipulation. These steps would remove a significant source of pressure and misery for many human beings, as well as reducing an important driver of obesity.

- **Promote healthy foods** – producers and sellers should be encouraged to spend more marketing budget promoting healthy foods, and to make them as attractive and convenient as possible. Actively promote healthy foods and subsidise this promotion, both in overall campaigns and in individual contexts.
- **Ban upselling strategies** – portion sizes and upselling strategies have become highly effective tools to encourage people to eat more food, as they tap into our vulnerabilities to seek more calories and greater value. Standardising portion sizes and removing food sellers 'ability to use upselling tactics could therefore make a significant impact in reducing people's calorie consumption. First, portion sizes for unhealthy foods, including fast food servings and meals, should be standardised across the industry, and set by independent nutrition experts. It should be clear what the recommended intake of a product is. Second, fast food retailers should be prohibited from the practice of upselling – of verbally offering larger portions or advertising meal deals beyond standard sizes. At this stage this is not a call to prohibit larger sizes of individual items, but to start by removing additional marketing and incentives to purchase

them. Prohibition could be considered however at a later point.
- **Provide pro-health nudges** – as the converse of the previous point, there are many possibilities for nudging customers towards healthy options in food retailers, shops and restaurants, such as offering salad, fruit or vegetables as extras with a meal at a reduced price. These could be used to replace the upselling tactics above.
- **Regulate retail and restaurant environments to promote healthy foods** – the layout of food retailers and the items within them should be regulated to ensure that healthy, non-processed foods rather than unhealthy foods are the most visible and easily accessible as customers navigate the shops and restaurants. This might include having fruit and vegetables at the entrance to a shop, putting healthy foods on more prominent display in menus and shops, and offering an extra-convenient 'health route' around a supermarket, so that a healthy shopping trip is also a quicker and more convenient one for the customer. A study in The Netherlands tested whether moving healthier food products to a more prominent position at a food kiosk would encourage people to buy more of them. It not only found that more customers bought more healthy foods when this 'nudge' was instigated, but also that they approved of this nudge being used[246]. This not only shows the potential effectiveness of such interventions but also that public opinion may be in favour of them.

At the same time, the financial incentives and offers provided by retailers and restaurants on food need to change to favour healthy foods. Retailers and restaurants could be regulated to implement a 75/25 rule on promotion and pricing offers on food, whereby any promotion or reduction of an unhealthy food product has to be balanced with similar promotion or offers on 3 healthy products. A balance of discounts and offers in favour of healthy products could help to encourage healthier food choices and make them more affordable. Food producers and retailers could be incentivised to provide these. Offers of unhealthy food products for children should be stopped.

Regulate food packaging and labelling to inform consumers – the packaging and labelling of food has become an important component of the marketing strategies used by food companies to convince consumers to buy their products. It should be used instead as a way to help consumers make informed choices about their food. This is not to suggest that all products must be presented in plain white boxes. Manufacturers should be able to make their products attractive as consumers get pleasure from this. We should however eliminate packaging that exploits people's biology or LASID status as creatures to manipulate them into buying unhealthy food. We should therefore apply the same principles of regulation to food packaging as to its marketing, and increase its use to consumers by making it a source of clear, unbiased information that is as useful as possible in helping people make informed decisions. The steps below should be implemented in any context in which food is sold or served, including product packaging and restaurants.

- **Ban the use of manipulative marketing techniques on the labelling and packaging of unhealthy food products** – instead, simply present a context-free picture and limited factual description of the product. This means removing promotional incentives such as free toys and characters that will appeal to children independently of the product, whether these are Tony the Tiger or Happy Meals. It also means removing any marketing health claims on products, including phrases such as '0 percent fat' or 'wholesome', and images that imply its status as a healthy product, such as use by athletes, in order to avoid biasing people's perceptions of the healthiness of the food.
- **Standardise food labelling on the front and back of packs** – nutritional labelling on the back of food packaging packs is mandatory and reasonably consistent in the UK, so this should be continued and applied globally. The summarised nutritional labelling on the front of packs needs to be tightened up to meet this standard, as it may be the way that many people make their buying decisions, rather than using the more detailed information on the reverse. Front of pack nutritional information needs to be mandatory and standardised, with a labelling system (such as the colour-coded 'traffic light' system sometimes used now) that enables people to make quick but accurate decisions. This labelling needs to be prominent and include the key nutritional information consumers need, including calories, sugar and fat per 100g, rather than per serving, to make all products easily comparable. Clear standards should be set for the definition of each colour level by independent

nutritionists rather than the food industry, that cannot be manipulated by manufacturers. As part of this mandatory information, but secondary to the main 'per 100g' information, it should be clearly displayed what one portion consists of, people's daily recommended intake and how many servings are contained within a pack. A consistent, mandatory global food labelling system like this would help people make better food choices, regardless of which country they lived in or bought their food from.

- **Ban spurious health arguments** – do not allow food manufacturers to use the obfuscating claim that 'any food is acceptable as part of a balanced diet'. Instead, introduce a clear additional warning on packaging (possibly in the form of a black mark) to state when a food has unhealthy levels of sugar, salt or fat, and to identify ultra processed foods – in other words, help people discriminate easily between healthy and unhealthy foods.

These labelling principles should be standardised across all food products in order to keep nutritional information as consistent and understandable as possible for consumers.

Tackle food availability and pricing – another way to tip the balance from unhealthy to healthy foods is to incentivise and increase the availability of healthy food, whilst disincentivising and regulating unhealthy food – both for food producers and consumers. There are a number of ways to achieve this, including laws, taxes and financial incentives. Below is a small selection of steps that have potential to be effective.

- **Tax unhealthy food and drink** – this strategy has proved to be highly effective in both reducing people's consumption of calories and achieving positive change within the food industry. A tax on sugary drinks has been implemented in a number of countries, including Mexico (where it reduced soft drink purchases by 6 percent) and Saudi Arabia (reducing sales by 36 percent)[247]. A similar intervention in the UK aimed to reduce the amount of sugar in drinks rather than reducing sales, and achieved a decrease of 34.4 percent in the total sugar sold in soft drinks by retailers and manufacturers between 2015 and 2019[248]. Higher taxes should therefore be applied on unhealthy food and drink, including those high in sugar and fat, and ultra processed foods. Financial disincentives like this can be regressive for people on low incomes, but this can be addressed by using the tax revenue to pay for measures that will improve people's health, such as subsidising the cost of healthy foods[249]. This helps to bring the prices of foods closer to their real cost to society[250].
- **Subsidise healthy foods** – political policy should be adjusted to subsidise and promote healthier foods so that people at all socioeconomic levels have the opportunity to eat healthily and are incentivised to do it. This not only includes reducing and subsidising the cost of these foods, but also developing publicity campaigns to promote them to people as cheap, easy and convenient, and giving support and advice on how to use them in their diets.
- **Increase the convenience of healthy food** – steps have already been set out for how to increase the convenience and

accessibility of healthy foods within retail environments, but food manufacturers can also assist in this process. For example, a recent report found that healthier ready-to-eat meals could make a substantial contribution to improving people's diets, as fast food and ready meals provide more than a sixth of the calories that people consume within the EU[251].

Refocus and regulate the food industry – the food sector is the (obese) elephant in the room on this issue, as its marketing tactics, exploitation of people's health for profit and lobbying of politicians to maintain the status quo all play a significant role in driving the obesity crisis. We must therefore take steps to reduce its power to steer people towards unhealthy food, and these have been set out in other points above. We also need to:

- **Reduce its lobbying power** – strong regulations are needed to prevent lobbying activities by food companies that obstruct obesity prevention strategies. This includes demanding greater transparency and an end to financing of politicians and political parties by these, and other, companies. It also includes stricter standards on public-private partnerships – for example, preventing the food industry from helping to set national obesity strategies[252].
- **Review its role in the health of nations** – the recommended steps outlined in this chapter will affect the food industry in a substantial way, but they must be undertaken to protect the health of human beings. The food industry therefore has a choice – to get onside with these changes and fulfil its role in enabling public health or to

continue to block progress and, in some circumstances, work against people's health. It is not clear which side it will take, but it has the potential to play a fundamentally positive role in changing the health of millions of people around the world, and to continue to earn strong profits whilst doing this.

- **Agricultural policy** – we will need to transform our obesogenic food supply into one that promotes healthy eating habits among the population at large. The steps to achieve this are complex and substantial but include increasing funding to support fruit and vegetable production both globally and within individual nations[253], and refocusing financial incentives away from producing meat and dairy products and their crops. A drastic global reduction in meat and dairy consumption is a key step in addressing climate change, and doing so would also help to move populations on to a more plant-based diets, which have been linked in a number of studies to lower Body Mass Index (BMI)[254] and improved cardiac health[255].

Build a more physically active infrastructure for human beings – we do not all need to run a marathon every month. We just need ongoing, regular physical exercise. Structures therefore need to be created in people's lives that make it easy for them to become more active – whilst of course enabling people with disabilities to participate equally in society. A number of suggestions have been made above as to how this could be achieved within people's everyday lives and our institutions, and below are some further steps to help us achieve it:

- **Promote physical activity** – build an ongoing national mass media and social media campaign to promote physical activity[256], including highlighting the variety of activities open to people to 'get active their way', and the various opportunities and incentives there are to do this – see next point.
- **Incentivise and promote physical activity** – because just promoting it is not enough. People of all ages and demographic groups could be encouraged to undertake regular physical activity through the use of incentives, beyond the additional opportunities and subsidies that have already been discussed in this chapter. For example, using behavioural 'nudges' such as apps or watches that notify users when they have been sedentary for too long and encourage them to get active by gamifying physical activity – such as online treasure hunts or gaining 'rewards' for achievements, including taking more steps each day or climbing stairs rather than taking the lift. Technology could be harnessed to promote exercise and make it fun for a wider range of people, including children used to sedentary activities such as gaming or screen watching[257]. At a broader level, ideas such as offering people tax reductions for maintaining a certain level of ongoing physical activity may be reasonable, given that the health benefits of physical activity are so significant and the costs of inactivity are so great for the nation.
- **Remove the barriers to physical activity for people in poverty** – many of the other suggestions in this chapter will assist this process, including a universal basic income and

improvements to local infrastructure. Other steps can also be taken however, including investing more in safety and facilities in poorer neighbourhoods, as well as subsidising opportunities for exercise for people with lower incomes. For example, a means-tested regular 'physical activity' payment could be distributed to pay for any form of sport or physical activity, so that people have the chance to find the forms of activity that they enjoy, and then access them, even if they are on a low income.

- **Promote the social side of exercise** – social connection and fun can be important incentives to encourage people to take up and continue physical activity, as demonstrated by the success of the Parkrun movement. More focus could be given to promoting social groups for physical activity, such as local 'walk and talk' groups for different ages, and organised lunchtime walks in green spaces in towns near offices.

Make health a political priority – the health and obesity crisis needs to become a core political issue and matter of concern for the public, and policy makers need to put in place the frameworks needed to address the issue properly, including an integrated national plan.

- **Make obesity a key political issue** – build political support for the idea that the central priority of a nation and a government is to promote the health of its citizens. Raise awareness of the idea that the continual rise in obesity is a political scandal, in which governments are failing to protect their citizens from the environmental threats that lead to obesity, leading to millions of deaths and cases of chronic diseases, whilst wasting taxpayers' money on treating the symptoms rather than the cause. Provoke a public sense of outrage at this situation and show political parties that this is a platform on which they should all stand and a vote winner, as it involves protecting children, promoting longevity and spending public money more effectively. Public pressure could be built through the development of a social movement for healthier lives.

– **Build a national plan for healthy lives** – the recommendations in this chapter involve a high level of state involvement, from establishing local community infrastructure that promotes more exercise through to regulating the food industry. As a result, these steps should all be built into an integrated plan to tip the balance of the environment around every citizen towards healthier living. It would essentially set healthy living as the cultural default and the cornerstone of flourishing lives for all, and ensure that the structures, institutions and communications that surround us in our daily lives operate in a way that is consistent with this aim, rather than acting against it as they currently do. If each country produced a plan of this nature, it could save them billions of pounds in healthcare costs, and result in a happier, healthier and more productive citizenship.

Prioritise human flourishing and health above the motive for financial profit – a short final point to this section. The recommendations outlined in this chapter demand that we challenge some of our most basic assumptions about how we prioritise people's health, how we should shape the environment around us and how much we should spend on doing this. At the broadest level, it demands that we prioritise human wellbeing and health above the drive for financial profit and use redistributive financial policies rather than food industry profits to invest in our institutions and surroundings. This may sound simple, but it challenges one of the most basic tenets of our current economic and political systems. If we can make this change though, it could open up the possibility of healthier, longer and better lives for millions of people.

Conclusions

Our toxic food environment surrounds us with, and promotes, an enormous range of unhealthy, high-calorie density foods, and makes healthy foods harder to access and buy. It also makes it increasingly difficult for people to make informed choices about the food they should eat. This is exacerbated by our increasingly sedentary lifestyles, which have led us to expend far fewer calories than our ancestors living even a couple of generations ago. Together these and other factors have created a global obesity epidemic, which is not simply about increasing numbers of people becoming overweight – it is leading to a range of life-threatening diseases, killing millions of people, reducing quality of life and happiness and costing individual countries billions of dollars as they struggle to treat its manifold consequences. But to tackle this challenge to humanity, we need to tackle its causes – not just its symptoms.

We have made much progress in improving human health and longevity through applying scientific knowledge to achieve technological breakthroughs in areas such as vaccines, hygiene and surgery. We can now do more to apply our knowledge of the science of how human beings think and behave to help us deal more effectively with the modern health challenges that are shortening and destroying people's lives around the world.

There are a few steps we can take to change the way we think and behave towards food as individuals, but largely the solutions to this global problem require us to change the environment around us. Given the creatures we are, including our biology and tendency for LASID thinking and behaviour, we need to not just level the playing field but skew it in favour of healthy living and away from unhealthy foods and sedentary lifestyles, as human beings evolved to prefer calorie-rich, high sugar and high fat foods, and are vulnerable to many forms of manipulation that make us consume them – from the structure of our local communities to advertising.

Changing our environment will require a wide range of steps across many aspects of our lives and societies – there is no single solution to address this issue. We need to build a culture that consistently promotes and delivers healthy eating and physical exercise across the institutions that surround us, not just in isolated contexts such as sports clubs or doctors' surgeries. This will involve substantial changes to many things we take for granted, from regulation of food marketing and packaging to subsidising physical activity, in a bid to promote and increase the availability of healthy foods and physical exercise, to move our societal default towards this and away from unhealthy lifestyles. These changes will prolong and improve millions of lives and save billions of dollars each year, as well as having a number of wider positive impacts, from increasing the environmental sustainability of our food through to improving school attendance and the life chances of our children[258].

It should be a no-brainer. We know what needs to be done to save and prolong lives and improve the health of future generations – the question is whether we are prepared to change the structures and systems that surround us to do it.

Truth

In brief – human beings are not built to seek the truth, but to make sense of the world in an efficient way and protect the beliefs and existence of the groups we belong to. This can make it difficult for us to maintain global consensus on the truth, especially when external structures and actors overwhelm, influence and exploit the way we seek, interpret and act on information. A shared conception of the truth is vital for human beings – so, to maintain it, we need to prioritise and reshape our relationship with information.

Chapter 9
Can we protect the idea of the truth?

Truth is critically important for human beings – in our individual lives, in our societies and for our species as a whole. The accuracy of the information we receive, the level of trust we have in our political leaders and the institutions that surround us can be a matter of life or death. For example, a study in the American Journal of Tropical Medicine and Hygiene found that around 800 people died and 6,000 were hospitalised in the early months of the Covid-19 pandemic[260] as a result of drinking methanol – a toxic, highly concentrated, alcohol commonly found in household cleaning products[261]. This was a direct result of exposure to misinformation – specifically, a popular myth that drinking methanol could kill the virus by disinfecting the body. This is just one minor piece of misinformation among many that circulated during the pandemic – just consider how many of the 234,000 Covid-19 deaths of unvaccinated people in the US between June 2021 and April 2022 might have been prevented if conspiracy theories hadn't influenced some of these people to avoid vaccinations[262].

Human beings have a strange relationship with the truth. Each of us feels a strong motivation to seek it – to understand things 'as they really are' and to have clarity on the world. When we think we know the truth on a particular issue, it can be a source of great emotional stress to us when other people hold differing views and seemingly have an incorrect view of reality. So, truth really matters to us in itself, beyond its important role in affecting our behaviour and the choices we make.

Yet we are living in a world in which our general consensus on what constitutes the truth is under threat, and where many people are struggling to accurately navigate their way through the information around them. This chapter will explore why people hold beliefs about the world that are biased or inconsistent with reality, even if there is no evidence for them and plenty of evidence against them. Causes will include some features of our thinking and behaviour as LASID creatures that can actually divert us away from the truth, as well developments in our society that create a hostile information environment where it's difficult to separate fact from fiction. It will also explore what steps we can take to change this and preserve the importance of the truth as an idea in our society. As the chapter will show, this matters a great deal, as a shared conception of the truth helps each of us to survive, binds our relationships and maintains our democracies, and losing it risks all these things, and more.

How bad is the problem?

A significant proportion of people have inaccurate beliefs about the world. In 2009, the Pew Research Center in the US[263] found that, while 97% of scientists believe humans and other living things have evolved over time, only 61% of the American public believe this, with a third of this group (22% of the overall sample) believing evolution was guided by a supreme being rather than natural processes. Also, nearly a third of the American public believe that human beings have existed in their present form since the beginning of time. Remember, these are not the beliefs of extremist groups, like the young Earth creationists, who believe that the earth was formed only 6,000 years ago, but of ordinary members of the public.

There is also widespread belief in conspiracy theories. For example, 19% of Americans in 2020 believed that climate change is a hoax set up by corrupt politicians and scientists. This scale of misbelief can have significant consequences for society, and can hamper our ability to make progress on key issues such as the environment. In addition, some of the conspiracy theories people subscribe to have links with dangerous prejudices and stereotypes, which can fan the flames of hatred – for example, 26% of Americans in 2021 believed that the billionaire George Soros is behind a secret plan to undermine the US government, control the media, and dominate the world. This is a theory commonly linked to anti-Semitism – of 'Jews taking over the world'.

Scholars have argued that something has changed about the world in recent years – that we now live in a 'post-truth world' where the idea of truth itself is under threat[264]. Various things have shifted, including the movement of misinformation from the fringes of the internet into the mainstream[265] and a change in politicians' conceptions of what constitutes honesty[266]. Some of the causes of this shift will be explored later in this chapter, but they include growing economic inequality, political polarisation and increasingly siloed media channels.

One of the most visible and disturbing examples of this change in our relationship with truth is how misinformation has increased in American politics in recent years. The 2020 US Presidential election was won by Joe Biden, yet the then incumbent President, Donald Trump, continues to this day to claim the election was rigged, subject to voter fraud and ultimately won by Trump himself. These claims contesting the election have collectively become known as the Big Lie by journalists, as they contain hundreds of inaccurate or unevidenced accusations – from voter fraud through to observers not being allowed into vote counting rooms.

These falsehoods about the election have had appalling consequences. Millions of people believed Trump's claims, and a CNN poll in 2023 revealed that 63% of Republicans still believe Biden did not win the election legitimately (although only 52% of these think there was any clear evidence of the election being stolen). These inaccurate claims fuelled the Capitol riots of January 6 2021 in which five people were killed as 2,000 Trump supporters stormed the Capitol building in Washington DC in an attempt to prevent Joe Biden's victory being formalised. Perhaps of longer-term consequence is that these falsehoods have been weaponised by Trump and his acolytes in order to sow mistrust among sections of the American public about the entire democratic system in the US. This is a politically-motivated move designed to further his ambitions to regain and consolidate power in future, which could potentially lead to the death of democracy in the US. These are just some of the consequences of several years of misinformation from Trump – The Washington Post found that he made 30,573 false or misleading claims in the four years he was in office as President[267].

The threats to our conception of the truth in modern society extend way beyond one single category, such as political lies, fake news or conspiracy theories. We are surrounded by partisan views, manipulation of news and half-truths. Psychologist Sander van der

Linden is the Professor of Social Psychology in Society at Cambridge University and is known as their 'Defence Against the Dark Arts' teacher for his work on fake news and misinformation. He notes that even information from mainstream sources can be misleading whilst not being completely fake – for example, a 2015 article in British newspaper The Sun misrepresented the results of an opinion poll to suggest that Muslims had a disproportionate level of support for terrorists, when the results did not show this[268]. Even the terms describing these types of misinformation can be disputed territory leveraged for political ends. The term 'fake news' has become a rhetorical device that people (including politicians) use to invalidate and dismiss information that goes against their attitudes and values[269].

This chapter will collectively describe these threats using the term 'misinformation', which means any information we consume that turns out to be false[270]. Misinformation can be spread unintentionally (for example, people sharing tweets thinking they are true) or with the intention of misleading (for example, lying in order to seek power), and in the latter case it is sometimes called 'disinformation' or 'propaganda'.

So, there are significant threats to our conception of the truth. But is truth really that important?

Why truth matters

To start at the most basic level, an accurate reflection of reality is important to us as individuals to make good decisions. These include big political decisions about who to vote for, but also important personal decisions, such as our health choices. For decades tobacco companies misled the public about the effects of smoking on health, and this has led to the loss of millions of lives through smoking and exposure to second-hand smoke[271]. Evidence also shows that exposure to conspiracy theories about the use of antidepressants reduces the intention of participants to seek help, due to decreased levels of trust in health authorities[272].

Belief in conspiracy theories can have particularly serious consequences. In an academic review paper[273], psychologist Daniel Jolley and colleagues found plenty of evidence linking beliefs in conspiracy theories with consequences across a number of important areas, some of which relate to the challenges discussed in this book, including health, extremism, prejudice and climate change. For example, a 2019 report by the US Federal Bureau of Investigation (FBI) found that 24 out of 52 lone terrorists (46%) either consumed or discussed conspiracy theory information, supporting the theory that conspiracy theories can act as a radicalising agent for extremism[274]. A further study examining the effects of conspiracy theories about Jewish people found that exposure to such theories not only increased prejudice towards this group, but also had an indirect association with greater levels of prejudice towards several other groups including Asians and Americans[275].

As a broader point, Yale historian Timothy Snyder points out that when we fail to identify facts, we can lose our freedom[276]. Truth is the common view of the world on which we build our lives, relationships and societies. If we can't agree on what constitutes truth then it is impossible to criticise people in power, as there is no basis on which to do this. Without the ability to separate facts from fiction, we can also become open to manipulation from other people, including those with malign intent.

As will be shown later in this chapter, creating a sense of disagreement about facts among the public is therefore a useful tool in the anti-democratic playbook. This is one of the reasons why fake news is often used not simply to spread misinformation about a particular issue, but to polarise people[277]. When we lose our shared conception of the truth, we therefore lose not just our freedom but our power.

Truth is also about trust – the bond that binds us together in our relationships and societies. If we lose a shared conception of the truth and our trust in it, we lose our trust in each other. We can see this at a simple level in our relationships. When we find that someone close to us has not been telling the truth, we can feel betrayed – an emotional sense of hurt. This is partly because telling the truth is part of the unwritten social contract we have with each other, and breaking this contract is socially unacceptable. As tribal creatures, honesty is needed to maintain trust and co-operation in our groups, so when this trust is broken it can lead the perpetrator to be ejected from the group, which, as we have seen in Part 1, was equivalent to a death sentence for our hunter-gatherer ancestors.

A shared conception of truth also helps to maintain relations between different tribes, despite any tendencies we may have as LASID creatures to be less trusting of those outside our own in-group. If this shared conception of truth disappears however, then it can lead to a breakdown of trust and a risk of greater conflict between groups. This building of trust through a shared picture of the truth also enables us to cooperate – probably the most important human ability that separates us from other animals.

It is possible for humans to cooperate without a shared vision of the truth, say around a complete fantasy – but this is not enough to help us thrive in the environment we actually find ourselves in; we need our shared vision to be based on the truth, as far as we can see it. For example, if we reached global agreement that the Earth was flat, this might help us cooperate, but the reality of the Earth being spherical would prevent this cooperation from being effective, as it would prevent us from navigating internationally, undertaking global trade and achieving many other practical goals we now take for granted. So, in some cases, cooperation alone is not enough – we need a shared conception of truth, and one that is as accurate as possible.

If we lose this capacity for co-operation based on a shared conception of the truth, we compromise our ability to maintain or build upon many of the lifestyle changes we have gained, from mobile phones to food production, and to respond to issues that affect us all – whether nationally or globally, including the challenges explored in this book. The Covid-19 pandemic was a good example of this. There was sufficient consensus and trust in both the scientific advice and our political leaders for most people to follow the actions they prescribed, but, as was shown at the start of this chapter, those who didn't trust the scientific advice essentially formed a different tribe and this prevented their cooperation – with deadly consequences for tens of thousands of people.

The stakes are therefore incredibly high for us both as individuals and as a global society if we were to lose our capacity to tell truth from fiction or fail to maintain a broad consensus on the truth.

What is the truth?

Before exploring the factors that are threatening our relationship with the truth, it is important to be clear as to what we actually mean by 'the truth'. The traditional idea of the truth could be defined as 'the accurate reflection of reality'. In other words, when a belief that someone holds or a statement that they are making reflects how things are in reality.

As shown in Part 1 though, it is impossible for us to represent exactly 'how things are' in reality as it is way too complex. We therefore construct simplified models of this reality in our heads for us to explain it. This affects what we can expect from the idea of 'the truth', as, according to Professor Stefan Lewandowsky[278], although there may be a single reality 'out there', there is no such thing as 'the truth' in human terms, as the world is too complex and we all simplify reality in different ways.

So where does this leave our search for 'the truth' as human beings? Should we give up even trying to seek something that doesn't exist? No. First, although we may not have access to 'the truth' about our ultimate reality, it could be argued that there is another, more detailed, level of 'truth' beyond this that is available to human beings, consisting of 'everyday truths' about our immediate world and how it works, such as those established by the scientific method (which will always be temporary and subject to revision) and by well-informed, reflective consensus on information from our senses (for example, that a particular event happened) – both of which will be explored shortly. Second, as this chapter has argued, having a shared conception of the truth is critical in a number of ways to human society, including in building trust and cooperation between people. Our challenge is to build and maintain this shared conception of the truth, and to maintain people's trust in it as well as their appreciation of its importance to society.

One remarkable tool we have built to help us have a shared conception of the truth is the scientific method. It is a logical process that enables us to build the most objectively reliable picture of reality we can from a position of ultimate uncertainty – which is where we sit as human beings. It does this by making a hypothesis (an educated guess) about how a particular aspect of reality works, and then conducting experiments to test whether this hypothesis accurately describes how things work in reality. If the evidence from the tests shows that the hypothesis is accurate, you can 'bank it' as a piece of new knowledge about the world, and then if you want to, undertake more experiments to refine it and learn more or move on to explore another aspect of reality. If the experiments show that the hypothesis is inaccurate however, we can either adjust the hypothesis or abandon it and move on to something else. What's important about this method is that it's based on doubt – the awareness that we don't ultimately understand the exact detail of how reality works – so any theory is open to revision if convincing evidence is offered against it. Even our best sources of the truth will therefore be 'the truth – as far as we know it at the moment'. As human beings, this is the best method we have found to chip away at our lack of knowledge about the reality around us, and build models that represent it with incrementally greater accuracy, even if we will never be able to 'know reality', due to our status as individual creatures with particular capacities and perspectives.

Although we may have differing levels of knowledge about it, the vast majority of human beings have united behind the shared conception of the world that this scientific model has brought. Theories such as Newton's Mathematical Principles of Natural Philosophy and Einstein's theory of relativity have been posited, tested and then refined in the face of new evidence. They have greatly accelerated our understanding of the universe, from the minute to the massive, and have enabled us to build the society we live in today – from air travel to mobile phones.

We can also generate shared conceptions of the truth using evidence beyond the scientific method, based on the evidence of our senses – for example, we can taste that sugar is sweet or witnesses to an accident can agree that a cyclist was hit by a car. The objective model delivered by the scientific method, however, suggests that our own perceptions are subjective and fallible to a certain extent. For example, even if bystanders at the accident agree a cyclist was hit by a car, they may have perceived different versions of the same event and may not be able to build a shared conception of the truth of the event at a more detailed level than this.

It is not just the quality of our evidence that matters when evaluating the truth, however. A fundamental factor is how each of us perceive and interpret the evidence in front of us. Our beliefs can influence our perceptions. For example, a 2019 study showed that people's political orientation can bias their attention to scientific evidence about climate change – when a liberal looked at a graph showing changes in global temperature, they perceived a higher temperature change than a conservative individual looking at the same evidence[279].

So shared conceptions of the truth can be hard to reach even when the evidence is directly in front of us. To be able to reach useful consensus on evidence from people's senses we need to be aware of the biases we carry and account for these, choose well-informed participants and use samples of data that are as reliable as possible.

There can be even more room for variation of viewpoints when the evidence is one or more steps removed from us, such as when a newspaper, television station or government is broadcasting it. We need to have trust in these carriers of information if we are to believe the evidence they are putting forward. As will be shown later in this chapter, this trust has been eroded in recent decades, making it harder to gain shared conceptions of the truth.

In theory then, there *is* a basic version of the truth 'for humans' (with the necessary caveats noted earlier) that we each have access to and can build an all-important consensus on. We face a number of obstacles to reaching this consensus though, including aspects of our own LASID thinking and behaviour, as well as challenges from our modern environment. These will be explored now.

Why do people have inaccurate beliefs?

In this section, this question will be approached from two levels – first, by exploring some aspects of our mental makeup as individual LASID creatures that can lead us to struggle with misinformation and being influenced, then by looking at the role played by the context we live in and the external circumstances that surround us.

Our individual traits

Human beings are not built to seek the truth. As discussed in Part 1, we are built to try to make sense of the world, and to do this in a way that is as efficient as possible using the capacities we have. This can lead our minds into significant compromises in the accuracy of our thinking and judgements.

Many of the biases and heuristics discussed in Chapter 3 are important in driving how we interpret information, including framing and the mere exposure effect. This chapter will not revisit these, but will explore some more examples of traits that influence our response to information.

Our search for cognitive ease – as we have already seen in Part 1, we aim to minimise the cognitive effort we put into thinking. Our brains are constantly monitoring our internal state and external environment to assess whether further effort is required from our rational, energy-intensive System 2 thinking or whether we can continue to rely on automatic, efficient System 1. One area that we monitor as part of this is our level of cognitive ease – the level of effort and speed our brain is using to process information. A sense of cognitive ease signals that things are going well and there is no need for System 2 to step in, whereas a greater sense of cognitive strain signals that this might be necessary.

When we feel cognitive ease, we are inclined to feel comfortable, believe what we hear and trust our intuitions. This is also the situation in which we are more casual and less rational in our thinking, and more vulnerable to errors. There is a range of things that can make us feel a greater sense of cognitive ease, and these in turn can make us more likely to believe things to be true, whether they are or not. These are therefore powerful devices in the hands of people who wish to influence us, whether for benign or malevolent reasons. Anything you can do to increase someone's cognitive ease will help you influence them. One of these things is familiarity, which we explored in Part 1, and a reason why repetition can convince us of a belief's truthfulness – as familiarity is hard for us to distinguish from truth[280]. A font that is easier to read also produces greater cognitive ease than a less readable one. Mood also affects cognitive ease. When we are in a good mood, we rely more on System 1, and are more intuitive, creative and less vigilant – and therefore more prone to errors. When we are in a bad mood, our guard goes up, and we are more suspicious, careful and effortful with our thinking.

As demonstrated in Part 1, this idea of cognitive ease could be restated in a broader way. Our System 1 thinking is biased in favour of believing things. It could be seen as potentially gullible, with System 2 being the more questioning, doubting partner. Various factors can however affect the level of vigilance that System 2 maintains on the ideas of System 1, including things like those above that promote cognitive ease, plus when someone is tired, or when their System 2 thinking is distracted on a complex task[281]. In these situations, we are more vulnerable to poor reasoning or believing untruths.

The affect heuristic – psychologist Paul Slovak suggests we have an *affect heuristic*, in which the things we already like and dislike influence our beliefs about the world. Our political leanings and emotional attitudes towards things – and not just facts –

determine the arguments we find convincing. So, if we dislike something (like eating meat) this will drive our beliefs about its benefits and risks.

Confirmation bias – we also have a tendency to select information that supports our existing beliefs. This is known as *confirmation bias*[282]. This can affect the way we interpret information in a number of ways. One example is the *halo effect*, in which our initial emotional response to people or situations influences how we interpret later information about them. Another famous experiment by psychologist Solomon Asch listed descriptions of two people and asked participants to judge who they liked the most:

Alan	Intelligent, industrious, impulsive, critical, stubborn, envious
Ben	Envious, stubborn, critical, impulsive, industrious, intelligent

Most people viewed Alan more favourably than Ben, even though the adjectives used to describe them both were the same. The difference was in the sequence of the words, which made readers build a favourable impression of Alan initially (through being described as intelligent) and negative impression of Ben (envious) that influenced how they interpreted the later words. For example, it could be seen as a positive trait for an intelligent person to be critical, but for an envious person (as Ben is initially portrayed) it is a further negative quality.

Another example of confirmation bias is that the way in which a question is framed can influence how we answer it. If you were asked 'is John a kind person?' you are likely to draw upon different examples of John's behaviour in your judgement than if you were asked 'is John an unpleasant person?'. This means that the way information is framed can influence how we interpret it and make it harder to find the truth.

Our propensity for confirmation bias sheds some more light on how rational System 2 thinking interacts with automatic and instinctive System 1 – System 2 searches for arguments and information that are consistent with our existing beliefs rather than evidence that will challenge them. We have System 1 seeking coherence and then System 2 backing these views up. Together, these tendencies can make us less open to challenging the beliefs we hold, especially if they are driven by emotions. They can also make us less likely to consider any facts that go against our existing beliefs or political preferences. We can see how this might make us susceptible to adopting biased views or believing misinformation if it chimes with our existing emotions and beliefs.

The power of stories – as part of our attempt to make sense of the world, our minds construct stories and narratives. Daniel Kahneman suggested that the stories we find compelling can be biased in a number of ways, as we prefer explanations that are concrete instead of abstract, that attribute a greater role to ability and intentions than luck, and that focus on particularly striking events that happened rather than the many events that didn't happen[283]. Inaccurate stories of the past – known as *narrative fallacies* – can lead us to incorrect views of the present and faulty predictions for the future. This, coupled with our tendencies towards judgement of other people, can make stories very effective vehicles for transmitting information, and for making this seem coherent and believable, even if it is not true.

Social identity – to summarise this section so far, human beings have not evolved to seek truth. Instead, our minds have evolved to seek coherence – to build explanations and models of the world that help us make sense of it. As part of this we are meaning-making creatures, seeking convincing stories and patterns. We do not conduct this process of meaning-making as isolated individuals however. As 'contextuals' rather than 'individuals' we also search for coherence as groups, and as individuals we are strongly influenced by what psychologist Joe Forgas calls the 'consensual delusions' of the groups we belong to as part of our individual attempts to make sense of the world.

Evidence suggests that we tend to base our assessment of information – from empirical data to the credibility of particular sources – on goals other than forming accurate beliefs. This is called the *motivated reasoning thesis* (MRT). Such goals include maintaining our commitment to groups that we belong to[284]. For example, a study found that, when asked to assess whether a group of scientists were 'experts' on three culturally divisive issues (global warming, nuclear power and gun control), people's answers depended on how closely the scientist's apparent views on each issue aligned with those of the cultural groups that the participant was part of. For example, when a scientist endorsed a position that climate change was a low risk, participants with 'hierarchical individualist' views similar to those of the scientist were 54% more likely to view them as an expert than participants with 'egalitarian communitarian' views that conflicted with those of the scientist.

This is part of a broader tendency to engage in what Yale University Psychology Professor Dan Kahan calls *identity-protective cognition*. This is where we mobilise our mental resources to avoid cognitive dissonance and rejection from the groups that matter to us, and this could be achieved through tactics such as dismissing or belittling information that conflicts with our group's values and rationalising information that fits them. We are often not aware that we are enacting these behaviours or patterns of thinking. Interestingly, this tendency to protect our identity seems to exist on a spectrum, from one end, where an issue isn't important to our identity and the truth matters more to us, through to the other end, where our identity feels more strongly under threat and thus the truth is less important to us (for example, a culturally divisive issue like gun law)[285]. One potential tactic to build greater consensus on the truth may therefore be to make people aware of issues that are likely to provoke identity-protective cognition in them than others, and focus on ways to reduce this pressure to conform.

Another aspect of identity that can affect our relationship with the truth is our ability to deal with contradictory evidence. As we have seen, we have developed defence mechanisms such as confirmation bias that can steer us away from information that potentially conflicts with our beliefs and those of our group, or lead us to interpret it in line with our beliefs. We are inclined to muster further intellectual resources to defend our beliefs, identity and place in our group when our version of the truth is threatened. In cases where someone realises that the truth goes against their previous beliefs and those of their group, they face a difficult choice: either double down on their position and maintain their group membership or go with the truth and put it under threat. The consequences of the latter can often be too great to endure, as they not only imperil their group membership but also their sense of personal identity by implying they were wrong and are not intelligent. So, admitting we are wrong about facts is harder than it seems to be – especially when those facts matter to our group identity. This can 'trap' us into sets of beliefs and make us dig even deeper into them – regardless of how wrong they are. This is a common way people can get trapped in a web of conspiracy theories.

These identity-protective behaviours are a significant contributor not just to biased or inaccurate factual beliefs but also to polarisation between people on major issues such as climate change or politics and difficulties in gaining consensus on what constitutes the truth. As a result, they will emerge again within other topics in Part 2.

Summary of our relationship with truth as individuals – from the discussion so far, it can be argued that human beings have two relationships with truth. The traditional view held by most people is that we are each searching for the truth – a sense of objective reality – when we build up our beliefs about the world. This however is not the everyday relationship most of us have with the truth as LASID creatures. It is the domain of scientists, looking to use an objective methodology to build as accurate a model of reality as possible. The assumption that we are 'objective truth-seekers' stems from our incorrect, Enlightenment-led view of human beings as rational creatures.

In reality, there is a range of motivations behind our beliefs – including a search for coherence, belonging and meaning – and not just need to seek the objective truth. Our day-to-day relationship with the truth is informed by our desire to make sense of the world both as individual LASID creatures and as members of groups. Our individual beliefs about 'how things are' are influenced and reinforced by the groups we are part of. We have therefore evolved to find agreement and conformity within our groups, rather to seek an objective sense of the truth. Our shared group beliefs can be seen as shared perspectives as to how things are and how they should be – or 'consensual delusions' – ideas that bind our societies together, for better or worse.

The way we form our beliefs as LASID creatures can therefore be helpful in enabling us to cooperate, binding us together in our tribes and overcoming individual and intragroup differences. They can also however lead us away from the truth in several ways, including preventing us from seeing other options and the fact that the assumptions that overarch us are arbitrary.

We can illustrate some of these traits at work by briefly considering why some people believe in conspiracy theories. Evidence suggests that people adopt conspiracy beliefs when some of their important psychological needs are not being met, such as when they are feeling anxious, uncertain or threatened[286]. People use them to make sense of the world in a way that chimes with their existing beliefs, and to feel in control of their environment. These beliefs are also driven by social motives, including the need to belong and to keep a positive image of themselves and their in-group. All of these drivers are consistent with the traits we have discussed so far.

It is therefore easy to see, as LASID creatures, how we can be led away from the path of truth and be vulnerable to influence and misinformation, which can in turn lead us to different conceptions of the truth according to our beliefs and identities. The next section will explore how the structures, institutions and ideas of the modern world around us are making it increasingly difficult to defend ourselves from these forces and to maintain a shared conception of the truth.

Our external context

We are creatures that evolved to live in small tribes and to deal with our immediate surroundings. Our world, and our relationship with information, has changed enormously since this time, including the amount and complexity of the information that is available, the number of communications we receive and the range of sources of these messages and information. Circumstances have also been building around us that put our ability to navigate and gain consensus on the truth under even greater threat, and these have led us towards a 'post truth world'. This section will investigate some of the factors that are responsible for this.

Information overload – the information processing demands on human beings have risen enormously since our hunter-gatherer ancestors moved towards settled agricultural societies. We are surrounded by an enormous amount of information on a wide range of subjects, and it is almost impossible to be well-informed about every issue affecting our lives, from the workings of DNA to how sustainable tuna fishing is. We are therefore reliant on secondary information to inform our views of the world, and are vulnerable to manipulation or misrepresentation of this data. Information overload has been shown to cause a range of problems for our ability to think effectively, including what to what to look at, what to share and what to believe[287]. For example, a survey of business managers by Reuters found that important business decisions were either delayed or adversely affected by having too much information[288].

We therefore have to make choices about what information is important to us to give our attention to, as well as where to find reliable sources of information and how to interpret this information accurately. Most of us are not born with these skills, and without them we are at risk of biased thinking, errors of judgement, misinformation and all the consequences that these bring. Yet in the UK, information management skills are not sufficiently prioritised in education.

So, even without considering the other external factors that make it hard for us to see the truth, we face an information environment that we are not naturally prepared to handle as LASID creatures, and we are not doing enough to equip our children with a sufficient range of appropriate skills in our education system to be able to manage information effectively in their lives.

The attention economy – in recent decades the internet and social media has grown from nothing to become one of the main sources of information for human beings. The majority (62 per cent) of US adults get their news from social media[289].

The business models of many internet and social media companies rely on the commodification of our attention[290]. We are offered the benefits of 'free' products such as communication platforms (including X and Facebook) and media services (such as YouTube), and these companies make money from selling advertising space on these platforms. These services are not truly free however, as they monetise our attention in order to generate as many viewers as they can for this advertising – which leads these online companies to produce and prioritise content that retains our attention for as long as possible. Unfortunately, many of the things that retain our attention as LASID creatures can work against truth and accuracy, so this produces a problematic incentive structure for these companies. For example, people are more physiologically activated by negative than positive news[291], and have a tendency to share messages more that are in moral-emotional language[292]. This creates an incentive for media companies to promote and allow content that has these qualities – for example, in the 2016 US election campaign misinformation on Facebook was found especially likely to provoke outrage in voters, and evidence suggests fake news titles are considerably more negative in their tones and emotions (including anger) than real news. The attention economy therefore creates incentives that contribute to the spread of misinformation.

Social media companies are aware of this dilemma. When Facebook tested changing its algorithm to downrank content that was 'bad for the world' it produced fewer engagements from its audience – and therefore less profit for the company[293]. The need to stop misinformation therefore appears to conflict directly with the commercial aims of many internet and social media companies.

Another feature of the online attention economy that exploits our cognitive systems in problematic ways is the use of algorithms. Media companies use these to curate and prioritise the content we receive so that it is most relevant to us – but the key aim again is to further their commercial goals by maximising our attention. Many companies keep their details of their algorithms as closely-guarded secrets, so they are not open to public scrutiny. But a Facebook whistleblower revealed that content that made people angry was particularly prioritised in people's newsfeeds, even though it was also significantly more likely to include misinformation and poor-quality news[294]. In other words, lower quality, potentially incorrect information is being pushed at us for commercial gain.

The evolution of the media landscape – the global media landscape has changed dramatically in recent decades, with some of these changes contributing to the spreading of misinformation and distortion.

Journalist Nick Davies has written extensively on misinformation and the media, and his book *Flat Earth News* exposed the decline of the news media in the UK. He outlines a number of changes in journalism over recent decades that have made access to truth more difficult for the public[295]. Local newspapers used to be owned by individual companies and employed journalists who used to gather first-hand evidence for their own stories, as well as supplying this information to national titles. This changed towards the end of the twentieth century when these independent companies were swallowed up by large corporations. In 1992, 200 companies owned local papers in the UK, but by 2005, 10 corporations owned nearly three quarters of them. This was accompanied by the loss of hundreds of local titles – 24% of local newspapers closed in 10 years. To boost profits for newspaper corporations, newsrooms have also been stripped of their reporters – a key source of evidence-based news. Between 1986 and 2000, over half the provincial members of the National Union of Journalists (amounting to over 4,000 journalists) lost their jobs. A similar pattern has taken place in the US[296]. This means that the remaining reporters have no time to research or produce quality stories. Davies notes one reporter he spoke to had to produce 48 stories in a week, but spent only three hours out of the office and spoke to only four people face to face. As a result, journalists end up churning out any stories they can find from other sources in order to meet their quota. Journalism is replaced by what Davies calls 'churnalism' — a relentless regurgitating of poor-quality information that now stands in as 'news'.

Most national titles and global news websites are now reliant on a handful of the same news agencies — primarily Associated Press and Reuters. This not only results in the homogenization of news stories, but also gives an unrepresentative global view, as 40% of countries in the world have no print bureau to gather stories for either agency — and their coverage for television news is even worse. This situation is exacerbated by the rise of public relations in the news and journalism industry. Davies found that 54% of home news stories from some of the most highly regarded papers in the UK (including *The Times, Telegraph,* and *Guardian*) included PR material, with the tabloids including a much higher proportion than this, dominated by celebrity stories[297]. The media themselves have become so hollowed out that they do not have the staff to check for the influence of PR before they pass these stories on to their readers.

All of this leads to unrepresentative and inaccurate news reporting, tainted by PR hype and pandering to the tactics that will generate the largest audiences and profits, from emphasising moral panic to removing contextual information from stories that will inform readers. Instead, reporting just becomes about 'events'. We end up with a situation in which we have multiple news and information channels, each projecting their own version of the truth to an audience that already holds these views, all in the name of profit. Independent journalism and information provision are key ingredients in a society seeking to help people build a realistic view of the world as well as a consensus on the truth. They are also core aspects of a democratic society.

Media ownership – of newspapers, television and other broadcast media – has also changed. Some media (such as the BBC in the UK) attempt to maintain editorial objectivity and balance, but not always with great success, as this is difficult to do. Others can be regarded as tools of manipulation for political purposes. For example, the billionaire Rupert Murdoch owns a stake in some of the most influential media in countries around the world, including *The Sun* newspaper in the UK and the Fox News television channel in the US. Over many years he has routinely appeared in the top 10 rankings of the most powerful people in the world. He is known for his right-wing views, and his dominance of the media landscape has enabled him to promote these views (and his interests, political or financial) to his millions of readers and viewers. A study by political scientists David Broockman and Joshua Kalla showed significant differences between Fox News and competitors such as CNN in the topics they cover, the information they give viewers and how they frame this information. For example, during the Covid-19 crisis, CNN included details about the severity of the pandemic and criticisms of President Trump's response to it, whereas Fox News discussed why the virus was not a major threat[298]. The study also demonstrated the impact of these partisan media on viewers. They paid 304 Fox News viewers to watch CNN for a month, and found some significant changes in their attitudes, despite the fact that nearly all the participants were very strong Republicans. For example, by the end of the study the CNN test group was found to be much more supportive of electoral voting by mail (a practice commonly and incorrectly accused by conservative channels of being susceptible to fraud), and much less supportive of Donald Trump and other Republican politicians than the control group who just watched Fox News. Media like *The Sun* and Fox News are therefore not simply messengers of information – they are channels through which powerful and wealthy people can influence people in order to gain and maintain more power and wealth. So, partisan commercial media can lead to significant spreading of misinformation – for example, studies repeatedly show that people who gain their news information from public service media in the US (such as PBS or NPR) become better informed the more they pay attention to the news, whereas those watching Fox News become less informed[299].

The fragmentation of the media landscape that occurred in the 1980s with the advent of cable television was accelerated by the birth of online media. This has enabled the public to gain information that is slanted towards their existing beliefs and preferences, whilst rarely being exposed to other viewpoints. Exposure to these 'echo chambers' has been shown to lead to inaccurate beliefs even when people understand the appropriate evidence correctly. For example, a Republican who knows the evidence will give incorrect answers only 3% of the time to questions about Barack Obama's place of birth or Iraqi weapons of mass destruction. Someone with similar knowledge and political views will give incorrect answers more than 30% of the time if they are a regular user of conservative websites[300].

Societal conditions – another contributor to the rise of 'post truth' politics and misinformation is our political and economic conditions. For example, there is evidence of a decline in civic engagement since the 1960s and 70s, including factors such as empathy and trust among people, as well as trust in public institutions[301].

One reason for people's distrust of mainstream information may be that they feel the overall political system around them has let them down. For most people, real income growth has generally stagnated since the 1960s, with 85% of any growth in income largely being taken by the top 1% of earners. Many experts have suggested that the economic conditions of the last 40 years (including the neoliberal economic system that took root from the late 1970s and the 2008 economic crisis) have proved to be disastrous for the lives of ordinary people.

These economic conditions are one of the reasons why people have lost trust in mainstream politicians, journalists and other media. When people feel that the consensus of how to run the world is failing them, they lose trust in it. This leaves them vulnerable to messages from alternative sources, which could include those that present an inaccurate view of the world, of which there are many, especially online – for example, certain social media influencers. More than one leading academic has suggested to me that some of the political shocks of recent decades, such as the election of Trump in the US and Brexit in the UK, would not have happened in happier economic times.

The evidence bears this out. For example, inequality in the US has also grown since the late 1970's[302], with the richest 1% of the population now making more than 25 times as much money as the other 99%[303]. A recent study showed that both perceived and actual economic inequality are associated with greater levels of conspiracy beliefs[304]. The same study also suggested that feelings of anomie – the sense that society is breaking down – also influenced a tendency towards conspiracy theory beliefs.

Aside from the other negative consequences it has been found to bring[305], evidence shows that inequality is associated with political polarisation. James Garand, Professor of Political Science at Louisiana State University, found that high levels of income inequality within US states bring high levels of political polarisation within the electorates of those states, and that both this income inequality and political polarisation have a significant influence on senators within these states, making them more polarised too. As inequality rises, Republican senators become more conservative and Democratic senators less so[306].

In summary, poor economic conditions and greater inequality can create the conditions for greater polarisation of views and for people to be more open to untruths. They can also create the conditions for political actors to move towards more extreme ideological positions. As will be seen shortly, there are now also more opportunities at their disposal to exploit these positions.

Mass persuasion techniques – we are surrounded by actors, including politicians and companies, who use mass persuasion and influence techniques to attempt to convince us that we should think and behave in the ways they want – including buying products, voting and spending more time glued to our screens. Given what we know from Part 1 about the vulnerabilities of human beings as LASID creatures, many of the influencing techniques used today can be seen as manipulation rather than simply persuasion – whether they are off-line or online.

One example of this set of techniques that has emerged with the development of the internet is micro targeting, where companies use your data trail to make inferences about you and direct highly targeted advertising and messages at you. For example, the 'likes' you give on Facebook enable the company to make inferences about your personality and interests. These can then be used by advertisers to target you with political and commercial messages through the use of complex algorithms. A Dutch study showed that people's voting intentions could be raised significantly if a political advertisement with an extroverted message ('bring out the hero in you') was sent to extroverts rather than introverts, and the reverse was also the case for an introverted message[307]. This practice represents manipulation, as people don't know they are being selected and targeted, as the algorithms are often secret. It can also spread misinformation because monitoring agencies and political opponents don't know what is being said in each variant of an advertisement if they can be targeted down to the level of individuals or small groups of them[308]. In addition, political groups can target conflicting messages at different audiences – as the Liberal Democratic Party (FDP) in Germany was found to have done in the September 2021 elections, where it targeted 'green' Facebook users with an ad promising greater climate protection, whilst promising 'frequent traveller' users with one promising no restrictions of freedom to address climate change[309].

Microtargeting was used to help win some significant recent political battles. The Vote Leave campaign used a billion targeted digital ads in its successful efforts to win the Brexit referendum. The extent of its use of user data and models is still a matter of controversy, but the micro-targeting services company it engaged (and spent 40% of its campaign budget on) was found to have failed to verify that informed consent had been gained to use personal data for micro-targeting UK citizens on Facebook in the Vote Leave campaign. Donald Trump's 2016 presidential election campaign also invested in millions of Facebook ads, at a cost of over $40 million. Evidence suggests that microtargeting can be effective in influencing voting if the right people are targeted with the right message in the right context – for example one study showed that targeting abortion rights ads to female voters in competitive districts in the 2018 Texas midterm elections helped to increase voter turnout by 1.66 percentage points – a margin that could make a difference in a tight race[310].

The practice of microtargeting is likely to become more effective, as more data is obtained about users and algorithms become more sophisticated. If we see misinformation as a virus, microtargeting can be a way of spreading it in concentrated forms to the people most susceptible to it. Such practices are therefore clearly of major concern as sources of influence in future elections, as well as in any other context, such as advertising.

The rise of populism – the examples above show how commercial forces in the media sector, alongside developments in technology, have increased the potential for misinformation. In addition, the economic and social situation of the public in several countries has created conditions that could be exploited by leaders and political groups who want to use the new 'misinformation-friendly' environment to seek power.

History shows us that populist and autocratic leaders can emerge when there is popular discontent with the status quo. A core driver of the rise of the Nazi party in Germany in the 1920s and 1930s was public dissatisfaction with the economic crisis that the country was in and the diminished quality of life that its citizens faced. Populist leaders have duly emerged in various countries recently under the more recent conditions of economic dissatisfaction outlined above, including most notably Donald Trump in the US.

The abuse of truth and use of misinformation is a common part of the populist playbook. The Nazis were vigorous proponents of the machinery that existed at the time for spreading propaganda and misinformation, including radio and newspapers. Their attitude to the truth is summed up by a quote attributed to Joseph Goebbels, chief propagandist for the Nazi party: 'repeat a lie often enough and it becomes the truth'. Under the Nazis the truth was something malleable – an idea that could be manipulated for political gain. If they could control the means of communication, then the truth was whatever they wanted it to be, and whatever they wanted people to believe.

One of the more worrying aspects of the modern rise of populism is that it is creating alternative visions of reality and the truth, and Trump is not alone in his embracing of these principles. There is evidence of a cultural shift in attitudes towards evidence and truth in certain sections of the political elite in the US. A team led by Jana Lasser, a Professor at Aachen University in Germany, examined over four and a half million tweets by members of the US Congress between 1st January 2011 and 31st December 2022 and found evidence of a shift in behaviours from both Republicans and

Democrats based on the language used in these posts[311]. Over this 12-year period, these politicians had moved away from a conception of honesty based on evidence (known as 'fact-speaking') towards one based on personal feelings and intuition ('belief-speaking'). The study also found that Republicans tended to share lower quality information than Democrats, and that this could be associated with their belief-speaking. In other words, belief-speaking could lead to greater sharing of low-quality information by Republicans, as the more they appeal to beliefs rather than evidence, the easier it is for them to rely on less credible evidence to justify their beliefs. There is no evidence of this trend for Democrats.

Critically, this increase in belief-speaking information did not appear to deter voters, and did not result in a drop in vote share for Trump. The authors of the study argue that belief-speaking can be seen by voters (particularly partisans) as a sign of authenticity, of 'speaking one's mind', and that they may feel this is better than factual accuracy as a marker of the politician's honesty. So, a shared experience of feelings and intuitions becomes 'truth', even if it is factually inaccurate. This, of course, presents a significant danger to our shared conception of the truth based on facts – as well as to democracy itself.

Summary of how our context affects our relationship with truth – this chapter has explored just a selection of the external factors that make us more susceptible to misinformation and that drive apart our consensual beliefs about truth and reality.

Money and power are at the heart of some of these contextual problems. They are also central reasons as to why we struggle to address them with sufficient strength. As with all the other challenges discussed in this book, we need to ask what matters most to us – the damage caused by a breakdown in our consensus on truth, or the maintenance of old dogmas such as 'unconstrained financial markets = human freedom' that have been discredited by our new picture of human beings as LASID creatures. This book argues that we need to start putting human flourishing first.

Another reason for our failure to act on some of these external sources of manipulation and misinformation is that policy makers, along with most of the public, still carry an inaccurate view of human beings as purely rational creatures, which leads them to believe that we can protect ourselves from misinformation or any attempts to influence us. Once we start to see human beings as the LASID creatures we are though, we can see how vulnerable we are to these factors and how we need support to defend ourselves against them.

Could truth become tribal?

It could be argued that the post-truth era is, at its centre, a fragmentation of the consensus on what constitutes the truth. Groups (such as the Republican Party in the US, led by Donald Trump) have created alternative realities and stories about the world that contain inaccuracies (for example, the belief that human-made climate change is a hoax, or that former US president Barack Obama was born in Kenya rather than the US) but that are believed by millions of people[312]. These groups have become more influential and are capable of building societies around their beliefs if their leaders are elected. This in turn can lead to a 'battle of realities' – of competing views of how the world is, and as a result, of how it should be.

This troubling situation may however be reasonably consistent with how we deal with information as the LASID creatures we are, as we have set out in this chapter. We have essentially evolved to deal with information and build a sense of the truth not as an objective reality but according to the beliefs and needs of our tribe. Our hunter-gatherer ancestors only needed a conception of the truth that enabled their limited individual tribes to survive and thrive – they did not need a shared conception with other tribes.

The idea of finding a global, objective, humanity wide conception of truth is therefore a relatively new one, born from the Enlightenment and the scientific, technical and social developments that followed it. It asks a lot of human beings to maintain it, given the LASID creatures we are, including our susceptibility to follow tribal beliefs and behaviour.

The danger we currently face is that the truth becomes tribal again, where each 'tribe' simply sees the world in different ways, with its own truths and beliefs. This is of course disastrous for human beings as a species, for the many reasons outlined at the start of this chapter. Our shared conception of the truth has led us to cooperate and build a globalised world that needs us to maintain this cooperation.

One of the key challenges facing humanity in the modern world is therefore to restore and maintain this consensus on truth between human beings. The good news is that for hundreds of years, we have already been doing this. One of our greatest achievements as a species has been to cooperate and build a consensus as to what the truth looks like on some basic beliefs, such as the primacy of evidence and the scientific method as identifiers of truth. This has enabled us to build the globalised, technologically advanced world we have now.

We therefore need to take action to maintain this global consensus on the truth – and the next chapter explores how we can do this.

Chapter 10
How to defend the truth

What can we do then as individuals and as a wider society in the face of this onslaught of misinformation, and the worrying consequences it brings? As with all the other challenges we discuss in this book, there is a range of possible solutions, but each will bring advantages and disadvantages. Two types of solution will be explored in this chapter – equipping people with the skills to seek the truth and defend themselves against untruths, and changing the context that surrounds us to ensure it supports us in seeking truth and avoiding misinformation, rather than exploiting the vulnerabilities of our LASID thinking for power, profit or other motives unaligned with human flourishing.

Building individual capacities

We can build our capacities as LASID creatures to seek truth and recognise and resist misinformation. This includes helping people understand how we think as LASID creatures and the vulnerabilities this leaves us open to in dealing with information, and equipping them with the skills to know when and how to move from automatic System 1 thinking when they encounter information to System 2 thinking, in order to apply more analytical, rational thought to evaluate it.

Dr Anastaisia Kozyreva is a Senior Research Scientist at the Max Planck Institute in Germany and, along with her colleagues, argues that it is not enough to simply use the tools employed to combat offline misinformation in online settings (such as critical thinking), as online settings are different from them in a number of ways, both structurally and in the way people perceive and behave in them – for example, online material often lacks cues as to its quality that one might find offline, such as a list of sources or authors[313]. Any skills of critical thinking and information literacy we teach people should therefore include or be accompanied by other skills that equip them to deal with information in online environments too, such as critical ignoring. This is an information management technique that could be taught to help people deal with the vast array of information they encounter, particularly online. It is about choosing what information to ignore, so we can focus our limited cognitive capacity on information that matters. It could be seen as a version of mindfulness, but rather than letting your thoughts drift by and choosing which ones to engage with, you are letting information drift by. Dr Kozyreva and colleagues recommend three strategies for critical ignoring: *self-nudging*, where one removes any distractions and temptations from one's online environment; *lateral reading*, where one vets the source one is reading by checking its credibility via other sources, and the *do-not-feed-the-trolls heuristic*, where one ignores communications from malicious actors rather than giving them attention[314].

Improve information literacy – as the previous chapter demonstrated, many of our biases in perception and interpretation of information are caused not by people's capacity to understand that information or their access to unbiased information, but by their tendency to reject information that doesn't confirm their existing views or that threatens their sense of identity. We need to take action to address this, and one way to do so is to make training in information literacy an essential part of the education curriculum so that people can make better decisions for themselves, starting in primary school, from the moment children begin to encounter differing sources of information from the outside world. This training could include how to evaluate the information we receive for biases or validity, how to find trusted sources of information and how to think critically. It needs to cover all sources of information, including newspapers, television, friends and family – not just digital channels, where much of the existing training in this area appears to currently be focused. Information discernment is already being taught in subjects across the curriculum in schools in Finland, and the country now has the highest media literacy index among 35 European countries[315].

'Inoculate' people against misinformation – 'prebunking' is a method of immunising people against the effects of misinformation that follows a similar approach to vaccinating people against a biological virus. The aim is to expose people to small quantities of misinformation (by making a relatively weak challenge on their beliefs) and then refute that challenge. The idea is that this weakened attack on their beliefs and subsequent refutation of it will activate their psychological defences against it in the future – just as exposing people to a drastically weakened version of a virus activates the production of antibodies to fight it off at a later point. The 'vaccination process' consists of two stages – first, warning people that attempts to persuade them may be imminent, and second, giving them the tools and arguments they need to resist and argue against the message.

This technique, and its effects, can best be shown with an example of a study from Professor Sander van der Linden and his team at the University of Cambridge[316]. They exposed participants to a misinformation campaign about the level of scientific consensus on climate change, but before doing so split them into groups including those without any inoculation, and those given the full 'prebunking' inoculation treatment. Participants in the latter group were warned that some politically motivated groups try to mislead the public about climate change (the warning), and were then told that they might hear about this campaign online but that it was bogus and included dubious signatories (the tools). The results of the study were clear – participants who had been inoculated increased their estimate of the scientific consensus on climate change by 13 percent. Those presented with no inoculation *reduced* their estimate of the consensus by 10 per cent. The inoculation did not change people's world views about climate change, and it was not meant to, but it did protect them from misinformation on the subject – even climate sceptics.

These inoculation techniques could be taught in schools, and delivered at scale to the population through online tools such as the 'Bad News' app[317], which has been shown to be very effective – boosting immunity to misinformation by 20-25 percent, regardless of people's age, intelligence, political views or other variables. More recent work on pre-bunking has found that it is most effective when a 'booster' is given regularly in order to maintain immunity – for example, in the form of social media posts to simply remind people that misinformation exists and to keep a look out for the tell-tale signs when they encounter messages. It is also most effective when it is taught as a general skill rather than focused on one issue (as in the climate change example above), as it enables people to deal with misinformation generally rather than just on one topic.

Professor van der Linden suggests we need a society-level 'Misinformation Defence System', which inoculates the population against misinformation through a multi-layered approach, including the inoculation techniques above, plus others that will be explored shortly, including fact checking and debunking information in real time[318]. He argues it may be possible to ultimately develop 'herd immunity' to misinformation through these methods, but this is likely to take some time to achieve as the percentage of the population we may need to inoculate to achieve this could be as much as 90%.

Changing our context

We need to create structures and values around us that recognise the LASID creatures we are and prioritise the idea of the truth as a form of glue that binds a safe, co-operative and trusting society together. These structures need to help people gain access to reliable information in a way that demands relatively low cognitive effort, and need to take at least some steps to prevent and filter out inaccurate or manipulative information. These measures will help give people a fighting chance to cope within the information chaos that surrounds them, and so that they don't have to access energy-intensive, rational System 2 thinking all the time. These steps will also cumulatively help to rebuild a sense of trust in people towards their sources of information and the institutions that surround them. Some suggestions for this will be set out below – but first, a couple of impediments facing our attempts to make large-scale improvements in this area should be acknowledged.

A central challenge in moderating any form of content is striking a balance between protecting people's freedom of speech and preventing harms caused by the content. One approach to protecting free speech is to allow people to say what they wish but have structures in that communication channel that can automatically challenge the factual accuracy of the content, or simply remove it if it is inaccurate. In the UK however, our legislation already goes further than this when the content of a post is hateful or harmful, and we ban people from being able to say certain things in the first place (such as inciting hate or violence towards a particular racial group). A challenge is therefore to identify how far this 'censorship' can go – in other words, at what point a piece of content becomes sufficiently harmful to be banned before it is expressed.

Evidence from the USA[319] suggests that there is strong public support for making interventions to tackle the spread of harmful misinformation on social media. In a study of 2,500 Americans, 66% of responders supported the idea of deleting a social media post containing harmful misinformation and 78% supported an additional intervention on the social media account of the person who posted it – from issuing a warning to suspending the account. Interestingly, responses varied according to the topic within the post, with more support for penalising misinformation on Holocaust denial (71%) and disagreement on Joe Biden's win in the 2020 US election (69%) than on climate change misinformation (58%). These results suggest that the public may be willing to support more scaffolding and regulation in the management of misinformation.

Another challenge facing any large-scale attempt to regulate information flow or provide more accurate information is the question of who should be in charge of this. Should it be an independent body, free from governmental or corporate interference, or should it be simply the consensus of other members of the public? Both options have substantial advantages and disadvantages. A powerful, independent and well-funded international institution (for example, a new wing of the United Nations) could potentially manage and set standards for global information flow, as well as ensure any agreements and rules are enforced. Although this could be the most effective way of carrying this out, it also seems to go against our traditional views of freedom – carrying the uncomfortable whiff of Big Brother, where the information we have access to is regulated by a powerful external party. It can be argued however that our traditional views of freedom as 'non-interference' are based on an incorrect picture of human beings (something that will be explored more in Part 3), and as LASID creatures we need some regulatory structures around us to protect the freedoms that actually matter to us, such as the freedom to not be manipulated. The alternative 'public consensus' approach to regulating information flow seems to be less restricting on people's liberties, but may be less accurate and could be open to error or manipulation by people in power as a result of group dynamics (just recall the Solomon Asch conformity experiments). This book argues that we need both of these arrangements – centralised and people-driven – to move forward, but we need to acknowledge immediately that there is no perfect solution to this. As with many aspects of attempting to change the world, it's a question of arbitrary grey areas that need to be decided by negotiation.

Manage information more effectively – first, there are a range of ways that we can manage information more effectively, including fact checking, content moderation and flagging misinformation:

- **Provide labelling of information sources** – this is another option with significant potential to help members of the public make informed decisions about the information they are choosing and consuming. Labelling of this kind is a form of nudging – a strategy that aims to change people's choice architectures in a way that changes their behaviour in positive ways without changing their minds. Evidence shows that people prefer nudging techniques that respect their autonomy and provide some form of education rather than simply guiding their unconscious reactions to desired outcomes[320].

    The labelling measures suggested below, as well as some of the others mentioned in this section such as fact checking, could be implemented and monitored by an independent international 'Information unit' (such as an arm of the United Nations) in order to be independent of government or corporate manipulation[321]. In theory, labelling could be applied across various information sources, for example:

    - **Websites, broadcast media, newspapers and magazines** – in the UK, businesses selling food (from pubs to takeaways) are legally obliged to

display a 'food hygiene rating' prominently in their windows after inspection from the Food Standards Agency. This makes potential customers aware of the standards they adhere to. A similar 'information accuracy index' rating could be allocated to every information provider – including newspapers, television channels and websites – following inspection of their output by an independent organisation. This accuracy index could be on a scale up to 100, with ratings based on a combination of factors including accuracy of reporting, quality of sources, and levels of bias. It would account for misleading information, such as when media titles use reputable sources but employ emotion or exaggeration in their headlines to get more clicks[322]. A simple label could accompany the index to show the political orientation of the information source. Each of these steps could help users become more effective at selecting and interpreting the information they are receiving.
- **Social media accounts** – individual social media accounts could receive a rating similar to the 'information accuracy index' above, based on a range of factors including the sites they visit, where they get their information from and the quality of the information they share and like.
- **Extend the reach of fact checking** – fact checking in real time is a major challenge due to the sheer amount and

complexity of information that is being distributed each minute, particularly online. Algorithmic fact checkers are however becoming a reality, and they will boost our ability to check and flag social media and other content for accuracy. Steps are already being taken to challenge some of the most misleading posts on social media by turning to the online communities for help – for example on X (formerly Twitter) the Community Notes function enables other users to place a note of context on a particular post if enough users rate that note as helpful. Ideas such as these are helpful and should be developed further.

- **Make information clearer** – known as 'boosting', this type of intervention aims to change the environment to empower people to use their cognitive capacities to make better decisions and judgements for themselves[323]. A range of boosts could be applied within both online and offline environments to make information clearer and help people interpret it more accurately. One example is forcing media companies to be transparent about their targeting techniques, such as the algorithms they use. Another, more niche, example is to ensure health statistics are presented as absolute numbers ('Medicine X reduces the risk of heart disease from 30 per 1,000 to 12 per 1,000') rather than the way they are commonly presented with incomplete information ('Medicine x reduces the risk of heart disease by 60%') which leads us to an inaccurate impression of its effectiveness, as in this example, where the real effect of the medicine is only 18 in 1,000 – 1.8%.

- **Make it harder to share misinformation** – known as 'technocognition', this step involves using insights from psychology to design information architecture that slows the spread of false information. Some of these technocognition solutions introduce the idea of 'friction' into online processes – to make it slightly harder to share or post dubious content so that we have to pause and engage our more considered System 2 thinking. For example, evidence suggests that making people pause and reflect to explain why a particular headline is true or false can make them less inclined to share false headlines, whilst not affecting their desire to share true ones[324]. Another example of this is the prompt system tested by Twitter (now X) in 2020 that asks people who are trying to share an article they have not read to read it before sharing[325].
- **Introduce 'inoculation' into the media environment** – media channels could be compelled to incorporate the principles of 'prebunking' discussed earlier into their infrastructures. X (formerly Twitter) has already started doing this, to some extent. For example, in October 2020 they took the step of prebunking misinformation about the US election results by warning people at the top of their feeds that they might encounter misinformation about the election process, and provided refutations of some of the potential false claims, such as 'voting by mail risks election fraud', as well as a button where they could seek further information[326]. This sort of approach is needed on all channels, but as noted previously, not just in relation to individual issues like specific elections. It needs to be

extended in all media channels to a broad-spectrum approach – equipping people to defend themselves against misinformation more generally, not just on specific issues. For example, as Professor Sander van der Linden suggests, YouTube could insert an inoculation video in the unskippable advertising space that occurs a few seconds before a video plays.
- **Provide easy access to independent sources of information** that people can trust. Again, it would make sense for this service to be run by an independent, international non-governmental organisation in order to minimise the influence of political actors in this service. The organisation could be tasked with providing basic objective information about the world – from population levels to scientific facts – and this information could be the default choice that other information is evaluated against when being evaluated for accuracy. It could also represent the default choice when people are searching for information – whether on or offline. A central repository of information like this could contribute to the sense of a global bank of accepted knowledge – of consensus on the truth.

Structural changes – we also need to make some bolder, larger-scale changes to the structures that surround us in order to address some of the causes rather than the symptoms of misinformation and a lack of consensus on the truth:
- **Reinforce the primacy of the truth in human society** – as an initial, overarching point we need to collectively remember why the truth matters in society, and that the

consequences of not supporting this are grave, including ultimately the potential breakdown of society. As LASID creatures we need to respect the idea of free speech, which is important for a free society, but given the creatures we are, we also need to tip the balance back towards reasserting the importance of truth – one view is sometimes not as valid as another. Reinforcing the primacy of the truth needs to take several forms across a range of structures and institutions – for example, through our political leaders setting an example of a high standard of honesty and by promoting the importance of truth within education.

We also need to be clear about what constitutes truth or accuracy – and to establish social norms that prioritise beliefs that are based on this. There are certain areas in which particular types of knowledge can be classed as 'truth' – or at least the closest we have to it at this point. These areas are based on evidence gained from the scientific method – and can include knowledge from global temperature rises through to the distance from London to New York. Beliefs based on evidence-driven knowledge include the fact that the Earth is around 14.5 billion years old (not 6,000 years), is spherical (not flat) and has an atmosphere that is warming due in part to human activity (climate change is not a hoax). Even beliefs based on this evidence should be reviewed and revised if the evidence changes – and this continual willingness to be open to doubt and to revise our beliefs in the light of evidence is one of the great ideas within the scientific method. But what about beliefs that aren't based on evidence, as the scientific method suggests? These beliefs should be treated with less certainty, and those that run contrary to it should be treated with suspicion and caution. There are of course many beliefs that can't be based on evidence – for example, the belief that The Beatles are a better band than the Rolling Stones is based on subjective taste in music – and these can simply be seen as opinions. We can continue to have a society that values and protects freedom of speech, and allows people to express their beliefs, whilst being clear that some beliefs are based on a stronger conception of truth than others.

- **Establish a global information charter** – a set of principles and standards could be established for how information should be used and communicated by public institutions around the world, including governments and companies. These would recognise the importance of open, clear information and the corrosive effect of misinformation on society, by prioritising it above other business goals, and ensuring that the promotion of clear information and avoidance of misinformation is one of the core parameters that every organisation works within. This charter could provide the moral impetus and regulatory framework for many of the other structural recommendations that follow in this section. It could be enforced through incentives and penalties, such as an 'information pollution charge' – penalties for polluting the information environment comparable to those for polluting the natural environment. These could include a series of taxes or fines for structural inadequacies in companies that lead to the spread of misinformation, as well as for levels of misinformation and any consequences of this. This charter could be established and monitored by the global information organisation discussed earlier.

- **Demand a reshaping of how social media companies work** – As Professor Sander van der Linden notes, although social media companies are starting to take a few steps to combat misinformation, there is a fundamental conflict between the business models of these companies (which aim to maximise people's attention, dwell times and conversations in order to maximise profit) and the aim to promote more considered, tolerant and evidence-based sharing of information. We therefore need to tackle these business models to change the incentives for these organisations.

  Some commentators[327] have suggested that social media companies should move away from a model that seeks to maximise engagement, as this encourages tactics (such as prioritising content featuring moral outrage) that promote misinformation. Moving away from this model would require companies to find another source of revenue than advertising, such as the monthly subscription model used by Netflix and other streaming services. Alternatively, it may be possible to keep a model that aims to maximise engagement if this has to take place within the strict parameters of the global information charter (see above).

  Second, we need to ensure that social media companies (and indeed, all communicators and media providers) are held accountable for the information that is spread on their platforms – and its consequences. This could take the form of economic incentives and penalties, such as the 'information pollution charge' noted above.

- **Create a better media landscape** – we need to take steps to improve the media landscape in countries such as the UK, and a range of measures are needed to achieve this. We need to establish a sense that information is a community asset that is essential for individual welfare and social cohesion, not simply a resource to be exploited for profit.

Journalist Nick Davies suggests that the current business model for journalism needs to be completely changed. One possibility he suggests is for governments to contribute money to an independent fund that subsidises newspapers, rather than them being run as commercial operations. He acknowledges however that this opens up the risk that governments that are unfriendly to the idea of a free press could close them down or manipulate them. Media ownership should also be challenged, in order to prevent an over-accumulation of power and influence in the hands of a few individuals and corporations. There should be far more restrictive limits on the number of media titles (and audience sizes) that individual organisations can own.

News outlets also need to reinvest in staff – both to improve reporting and news gathering, and to establish greater levels of fact checking and monitoring of misinformation. For example, Professor Stephan Lewandowsky and colleagues suggest that news media companies should invest in 'Anti fake news editors' to counter the spread of misinformation by identifying disinformation that is circulating around the public and using their platforms to debunk it[328].

- **Prevent people from exercising power over each other by exploiting their vulnerabilities** – this is a principle that could be established as part of the global information charter mentioned earlier, but is worth noting in its own right. Our inaccurate view of human beings as rational creatures has led us to assume that many activities that seek to persuade people (such as advertising) are harmless, as we have the mental tools to defend ourselves against them. As we have seen, the reality of our LASID thinking shows that this is not true – we are vulnerable to many of these influences and this misinformation, and we therefore need to be protected from them to avoid manipulation and enhance our ability to process information effectively and gain consensus on the truth.

    We therefore need to significantly step up the regulation of these forms of manipulation to give us this protection. This includes banning institutions and companies from any form of communication that is deemed to be exploiting people's cognitive vulnerabilities for their gain – whether it is political, financial or other. For example, advertising that seeks to create wants or needs in people rather than simply informing them of the existence of a product. Or political campaigning that seeks to motivate voters using 'dog whistle' messages to appeal to their most tribal instincts, and newspaper headlines or articles that seek to increase circulation with the same tactics. Or the use of microtargeting to target people with personalised messages when they are unaware of how and why they are being selected. These steps are substantial and will transform communication industries such as advertising – but not before time. X (formerly Twitter) has already taken the step of banning political advertising from its platform[329]. Rolling out this step will require both regulators and communicators to adopt a clear, up-to-date understanding of how human beings actually think and behave.

- **Build more informational checks and balances into the democratic system** – we should apply the principles of the global information charter to political messages and communications, including common sources of bias or misinformation such as think tanks and politicians themselves. Specifically, we should make political communication subject to the same rules as any other biased or incorrect information – or even tighter rules as these bodies are meant to be setting our standards. For example, make it illegal for any employee of a government agency to knowingly publish incorrect information, except for genuine reasons of national security – and ensure the latter are not manipulated simply to prevent the communication of the truth. Political campaigning of any sort (whether by politicians, campaign groups or other agents) should also be subject to these rules, as should political leaders, who we should be required to set the highest standards of honesty, in order to drive greater trust in our institutions and information. These steps, plus others already mentioned such as stronger regulation of media ownership, could also help to reduce the capacity of potential populist leaders to build their power on the basis of spreading misinformation and hate.

- **Change our economic thinking** – the previous chapter showed how inequality has contributed to the emergence of the post-truth world, and in particular the feeling of certain groups that they have been let down by the neoliberal agenda. If we are serious about dealing with the role of truth in our lives, we therefore need to address these issues. First, we need to change the fundamental conditions that people live in. We noted that one reason why people adopt conspiracy beliefs is when some of their important psychological needs are not being met. Similarly, we have seen how a feeling of being forgotten, not respected or not given fair resources or opportunities by your government can lead to growth in alternative conceptions of truth. We therefore need to reduce inequality and ensure that everyone has the basic goods they need to build a reasonable life, and greater access to economic opportunities that give their lives meaning, dignity and a sense of agency. This requires some big political and societal changes – from higher taxation to ideas like a Universal Basic income. These ideas will be explored in more detail in Part 3.

We also need to rethink the neoliberal economic principles that have dominated our world since they were introduced by Thatcher and Reagan in the 1970s. These can be regarded as an extreme form of capitalism that believes 'financial markets know best 'in how to organise the world, and that any interference with these (such as the regulation of commercial activity) is harmful. As will be shown in Part

3, this dogma is flawed in a number of ways and has resulted in many negative consequences for human beings, including greater inequality. It also makes it difficult for us to regulate structures such as corporate behaviour, which we need to do to make life better for the LASID creatures we are.

- **Give people more power** – we need to give people the chance to be the enlightened, rational beings that we want to be, by improving their access to power and their ability to have a say in how their lives and societies are run. We need to do this in a way that uses our deliberative and collaborative capacities rather than our unrestrained instincts. This does not preclude some of this activity from taking place online, but it should lean towards the cooperative philosophy of Wikipedia rather than the relatively unrestrained environment of X (formerly Twitter). This activity should cover structures from the global to the local level. For example, we could give people more opportunities to get involved in shaping local and global issues by taking part in citizens' assemblies, which make recommendations on political issues following a collective process where the group takes the time to understand the issue, including different arguments for and against it. We can also improve our access to power via voting. In the UK, the First Past the Post (FPTP) voting system has been criticised as being undemocratic as only the votes for the winner in each constituency count, with one MP selected from each constituency to sit in the national Parliament. Changing to a different system such as Proportional

Representation (PR) would ensure that every individual's vote counted in the national vote, as the distribution of seats would correspond to the national distribution of votes. This is just one of many actions that could help to build people's sense of agency and capacity to seek a more accurate view of the world.

Conclusions

The search for truth is another example of an issue in which our cultural expectations are at odds with the reality of the LASID creatures we really are. Contrary to popular belief, human beings are not built to seek the truth, and are not 'failures' or 'weak' if we struggle to do so. We are built to make sense of the world in an efficient way within our capacities, as well as to preserve and protect the beliefs and existence of the groups we belong to. This can lead us to a range of thinking and behaviours that make it hard for us to naturally gravitate towards a global consensus on what constitutes the truth and to seek this. The search for the truth and consensus on it is made even more difficult by the structures, institutions and other actors around us in modern society that overwhelm, influence and exploit the way we seek, interpret and act on information.

Despite all these factors, a shared conception of the truth is important for human beings – both individually, as groups and as an overall species. So, the stakes are high. Given the way we think and behave as LASID creatures, consensus on the truth is something we have to continually work to maintain as a global society. If we fail to maintain this consensus, we risk our conceptions of the truth being fragmented into the various tribal in-groups around the planet, and as a result some of the important benefits of our capacity for global cooperation could be compromised or lost.

Prejudice

In brief – Prejudice, hate and discrimination stem from aspects of our nature as LASID creatures including our capacity for stereotyping and our tendency towards tribalism and conformity. Our inclination towards prejudice and hate can be increased by the structures, norms and messages around us, and exploited by people seeking power, money or other ends. To significantly reduce prejudice, we need to develop new thinking skills and change the institutions and society around us to promote cooperation and positive views of out-groups, and avoid prejudicial communications, structures and ideas.

Chapter 11
Where do prejudice, hate and discrimination come from?

In 2020, Rose Wakefield, a black woman, stopped to buy petrol from a store in Beaverton, Oregon. In this particular US state, it is illegal for drivers to use self-service pumps to fill their own cars, so she waited for an attendant to help her. After waiting a while to be served, she noticed that the attendant on duty was pumping petrol for white customers that had arrived after her. She complained and was eventually helped by another attendant. Once her tank had been filled, she asked the original attendant why she'd had to wait so long and they told her 'I don't serve black people'[331].

Prejudice means 'prejudgement'. It is a negative or hostile attitude towards particular groups of other people that can then build into behaviours of discrimination, conflict and violence. Prejudice is therefore often a starting point for other negative behaviours. Many human beings still have the expectation that we should be able to show each other greater respect and compassion than we do, and that we should be able to live without prejudice. But how likely is this, and what are the drivers of human prejudice and hate?

This chapter will explore different ways in which prejudice and hate can manifest themselves, and the aspects of our psychological make-up as human beings that can lead people to adopt prejudiced or hateful views – including social identity and our tendency to feel more positively towards people in our own groups (in-groups). It will also look at how prejudice can lead to the problem of discrimination. The next chapter will consider whether there is anything that can be done about these challenges, given the creatures that we are. The limited space available in this chapter will mainly focus on a particular type of prejudice and discrimination – that relating to race. This is not to deny the existence or importance of other forms of prejudice beyond racism, but focusing on one variety of the phenomenon can be a useful way to understand the others.

Later chapters will explore how prejudice and discrimination contribute to other major human challenges, including their roles in some of the worst episodes in human history – including genocide and violence.

How bad is the problem?

Prejudice

In liberal societies in the modern world, we see prejudice as an extremely negative phenomenon. Being called intolerant or a racist is a strong insult. Yet it is common in modern society, and many of us have first-hand experience of it or the discrimination that results from it – whether as a woman overlooked by a male-biased society, a black person affected by racism or an older person looked on as a burden or 'past it' by other people.

Human beings have an unfortunate ability to make any group the potential object of prejudice, including but not limited to those based on class, age, sex, race, sexual orientation, ethnicity, physical health and mental health. Each of us therefore has the potential to be prejudiced about others, and to be the victims of prejudice. Research suggests that certain groups are more likely to be the objects of prejudicial stereotyping – those based on race, sex and age[332]. Given that prejudice is such a broad concept and happens so commonly in everyday life, it is difficult to quantify the scale of the challenge or identify whether things have improved or got worse over time. We can consider a couple of the areas above though to get a sense of how attitudes have changed.

There is evidence that some forms of obvious sexual discrimination have reduced over time, such as women being granted the right to vote. Even in this one specific area, however, there is still much variation – for example, women gained the right to vote in New Zealand in 1893, but not until 1971 in Switzerland[333]. Attitudes have also changed to a certain extent – for example, research in the 1970s[334] suggested that female leaders in companies were valued less than their male counterparts, but by the mid-1980s, evidence suggested this bias was no longer present[335]. Sexism is now illegal and in many areas of society is seen as unacceptable, so explicit sexism can be harder to detect than before. This of course does not mean that it has disappeared – it has instead taken new forms. For example, research has shown that sexism can take the form of both hostile and benevolent attitudes towards women, which play an important role in driving gender inequality[336], and which are based on stereotypical views of women, relating to characteristics such as their attractiveness and perceived identity. People with these sexist views take a benevolent attitude (attraction, protection etc.) towards women with traditional characteristics (such as housewives) and a hostile attitude towards women with non-traditional traits (such as career women or feminists)[337]. Evidence suggests a reduction has taken place in explicit sexism in certain areas of society over time, but that sexism remains, just in different forms, as it has become less culturally acceptable[338]. It is important to note however that this evidence relates to the situation of women in the democratic West, and considerably more negative attitudes and policies towards women exist in some cultures and countries beyond this – for example, in Taliban-controlled Afghanistan, where women have been denied the right of education.

Racism is a form of prejudice that has played a role in some of the most shocking forms of discrimination and human violence in our history, from the slave trade to genocide in countries such as Germany, Rwanda and Bosnia. A range of sources of evidence suggest that there has been a significant reduction in expressed anti-black attitudes in the United States since the 1930s[339], when such attitudes were prevalent among the white population[340]. Similar reductions in negative attitudes towards ethnic minorities have occurred in western Europe and the UK. This is believed to be due, in part, to the civil rights legislation of the 1960s which made racial discrimination illegal and helped to build more egalitarian standards of personal conduct on this issue[341]. So, like explicit sexism, blatant forms of racism (such as name calling, abuse or discrimination) are now illegal and culturally unacceptable. Just because racist attitudes aren't being expressed doesn't mean they have disappeared, however. Various theories suggest that people want to be seen to be keeping up with modern social norms to behave in a non-prejudiced way, but at the same time, still harbour an antipathy towards racial out-groups. This means that people have changed how they express their racist attitudes, with modern racism taking more subtle forms[342]. For example, psychologist Teun van Dijk argues that people's communication and storytelling can reveal prejudices, sometimes simply acting as contexts to voice racial grievances, such as an incident from their research in which a participant was telling a story about a car accident in which their car was scraped by another driver, but the storyteller's main aim was to mention that the other driver 'didn't speak a word of English' and that it was dangerous to drive a car when you don't speak the language. The other driver's minority status and inability to speak English was therefore the point of the story rather than conveying the car accident[343].

Racial prejudice can also be expressed in non-verbal forms. For example, psychologist Birt Duncan set up an experiment in which white students witnessed an interaction between two males, with one shoving the other in an ambiguous way at the end, and tested how the observers interpreted this shove when the shover was white and when they were black. The study found that, when the shover was black, the act of the shove was seen as more violent than when they were white, with it being seen as 'playing around' in the latter case[344]. Prejudice can also be concealed to the conscious mind of the person who feels it. Chapter 4 showed how even people who regard themselves as unbiased and non-racist can be seen to have prejudiced views through the implicit association test (IAT).

In conclusion, racism, like sexism, is now socially unacceptable, so the more blatant examples of it are more difficult to find than they were. They have not gone away though; they just exist in different forms. These deep prejudices also have the potential to be ignited when the external circumstances and norms surrounding the individual are more sympathetic to their values. The consequences of this will be explored later in Chapters 13 and 14.

Hate

Prejudice can be defined as a set of unwarranted negative attitudes towards other people based on their membership of particular groups. But what about hate? In the 1950s, psychologist Gordon Allport described it as 'extreme dislike associated with prejudice that produces impulses of aggression'[345]. Since this time, a more nuanced picture of hate has developed, consisting of several components, which can express themselves differently on different occasions. These include a lack of desire for intimacy with the other group, a feeling of emotion such as intense anger or fear when feeling threatened by the other group, and the devaluation of the other group through contempt[346]. So, hate can be motivated by an emotional form of prejudice, and brings the potential for negative action towards the victim.

Another feature of hate can be seeing particular groups as inferior and less than human. This process of dehumanisation is particularly dangerous as it has been shown to predict certain forms of violence towards these groups[347]. This will be explored in more detail in Chapter 13.

The charity Stop Hate UK reports that over 100,000 racially aggravated hate crimes were committed in the UK in 2021/22. Even though the overall trend may be for a reduction in overt prejudice, hate and discrimination, these harmful phenomena therefore remain significant problems in society – particularly for the groups that are most commonly the victims of them, including black people and women.

Discrimination

Discrimination can be defined as the unfair treatment of particular groups of people, often based on prejudicial views of them – whether or not the discriminators are aware of having these prejudicial views. Whilst some of the most blatant forms of discrimination (such as racial segregation of public places) have reduced for the reasons discussed earlier, various types remain, some of which may conceal underlying prejudices[348]. Nearly half of all black respondents to a 1997 Gallup poll said they had experienced discrimination in one of five common situations at least once in the previous month[349].

One form of discrimination is a reluctance to help a particular group in society to improve their situation or gain more equal rights. This can take place at various levels in society – including between individuals (for example, a landlord not being prepared to rent their property to particular ethnic minorities) or embedded within institutions or societies (for example, a government being prepared to accept refugees from one country but not another, despite similar circumstances). Another example is tokenism, in which minor, relatively meaningless positive acts are taken to help minority groups, and are used to justify failing to undertake larger, more beneficial acts. For example, universities in the UK have been accused of tokenism for their support of the Black Lives Matter movement whilst failing to address underrepresentation of Black and minority ethnic (BME) staff[350]. Reverse discrimination can be seen as a more extreme form of tokenism, in which people with prejudiced views attempt to favour those from groups they are prejudiced against over others. For example, a study investigating the relationship between race and essay quality on the marking behaviour of teachers found that there was a tendency for the participant teachers to rate papers they knew were from black students higher than those from students whose race was unknown. In other words, they used reverse discrimination[351].

The picture presented so far may give the impression that the fight against prejudice and discrimination has been a path of continual, incremental improvements. This is not the case. As LASID creatures, we are subject to negative as well as positive traits being activated by the context in which we live. So, if the conditions and structures around us in society change for the worse, this can bring about negative changes in our behaviour such as increases in prejudice and discrimination. A recent example of this is the significant increase in antisemitic abuse that took place in the UK following Hamas's attack on Israel on 7th October 2023. This rise took place before Israel had launched any military response. There had been an average of 5 incidents a day in 2023 before this point and on the 7th October, this rose to 31, with 416 the following week, including a peak at 80 in one day on 11th October[352].

The idea of human moral progress can therefore be seen as a myth, based on an incorrect view of how human beings think and behave. It can lull us into a false sense of security that the world is automatically getting better without any effort from us. When we understand that human beings are LASID creatures however, we can see that our thinking and behaviour are dependent on our context, and therefore that we need to put continual effort into building and maintaining the contextual structures around us (from institutions to social norms) that will promote the progressive behaviours we want to see. The next chapter will explore some specific ideas as to how we can do this.

The effects of prejudice

Prejudice and discrimination can have a wide range of effects on people – from causing minor inconveniences to horrific acts of violence such as genocide and lynchings. Chapter 14 will examine a particular example of mass violence, and the section below will explore a selection of the other effects of prejudice.

A central effect of prejudice is that it stigmatises particular groups and the people who belong to them[353]. It creates an aspect of their identity that devalues them in comparison to others. This can lead to the group having lower status and less power than others in society, and can bring a range of disadvantages and negative outcomes for members of that group, including economic disadvantage, fewer opportunities, less political influence and poorer access to services. For example, a survey in 2001 found more than one-third of black people reporting that they had failed to get a job or promotion due to their ethnicity or race[354]. These disadvantages can then serve to reinforce the stereotypes of that group – such as being lazy or less intelligent.

Stigma can also have profound negative effects on the mental lives of individuals. It can cause low self-esteem – for example, several studies show a connection in African American children between experiences of discrimination and feelings of low self-esteem and depression[355]. Some of these effects can be mitigated to a certain extent however through steps such as equipping children with a sense of pride in their racial group[356].

Members of groups subject to stereotyping are often aware of the stereotypes others use to view them – for example, African Americans over 14 years old are aware that other people carry negative impressions of them[357]. This can make them vulnerable to stereotype threat – worrying that they may confirm the stereotypes other people feel about them[348]. For example, some students from particular backgrounds feel stigmatised and devalued by their social identity and feel that it is not compatible with someone who does well in education[358]. This psychological barrier is associated with poorer academic performance[359], and is an example of how our beliefs can become self-fulfilling prophecies – a factor that can have a significant effect on our life outcomes. A famous experiment that illustrated the power of our expectations was run in 1968 by psychologist Robert Rosenthal and teacher Lenore Jacobson, who gave an IQ test to a group of elementary school children[360]. Their teachers were told the test showed that 20 of these children would bloom (in other words, would shortly have a strong rise in their intellectual development) – when, in reality, these 20 were randomly selected, with no IQ difference between them and the other students. Over the following period of time, the teachers reported less curiosity and interest from non-bloomers in their classes – reinforcing the stereotypical expectations they had been set. When they measured the students' IQs again at the end of the first and second years, they found that the bloomers showed a significantly higher growth in IQ levels than the non-bloomers. So, expectations create reality, and low expectations through prejudice can lead to poor life outcomes.

Where do prejudice, hate and discrimination come from?

Given the negative consequences of prejudice, it may seem difficult to imagine how it could have emerged from traits in humans that are evolutionarily adaptive (i.e. evolved to bring benefits to us). This section however will explore some of the factors that combine to produce prejudice, hate and discrimination within us as individuals and groups – including aspects of our nature as LASID creatures that are evolutionarily adaptive in some ways but can result in negative consequences for our judgements and behaviour towards other people. It will also explore contextual factors in the modern world that can fan the flames of this prejudice.

Our individual traits

Below are a range of factors in our nature as LASID creatures that can contribute to the development of prejudice, hate and discrimination.

Stereotyping – Part 1 explored how human beings use categorisation and stereotyping to help us to make sense of the world and make decisions quicker. Studies show that we learn to assign characteristics to people and groups from a young age[361]. Stereotyping can be an important tool to help us deal with a complex world, but it can also result in prejudice if it makes us unable to notice individual differences between people in different groups. So, this evolutionarily adaptive trait for making sense of the world can have maladaptive and dangerous consequences for our perceptions of, and behaviour towards, other people.

Stereotyping is part of our tendency towards attribution – to ascribe causes to events when they occur. If someone performs an action, we will want to find a cause for it, and this will often involve us going beyond the information we are given. If a situation is ambiguous, people will make attributions that fall in line with their existing beliefs or prejudices[362] – and these can affect our behaviour. For example, if your existing belief is that black people are violent, you may feel more threatened when you see a black stranger walking towards you than a white one, and may be less friendly towards them. Our negative stereotypes of people are fuelled by a range of factors, from aspects of our tribal identity to perceived threats, which we will explore shortly.

We don't all hold rigid stereotypes like this, and people are often prepared to test their beliefs about what other people are like. We can however use biased strategies to approach this testing process that just confirm these beliefs. For example, when participants in a study were asked to test whether particular people fitted the profile of an extrovert they asked 'extroverted' questions such as 'How would you liven up a party?', whereas when they were asked to identify introverts they asked 'introverted' questions such as 'What things make it difficult for you to open up to people?'. The nature of the question affected the response – as people who were neither extroverted nor introverted would seem extroverted if they answered the first question and introverted with the second[363].

Personality traits – the idea that there could be an 'authoritarian' personality type was first suggested in the 1950s by

Theodore Adorno and colleagues working at the University of California in Berkley, who wanted to investigate the factors that had led to the rise of fascism and authoritarianism in Germany in the Second World War. They argued that children subject to extremely harsh parenting felt anger that they weren't able to express directly to their parents, so they came to idolise and identify with authority figures instead – an argument based on the psychodynamic ideas of Sigmund Freud[364]. The authoritarian personality can be characterised by a number of traits – deference to authority, intolerance of weakness[365], aggression against out-groups and a firm adherence to conventional values[366]. This specific model has been discredited over time, in part because receiving conditional rather than unconditional love from their parents is not the only reason why these people became prejudiced. It was found that the parents of these people often tend to be highly prejudiced, and therefore the children may have grown up to identify with these beliefs – and we will consider this idea of conformity shortly[367].

There has however recently been a revival in interest in the role of personality and values in forming prejudice. Research has shown a strong association between prejudice and attitudes such as Right-Wing Authoritarianism (RWA – a belief in the need for social cohesion and security) and Social Dominance Orientation (SDO – a belief that the world is hierarchical). RWA is associated with specific personality attributes – those of low Openness to Experience and high Conscientiousness, whereas SDO is associated with low Agreeableness[368]. Evidence suggests that these traits are activated further by our environment, including the type of out-groups we encounter[369]. For example, a study found that RWA attitudes (but not SDO) were found to predict negative feelings towards groups perceived to be deviant – and this study, these were drug dealers and rock stars. SDO (but not RWA) attitudes predicted negative feelings towards groups felt to be socially subordinate, including housewives and people who were unemployed or physically disabled. Both attitudes predicted negative feelings towards feminists – a group felt to be both deviant and socially subordinate by people with these attitudes in the study.

Our tribal tendencies – Part 1 discussed how human beings favour members of their own groups ('in-groups') above those in other groups ('out-groups'), as well as how our social identity and sense of belonging to particular groups can influence how we think and behave towards other people – even in how we perceive them. These factors are particularly important in explaining our capacity for prejudice, hate and discrimination. A simple example of this is the fact that we judge people from other groups to be more similar to each other than members of our own groups. This is called the *out-group homogeneity effec*[370]. This means that, before we even begin attaching specific judgements to members of these out-groups (such as 'lazy', 'unclean' or others) through other stereotyping processes, we have already made the judgement that the individual members of those groups are more likely to conform to blanket judgements than the members of our own group. In other words, they are less 'individual' than members of our group. This is of course completely incorrect, and is a bias that can contribute to prejudice.

We therefore don't just favour people within our in-group above those in out-groups – we also perceive them differently. Another compelling example of this is from a 2014 study by social psychologist Leor Hackel and colleagues, which asked participants to analyse a number of faces, ranging from human to artificial and doll-like, and found that people more readily saw human minds within the faces of in-group members than those of out-group members[371]. We therefore even have a bias in how we perceive the humanity and minds of others.

Our tendency to feel more negative and hostile and less open towards people in out-groups can be activated in stronger ways by changes in our environment, such as perceived threats and competition, which can lead to prejudice, hate and discrimination. As we will see shortly, we can also be influenced by other people who may exaggerate these threats and try to activate our automatic, instinctive and tribal thinking to achieve their own ends. Teun van Dijjk, former Professor of Discourse Studies at the University of Amsterdam, suggests that political leaders who push racism and prejudice could be seen as enacting a form of group dominance by white people over other ethnic groups – a type of power abuse that seeks control over valuable social resources – including jobs, housing, respect and wealth[372].

Conformity – it has been argued that one of the strongest drivers of prejudicial behaviour is conformity to social norms[373] – in other words, many people adopt prejudicial views in order to conform to the norms of their social groups. This follows on from the exploration in Part 1 of the power of social conformity as an influence on our beliefs and behaviour.

This conformity might take the form of being more likely to adopt the beliefs of the groups we belong to, due to our desire to maintain our sense of social identity and be part of a group. For example, it has been shown that when people move into an area where there are higher levels of prejudice, they show increases in their own prejudice levels. In one study, people who had moved recently into New York City and had direct contact with anti-Semitic people became more anti-Semitic themselves[374]. Some people might also have a more general propensity to conform. A study in South Africa showed that people who were most likely to conform to a range of social norms also had a higher level of prejudice against black people. In other words, a prejudicial attitude is just one of many things that these strongly conformist people conform to[375].

Even casual exposure to prejudiced behaviour can affect our own attitudes and conduct towards a group that is the object of prejudice. In one experiment[376], participants were asked to read an outline of a criminal trial in which a defendant was represented by a black lawyer. While doing this, one group of participants was exposed to 'overhear' a racial slur against the lawyer by a couple of other subjects, who were actually confederates of the experiment. At the end of the study, the participants who had been exposed to the racial slur rated the black lawyer more negatively than those who'd been exposed to a negative comment unrelated to race. Worryingly, the group exposed to the racial slur also produced harsher verdicts for the defendant that the black lawyer was representing – showing the potential for negative consequences of prejudice beyond its immediate victims.

A final example of conformity is in our varying capacity to self-police our prejudiced attitudes. This has been found to relax when people are in situations with weaker egalitarian values, with people being more willing to open up into overt racism in this situation[377]. This shows the dangerous potential for releasing suppressed prejudiced views in people when they are surrounded by a context that condones and supports such views – such as a government with an agenda that is hostile to out-groups (such as refugees) or that fans the flames of racism.

Perceived threats – one theory suggests that when an individual or group feels threatened, this can lead to prejudice[378]. Several types of threat can contribute to this. The first consists of threats to the welfare of in-group members and the political and economic power of the in-group – known as 'realistic threats'. Another is symbolic threats, which play a significant role in modern racism, according to many studies. These are where an in-group's symbolic beliefs are seen to be under threat, including its norms, values and ideas of how the world should be. For example, one contributor to Islamophobia in Western countries could be the perception that Western values are under threat from Islam – one of many fears that can be exaggerated and stoked by external forces wishing to influence people, from newspapers to political leaders, which we will explore shortly. Anxiety between groups also contributes to a sense of threat, when people feel discomfort engaging with members of other groups – often due to concerns about being rejected or ridiculed by them[379]. Negative stereotypes, such as the belief that out-group members are unintelligent, unclean, untrustworthy or hostile, is another category of threat that has been shown to contribute to prejudice.

Political and economic competition – another influence on prejudice is competition for economic and political resources. Prejudiced attitudes tend to increase when there is conflict between groups over a set of mutually exclusive goals (ideological, political or economic), or when there is competition for resources. For example, when there is increased competition for a small number of jobs, prejudice, discrimination and negative stereotyping increase considerably[380]. Research suggests that prejudice and hostility towards Chinese immigrants in the US in the nineteenth century fluctuated according to the level of economic competition that existed at particular points in time. When they were attempting to join the gold rush in California, Chinese immigrants were described as depraved, vicious, gluttonous and inhuman. But when they helped to build the transcontinental railroad, taking on dangerous jobs that white Americans were unwilling to do, they were described as trusty, intelligent and equal to the best white men[381]. This example shows how prejudice towards immigrants (including refugees) can often be built on false premises – that it is a zero-sum game or that there is competition for very limited opportunities. This is often not the case, such as in the above example, in which immigrants even in the worst economic times were prepared to undertake jobs that the local population would not do. As we will see shortly, the falsity of these premises does not stop various actors from using them in attempts to stir up prejudice in people.

Scapegoating – the final example of a contributor to prejudice is scapegoating. This is where an innocent but relatively powerless party or group is blamed for something that is not their fault. This can be illustrated by a study in which psychologists Carl Hovland and Robert Sears compared the fluctuations in the price of cotton in the American south between 1882 and 1930, and the number of lynchings of black people. The study found that as the price of cotton fell, the number of lynchings increased[382]. Black people became scapegoats for the economic woes of whites. Evidence suggests that this scapegoating is not just caused by economic competition – frustration and the displacement of aggression are also at the heart of it. The example above showed how the number of acts of racial aggression increased against one group when the frustration of another increased. Many other examples of scapegoating have taken place in human history, including Jews being scapegoats for a host of perceived problems in Nazi Germany in the 1930s – a period that will be examined in more detail in Chapter 14.

Summary – overall, research suggests that any particular form of prejudice, such as racism or sexism, is driven by a range of processes, including the thinking, emotional and group-related factors we have discussed here, rather than by one in isolation[383].

Our external context

As previous chapters have demonstrated, to understand human thinking and behaviour on a particular issue we have to also consider the context each of us lives within, as this has a powerful influence on us as LASID creatures. Some of the major external factors that can influence our levels of prejudice, hate and discrimination will be explored below.

Mass media – Professor Kim Bissel argues that the mass media sources around us shape prejudice in two ways – spreading inaccurate information (such as stereotypes) about social groups, and telling audiences how society thinks about and behaves towards different groups and categories of people[384].

Inaccurate and biased information about social groups often appears in the media, across a range of channels and in both news and entertainment. Stereotypes based on sexuality, race, age and gender are promoted[385] – for example, a study of newspapers in the US found that the most common theme in articles related to mental health was 'danger', whereas stories of achievement or recovery were rare[386]. Another study examined a representative sample of fictional programmes from several major US television networks (ABC, Fox, CBS and NBC) and found that African Americans were portrayed more negatively than white characters. They were seen as the least respected and laziest, with their clothing the most dishevelled and provocative[387]. News reporting can also promote prejudiced or stereotypical views of people – for example, a 2016 article in the British tabloid *The Daily Star* noted that Prince Harry's new, biracial girlfriend Meghan Markle was 'gangster royalty'[388], with the *Mail Online* remarking she was '(almost) straight outta Compton'[389].

Some mass media output can go much further than simply reinforcing negative stereotypes, and can move towards hate speech. An article in UK newspaper *The Sun* by journalist Katie Hopkins in April 2014 called migrants 'cockroaches' and 'feral humans'. Hopkins was not censured for this by either her employer (one of the largest circulation papers in the UK) or by the journalism regulatory body the Independent Press Standards Organisation[390]. It was left to no less a figure than the UN High Commissioner for Human Rights, Zeid Ra'ad Al Hussein, to condemn her article's vilification of a marginalised group. The UN argued that the article had used language resembling that used by Rwanda's Kangura newspaper and Radio Mille Collines in the lead up to the 1994 genocide, and for which these organisations were convicted by an international tribunal of public incitement to commit genocide[391].

The substance and presentation of any content that is broadcast to us can affect how we see and respond to other people. For example, a study carried out in 1997 found that white television viewers who were exposed to comedy sketches featuring negatively stereotyped portrayals of African-American characters were more likely to find a black person guilty of assault than those who had watched neutral portrayals[392]. Even advertising can have significant impacts on how people perceive each other. One study investigating the influence of advertising found that, in comparison with people in a control group, male interviewers who had watched sexist television advertisements then judged a female job applicant as less competent, whist remembering less of her biographical information, and more about her physical appearance[393].

Social media – as has already been seen, many people, including 62 percent of adults in the US[394], now get their news and sense of the world from social media. There is a concern that social media as an information channel amplifies people's prejudices. For example, a study of Polish adults found that that people who use social media regularly as their primary source of news information showed higher levels of anti-Muslim prejudice than those who obtained their news through traditional mass media channels such as newspapers[395].

There are a number of reasons why this could be the case. First, when you search a social media platform like YouTube, its algorithm aims to provide you with the most relevant results that will maximise your viewing time, based on your past digital footprint[396]. If you watch news or any other videos that are biased or prejudiced in some way, it is likely that the next video you are recommended will be similarly biased[397]. This 'filter bubble' effect serves to reinforce beliefs we already have, as it drives us towards similar content. Second, as Chapter 9 argued, the business model of social media companies incentivises them to prioritise provocative, emotive content on their platforms, as this secures greater attention from people and therefore higher advertising revenue. This rewards not only more sensationalist, emotive news headlines and content but also more emotive and controversial posts. The attention economy therefore doesn't just contribute to misinformation, but to the development of prejudice.

People's behaviour online can also contribute to prejudice. For example, evidence suggests that people are more likely to share moral content through online rather than offline interactions, especially when it sows moral outrage. This provocative and one-sided content could stifle debate and lead people towards simplified, emotionally-led views of issues[398]. Research overall suggests that the anonymity of the internet may increase people's expressions of prejudice, but may at the same time reduce discrimination as this anonymity can hide social cues that might lead to discrimination – for example, when people are trying to access services. As the internet becomes less anonymous and more information about users becomes available, these trends might change to more resemble the offline world[399]. One study suggests that people wishing to express prejudice may seek anonymous ways to do this online, just as those wishing to reduce their exposure to discrimination may do the same[400].

These factors are accompanied by the presence of prejudiced and hateful material online. Some social media companies (like X) have been heavily criticised for being too lenient on hate speech[401], and greater pressure needs to be put on them internationally to tighten up this monitoring and increase the severity of consequences for any perpetrators.

Political parties and leaders – another source of prejudice is political parties and their leaders, who have the capacity to not only spread prejudicial ideas among their supporters and within the population, but also to implement prejudicial and discriminatory policies. At its most extreme level, this can be seen in the ideas of the Nazi Party in Germany in the 1930s and 40s, which not only campaigned on an anti-Semitic platform, but even before its systematic attempted killing of an entire race, introduced policies to indoctrinate anti-Semitic beliefs into its population and to essentially close down the lives of Jewish people with a programme of extreme discrimination.

The political tide within individual countries can ebb and flow over time between moderate and more extreme parties, and this can have a significant effect on levels of prejudice and how they are expressed and acted upon within a population. In the UK, less moderate politicians within mainstream parties routinely invoke 'dog whistle' messages and policies to arouse or appeal to people's prejudicial feelings against minority groups without explicitly attacking them – for example, in 2021 then UK Home Secretary Priti Patel's immigration policy was accused by many political commentators of inflaming prejudicial attitudes rather than reducing them[402].

In more recent times, the political rhetoric and policies of the Republican Party in the US has shifted from coded references to race towards a much more aggressive and openly racist position following the election of the country's first black President, Barack Obama, in 2008[403]. For example, Donald Trump has used highly prejudiced rhetoric over many years, from threatening to ban Muslims from entering the US to building a wall against Mexico. It has been argued that Barack Obama's election in 2008 gave some whites in the US licence to show more negative opinions towards minority groups – and this has helped to fuel the lurch to the right that we have seen since this point[404].

This change in political leaders and rhetoric has an impact on the thinking and behaviour of populations. A number of studies have linked Trump's rise in popularity with a greater propensity within people to express xenophobic views or prejudiced statements, especially by people who are already prejudiced[405]. Reported hate crimes against black people rose after Donald Trump's US election victory in 2016[406]. A 2023 study entitled 'Trickle-down racism' also found that Trump's election victory made his supporters more likely to express dehumanising attitudes about black people than they were before[407].

It has been suggested that people's views about race are influenced by the political environment, including their leaders. As part of this, prejudiced rhetoric from leaders like Trump helps to establish new social norms, and legitimises the expression of dehumanising beliefs by white people[408]. This change in the tone and content of social and political views is then diffused to the public via mass media channels, some of which find this change convenient, such as those that will make increased revenue from this inflammatory content and those with existing attitudes and biases that match those of the leaders. Politics and political leaders can therefore be influential in stoking prejudice and discrimination, aside from the more obvious impacts governments can have in implementing discriminatory policies.

Culture and institutions – prejudiced and discriminatory attitudes can be ingrained within our cultural thinking without us noticing. For example, in recent years, the UK has been forced to start facing up to its history of colonialism, including the question of whether some of the nation's most famous historical figures should continue to be celebrated and honoured in the light of their links to racial oppression. In 2020 a statue of slave trader Edward Colston was pulled down by anti-racism protesters in Bristol – an act that received mixed public support, with a subsequent YouGov poll showing 53 per cent of the public supporting the removal of the statue, but only 13 per cent approving the manner in which it was removed[409]. This illustrates the controversial nature of such issues of cultural prejudice and discrimination, with differences between people's conceptions of prejudice and the impact this has on groups and society.

Our institutions can also be sources of prejudice and discrimination – partly in their purpose and the way they are set up, but also in the way they operate and the views and practices that they promote or allow. For example, a survey by the University of Manchester in 2019 found that racism remains a widespread problem in UK workplaces, despite the fact that racial discrimination in employment has been outlawed in the UK for over 50 years[410]. Over 70% of Asian and Black workers who took the Racism at Work survey reported that they had experienced work-based racial harassment in the previous five years[411]. 46% of respondents with a Black, Asian and Mixed heritage said they had been subject to racist jokes and verbal abuse in this time, and a third had been bullied and/or subjected to ignorant or insensitive questioning. Around half the respondents said this racism had affected their ability to do their job, with others also noting it had negatively affected their mental and physical health, increased their amount of sick leave and, for 15% of ethnic minority women and 8% of ethnic minority men, caused them to leave their job. All this goes to show that prejudice and racism remain an integral part of working life for many people.

Even our social institutions – the sources of support and care that we should be able to trust and gain equal treatment from – can have high levels of prejudice and discrimination that result in worse outcomes for minority groups. A 2022 report from the National Police Chiefs Council and College of Policing[412] showed significant evidence of prejudice, bias and discrimination within Britain's police force. It noted that black men are over three times as likely to be arrested than white men, and nine times more likely to be subject to stop and search. In early 2024, the leader of Britain's police chiefs' organisation admitted that the British police force was fundamentally racist[413].

Racism has also been found to be present in health care. A 2022 report[414] found that racism affected the health care systems of countries around the world, including the USA, UK, France and New Zealand. The racism took many forms, including racial slurs from healthcare staff towards African American women in the US and Aboriginal women in Canada, and non-European migrants in Germany, Portugal and Sweden feeling that their symptoms and complaints are not taken seriously by health staff. Aside from the obvious emotional harm this brings, this racism leads patients from minority groups to experience inadequate healthcare for various reasons, with some avoiding healthcare due to fear of racism, and others receiving worse treatment. For example, a US study found that implicit racial bias towards white people is associated with less serious diagnosis for Black and Hispanic patients when emergency units are crowded. The report shows many examples of minority staff experiencing racism too, including Arab nurses in Israel subject to verbal and physical violence from healthcare users.

Summary of this section – human beings have a set of tendencies (including stereotyping, a preference for our in-groups and a sensitivity to threats and competition) that can make us vulnerable to adopting prejudiced views of others. These tendencies could be exploited with some ease by external parties who wished to build prejudice for any reason. These parties exist in a range of forms around us, including politicians who wish to seek power through people's prejudices and media that make more money through stoking people's emotions. Prejudice and discrimination are also stimulated and maintained in subtler, perhaps less deliberate, ways though the culture and structures that surround us, including the assumptions we carry about other groups of people (such as 'blue for boys and pink for girls'), how the information around us is prioritised and presented, and the way our institutions – from policing to education – are set up.

The bad news then is that it is easier to get people to adopt and maintain prejudiced, tribal views than it is to ask them to reserve judgement and treat people individually – a point that newspapers and unscrupulous politicians know and exploit. The good news is that we can use our knowledge of our vulnerabilities to prejudice to make changes to the context in which we live, in an attempt to reduce prejudice and discrimination.

What can we realistically expect to change?

If you were to ask someone with a liberal mindset what their overall aim might be for addressing the challenge of prejudice, they may well argue that they want to see it eliminated – in other words, for all people to judge each other as individuals on their own merits at all times. But is that actually possible, or a realistic goal to set? The thinking and behavioural traits we have that leave us open to prejudice and discrimination play an important role in helping us navigate the world and survive, so we aren't going to change from being the creatures we are any time soon.

Prejudice reflects an unwillingness or inability to judge an individual person on their own merits – their character, abilities, weaknesses and other factors – and instead ascribe a generalised profile to them. When we describe prejudice like this, it may feel that we're not just describing an undesirable trait, but also a standard aspect of human behaviour – part of who we are. If we are discriminating creatures by nature, how can we stop ourselves from doing what is in our nature and can actually help us in our lives?

One potential answer to this is just to concede that prejudice is part of what it means to be human and to leave it at that. But this would not be satisfactory for many people. Prejudice and its consequences result in a large amount of human suffering, and it can be seen as an aim of a good society to reduce suffering as much as possible. Perhaps it is this attitude of acceptance – 'this is just how we are' – that has prevented human beings from having the commitment and vision to take the radical steps needed to reduce prejudice in our world as much as possible.

The evidence in this chapter so far however suggests that we could do a great deal more to address prejudice, hate and discrimination. Our knowledge of human beings as LASID creatures tells us that we have certain thinking and behavioural traits that make us vulnerable to prejudice. This knowledge suggests that we need to surround ourselves with structures and ideas that support us in challenging and avoiding the thinking and behaviours that result in prejudice and its negative outcomes such as hate and discrimination. As will be shown in the next chapter, this involves a wide range of major steps, from education to help humans de-bias ourselves through to challenging the assumptions that our institutions make about different groups of people. It also includes removing incentives to exploit our vulnerabilities towards prejudice for political or financial gain, for example preventing politicians stoking fear of particular minority groups.

There is therefore a great deal more that we can do, and our first step is to realise just how far away our modern society is from where we could be. For example, people are not generally aware of the biases they carry or how to prevent them, our institutions, assumptions and flows of information are biased in many ways, and we allow prejudiced ideas and language to be communicated by mainstream media.

Perhaps we should therefore not get caught up with the big idea of 'eliminating' prejudice and its consequences, but instead focus on the radical steps we could take to build a society that recognises our vulnerabilities to prejudice as well as the negative consequences this can have and is structured in a way that steers us away from them.

Chapter 12
How to reduce prejudice and hate

This chapter will explore some steps we can take to build a society that steers us away from prejudice and its negative consequences through changing how each of us thinks about other people and re-shaping some of the structures and institutions around us to promote less prejudicial messaging, thinking and behaviour. These incorporate some of the insights about our vulnerabilities towards prejudice from our LASID thinking that have been explored in the previous chapter.

It is important to note that this section aims to discuss how to address some of the causes of prejudice and discrimination – not the symptoms. For example, there are many important ideas and schemes that can help victims of discrimination, such as social support to reduce stigma[415] – but these will not be discussed here, as the focus is on preventing the causes of this discrimination.

An important principle should be constantly borne in mind when considering how to address each of our challenges in the modern world. This is the need to balance our aims to improve society with the need to protect people's important freedoms. This will be explored in more detail in Part 3, but it is worth mentioning briefly now. The freedoms we deem important will differ for each of the challenges we discuss in Part 2. For example, in suggesting solutions to the problem of obesity in Chapter 8, it was necessary to strike a balance between helping people to live healthier lives and protecting people's freedom to choose the food and drink they want to consume. In this chapter, one of the relevant freedoms we need to think carefully about how to protect is people's freedom of speech and ability to say what they wish, whilst steering their behaviours and the structures around them to promote the non-prejudiced behaviours we desire. For example, censoring and cancelling particular voices and views (such as those that could be seen as prejudiced) can be counter-productive, as it can stoke the resentment of individuals and groups that hold these views. But at the same time, given the LASID creatures we are, we may need to promote certain behaviours or ideas in order to counteract our tendencies as creatures — for example, our tendency to stereotype. In the end there is no 'right' answer to this balancing act, and the recommendations should always be open to debate and adjustment.

Building individual capacities

Below are some steps that can be taken to reduce our tendency towards prejudice and hate as LASID individuals:

Train people in non-stereotypical thinking — studies have shown people can be trained to break their traditional stereotypical associations and adopt more balanced viewpoints[416]. For example, in a study with employers, participants who practised associating women with attributes that run counter to stereotypes (such as dominance and strength) were more likely to offer a job to women than people who had not received such training[417]. It would therefore be possible to build this type of non-stereotypical thinking into our education system, in order to balance out some of the negative stereotypes that people may have acquired from other areas of their lives.

Another way to help people to overcome their tendency to stereotype is to encourage them to override this automatic System 1 process using their System 2 rational thinking[418]. This process of inhibiting stereotyping can require effort and self-control however, due to the greater cognitive effort associated with System 2 thinking[419]. One study showed that this inhibition training can be most effective in people who already have aspirations to have low prejudice, and are shown situations where they are most vulnerable to prejudiced thinking. They can then develop what the experimenters call 'cues for control' which can alert them to the fact that they may need to exercise particular care and rational thinking in a forthcoming situation. People could be trained to develop this capacity for stereotype inhibition.

Teach and practise the art of perspective taking – we can train people to use System 2 thinking in other ways to help them override their automatic System 1 stereotyping tendencies, for example by helping them get into the practice of seeing things from another person's psychological perspective. Perspective taking can help us understand the diversity of experiences that people have of the world, the fact that other, legitimate viewpoints exist beyond their own and help us to see other people not just as stereotypes but as complex individuals in their own right[420].

Studies have shown that perspective taking can reduce bias and stereotyping. For example, a study in the US in 2016 found that levels of prejudice against transgender people could be reduced significantly for at least 3 months just through a 10-minute conversation that encouraged people to take the perspective of a transgender person[421]. The simplicity and effectiveness of this solution may seem surprising – and it surprised the academics responsible for this experiment too. As with any psychological phenomenon though, the effective use of perspective taking gets more complex as you explore it in greater detail – for example, being heard seems to be more important in reducing prejudice in members of minority groups, and listening is more important for majority group members. A 2012 study showed how perspective taking of this type proved effective in reducing prejudice between Israelis (the majority group) and Palestinians (the minority group)[422].

This example illustrates how the practice of greater perspective-taking also needs to be dramatically increased and embedded on the international stage, with countries, religions, parties and every variety of group adopting operating principles that seek to understand the perspectives of other comparable groups rather than simply see them as competitors or out-groups. We don't need to look too far for a powerful example of this in practice, as a few decades ago it possibly saved the world from nuclear war. In the Cuban missile crisis of 1962, Soviet Union leader Nikita Khrushchev had moved a number of medium-range nuclear weapons to Cuba, within striking range of the US mainland. Over the 13 days of this crisis, Khrushchev and US President Kennedy were involved in ever-escalating and dangerous negotiations as the world moved towards nuclear war. Kennedy was under great pressure from his military advisors to invade Cuba or strike the missile sites. Kennedy, however, used perspective taking at this crucial moment to try to see things from Khrushchev's point of view. Kennedy believed the Soviet leader didn't want a destructive war, but needed to save face if he was to remove the weapons from Cuba. So, Kennedy gave Khrushchev more time, and they agreed that the Soviets would remove the missiles, and the US would not invade Cuba. They also reached a secret agreement that the US would remove its missiles from Turkey, which the Soviets perceived as a similar threat to them as the US saw the missiles in Cuba. This part of the agreement was not made public so that both sides could save face, and the US would not be seen to be letting down its NATO allies[423].

Perspective taking therefore has potential to reduce both prejudice and conflict, and we need to adapt our institutions to encourage people to adopt this skill individually, as well as to adjust our local and international institutions to enable perspective taking to happen as part of their best practice. This could include schools helping children to use it to deal with conflict, local councils providing opportunities for people of different ethnic groups to understand each other and international institutions building perspective taking into a prominent role in their operations, especially in their relations with other groups.

Provide 'thinking training' to de-bias ourselves and unleash our superpower – this section has discussed the need to teach people specific skills that can help them avoid prejudicial thinking, but these ideas could be applied in a broader way to help us deal with a bigger issue that is a core focus of this book – the biases in our thinking generally.

There is a strong argument for 'thinking training' for human beings – from childhood and throughout adulthood – to help people understand the creatures they are, how they think and behave, and the biases and tendencies this results in. Essentially, how to manage your mind in different areas of life – from prejudice to mental health to food choices. This training can help people to identify situations in which these biases are likely to be present or these tendencies activated, and provide people with strategies to overcome them. For example, if we can identify that there may be a temptation to conform to the views of the most senior people in work meetings, we can train ourselves to develop, communicate, and have confidence in our own opinions with this in mind. In other words, the 'thinking training' would help us to think more like the self-aware, rational creatures we aspire to be.

We already provide fragments of this training in society, but only on a limited number of topics to a small audience – for example, in cognitive behavioural therapy, patients are taught to understand how their thinking processes work and to develop habits to move them away from destructive negative thoughts. There is a wide range of other elements of mind management that could be covered within a lifelong 'thinking training' programme, including managing our biases. This could be split into several core components of human life, for example, managing information, aggression and violence (as we will explore in the next chapter) and prejudice (including the skills of non-stereotypical thinking and perspective taking and the anti-prejudice teaching already mentioned in this chapter).

This could be a lifelong form of education for both children and adults that is built, reinforced and practised throughout our lives, as it never ceases to be valuable. This training should not just be a core part of the national curriculum for children and young people – it should also be embedded in adult life, including within the structures and institutions that surround us, from workplaces to governmental departments.

Framing this as 'thinking training' could help to make it more palatable to those people who may feel the idea of 'anti-bias training' is politically-led and unnecessary. It can also be presented as skills with a number of useful practical applications, such as helping to make people more productive and successful, not just as a 'woke' idea to make us less biased on race or gender issues. In fact, it could be a way to make people think differently about themselves, so that bias is not something people feel criticised, blamed or demeaned for but is just part of being human – a tendency we all share. We could promote thinking training as a chance to make human beings more powerful and to 'unleash our human superpower' – our ability to cooperate and build better lives for ourselves.

Changing our context

Aside from finding ways to change our individual responses to other people, we can also change the context around us, including our structures and institutions, to make it an environment that promotes more positive and less biased judgements of others. One principle central to the suggestions that follow is that we have seen various ways in which prejudice can be activated in us as LASID creatures, but there are plenty of counter examples in which co-operation can be activated. We therefore need to change our context in ways that activate our cooperative rather than prejudicial capacities.

Build more anti-prejudice teaching into the education system – a range of steps can be taken within the education system to reduce prejudicial and discriminatory thinking and behaviour. These include introducing teaching non-stereotypical thinking and perspective taking as just mentioned as well as the anti-bias training that will be explored shortly. These would form part of a broader range of skills we should teach our young people to understand and manage their mental and behavioural patterns as LASID creatures. The full range of these broader skills will be explored in Part 3.

These skills also include promoting understanding and tolerance of diversity, as studies suggest that prejudice partially stems from ignorance[424]. Knowledge and understanding of differences as well as similarities is important in reducing prejudice[425]. We need to teach children about the fact that we are different and have different experiences of the world (and to understand others' experiences as part of perspective taking, mentioned above), but are part of one species and need to unite together to stop prejudice. This encourages people to adopt multiple identities – seeing themselves and other people as members of several groups rather than just one in-group, and this can help to reduce intergroup bias[426]. The need to unite to achieve the common goal of reducing prejudice, discrimination and suffering is also important, as it has been shown that shared goals that require people to cooperate help to reduce hostility between groups[427]. We must also build a sense of agency in young people that they can do something about these problems.

In 2020, the UK television series 'The school that tried to end racism' explored what happened when this type of anti-prejudicial training (in this case to reduce racial bias) was tested in a secondary school in south London. At the start of the training, the children were given an implicit association test (IAT) which found that the majority of the class had a pro-white unconscious bias, but when tested again at the end there had been a significant drop in this bias, towards a neutral, non-biased position. This was clearly a broad and illustrative study, but its positive results and emotive content amplified the calls to implement this substantive training across the curriculum. Unfortunately, Professor Rhiannon Turner, one of the academic consultants in the series, noted that there was a reluctance from politicians to take this action after the programme had aired, as there was a view that sufficient steps were already being taken on this issue[428]. Professor Turner believes that this is not the case, and that teaching on this topic needs to be fully enshrined in law, with clear teaching requirements and standards[429]. These principles and skills to reduce prejudicial thinking also need to be embedded across the whole curriculum – not just isolated within one subject of anti-prejudice training or thinking skills.

Teachers also need to be trained to provide this teaching and work within these new processes, as these can currently be a source of anxiety for educators – for example, they may feel they don't understand the topics well enough or feel that they will get into trouble if they make a mistake. Teachers need to feel confident in delivering these changes, and that confidence comes from clear guidance and training from government and educational policy makers, as well as a strong sense of commitment that this issue matters.

Promote intergroup contact – negative attitudes to out-groups can be maintained by a fear and lack of understanding of them, as well as a lack of access to information that may help to reverse false beliefs. This lack of understanding is often exacerbated by a lack of contact with these groups. A range of research shows that giving people the chance to meet members of out-groups can produce a positive change in attitudes towards them. Psychologists Thomas Pettigrew and Linda Tropp analysed the findings of over 500 studies and found that intergroup contact not only reduces intergroup prejudice on matters of race and ethnicity, but could also do the same on other topics, such as sexual orientation and mental and physical disability[430]. The authors suggest that this intergroup contact makes people familiar with each other, which leads to liking. As we saw in Part 1, human beings tend to like things (including people) the more familiar they are – known as the *mere exposure effect*.

A reasonable question to ask is how this idea of intergroup contact can be rolled out across populations in society, as it is simply not possible for everyone to have face-to-face contact with every type of out-group they might encounter. A promising solution to this is the idea of 'indirect contact' – various methods of non-face-to-face contact that have shown positive results in reducing prejudice and in-group favouritism[431]. The first method is extended contact – knowing an in-group member who has out-group friends, for example, knowing a white colleague has black friends. When people see this intergroup contact in a positive way it can reduce intergroup anxiety and reduce prejudice. Imagining social contact with an out-group member has also been shown to promote better relationships with out-group members. Online contact through chat software has also been shown to improve intergroup relations. For example, Protestant and Catholic students in Northern Ireland who undertook a short cooperative online interaction with a student from the other community reported more positive expectations and lower levels of anxiety about intergroup contact[432].

These steps for intergroup contact could be built into many of our institutions as well as the structures in our daily lives. For example, the education system and workplaces could implement contact and cooperative activities between pupils or workers from different groups and backgrounds into the fabric of their processes, and social media platforms could promote online interactions between people from different in-groups through targeted prompts to all users or setting up new online spaces. Studies suggest that the potential success of these steps can be maximised by making sure that people are fully ready to take part in this intergroup contact[433]. This includes being equipped with positive expectations about the experience and the people they will meet, a sense of self-efficacy, and skills such as perspective taking and empathy – all factors that could also be nurtured within the institutions themselves.

Implement steps to prioritise the truth in society – Chapter 10 outlined a number of changes to the structures around us that could be made to prioritise the idea of the truth in society, help people gain access to reliable information and filter out inaccurate or manipulative information. These included managing information more effectively, reshaping how social media companies work and creating a better media landscape. Each of the steps in that section could also play an important role in reducing prejudice and is worth revisiting in this context.

A couple of these points can be expanded further to apply them more specifically to reducing prejudice:

- **Establish a global information charter** – this could include monitoring and preventing prejudicial messages or information as well as misinformation. This point might be subtle in how it appears in daily life – for example, criticising billionaire George Soros is not in itself antisemitic, but using him as a symbol of Jewish wealth, power or control may well be[434] – and challenging these subtle uses of prejudicial tropes is just as important as preventing the spreading of more obvious ones.

- **Prevent people from exercising power over each other by exploiting their vulnerabilities** – this includes much stronger regulation to prevent messages or framing that use biased, stereotypical or prejudicial portrayals of people or groups of people in order to influence others. This includes blaming or scapegoating of particular groups. This principle should be rigorously applied to the media and politicians as much as anyone else, as these actors set the standards for our discourse in society, and as we have seen, have an influence over the social norms that other people adopt in relation to prejudicial language and attitudes, and have the potential to build public support for prejudicial, hateful or potentially violent views and policies.

Promote positive and penalise negative representations – following on from the need for positive narratives, one way to help people overcome their tendency to stereotype is through priming our System 1 processes. For example, one study found that exposing people to well-liked examples of black people (such as Denzel Washington) reduced their levels of race bias compared to people who had not been exposed to these examples[435]. This study has a range of implications, including for the mass media. It suggests that more balanced representations of minority groups (especially those vulnerable to prejudice) that remind people of well-liked examples of these groups as well as the usual groups (for example, disabled as well as non-disabled athletes) could help to reduce negative stereotypes and prejudice. Steps like this to promote positive representation should be taken in all institutions, including politics, education, workplaces and sports teams – not just the mass media. This is a more radical recommendation than it may seem, as we live in a world where negative stereotypes of various groups are routinely communicated to the public. To achieve this transformation in positive representation we need to change the culture of all institutions. This includes stricter monitoring and penalties for spreading negative stereotypes and legislating to actively promote positive representations of minority and out-groups.

In tandem with this recommendation, steps that can reduce the perceived threat of out-groups and increase their familiarity can also help to reduce prejudice. Mass media therefore have an important role to play in this step through their choice of content (for example, more news stories of people beyond our in-group) and framing of people and groups in that content (for example, non-prejudiced portrayals of minorities).

Create a new narrative of interdependence and cooperation – the steps listed so far in this section are a start, but they are not enough to reduce prejudice to the lowest levels possible. Nor is the broad global idea that most people already subscribe to in principle – that every human being is equal. To gain significant social change we need to change our cultural ideas to recognise the fact that, as LASID creatures, the process of reducing prejudice in society requires sustained effort – it is an active process, not a passive one. Everyone needs to play a part in maintaining a co-operative, less prejudiced world from the way they think about and relate to people in their daily lives through to the information they consume and politicians they vote for. If we don't maintain this effort to balance and overcome our tendencies towards prejudice, then prejudice and discrimination will become stronger.

We also need to be clearer about the rewards of building a more cooperative world and the consequences of allowing prejudice to continue. We must not allow prejudice and bias to be seen as an annoying, lofty and minor liberal 'woke' principle. Instead, we should see it for its fundamental, existential and practical consequences – for example, preventing conflict, violence and suffering, as well as building cooperation and a society that is better for everyone – not just the victims of prejudice and discrimination.

A central idea we need to establish within this new cultural vision is our mutual interdependence as human beings – the idea that we need each other to accomplish our goal (of flourishing, or even surviving, as a species), and need to cooperate together to achieve it, regardless of the different groups we are members of. This principle has been found to be key in reducing hostility and increasing cooperation between groups[436]. It could also be at the heart of a new approach to reducing prejudice and increasing human flourishing, whether in classrooms or in international political settings.

This approach would require the re-calibrating of our institutions and social arrangements to promote cooperative principles – essentially, a way of bringing the values of a small tribe to a large, complex society – ensuring everyone plays a role and that we are bonded closer in our group. To see how unusual this idea is, compare it with how schools operate at the moment. Psychologist Elliot Aronson[437] argues that school classrooms are highly competitive – children are competing for the approval of their teachers and only some will be 'winners' in this contest (e.g. getting questions right) and many will be 'losers'. In this competitive environment, Aronson argues, friendliness and cooperation between children is rarely fostered. The same observation could be applied to workplaces, financial markets and many other institutions. It doesn't have to be this way, Aronson argues. We can choose to design lessons in which children have to cooperate in order to learn and succeed – he calls this the 'jigsaw method'. For example, using this teaching approach to study the background of a famous American, each child was given a different section of the person's overall biography, and the children had to work together to construct and learn the full picture. Each child had the same importance in the task and needed to play a role. And each child relied on the others succeeding. So, cooperation was essential. This cooperative approach to learning produced clear results when it was tested in classrooms across America. Children in jigsaw classrooms liked each other more (including across racial groups), liked school more and had better self-esteem than those taught in traditional ways. Ethnic minority children achieved better exam results too. This principle of rewiring our education institutions for cooperation rather than competition could be applied to other institutions and relationships, including workplaces, politics and interpersonal relationships. For example, an office that recognised the mutual interdependence of fellow workers might include different incentive structures, working methods and staff performance measurements than one based on individual performance and competition.

This new narrative of cooperation needs effective leaders and communicators to promote it and to mobilise collective action. The people who can define our social norms have social power – for better or for worse. As we have noted, leaders that stir prejudice and discrimination have an easier task than those seeking to build cooperation and reduce prejudice, because the former appeals to our laziest instincts, whereas the latter requires more cognitive effort from human beings. We therefore need to identify, and amplify the voices of, leaders and communicators who can set norms of cooperation and, where possible, encourage all political leaders to act in line with this more positive narrative.

De-bias our institutions – we need to use our knowledge of how people think and behave to rewire our institutions to become less biased – from companies to social care providers. One initial ingredient in this is to embed the anti-prejudicial training discussed above into our institutions, from workplaces to the police force. Adult attitudes can be changed, even if not as easily as children's. Such training should become a legal obligation for any company or institution.

Embedding anti-prejudicial training won't be enough on its own if an organisation is structurally biased though. Professor Rhiannon Turner suggests that many organisations don't do enough to monitor or combat discrimination. They may carry out an annual survey on discrimination, but this can sometimes be just to avoid being sued[438]. To reduce institutional prejudice effectively, we need to review everything about our institutions. Essentially, just as we need to use our knowledge of how LASID creatures think and behave to help individuals think in a less biased way, we need to apply this principle to how our institutions think and operate too. This task requires us to challenge every aspect of an institution, including its leadership, structure, processes and assumptions. It is also potentially more complex than considering how to de-bias individuals, as organisations represent their own social communities, containing differing tribes and interactions between people. Part of the challenge organisations face in debiasing themselves is therefore to review how they can set up structures and expectations for these interactions between people and groups that will reduce bias – for example, possibly using cooperative rather than competitive working practices, as discussed earlier.

Progress is undoubtedly being made in some of the less complex aspects of this process, such as increasing the diversity of senior positions in companies. For example, the proportion of board positions in FTSE 350 companies held by women rose to a record 42% in 2024, from just 24.5% in 2017[439]. Many of the most publicised progress reports on diversity tend however to focus on the few hundred largest companies in each country, rather than the vast majority of other organisations and institutions, and these often have lower diversity rates than the larger ones – for example, in 2020, only 16% of small small-to-medium sized businesses were led by women[440]. The diversity of boards of directors and senior management teams needs to be representative across gender, race and other variables, in order to reflect the diversity of society.

Initiatives such as the Parker Review of ethnic diversity on boards in the UK are setting voluntary standards, but these measures need to have more legislative strength, be applied across key areas of prejudice and be applied to all companies, as the largest companies tend to be further ahead than the majority in implementing these policies.

As noted above though, the changes required to our institutions go way beyond diversity of leadership. For example, processes should be implemented that help to circumvent our tendency for biased thinking, such as blind recruitment, in which a candidate's identity isn't revealed until interview shortlisting has been completed. Cultural changes will also be required to re-examine the assumptions that the social norms and expectations of our institutions make about different groups of people. There is much work to do.

De-bias society – we need a rethinking of the assumptions and biases overarching our society along similar lines to the process outlined above for our institutions. For example, in the UK we should continue to review the way we perceive our history of empire and the attitudes it involved towards other groups of people (such as slaves). We should be clear when these attitudes, policies and behaviours are inconsistent with our values today, as this helps to reinforce the importance of less prejudicial ideas. Similarly, we should consider whether our international or immigration policies today are consistent with the non-prejudicial values we are aiming for, and if not, change them.

We can also embed processes in society and our institutions to identify biases and correct for them, in order to support (rather than just penalise) people in avoiding prejudiced thinking and behaviour. For example, through labelling, signage or pop-up windows online, we can help people identify situations in which they might be most prone to bias, discrimination or prejudice, so that they can pause, activate their System 2 thinking and quickly consider how to avoid it. These 'prejudice danger moments' might include when we're in social groups (danger of conformity or being affected by our social identity), online (danger of anonymity or increased likes for more emotive content), chairing meetings or employee recruitment at work (danger of unconscious bias affecting our decisions).

Address economic inequality – to truly address some of the drivers and effects of prejudice, we need to deal with the issue of inequality. We need to ensure that every individual, regardless of their background, has the basic resources to enable them to live self-determined, well-informed and dignified lives, where they are not living in fear or resentment of others.

This step would assist not only those who have been the victims of discrimination, which can lead to unfair and unequal economic outcomes, but also those people who may be at risk of entering into prejudicial or more radicalised behaviour, due to their disenchantment with the status quo and a desire to search for scapegoats to blame their own situation on. See Chapter 10 for more details on the need to address economic inequality.

Conclusions

In summary, if we want to reduce prejudice in human society, we need to become more aware of how it can be triggered in people, as well as how its counterpoint of cooperation and inclusion can be activated. We then need to arrange the institutions and systems around us in society to promote cooperation and prevent prejudicial reactions. This involves a range of steps, some of which seek to rewire our automatic System 1 tendencies to different ends (such as promoting more positive views of out-groups), and others that seek to override our System 1 tendencies with rational System 2 thinking (such as teaching people thinking skills).

Many of the ideas and institutions that surround us in society also promote or allow prejudicial thinking to emerge, and we need to challenge and adapt these basic assumptions and structures if we are to address this issue in the most effective and meaningful way. Key to our success is recognising that reducing prejudice, hate and discrimination requires ongoing, active work from all of us. The next chapter will examine what can happen if we aren't willing to put in this effort.

Violence

In brief – Conflict and violence have been features of human societies since they first existed. Yet in the twentieth century, over 100 million people died violently at the hands of other human beings. Our levels of violence and aggression are influenced by a range of things – from learned behaviour to uncomfortable levels of heat. We all have the potential for acts of extraordinary and shocking violence, depending on the situation we find ourselves in. We can however reduce our potential for violence and make the world safer through a range of steps, including stronger licensing of weapons, changing conditions that promote violence and creating environments of cooperation rather than conflict.

Chapter 13
Where do violence and aggression come from?

On July 13th 1942 a group of men gathered in the forest a few kilometres from the village of Józefów in southeastern Poland. Most were ordinary people of a working-class background, recruited relatively recently as civilians into a reserve police battalion to support the German war effort. They included a tailor, a cigarette salesman and a metalworker. They waited for the first truck of around forty women, children and men to arrive, and when it did, each of the police paired off with someone from the truck and marched them down the forest path. At a certain point in the woods, the people from the truck were ordered to lie face down in a row. At this point, the policemen – including dock workers, truck drivers and waiters – stood directly behind them, placed the tips of their bayonets in the backbone above the shoulder blades of their victims, and shot them in unison.

How could ordinary human beings like you and me behave like this? This chapter will examine the challenge of human aggression and violence, and explore some of the factors that drive these behaviours within people. The next will take a more detailed look at an example of extreme violence – the mass killings perpetrated by Police Battalion 101 in Poland as part of the Holocaust – in order to understand what human beings are capable of and the factors that can drive this behaviour. By facing up to the reality of our capacity for violence and understanding it, we can learn lessons that could help us to build a less violent and more peaceful world. The final chapter on this theme (Chapter 15) will then consider what steps we can take to build such a world.

How bad is the problem?

We all want peace. The idea that we can just get on with one another and live harmoniously together is an incredibly attractive idea for human beings across the world, and for good reason. As an aspiration, it is a state of affairs in which we avoid a range of significant harms, and experience a range of profound positives in our lives, as can be illustrated with a couple of the definitions of the word 'peace':
- Freedom from quarrels or dissension between individuals (or, esp. in early use, between an individual and God); a state of friendliness; amity, concord.
- Freedom from anxiety, disturbance (emotional, mental, or spiritual), or inner conflict; calm, tranquillity[442].

As a result, it is one of the most enduring themes in our cultural heritage as human beings, and runs through many of our stories and songs – from 'West Side Story' to Marvin Gaye's 'What's going on'. We aspire to peaceful global existence, and are profoundly hurt and disappointed when we see conflict and violence between people. But is it realistic to expect or even hope for harmony among human beings? Depending on your outlook (and perhaps your musical taste) the sentiment of John Lennon's song 'Imagine' might be cloyingly sentimental and unrealistic or a brave and visionary statement of how the world could, and should, be.

Conflict in itself, however, may not be the problem. It could be seen as a natural state of affairs among social animals with differing interests living in close communities. Perhaps the problem is keeping conflict as non-violent as possible. Similarly, it could be argued that human aggression and violence can serve a purpose beyond their potential evolutionary value. For example, they help to regulate relationships and enforce rules to maintain an orderly, peaceful society. The challenge we face may therefore not be to eliminate aggression and violence but to reduce them to levels that will minimise human suffering and death. The question is what level of aggression and violence is needed to do this.

A first step is to ask whether things are really as bad as we think. Our newspapers and screens are filled with stories of conflict and violence, showcasing the worst sides of human nature. But are things any better now than in the past?

This question is more complicated than it appears, although the answer may initially seem to be a firm yes. The UN Global Study on Homicide[443] suggests that homicide rates – the intentional and illegal killing of one person by another – have declined significantly over the past few hundred years. There are a range of reasons for this long-term reduction on an international level, including the development of democratic societies, the building of social and political institutions (from the judiciary to the police force) and the spread of trade and tourism. Interpersonal violence has also declined – a point illustrated by the 90 percent reduction in deadly violence between individuals in Europe between the 15th and 20th centuries. The social psychologist William von Hippel suggests that this is for two principal reasons. First, the presence of stronger and reasonably impartial law enforcement in states has reduced the need for people to take the law into their own hands and take personal action to attack or defend themselves or their property from others. A second possibility is that we have become more sensitised to violence since the world has become a safer place[444]. In other words, the less violence there is, the more it affects us when it does occur.

Ultimately then, it appears that various forms of social, cultural and legal 'scaffolding' around us have helped to dampen our capacity for everyday violence and nurtured our capacity for cooperation. That is the positive side of the picture. But there is a counter argument. A great deal of violence still takes place in the world and causes desperate suffering for millions of people as a result. Around 440,000 people were killed through homicide in the period 2019-21[445], and these deaths are just the tip of the iceberg in terms of the total number of acts of aggression and violence between people around the world.

Large-scale violent conflict also remains a feature of modern human society. In the 40 years following the end of the Second World War, there were 150 wars and only 26 days of global peace between nations. In the 20th century, over 100 million people died violent deaths at the hands of other human beings – a figure more than five times that of the 19th century and more than ten times that of the 18th century[446].

Beyond wars and conflict, the 20th century also witnessed the largest number of systematic killings of human beings in any century in history[447]. So extreme was the level of slaughter in particular events (such as the Holocaust) that a new term was coined to describe this form of deliberate mass killing – genocide. This refers to acts committed with the intention of destroying, completely or partially, a religious, ethnic, national or racial group. Massacres and mass killings were nothing new before this point, from the destruction of Carthage by the Romans that left 150,000 people dead to the slaying of 'infidels' by both sides in the Crusades in the 12th and 13th centuries[448]. But the 20th century lived up to its naming as the 'age of genocide'[449], despite a continuing debate as to which events fitted the exact definition of this term. Several periods of violence took place that can be argued to have fitted into this category – including the starvation of 6 million Ukrainians in 1932 by Stalinist Russia, the killing of 6 million Jews by Nazi Germany during the Holocaust of 1939-45 and the massacre of 500,000 people in Indonesia between 1965-66[450] [451]. Other forms of mass killing also took place, including the 'Rape of Nanking' in the Sino-Japanese war in 1937, in which Japanese soldiers raped and killed around 250,000 Chinese soldiers and civilians[452]. Overall, it is estimated that 60 million people – men, women and children – were the victims of mass killing and genocide in the 20th century[453].

Advances in technology have also driven the development of weapons of greater destructive power than ever before. Nuclear weapons are the obvious example here, with the bombing of Hiroshima in 1945 alone killing 69,000 people and injuring a further 69,000[454]. Other destructive technologies of recent centuries have caused greater death and suffering than these however, including the use of machine guns from the late 19th century, which have killed millions of people in the two world wars and other conflicts around the world, and which still constitute the weapon of choice for armies around the world, such as the US[455]. The cumulative death toll from the use of machine guns is not known, but its scale can be illustrated by the estimate that 100 million of these weapons are in existence around the world today[456].

In summary, whilst rates of certain forms of lethal violence have decreased over the past several hundred years, violence still remains a substantial challenge for human beings as it causes death and suffering for millions of people. In addition, incidents of mass violence such as genocide appear to be showing no signs of reducing, and our potential to kill even larger numbers of people is increasing with ever more sophisticated and devastating weapons of mass destruction. Our capacity for aggression and violence has therefore not gone away – and there is clearly an urgent need to address this challenge.

Where do violence and aggression come from?

What are the factors that lead us towards aggression and violence? The first point to note is that aggression and violence are incredibly broad ideas, covering a wide variety of actions, including verbal abuse, smacking a child and acts of genocide. This section will simply examine some of the factors that are connected with aggression and violence in human beings generally. It will examine those related to our individual psychological makeup as LASID creatures, as well as external factors that can influence our levels of aggression and violence. The next chapter will then focus on one specific example of extreme violence – the behaviour of the members of German Reserve Police Battalion 101 during the Holocaust – in an attempt to understand the factors that could drive ordinary, law-abiding people to commit acts that we may think only psychopaths are capable of.

Our individual traits

Below are a number of factors relating to our psychological makeup as creatures that can contribute to aggression and violent behaviour.

Personality – perhaps the most tempting cause to attribute aggression to is someone's personality – 'they are just a naturally aggressive person'. Research suggests that some people show behaviour patterns that can be described as a 'Type A' personality, including being over-competitive in their relationships with others[457] and showing greater aggression than other people when they are unable to achieve tasks[458]. It is however, over-simplistic to suggest that natural tendencies are the sole reason why people behave aggressively, as many other factors can influence this behaviour[459].

Biology – scientists have found that certain biological factors play a role in aggression. For example, the MAOA gene, which regulates serotonin, a neurotransmitter that helps to control aggressive behaviour[460]. This has been shown to be involved in aggressive violence and has been termed by the media as 'The warrior gene'[461]. The hormone testosterone has also been found to have a minor correlation with aggression. Males have more testosterone than females, and men commit many more violent acts than women. A 2022 survey in Scotland found that 73% of violent crimes in 2019-2020 were committed by men – just under three times the number committed by women[462]. The relationship between testosterone and aggression is both small and unclear however[463], and it is unclear whether it is causal, or if so, in which direction the cause-and-effect relationship runs. For example, competing in both physical and non-physical competitions can influence testosterone levels, and winning a game of chess can increase testosterone levels[464].

But why do we show aggression? Evolutionary social psychologists suggest that it has survival value to human beings, as well as other animals, as it helps us get access to, and protect, the resources we need, such as food, mating partners, offspring and territory. They claim that aggression is instinctive in human beings – as is all other social behaviour – and developed as a means of enabling us to successfully pass on our genes to our children[465]. Most modern social psychologists however don't favour explanations of how aggression occurs or is maintained that are based exclusively on instinct[466]. They prefer to explain it as a combination of traits in us as LASID individuals that can be activated or suppressed by the environment we are in – for example, if someone is naturally irritable, this could turn into aggressive behaviour when activated by a dispute with another driver over who found a parking space first[467].

Learned aggression – research suggests that we can learn aggressive and violent behaviours during our lives. This can happen when we see others apparently being rewarded for behaving aggressively, or we experience this ourselves – for example, if a child takes a sweet from another, and is not reprimanded for doing so. Children can also learn aggressive behaviours when they are modelled by adults. A famous experiment that illustrated this was carried out by psychologist Albert Bandura and his colleagues[468], which tested the responses of groups of children aged 35-69 months to witnessing adult aggression in different settings. They watched an adult play with a 5-foot inflatable 'Bobo doll' before being left to play with it themselves. The first group saw the adult playing with the doll aggressively in the same room as them, including kicking it and hitting it with a mallet. The second group saw similar behaviour but on video, and the third saw similar behaviour but in a cartoon. The fourth, the control group, was simply allowed to play with the toy immediately. The study found that the children in all three groups that watched aggressive behaviour behaved more aggressively when they played with the doll afterwards than those who did not witness this behaviour. The 'live aggression' scenario (group one) brought the most aggressive reaction from the children, followed by the video and then the cartoon. Exposure to aggressive models of behaviour can therefore lead people to learn more aggressive behaviours themselves – regardless of the format. This suggests we need to be careful not just about the parental behaviour models children are exposed to, but also those from other external sources, such as the levels of aggression and violence on television and other media channels.

Aggressive behaviour can be learned early in life, and can then become a regular pattern[469]. Evidence suggests that an individual's level of aggression in relation to the rest of the population stays reasonably constant from childhood onwards – a more aggressive 8-year-old is likely to be a more aggressive 30-year-old[470]. This suggests that early intervention in reducing learned aggression may be effective. This is particularly important, as research also shows that aggression can end up being passed down through generations[471].

Stimulation – one theory (the *excitation-transfer* theory) suggests that if we have some history of learned aggression, a strong sense of arousal or stimulation from a previous source can increase the likelihood of an aggressive reaction in a new situation, as the 'excitation' is transferred to the new situation. For example, if you have been exercising at the gym and are driving home, you may respond more aggressively if another car cuts in front of you in the traffic. This heightened state of arousal could come from a number of sources that are unrelated to the event that is driving the aggressive response – including exercise, erotica or communications[472].

Disinhibition and deindividuation – we can feel a sense of disinhibition when we experience a reduction in the influence of social forces around us that restrain us from behaving in ways that conflict with established pro-social norms – such as antisocial, immoral or illegal behaviour – and aggression. Several factors can influence this sense of disinhibition, including the behaviour of groups we are members of (see next point on deindividuation) and the effects of alcohol. A number of studies have shown a link between alcohol and aggression[473] [474], as well as leading to a greater susceptibility to influence (including attempts to influence them into aggressive behaviour)[475].

Deindividuation is another form of disinhibition – in this case, when membership of certain groups makes people become less self-aware, and behave less like individuals, leading them to drop their usual individual judgements and self-imposed constraints on their behaviour. One example of deindividuation is the idea that people usually restrain their aggressive impulses because they are identifiable individuals in a society that has strong social norms against such aggressive behaviours. If someone is part of a group or a crowd however, they may feel released from these constraints due to just being one person among many – either through their anonymity (especially when wearing masks, uniforms or other anonymising items) or other factors such as the expectation of less personal punishment. This lack of individual identification may make people behave in a less self-contained way[476] – including both aggression and anti-social behaviour. For example, psychologist Philip Zimbardo conducted a study that tested participants' willingness to give electric shocks to someone (who was in fact a confederate of the experimenters). He found that participants who were deindividuated (with hoods and large lab coats) gave electric shocks of double the length than those who wore their normal clothes and were individually identifiable[477].

Dehumanisation – at the more extreme level of prejudiced thinking is the idea that particular individuals or groups of people are somehow 'less human' than others – an idea that can legitimise violence and ill-treatment towards them through the view that they do not deserve to be treated with the same respect, rights and consideration as other human beings[478]. For example, in Rwanda, before and during the genocide against them in 1994, Tutsi people were portrayed as 'cockroaches', 'snakes' and 'vermin' by their killers, the Hutus[479]. This illustrates the important role that prejudicial, hateful language can play in creating the conditions for later violence. Experiments by Abert Bandura and colleagues showed how dehumanization of participants through negative labelling led them to be punished considerably more than those who had not been labelled[480].

Dehumanisation is linked to our tendency to perceive those in our in-group more positively than our out-groups – a trait explored in Part 1 and the previous chapter. We tend to attribute more sophisticated and human emotions to our in-group members than those in out-groups, therefore potentially seeing the latter as less human and more like animals than our in-group – a process known as *infra-humanization*[481].

We can also call upon dehumanisation to help us justify ourselves and our actions. We want to maintain a positive sense of ourselves and our own identity. If we have done something cruel or unfair to another person or group of people, then we can justify our behaviour to ourselves by derogating that group[482]. If we are able to convince ourselves that a particular group is lazy, stupid, cruel or even subhuman, then we can not only justify our behaviour but also argue that it is virtuous. This sort of self justification can lead to an intensification of further hate and violence, as will be seen in the next chapter.

Dehumanisation can occur in a number of ways beyond seeing the victims as less than human. It can occur through removing the individual identity of victims, for example by shaving their heads or forcing them to wear the same clothing, both of which were implemented by the Nazis to dehumanise the Jews and other prisoners in their concentration camps. Depersonalisation can also occur through weapons that allow killing and violence to take place at a distance without the attacker seeing the impact on the victim.

Hearing and seeing the suffering they cause can make people restrain their actions more than they would do if they didn't witness these reactions[483]. Weapons of remote mass destruction such as bombs and drones can cause us to see victims not as individual human beings with valuable lives, but as faceless numbers.

Social identity – this is a factor that can influence our behaviour as members of a group. We usually find ourselves together in groups for a particular purpose. This might be for work, to support a football team or to undertake an activity. We share a sense of social identity with this group, and it provides a clear sense of the norms and expectations for acceptable behaviour. We look to others in our group for guidance on how to behave and we then conform to these norms. Just because we are football fans this doesn't mean we will be violent or antisocial. But if you are part of a specific faction of fans who have a norm of violent behaviour within their group, you are more likely to conform to this norm. Norms can apply more broadly to a cultural context too, such as regions of the world in which cultures of honour exist, where violence is seen as a means of restoring honour. For example, psychologist Professor Dov Cohen and his colleagues found that white males from the south of the USA were much more likely than those from the north to respond aggressively when they were publicly insulted by someone, suggesting a culture of honour in southern USA that leads people to attempt to restore their status through aggression or violence[484].

Social norms can act as restraining regents to stop us displaying extreme aggressive behaviours. People might show these instead through more subtle means such as words that are intended to harm or intimidate others[485]. For example, minor altercations between road users will result in the exchange of aggressive gestures or words rather than actual violence. Social norms can however be powerful forces in the other direction – towards aggression and violence – if the social norms around us are biased in favour of aggression and violence rather than against it. The role of social norms in driving violence will be demonstrated in the detailed example of Battalion 101 in the next chapter.

Our tribal tendencies – deindividuation, dehumanisation and social identity are just a few features of our tribal tendencies as LASID creatures that play a role in our capacity for aggression and violence, as well as in our capacity for cooperation to prevent it. These can be described as the factors that can bind us to our in-groups (such as conformity and obedience to authority) as well as those that can distance us from others (including in-group bias, prejudice and scapegoating). A number of these areas have already been discussed in this book, and their role in aggression and violence will be considered shortly in relation to extreme cases of killing and violence, alongside other factors.

Our external context

As LASID creatures, external factors can play an important role in influencing our capacity for aggression and violence. We will now explore some of the most important factors. Many of the points from the corresponding 'context' section in Chapter 11 on the subject of prejudice apply here, so it is worth taking another look at these before reading the points below.

Inequality and social disadvantage – this can be both a cause of aggression and of victimhood, with data from the Office of National Statistics (ONS) in the UK showing that people living in the most deprived areas of England were more than twice as likely to be victims of violent crime than those living in the least deprived areas[486]. Research from the United States suggests that levels of homicide and non-lethal violence are higher among young males living in poor urban areas, and this could be for a combination of reasons, including poverty, poor facilities, antisocial norms and dysfunctional families[487]. A sense of relative deprivation can be another driver of aggression – a sense that one or one's group is deprived compared to others and that there is little change of improving this situation. Under such circumstances an individual might be more likely to commit crimes or aggressive acts such as assault or rioting[488].

At a broader level, the frustration of people's basic needs, including material goods, opportunities and respect, can be a catalyst for aggression towards other groups. It can produce stronger in-group identification and sense of out-group threat, as well as a desire for a strong leader and aggressive ideology, especially among people with more authoritarian mindsets[489]. As one can imagine, this in turn creates the potential for greater aggression and violence on a broader scale.

Inequality is also associated with higher levels of violence. The UN Global Study on Homicide notes that societies with greater levels of income inequality tend to also have high levels of violence. For example, the subregion of Latin America and the Caribbean has the highest homicide rates in the world, and also has very high inequality – the income gap between the rich and the poor is twice that of advanced economies[490]. Poorer people are likely to have fewer resources than others to help them advance their interests and resolve their disputes, including money, access to legal representation and social networks with influence.

Our physical environment – certain aspects of our physical environment have been put forward as influences on our levels of aggression, including crowding and heat. The influence of crowding on our aggression levels is complex, as it can mean more than one thing, such as encroachment on our personal space, or a high level of population density, both of which may have some role to play in increasing our levels of aggression. For example, a study of a psychiatric ward in New Zealand found that a greater level of crowding on the ward was associated with a greater number of violent incidents – and particularly of verbal aggression[491]. We live in an unequal world in which greater wealth grants you greater physical space – households with lower income are more likely to be overcrowded than those with higher income[492]. This may be another contributor to the role of social disadvantage in aggression.

We already link heat to aggression in our everyday language – for example, describing anger as 'getting hot under the collar'. Evidence suggests that greater levels of heat increase our tendency for aggression, up to a certain point – suggesting that when heat is at extreme levels it saps our energy. For example, this trend was found in a study in 1980 that examined the levels of aggravated assault in Dallas, Texas over 8 months between March and October that year[493]. Various forms of aggression have been shown to rise as the ambient temperature rises, including collective violence[494], domestic violence[495] and violent suicide[496].

Society and institutions – the institutions and groups that surround us, from family life to workplaces and sports clubs, contain attitudes about aggression and violence, as well as structures and processes, that together have the potential to increase or reduce our levels of aggression and violence as individuals. Institutions may promote aggression and violence via their structures and assumptions or by failing to regulate it when it occurs within them. For example, we have already seen how exposure to aggression in our youth can increase our own propensity for aggression. Our family, friendships and social environments therefore all have an influence on this aspect of our behaviour.

The states we live in set the rules and expectations on how we should behave as citizens and how people are punished for infractions of these rules. There is sometimes the need for institutionalised aggression such as policing and punishment in order to protect people from greater harms, but the power of these institutions over people's lives mean that excessive brutality and violence from them can cause particularly high levels of suffering, and even cause further violence. For example, a 2019 report estimated that between 1980 and 2018 there had been 30,800 deaths across the USA as a result of police violence[497]. These killings disproportionately affected Black and Hispanic people, suggesting systematic racism in the police force. Such killings can result in further violence in the community – for example, the killing of George Floyd by police in the USA in May 2020 led to demonstrations in Minneapolis that resulted in lootings, buildings being set on fire and a further violent response from police with tear gas and rubber bullets[498].

As another example, education systems are thought to be forces for good – institutions that instil knowledge and positive values in our young people that will enable them to become kind, independent and effective adults. Yet they also have the potential to inflict violence as institutions and to impart ideas and models of behaviour that can lead to violence in students. Dr Conrad Hughes is Director General of the International School of Geneva, the oldest international school in the world, and suggests that violence brought about by schools can be symbolic, structural and physical[499]. Symbolic violence occurs through factors such as the hierarchical grading of pupils and judgements about them that can affect their self-image and life paths. It not only divides people into those who are formally educated and who aren't, but also ranks human beings through grades, a process that instils what Hughes calls an 'aggressive competitiveness' between them, and one that makes an arbitrary judgement about human value that can bring pressure to the brightest pupils and fear, humiliation and doubt to everyone else. It also priorities a certain set of academic disciples (such as mathematics and sciences) above others. Structural violence takes place through power relationships in the school – including expectations of pupil docility and subservience to teachers, and of being forced to conform to structures of power and particular roles – the latter of which, as we have seen in experiments by Milgram and Zimbardo, can promote the disinhibition of other social norms that help to hold back aggressive behaviours. Forms of physical violence are well known in schools, including bullying, which affects around 35 percent of children between 12-18 years old in US schools[500], and can cause both emotional and psychological damage to students. The negative effects of bullying on its victims can be significant and long term, including greater risk of depression, suicide, poor health, lower educational performance and lower earning later in life[501]. All of these aggressive and violent factors are woven into the institution before we even consider the values and ideas that the schools are teaching – which themselves are likely to instil and strengthen the social and cultural norms that surround us. Some of these values help to prevent violence (such as understanding other cultures and the importance of cooperation) and some can promote it, for example the promotion of particular definitions of competitive, self-driven success such as career achievement and material goods at the expense of others.

Military institutions sit at the sharp end of a country's approach towards the use of aggression and violence, and the manner in which soldiers are told to treat other people, including civilians and enemy combatants, is critical to the amount of suffering that might be brought about in a conflict situation. There is an enormous difference between the levels of suffering and death brought about by an army that works hard to avoid civilian casualties and treats enemy soldiers with compassion (such as not harming prisoners or those who have surrendered), and one that kills civilians and tortures and executes captured enemy soldiers, as the United Nations Human Rights Monitoring Mission in Ukraine (HRMMU) has found evidence of Russia doing during its 2022 invasion of Ukraine[502].

At a broader level, since the horrors of the First and Second World Wars, the development of international institutions such as the UN have helped to provide oversight and a means of dialogue on international relations, and protocols such as the Geneva conventions have established a set of rules and expectations as to how soldiers and civilians should be treated in conflicts. These have not however prevented the occurrence of many conflicts and flagrant breaches of these rules, as the many conflicts in the second half of the twentieth century and beyond have attested.

Culture and situation – a number of broader factors can encourage or legitimise violent behaviour more generally – for example, at the level of a society's culture. Levels of violence vary across cultures – and can change within cultures over time. For example, homicide rates are significantly higher in Brazil (21.3 international homicides per 100,000 members of population) than in its south American neighbour Chile (4.6 per 100,000)[503]. Differences like this may be due to differing cultural values – for example 'cultures of honour' referred to earlier, in which men are expected to show physical aggression to protect their reputations.

Extreme cultural or political situations can also generate new values and norms, which we might not be aware of at the time. For example, it could be argued that war creates a new set of social norms, in which killing other people is allowed and even encouraged in certain circumstances (for example, in the field of combat). In this situation, levels of violence can escalate and remain acceptable or justifiable, even up to the use of particularly extreme forms of aggression that take many lives, such as the firebombing of Dresden by the Allies in 1945 that killed at least 25,000 people[504]. Similarly, the aftermath of a major disaster is a time at which not only our emotions and prejudices can be aroused (in seeking out-groups to blame and punish) but also our capacity for aggression and violence in response to, and retaliation for, the threat – even if one group can't obviously be blamed for the disaster, such as in a terrorist attack. We should therefore be very sensitive to the tendency for conditions of conflict (and even initial conditions where there is a low-level threat of conflict) to change our levels of tolerance of aggression and violence.

Mass media – a range of evidence suggests that violent imagery in television, film and computer games has a significant short-term effect on the thoughts, emotions and levels of arousal of younger children, and boys in particular. This increases the likelihood of aggressive behaviour, as illustrated by the example earlier in this chapter of how watching a video of an adult playing aggressively with a toy brought out more aggressive learned behaviour in a child. The effects are less clear on older children and in the longer term[505].

A national survey on US television violence[506] found that 61 percent of programmes contained violence, but only 4 per cent had an anti-violence message. In the majority (71 percent) of scenes where violence took place in realistic settings, there was no criticism of the violence or remorse for it. So, we aren't just exposing ourselves and young people to violence in the media – we are also establishing values that don't condemn it, and are sometimes glamourising it or lacing it with humour.

The internet and social media have also become spaces in which acts of violence can be perpetrated and planned, including bullying, harassment, gang violence and political violence[507]. For young people, in-person acts of physical and verbal aggression are still more common than those carried out online, but online aggression is an area of growing concern, with 20 percent of young people in a 2013 survey[508] reporting that they had experienced cyber bullying. Instant messaging is the most common form of cyber bullying, and along with other online platforms offers ways for perpetrators to hide their identities by posting anonymously, adopting someone else's identity or using a false name[509]. This anonymity can potentially provide a form of disinhibition from refraining from aggression and violence, as has been shown earlier in this chapter.

Online platforms can also provide spaces for people with violent and extremist views to gather together. This can act as a source of recruitment for new members, as well as a breeding ground of increasingly violent views and space for building plans for action. For example, in the school shootings that took place in Finland in November 2007 and September 2008, both perpetrators had used the internet to share their views about violence and their intentions[510], and had taken part in pro-school-shooting groups that supported their ideas[511]. Social media is also used by gangs to support violence and crime – for example, posting videos of threats and violence, harassment and following up online conversations with real-life attacks[512].

Chapter 11 showed how prejudicial and hateful attitudes can be stoked by the mass media and in online spaces, which can also contribute to increases in violence and aggression.

The state and political leaders – the nature of the state and political leaders that rule us can also have a significant influence on our willingness to engage in violence. The findings from the 'Political parties and leaders' section on page 250 of Chapter 11 also apply to this point and are worth revisiting.

At a simple level in a democratic society, leaders can 'set the temperature' of the level of aggression in a nation. The language used in their speeches, their approach to political diplomacy and the attitudes they express towards groups within and outside their country have an influence on how its citizens feel towards each other and the outside world. A leader who sows division, uses aggressive language and stokes resentment can play a powerful role in fomenting violence. For example, former US President Donald Trump's long-term programme of stoking grievance and resentment amongst his followers reached a peak on January 6th 2021 when he asked those present at a rally in Washington DC to join him on a march to the Capitol building to protest against the election that he (falsely) argued had been stolen from him. In the speech, he attempted to pile public pressure on to his Vice President, Mike Pence, to reject the result of the election, and used language that denigrated weakness and invoked fighting, including 'You'll never take back our country with weakness', 'You have to get your people to fight', We're going to have to fight much harder', and 'We fight like hell. And if you don't fight like hell, you're not going to have a country anymore'[513]. Following his speech, 2,000 of his supporters stormed the Capitol building, in a violent riot that resulted in five deaths.

The policies that a ruling party enacts also help to shape the level of aggression of the political climate. For example, the attitude and policies towards people outside the 'in-group' of the nation can often tell us a great deal about the potential aggressiveness of that country at a given time. A conciliatory, integrated approach to refugees and living with its neighbours suggests a non-aggressive atmosphere, whereas a more hostile and protective approach (for example, strongly limiting immigration and building walls on its borders) suggests a more aggressive state.

At a more extreme level, if you live in a country with an aggressive, paranoid leader and a state that suppresses dissent, it may be difficult for ordinary citizens to hear any countervailing voices that moderate the leader's hate and criticism of other groups. Objecting to their policies and ideas could also put your life in danger. Such societies – both citizens and the groups surrounding the leader – can become vulnerable to 'groupthink' – when individuals override their usual desire to properly appraise different courses of action and end up following the solutions suggested by the leader[514]. This helps to set up conditions for extreme violence, as it did in Cambodia in the 1970s under the leader of the Khmer Rouge, Pol Pot, who organised the mass killing of 2.5 million members of his own country, on the basis of their educated status, which had allegedly led to their preferential treatment in a system he claimed to be unjust[515].

Situational factors – context not only affects our propensity for aggression and violence in a long-term sense (through factors such as learned behaviours, the groups we are part of, the roles we play, the influence of culture, the policies and rhetoric of political leaders), but also in the immediate situations we are placed in. This important factor will be examined in more detail in the next chapter.

Chapter 14
What are we capable of?
The case of Battalion 101

Up to this point, this section of the book has examined some of the factors that contribute to human aggression and violence. But it seems that not all killings are equal from a human perspective. For example, we see killings that have been sanctioned by the state (for example, a soldier killing another soldier) in a different way from those that randomly occur between individuals. The former appear more justified and less morally shocking than the latter, and even carry the weight of national and international law behind them. We also seem to have greater distaste for killings that are carried out face-to-face than those that take place remotely – for example, through the use of military drones.

Some of the most extreme and terrible acts of violence would therefore seem to be the face-to-face killing of innocent people on a large scale. How can human beings possibly do this?

To answer this question, this chapter will look to the Holocaust – but not to the organisers and managerialists, such as Adolf Eichmann, who oversaw the processes and machinery that enabled the near destruction of an entire race to take place, as these figures were at a position of removal from the killing. It will instead examine the behaviour and thinking of a group of people who picked up guns and shot innocent men, women and children at point blank range.

Police Reserve Battalion 101 was a group of German military police from Hamburg drafted in to assist the Nazi occupation of Poland in 1942[516]. This collection of 'ordinary men' became some of the most effective killers of the war, and was ultimately involved in the shooting of 38,000 Jews and sending a further 45,000 to extermination camps. Records left by German soldiers and testimony from some of the members of Battalion 101 following the war have provided us with insights on their actions, feelings and motivations, which have enabled scholars to piece together a fascinating and important picture of what happened and why.

Although it is a horrifying story, it is critically important to analyse. By focusing on these acts of extreme violence, we can start to build a more realistic picture of how and why they took place, as well as the tendencies in human thinking and behaviour that drove them and the steps we can take to reduce their likelihood in the future. We will also face the sobering truth that the capacity for extreme violence is within every human being, given particular conditions.

By 1942 in World War Two, the pool of potential conscripts to the German army was draining as it attempted to fight a war on two fronts in the east and west. They began to call up men who were too old for the army to reserve police duty, many of whom were not Nazi sympathisers or particularly prejudiced towards Jews. Reserve Police Battalion 101 consisted largely of men without any military experience. Most rank and file members of the group held lower-middle or working-class roles in Hamburg, such as dock workers, salesmen and waiters.

On June 20th 1942, having arrived in the Lublin district of Poland, the battalion received orders to carry out an unspecified 'special action'. It was unclear even to the officers what this meant, and the men were led to believe they would be performing guard duties. On 11th June their commander, Major Wilhelm Trapp, was told they would have the task on the next day of rounding up the 1,800 Jews of Józefów, a town around 15 kilometres southeast of Warsaw. Men of working age were to be sent to a labour camp, and everyone else – 1,500 women, children and elderly people – were to be shot. Major Trapp assembled the men early in the morning the next day and explained their assignment, telling them he had a 'terrible order' to give them. Unusually, he then made them an offer – anyone who didn't want to take part could step out, without any punishment. Only twelve people from a total battalion of over 400 men took up this offer to avoid the task at this point.

Some members of the battalion rounded up the Jews in the village and shot anyone trying to escape or who was too weak to walk to the assembly point at the marketplace. The 'work Jews' were marched to their camp whilst the rest were loaded onto trucks that shuttled to and from the forest, where other members of Battalion 101 – acting as the firing squads – waited for them. When a truckload of around 40 Jews arrived at the forest, each was paired off with a policeman and marched them down the forest path. Sometimes conversations took place between the Jews and their soon-to-be killers. When they had reached a certain point in the woods, the Jews were told to lie face down in a row. The policemen then stood behind them, taking aim by placing the end of their bayonets in the backbone above the shoulder blade of their victims, and shot them simultaneously. By the end of the day members of the three platoons in Battalion 101 had killed 1,500 people.

The effect of the killings on the policemen was massive. Some asked to be excused when they arrived at the forest, another group could not continue after their first shootings and others simply tried to avoid the task of shooting by doing other roles. Many arrived back at their barracks at the end of the day feeling shaken, demoralised and angry, and drank heavily from the large quantities of alcohol they were given that evening. Major Trapp circulated round the group, trying to console them and asking them not to talk about it – and no one wanted to anyway. It was simply not mentioned by the men. Some had nightmares that evening. But, despite these emotional reactions, at least 80 percent of those men asked to kill had done so repeatedly until 1,500 innocent people lay dead.

Battalion 101 took part in other mass killings after their first action in Józefów, including on 16th August the shooting of the 1,700 Jews of Lomazy, a town around 180 km southeast of Warsaw. The reaction of the men to these later shootings was very different, however. They didn't feel the same trauma when carrying out the killings, or recall them with anything approaching the same horror as the events of Józefów. This was partly due to the fact that some of the later episodes of killing were less personalised than the first one – the men didn't have to deal with their victims face to face. It was also however due to the fact that the men became habituated to killing – they simply got used to it. Historian Christopher Browning notes from their testimony that the men had strong memories of their first event of killing, but the later events became a blur – some men found it hard to remember which towns they had been in for each set of killings.

Ultimately the members of Reserve Police Battalion 101 were involved in the shooting of 38,000 Jews and in sending a further 45,000 to extermination camps.

Explaining the actions of Battalion 101

How could a group of 'ordinary men' commit the atrocities of Battalion 101?

Dr James Waller, an expert in Holocaust and genocide studies, has examined the testimony and actions of Battalion 101 as part of a wider research project to explain the behaviour of perpetrators in several genocides and mass killings in the twentieth century, including the Holocaust[517]. His findings dismiss some of the previous explanations for extreme acts of human violence, such as the idea that they stem solely from an extreme ideology within a society, such as antisemitism within Germany at the time of the Nazis. Waller argues that although antisemitism was rife in the country, it did not demand the elimination of Jews and does not alone account for the willingness of people to kill Jews personally. We can also see that the members of Battalion 101 were not particularly anti-Semitic or Nazi sympathisers[518]. This single-reason explanation also has the unfortunate side effect of making us believe that the potential for mass killing only lies within societies like Nazi Germany, which sit outside our normal world and as long as you don't have extreme societies like this, you can eliminate mass killing. The truth is sadly not that convenient for human beings.

Another discounted explanation is that the people who participated in these murderous actions were psychopaths. Whilst there may have been some individuals within the Nazi killing squads who were psychopathic (just as there are likely to be in any significantly sized group), the evidence from personality tests conducted on nearly 200 Nazis at the war crimes trials in Copenhagen in 1946 found that they did not display any particularly disturbed thinking or inclinations towards violence. So, the 'mad Nazi' explanation is also incorrect. A final debunked explanation for mass killing is that the perpetrators shared a common personality trait that predisposed them to this extraordinary behaviour, along the lines of the authoritarian personality proposed by Theodore Adorno discussed in Chapter 11. A single personality trait of this nature has not been found, however[519].

Moving beyond these more simplistic explanations, Dr Waller built a four-point model to explain the behaviour of perpetrators in genocides and mass killings, which we will use below to explore the actions of Battalion 101. Dr Waller describes it as a process through which the perpetrators themselves become changed.

1. **Evolutionary traits in thinking and behaviour** – this is the overarching explanation we can use to see how human behaviour can become shaped by the other three factors in this model. It essentially consists of the various LASID traits of thinking and behaviour outlined in Part 1 of this book, and the fact that these traits have evolved over a long time to give us an evolutionary advantage in a particular environment (the hunter-gatherer societies of our ancestors).

2. **The influence of cultural models** – the ways in which the identities of the perpetrators are shaped by the cultural ideas and belief systems around them, including world views, in-group and out-group biases and attitudes to authority.

3. **The 'othering' of victims** – the ways in which the group of victims becomes seen as 'the other' through 'us and them' thinking, and then dehumanised and blamed for its treatment at the hands of the perpetrators.
4. **The social forces influencing cruelty** – the power of the social context or situation to enable people to begin, sustain and rationalise their cruelty.

The first of these points has already been discussed in Part 1, so each of the other points will be examined below.

The influence of cultural models – the cultures and societies we live in carry a range of assumptions about the world and how to live within it, and we absorb these assumptions, sometimes unconsciously. The type of assumptions carried by the culture we live within can influence our propensity for violence.

Waller highlights some particularly influential areas:
- **The level of collectivist values** – cultures can exist on a spectrum between being highly individualist (valuing things like individual freedom and self-expression, like many Western democracies) and highly collectivist (valuing things like obedience, safety, order and conformity). We need a certain level of collectivist values to bind us together, but genocidal regimes have generally espoused collectivist values that make an individual's membership of the group central to their personal identity and indeed more important than the self. For example, in Nazi society, 'Aryanness', membership of a specific blood-based group, was central to someone's personal identity. This can provide a very sharp

definition of who is in the 'in-group' (our bias towards which we explored in Part 1), and can lead to greater in-group bias and feeling more distrustful and hostile to out-groups, seeing them a threat to the sanctity of the in-group. Somewhat perversely then, the very values that can strongly bind an in-group together can also combine to separate it from, and make it more hostile towards, other groups. Genocidal regimes have also used collectivistic values to build a sense of duty to the in-group – for example, a willingness to make sacrifices for the Fatherland was important in Nazi Germany.

- **Authority orientation** – this often sits alongside a strongly collectivist outlook, and describes a cultural model that orders the social world and the people within it according to where they fit in hierarchies. Societies with a strongly hierarchical model like this tend to cultivate citizens who respect and obey authority and enjoy exercising power over those below them. As shown in Part 1, human beings have a propensity to obey authority – something that can be leveraged further in societies with a strong authority orientation. Again, there is some value to hierarchy as it helps to order society and ensure people obey rules, but in societies with a strong authority orientation (such as Germany from at least the late 19th century to World War Two[520]) this can lead to unthinking adherence to authority, as famously illustrated in the war crimes testimony of Adolf Eichmann, one of the most influential figures in the implementation of the Holocaust, who argued that he was merely following orders. Most cases of mass killing and genocide have taken place in cultures with a strong authority orientation.

- **Social dominance and ideologies** – human beings compete with each other for scarce resources, so, like some other animals, we have a propensity for establishing social hierarchies to avoid ongoing conflict over these resources. Studies show that these hierarchies can be established within a minute of a group of strangers meeting for the first time[521]. Different cultures can carry different attitudes towards social dominance, which may be driven by ideologies, traditions and myths. As previously argued, extreme ideologies on their own are not enough to explain acts of mass killing and genocide, but they can play an important role in encouraging political violence. Jonathan Leader Maynard, Associate Professor in International Politics at King's College London, argues that there are a range of ways in which ideologies can influence people's willingness to kill. These include the perception that the victim represents a threat in the minds of the perpetrators, which establishes a motivation for killing, frames the victim as a legitimate target and provides perpetrators with a sense they are acting in self-defence[522].

The 'othering' of victims – in mass killings and genocide, the victims are seen as outside the moral community of the perpetrators, and not subject to usual moral rules. There are three aspects to this 'othering' process, some of which have already been discussed, but they are important to bring together here:

- **Us-them thinking** – Part 1 showed how humans have a tendency to favour their own in-groups (a trait known as *ethnocentrism*), even those that are assigned on the most minimal and irrelevant premises, such as supposed preference for the artists Klee or Kandinsky. We see our group as superior to others and can find it difficult to see people in other groups as worthy of the same level of respect and treatment[523]. Indeed, we have also evolved with a tendency towards *xenophobia* – a fear of outsiders and seeing strangers as a threat. These pro-in-group anti-out-group traits can be exaggerated and used by governments and propaganda to stir anger and reduce objections to violence against particular outgroups. In their analysis of extreme mass homicide, Psychologist Professor Donald Dutton and colleagues argue that the threat posed by an out-group often provides the first rationalisation for violence[524].

- **Moral justification and distancing** – perpetrators of extreme violence need to find ways to justify and distance themselves from the moral consequences of their actions. One way they can do this is through moral justification, arguing (usually incorrectly) that killing is the morally right thing to do – for example, their actions are helping to avert a terrible threat. This is essentially using their System 2 thinking to rationalise their behaviour. They might also use moral disengagement. As an example, some men from Battalion 101 justified their killing actions by saying they had no choice and that the Jews were going to die anyway[525]. Others took rationalisation to greater extremes, with one member justifying his shooting of children with the argument that their mothers had been shot next to them and by shooting the children, he was saving them from being unable to live without their mothers[526]. Another way to justify their violence is for perpetrators to dehumanise their victims using the methods we discussed earlier, from describing them in language that makes them subhuman (the Nazis described Jews as 'parasites', 'cancer' and 'excrement', among many other things), through to removing their identities (for example, through shaving their heads and giving them identical, grubby uniforms at concentration camps). The process of persecuting a group, as enforced by Nazi Germany in the years leading up to the Second World War, can reinforce their characterisation as subhuman, by leading to a degradation in the living standards and appearance of its members, making them look filthy, starved and desperate. A final way in which perpetrators can distance themselves from the moral consequences of their actions is using euphemistic language to describe them, to reduce their repugnancy – for example, the Nazis used phrases such as 'the final solution', 'evacuations', and 'special treatment' to describe aspects of their mass murder of Jews.

- **Blaming the victims** – we are creatures that aim to seek meaning in the events and world around us, including trying to understand why some people suffer. Studies suggest human beings have a tendency to believe the world is just, and that people deserve what they get[527]. If we can believe that victims have done things to deserve their suffering, we can retain our sense of a world that is just. Waller found that perpetrators of mass killings therefore often seek to blame their victims for their suffering. Nazis blamed Jews for their own destruction, including at a global scale by threatening the world (and Germany) through their domination of international capital and more locally by cheating people out of money. Some even blamed their victims for not showing more resistance during their persecution. Scapegoating, however factually inaccurate it may be, is therefore a common way for perpetrators to justify their actions and retain a sense of a just world.

The social forces influencing cruelty – this factor sits at the sharp edge of our capacity as creatures to be influenced by our context. Years of studies have shown that the situations around us are immensely powerful in influencing the thoughts, feelings and behaviours of human beings[527]. There are a number of ways in which an immediate social situation can make ordinary people cross the threshold of killing and then sustain this, and three key factors will be examined below:
- **Professional socialisation** – many genocides are carried out by military or paramilitary groups. Certain aspects of these groups can increase the chances of people carrying out violence within them. First, the path to violence and killing

often takes place through a sequence of small incremental steps, each one seeming relatively innocuous but which can ultimately lead an individual to become a perpetrator. When people agree voluntarily to an initial act this can make later, more extreme, actions easier to undertake, as it creates a new social context with strong pressures to continue. For example, once the men in Battalion 101 had killed for the first time, this appeared to be a pivotal moment on the path to mass killing, as they then became brutalised and habituated to the process. After that point, historian Robert Browning notes, they became increasingly efficient killers[528]. Second, ritual conduct can enable perpetrators to begin and sustain their cruel behaviour, as rituals such as the roll calls, parades and stripping of victims by the Nazis not only served to discipline and order their victims, but also humiliate them, helping to reinforce the self-image of the perpetrators and condition them to the bigger acts of cruelty they would be committing[529]. A third, and critical, aspect of professional socialisation is that people's roles and behaviours can become merged. Studies such as Philip Zimbardo's Stanford Prison Experiment[530], mentioned in Part 1, show that we can be shaped by the organisations we participate in and the roles we undertake, acquiring the attitudes and behaviours associated with them. In Zimbardo's experiment, a number of the participants quickly started to behave according to the roles they were playing. Prisoners became lethargic, submissive and depressed. Around a third of the guards became authoritarian, cruel and brutal in their roles – finding ways to humiliate and degrade the 'prisoners'. Zimbardo suggested that one of the most dramatic aspects of the study was how easily cruel and sadistic behaviour could be brought about in ordinary people who had shown no signs of this before. People had become their roles – and this process can have a significant impact on people's capacity to commit terrible acts, when they are part of a group or organisation seeking to harm others.

- **Identification with the in-group** – our emotional attachment to a group can have a strong influence on our thoughts and behaviours. Our group identity can be a critical part of our personal identity and, at extreme levels of identification with a group, can lead us to feel threatened by, and hostile towards, other groups, bringing the threat of violence. A couple of specific mechanisms can increase the power of group identification. First is the repression of individual conscience, where the group's values are adhered to rather than outside ones. Information about the crimes is not spoken about, and anyone that knows about the crime is called upon to take part. Perpetrators can also become desensitised to killing by the diffusion of responsibility – spreading the responsibility rather than focusing it on one person. For example, in giving Battalion 101 their orders before their first killing assignment, Major Trapp noted that if he had the choice, he would not give them the order – showing that the order did not come from him and that they shared responsibility for the action. Diffusion of responsibility can also occur by distributing the killing tasks to many people, or by splitting the process of carrying out the tasks – for example, so that the person opening the door to the gas chamber can claim they didn't personally kill the victims. In state sanctioned killing people can therefore claim to be just another cog in the machine and absolve themselves of moral and individual responsibility. Perpetrators can also become desensitised to violence by deindividuation, as discussed earlier in this chapter, where they cannot be identified as a distinct individual but as a group member. A second mechanism that can increase the power of group identification is self-interest – including protecting one's ego and maintaining a favourable opinion of oneself, particularly when this is threatened. Just as narcissism is associated with individual aggression, a sense of superiority from the perpetrator group is common in genocides. For example, Waller argues that Germans carried a very positive, romanticised sense of themselves as a race and culture, and the Nazis built upon this by claiming it was under threat[531].

- **Adherence to our in-group** – the final aspect of a situation that can influence people to commit acts of extreme violence is the group dynamics that bind people together and influence their behaviour. Perhaps most important among these is conformity to peer group pressure. The power of conformity was discussed in Part 1, and it played a critical role in the unwillingness of members of Battalion 101 to take up Major Trapp's offer that people who didn't want to take part in the killing action could do so without punishment. This offer was genuine – no officer who refused to shoot was punished; they were simply given different duties. The price of refusing the offer was great however. As has been previously shown, in a situation where people are uncertain of the action to take, some will conform with others as a guide to how to behave. Major Trapp had also set the group norm as performing the action, so anyone who wished to avoid it had to opt out (take action) which is harder to do than staying where you are (and not taking action). The pressure to conform socially was even greater. The men were part of a police unit in wartime, in which fidelity to their group and conformity would have been seen as critical in achieving war aims and in protecting other members of the group. Being held in high esteem by one's colleagues therefore mattered even more than normal, particularly as the group also had to live with each other for weeks to come. Although most of the group members were horrified by the idea of killing innocent people, refusing to conform to this behaviour meant risking rejection, isolation and ostracism from a group in which their belonging and standing mattered greatly to them[532]. So, most went along with the killing. Ultimately, and shockingly, the power of conformity appeared to be so strong in the situation Battalion 101 faced that some of the men preferred to kill innocent people rather than lose face in front of their colleagues.

Looking through these points of Waller's model that describe the behaviour of perpetrators in genocides and mass killings, one can see how each could have acted upon the men of Reserve Police Battalion 101, and other perpetrators of mass killings, to provide conditions for their appalling acts to take place. In the case of

Battalion 101, it is possible that the situation alone (including the strength of peer group pressure) could have been enough to induce some of the police to kill innocent people at point blank range. It can however be argued that the other factors in the list above, including the othering of victims over time in Nazi society and the state's determination to enforce orders to kill the Jews, helped to establish the extraordinary conditions that the men of Battalion 101 found themselves in.

A central point that emerges from this research is that the men of Battalion 101 were not monsters. Very few human beings are. We may want to 'other' them and say they are not like us, as this protects us from the possibility that we might be like them. But the truth is, as LASID creatures, we all theoretically have the potential to behave this way. The research shows the power of social influence, context, roles and other factors in driving the behaviour of what Robert Browning calls 'ordinary men' to become mass killers. In conclusion, this suggests that you or I might behave in the same way if faced with similar influences and circumstances. We all have the potential to commit almost unimaginable acts of violence, given particular contexts and conditions.

It is important to note though, as Waller does[533], that offering a psychological explanation for these brutal acts of killing does not condone or forgive them or the people who committed them. The perpetrators were not led blindly by instinct or fate to commit these acts. At each point in the process there were several opportunities to make different choices which could have greatly affected their actions and their outcomes. We have agency over our actions, and the perpetrators must take full responsibility for theirs.

Conclusions

The human capacity for aggression and violence is an incredibly complex topic, covering a wide range of behaviours and situations, from verbal hostility through to mass killing. This chapter, and the preceding one, have set out some of the most important aspects of our psychological makeup as LASID individuals and those surrounding us in our environment that contribute to aggression and violence. No single theory provides a comprehensive explanation for the full range of types of aggression, and our behaviour is often driven by a range of factors both within and beyond those explored in this section.

It is clear, however, that we are shaped more than we think by circumstances around us that we can't control, such as the groups we are in and our situation. We can use this awareness to help us structure our social world and institutions to prevent the most dangerous social situations from occurring where possible, or reduce the influencing power of these situations, and train people how to make better choices in such circumstances.

This variety of influences on aggressive and violent behaviour can be illustrated by the 4-point model used earlier to illustrate how ordinary people from civilised societies can find themselves committing acts of extraordinary violence. When we see human behaviour as multi-layered like this, including evolutionary, identity-related, social and situational factors[534], it can be seen how it is possible for anyone – even moral people like you and me – to be capable of extreme aggression and terrible violence when a certain set of conditions are met. Someone who had killed in the Rwandan genocide of 1994 told a researcher that at the time the killings were taking place, he didn't notice the small things that were transforming him into a killer[535]. Understanding this combination of 'small things' and its complexity helps us to build a richer and more realistic picture of ourselves as creatures, instead of over-simplified fantasies that label us as essentially good or essentially evil. It also shows how the small acts of prejudice or cruelty that we allow others to do or perform ourselves can be the seeds of ideas and behaviours that can have much bigger and more terrible consequences.

By understanding the perpetrators as human beings, we can understand ourselves better and put steps in place to address the factors that contribute to violent behaviour, and reduce the chances of it happening in future.

The next chapter will explore how we can use this knowledge to build structures, institutions and ideas around us that could help to reduce aggression and violence between people, as well as the chances of the worst excesses of human behaviour being realised.

Is it possible to stop human violence?

Before considering possible solutions, it should be asked what we can realistically expect to achieve in tackling the challenge of human violence. We look at incidents of genocide like the Holocaust and, with genuine determination and commitment, promise ourselves that we must never let them happen again. But is 'never again' an achievable goal? Is it realistic to expect an end to human violence? If not, what is the best we can aspire to?

A reasonable response to this question might be similar to the one to the same question in the previous chapter on prejudice. The potential for violence – even extreme violence – exists within every one of us due the ways we have evolved to think and behave as LASID creatures. The context we find ourselves in can have a substantial effect in determining our behaviour – both in terms of our immediate situation and the environment we have lived in that has shaped our thinking up to that point. This suggests, following the proposals in Chapter 12, that we need to surround ourselves with structures and ideas that support us in challenging and avoiding the thinking and behaviours that lead to violence, and particularly extreme violence such as genocide. There is much more we can do in modern society to achieve this, and in a similar way to tackling the issue of prejudice, we need to first realise just how far away our modern society is from where we could be. For example, although we know that reducing access to weapons reduces violent crime, guns and other weapons are still legally obtainable in the US and other countries. Or as another example, we know that dehumanisation fans the flames of violence by picturing certain groups as less than human and thus not deserving to be treated like other humans, yet as Chapter 11 demonstrated, we allow journalists and politicians, among others, to get away with this incendiary and hateful language without facing any consequences.

Rather than asking if we can achieve an end to violence, it may therefore be more useful to focus on the groundbreaking steps we could take to build a society that recognises our vulnerability towards aggression and violence, and is structured in a way that steers us away from these vulnerabilities. So, even if we cannot truly say 'never again', we will at least be able to reassure ourselves that we have done everything possible to prevent the worst excesses of human behaviour from manifesting themselves.

Chapter 15
How to reduce human violence

This chapter will explore some steps we can take to reduce both everyday and extreme violence. It will consider steps we can take to help individuals change their awareness of, and response to, their capacity for aggression and violence, as well as some broader ways we can shape the context around people, including media, cultural ideas and institutions, to move it away from the potential for violence and towards cooperation. Many of the recommendations from Chapter 13 on how to reduce prejudice will also apply here, as prejudice and aggression are closely related.

Building individual capacities

People can be given the resources and contexts they need to grow up in safe, healthy environments that promote non-aggressive behaviour They can also be equipped with the tools – both early in life and throughout it – to become more aware of their psychological tendencies as creatures, as well as mechanisms that could help them deal with situations or emotions that might lead to aggression and violence.

Give more help in the early years – given the importance of a child's early years to their later development, not just in relation to later aggression but a range of other psychological and behavioural factors, we should consider greater intervention and support for parenting at this stage of life to ensure all children get the conditions for the best possible start. This includes giving parents what they need to give their children a better start in life, including:

- The resources children need to have a safe, healthy and happy early life. This includes access to nutritious food, warm and safe housing and accessible child care. This point can be achieved through the step of addressing economic inequality noted in Chapter 13.
- The parenting skills and support to help them understand why this early stage of life matters so much in a child's development where they are developing attitudes and habits, and teach and model the non-aggressive behaviours that will help them to raise the cooperative, kind and emotionally intelligent humans we want our children to become. This will include helping parents to manage their own behaviours (see next point).

Provide 'Thinking training' – Chapter 12 discussed the need for an overall programme of thinking training to help us understand how we think and behave, the behaviours this results in and how to manage these in order to live better lives. This training should include a component relating to aggression and violence too, which could include the following areas:

- **How human beings think and behave in relation to violence** – understanding the factors that lead to our capacity for violence and the conditions that can make it happen, from in- and out-group biases to the power of the situation.

- **Identifying cues for aggression and violence** – helping people to identify the situations and contexts that can lead to aggressive or violent behaviour, so they are aware of how to avoid them, defuse them or adjust their own behaviour within them. For children, this might include how to deal with bullying and confrontation. For adults, this might include when they have become stimulated, disinhibited or confronted by a threat – for example in domestic arguments, social media arguments, or in potential road rage incidents.
- **How to manage anger and aggression** – teaching people how to recognise when anger and aggression may be rising in them and how to manage them in a healthy way. This is not through lashing out, 'rage rooms' or any other practice that could embed more aggressive behaviour. It is through methods such as breathing deeply to calm yourself down, removing yourself from the situation, taking some exercise, talking to someone or writing your thoughts down.
- **Challenging our prejudices** – in addition to the anti-bias components of this training from Chapter 12, we can ask people to honestly identify their own attitudes and prejudices, and moments when they have dehumanised others, whether consciously or unconsciously. They can then find ways to challenge and address these biases.
- **Perspective taking** – a practice discussed in Chapter 12 to help reduce prejudice, that can also be viewed as a thinking skill to reduce violence.
- **Teaching prosocial behaviour** – if we can learn antisocial behaviours such as aggression and violence (see learned behaviour section), we can also learn prosocial behaviour too,

such as non-violent communication, conciliation and cooperation. We can teach parents and leaders to model these behaviours for others.

This lifelong training, embedded in both the education system for children, and institutions for adults including workplaces, could help to teach children and remind adults of the expectations and best practices required of them for behaviour and relationships, and help organisations to become more effective in both harnessing the cooperation of their teams and preventing aggression and violence.

Changing our context

The steps above to build individual human capacities are a useful start, but need to be accompanied by broader structural changes. These range from establishing the human race as an in-group for us all to belong to, through to reducing the social power of the immediate situation to influence our behaviour.

Broaden our moral circle – we will not be able to stop the human tendency to seek membership of smaller tribes, be influenced by them or find them important in shaping our identities, and nor should we; it is a fundamental aspect of what we are as LASID creatures and can result in positive, cooperative outcomes as much as negative ones. But we can take some steps to see ourselves as part of a bigger group that transcends our own smaller tribes.

We should take every opportunity we can to find ways of transcending our individual in-groups and see commonality in ourselves. This could include football fans from different clubs uniting over a shared love of football or a set of nations uniting based on a shared history. It extends all the way up to the urgent need to establish among everyone on the planet the sense of a global 'tribe' of human beings – to see the commonality between all of us, as well as our interdependence. This is important not just to reduce our potential for prejudice and conflict, but also will be key in helping us address some other urgent global challenges such as climate change, as will be seen in the next chapter. An international organisation could be established to build this sense of a global in-group of human beings, and to foster cooperative values and activities between nations, groups and people.

Just to be clear, the recommendation is not to abolish the groups and nations we are part of in favour of one massive, homogenous superstate of human beings! It is about how we see ourselves and how we cooperate between groups. Even if we were lucky enough to establish a sense of common humanity among people, the blurring of in-group boundaries can backfire, as individual groups (such as nations) will want to retain their sense of identity – an effect that has been observed in studies[536]. Research therefore suggests it is best to strike a balance between an overarching common goal or identity that unites groups, and enabling each sub group to maintain a positive, clear sense of its own identity. Within this overall in-group we can celebrate the diversity of the people and groups within it – something that one psychology author suggests may be the answer to intergroup conflict[537]. Professor James Waller suggests we should also anticipate and identify the tensions that are likely to arise as we try to expand our sense of moral community[538].

Establish a culture of cooperation rather than competition – one way to solidify this sense of intergroup unity further is to establish a common threat. As will be seen in Chapter 16, such a threat already exists for human beings as a broad in-group in the form of climate change, and this could be one way of uniting our global human tribe. At a non-global level though, attempting to unite particular groups on the basis of a common threat may be dangerous as it may provoke prejudice, hate and violence – as the threat may well be perceived as another group of human beings.

There is another way to unify people though, as demonstrated by the work of psychologist Muzafer Sherif, who was responsible for some of the most famous studies demonstrating the minimal group paradigm, as discussed in Part 1[539]. Sherif took a group of schoolboys and separated them into two 'tribes', and it didn't take long for the groups to build hostile attitudes and negative images of each other. Their hostility escalated when the two groups were placed in competition with each other, and to such an extent that the experimenters had to intervene when the levels of fights and confrontations got out of hand. In the same 1950s experiments however, Sherif and his colleagues found that this hostility could be reversed to a certain extent by getting the groups to unite to achieve a common goal, such as helping to restart a truck that had broken down.

More recent research[540] has replicated Sherif's results, and suggests that this principle of setting shared (or *superordinate*) goals could be a powerful way of gaining greater cooperation and reducing conflict between both individuals and groups in a wide range of contexts.

This suggests then that the way forward is to change our culture into one based on cooperation rather than competition between human beings. Some initial ideas on what such a culture might look like were set out in Chapter 12. As was also noted in that chapter, this principle of cooperation could help us establish new ways for human beings to organise and interact with each other, including in education, workplaces, the economy and relationships – from those between individuals to international relations between states. To do this will require a rewiring of some of the structures and institutions around us – for example, reshaping the education system to use the collaborative 'jigsaw' teaching method explored in Chapter 12.

Minimise aggressive cues – we can remove or reduce the presence of factors in society that stimulate aggressive impulses. For example, when laws restricting handgun ownership were introduced in 1976 in Washington, DC, there was a quick and dramatic reduction in violent crime, including a 25 per cent reduction in homicides by firearms and 23 per cent reduction in suicides by firearms[541]. Restricting the availability of weapons is therefore a simple step we can take.

Make our structures and institutions less violent – this book has already argued that we need to rewire the structures and institutions around us towards promoting cooperation rather than competition. We also need to reduce their power to promote aggression and violence, whether this is intended or not – something that the promotion of cooperation will help to achieve, but further steps may be needed, some of which are outlined below.
- **De-bias the police** – the police force needs to be transformed to rid it of the systemic racism that independent reviews have found it to embody[542]. This is an urgent priority

in a number of countries, including the UK and United States.

- **Change how we educate children** – we need a review of the education system to explore its purpose, the methods it uses to assess children's progress and the messages it communicates to pupils implicitly through its structures and methods. For example, we need different ways of assessing the progress of children in education so that each builds a sense of confidence in themselves, an appreciation of their unique strengths and the agency to pursue the life they want with these skills. This forms one of the foundations of a sense of dignity and power – something that, if we lack it, can lead to frustration and aggression, as well as restricting people's potential.

- **Review the structure and values of the military** – although military institutions as a preventative force may be needed, we should review the decision-making structures and processes that exist within them to ensure they minimise the potential for violence – see the later point about 'defusing the power of the situation'. We should also review our attitude as societies towards state-sanctioned killing of any kind, including military operations. There is currently a greater public sense of shock and moral outrage at acts of violence and killing in civil society than those carried out by the state, and to reduce levels of violence, we should be equally sensitive to, and committed to preventing, each type.

Overall, the psychological evidence explored in this chapter suggests that the institutions that surround us play a much more significant role in our lives than many people realise. They do not simply provide us with essential services and support but also create the conditions people live their lives in, and influence our perceptions of the world and other people, which can have enormous impact on our experience of, and propensity for, violence and aggression. Greater funding and attention should therefore be given to the institutions that surround us to ensure that they are serving us properly and acting as a consistent force for good, rather than serving to reinforce inequalities and suffering for many, and allowing the conditions for violence to build.

Reduce the enabling role of mass media in violence and aggression – there are several steps that can be taken to achieve this, some of which mirror or build upon the recommendations in Chapter 12 relating to the role of the mass media in reducing prejudice:

- **Change the representation of violence and aggression** – violence and aggression are popular topics for newspapers, television programmes and other media channels to cover, as they make money for broadcasters. Violence is part of human life and it makes no sense to extensively censor it, and such a strategy could even be counterproductive. But we can reduce the amount of it on our screens and be aware of the impact it has on the learned behaviour of young children, and apply stronger restrictions to this. These restrictions may take the form of greater monitoring and awareness on behalf of parents rather than more regulation of the broadcast industry, as steps are already taken to advise viewers of the nature of content of programmes. In addition, all producers of media content should take more responsibility to understand their role in promoting aggression and violence, and do more to rebalance the way they represent these phenomena, away from the tendency to glamorise or humourise them. For example, mass media outlets could do much more to reinforce the negative consequences of aggression and violence, and promote the value of positive social norms such as kindness and cooperation, as part of a broader cultural shift to promoting a more peaceful and cooperative society. These may sound like minor details but they help to shape the border atmosphere and values we live within as a society.

- **Provide stronger regulation of dangerous speech and violence on social media** – dangerous speech does not have to be explicitly hateful or advocate violence, but can be defined as communication that could increase the risk of the reader condoning or participating in violence against members of another group[543]. This could therefore include labelling members of another group as 'cockroaches', specific incitement to violence, or many other things. Aside from taking a much stronger stance towards regulating such dangerous or violent speech on social media, communication platform owners need to take all steps possible to prevent them being used to organise acts of aggression and violence, and when they are, for the perpetrators to be banned indefinitely and their details passed to the police.

– **Prevent people from exercising power over each after by exploiting their vulnerabilities** – this was outlined on page 269 as a recommended step to reduce prejudice. It applies equally strongly to reducing aggression and violence, particularly against marginalised groups in society.

Equip groups to resolve intergroup tensions – we need to equip our structures – from small, local groups to international institutions – with the tools to help them tackle intergroup conflict and improve relations between individuals and groups. This includes the skills of mediation, bargaining and arbitration.

The capacity for conciliation is also important in helping to resolve conflicts and reduce violence in a range of settings, whether between individuals, groups or nations. When communication breaks down between conflicting parties, one of the greatest dangers can be escalation of the conflict into greater violence. For example, during the Second World War, Germany aimed to induce Britain to surrender by bombing its cities, and the Allies ultimately responded by bombing German cities, at enormous cost to civilian lives. The Allied firebombing of Dresden alone resulted in up to 25,000 deaths[544]. How can this cycle of escalation be prevented? Studies show that conciliation can work. In other words, one party tells the other it plans to make a concession to them, and then makes a small concession as promised, and then invites its opponent to do the same. The pressure is now on the other party to reciprocate this concession, as human beings have a tendency towards reciprocation – if others have done us a favour, we are inclined to reciprocate or comply with them[545]. Through gradual, reciprocated steps, tensions can be reduced and violence limited.

Create safer political conditions – we need to maintain political conditions that make it as hard as possible for political leaders and parties to emerge that can subvert democracy and build division, fear and resentment between people. This includes a number of factors:

- **Address economic inequality** – mirroring the same point in relation to reducing prejudice in Chapter 12, within each nation, we should ensure that every individual has the basic resources they need to live safe, self-determined and dignified lives. By doing this we can help to reduce the risk of resentment and scapegoating between groups, thereby avoiding a common building block for support of political extremism.

- **Maintain democracies** – at an international level we should be supporting any country that is seeking to build or maintain democratic government, as mass killings and genocide have occurred much less frequently within democratic regimes. We also should be heeding the warning signs and taking action when democracy appears to be under threat in other countries, as history suggests it is easier to intervene at this point than after authoritarian governments have got into power. Again, it is in the interests of the whole international community – not just citizens of the particular country – to protect democracies. The role of monitoring, nurturing and protecting democracies could be played by an international body such as the UN.

    A further action within this point is to ensure that political systems in each country are sufficiently robust to withstand the strains they are placed under when potentially authoritarian leaders and parties enter the system. For example, the democratic machinery of the United States proved only just strong enough to withstand the Republican party's assault on it during and following the 2020 presidential election that was won by Joe Biden. It needs to be strengthened, and in his book 'Why we are polarized' political writer Ezra Klein suggests a number of steps to achieve this, including removing the electoral college system that is no longer fit for purpose, introducing a voting system of proportional representation and removing the filibuster process from the Senate[546].

- **Take stronger international action to prevent and stop mass killing** – this is an important point at an international level, as the shocking fact is that no outside nation intervened in any of the nine episodes of genocide that took place in the twentieth century, at least not before the violence had ceased[547]. Writer and former US Ambassador to the UN Samantha Power suggests that the UN and the world's major powers had information on these genocides as they were progressing and yet chose not to act due to national self-interest[548]. We already have the technology and communication channels to identify situations around the world where the possibility of mass killing and genocide is building and when it is taking place. Our aim now must be to ensure that nations and international institutions have the incentives and processes in place to respond immediately and strongly to prevent these situations turning into mass violence and killing, rather than action being delayed due to national self-interest and political expediency. Professor James Waller recommends that the UN should mandate the development of a permanent international force that can be deployed in days or weeks to take action against regimes that are threatening or killing particular groups of victims[549]. There also needs to be stronger punishment and consequences for regimes found to be guilty of target mass killing. The International Criminal Court (ICC) was set up in 2002 as an international tribunal to hold to account individuals who commit the most serious violations of international law, including war crimes[550]. Although it is an important development, it needs strengthening in both its membership and its power to implement its judgements. For example, although it has 123 member states, some key global powers such as the US, Russia, China and India are not currently members[551]. Finally, further preventative measures can be taken by expanding peacebuilding activities within and between nations.

Defuse the power of the situation – the story of Reserve Police Battalion 101 demonstrated the devastating power of particular social situations to influence our behaviour for the worse as LASID creatures. We can take steps to prevent these situations from happening, and if they do occur, to help people identify the behavioural dangers of the situation and find ways to defuse them.

It may not be possible to apply this to all high-pressure social situations and we may not want to, as such situations can be the catalyst for exceptional pro-social actions, such as acts of generosity, for example when conformity within a group of wealthy individuals leads its members to make more generous charitable donations than they would otherwise do. We should therefore initially seek to apply these points initially to situations in which the likelihood of aggression or violence is high, and in which greatest negative consequences are likely to occur – which most obviously starts with our military institutions, both in groups of soldiers on the ground and military commanders making decisions. These principles could be applied to a range of other circumstances however, including political leaders, gangs, or corporate board members making major decisions.

- **Establish a clear sense of the 'broad humanitarian' moral values of the group** – we can ensure all group members are aware of the values expected of them in real life – those in which all humans are members of the same in-group – and encourage them to refer back to these in any moments when deciding a course of action – particularly when under social pressure.
- **Recognise dangerous social situations** – we can teach people, for example, as part of their military training, to recognise situations that could lead to unnecessary violence and cruelty, and to not only be extra vigilant of their behaviour and judgements at these moments but to flag to other members of the group that this is one of these dangerous situations.
- **Change how people handle the situation** – we can give people a toolkit of behaviours to use in such situations in

order to resist the lure of violence. For example, we can redefine heroism as speaking up in situations of social pressure and maintaining one's moral values.

Change the economic and political conditions that promote violence – as we have seen, some people and communities live in conditions that leave them vulnerable to regular violence and hostility. We need to change these conditions. One of the most influential steps we could take is to reduce poverty levels across our society, as poverty has been shown to be a driver of greater violence.

At the centre of all this is the need to reduce inequality, not just of economic resources but also of opportunity, dignity, safety and many other factors. This includes giving every individual with the basic goods and services they need – not just to survive, but to live healthy, dignified and self-determined lives, free from preventable harms. As various chapters of this book show, this is not just about providing people with material goods for the sake of it, but because economic inequality and poverty can be powerful forces making it harder for people to live safe, healthy lives – from staying healthy through eating well through to avoiding violence. They can also act as a catalyst for the emergence of greater violence from people who feel let down by the state, lack opportunities and resent others

As part of giving people a greater sense of dignity and agency we also need to give people more political power, as also outlined Chapter 10 as part of the recommendations on how to protect the idea of the truth. This must be distributed equitably across all groups in society. Giving people a greater sense of power – and making it clear they have this, and of the responsibilities this entails

– will work alongside the economic steps above to elevate people's conditions and status and reduce the potential to scapegoat or resent other groups of people.

Conclusions

We owe it to the victims of violence, hate, genocide and other human horrors to make sure we learn the lessons from their suffering, in order to reduce the chances of these things happening again. Unfortunately, such events continue to happen around the world, as we see in Ukraine, Israel, Gaza and other places. Also, despite our sense that everyday violence has reduced in modern society, it still affects millions of lives each year and leads to enormous suffering around the world.

Using the insights of psychology, this chapter has shown how a culture of violence can be reinforced by the assumptions, structures and institutions around us, as well as how all of us are capable of acts of extreme violence if particular conditions are in place. It is clear there are many more steps we could take to reduce the amount of violence in the world, as well as the likelihood of incidents of extreme violence and mass killing. These include providing the conditions in early life and beyond for people to live safe lives and develop non-aggressive habits, building societies and cultural norms that promote cooperation and work against division, and setting up robust international structures to prevent and quickly stop mass violence within and between nations.

Ultimately, violence and conflict are likely to be ongoing problems in a world of 8 billion or more human beings seeking access to resources, territory and opportunities. But we have the knowledge and potential to significantly reduce them if we are prepared to challenge some of our basic assumptions about how human beings should relate to, and look after, each other. The question is how much we want this, and whether we're prepared to take the radical steps needed to achieve it.

Climate change

In brief: Climate change is a threat to all human beings, and yet we are struggling to meaningfully tackle it as a global society. It is a uniquely difficult problem for human beings to solve, given the LASID creatures we are. We are stuck in a loop of inaction that is made even harder to break due to external structures and actors influencing us to avoid taking the necessary action. There are no guarantees we can solve this issue in time – but to do so we must act quickly and decisively as a global tribe to transform our structures and institutions so that they will enable us to lead good lives within the parameters of the planet.

Chapter 16
What is stopping us from addressing climate change?

We are in a climate emergency. Human activities have driven an ongoing rise in the Earth's air temperature beyond pre-industrial levels, and this is wreaking havoc across our planet, causing a transformation of our environment that is destroying lives. Ice sheets and glaciers are melting, oceans are warming to record-breaking levels and extreme weather events are taking place around the world, including floods, droughts and wildfires. The years 2014-2020 were progressively the warmest years on record[552], and 2023 has continued that worrying upward trend, with global temperatures moving to 1.26°C by the end of the year.

These changes have had a devastating impact on countries and communities around
the world, particularly those most vulnerable to the effects of climate change, in which more than 3 billion people live.

That is the first problem. The other problem is that we are failing to take the steps necessary to deal with this crisis within the timescales needed to avoid even greater disaster. Climate change can still be addressed, but we will need to make a number of major changes to our structures, institutions and habits as a species if we are to limit global warming to 1.5°C – the limit scientists suggest is necessary to prevent climate change from causing increasingly devastating and irreversible impacts[553], and the basis for the Paris agreement for climate change. This is the global agreement between nearly 200 nations to cut their greenhouse gas emissions in order to avoid the worst effects of climate change.

The State of Climate Action 2023 report produced by the World Resources Institute (WRI) provides a comprehensive review of whether we are on track to achieve the global changes we need to limit global warming to 1.5°C[554]. It finds that we are failing to take the necessary steps to achieve this – either in their pace or scale. The report largely serves to show just how far away we are from making effective progress to address the issue. It notes 42 indicators of progress that we need to have achieved by 2030 if we are to consider ourselves on track to keep within the limit of 1.5°C. We are behind – often way behind – on 41 out these 42 targets. For example:

- Target – reduce the carbon intensity of electricity generation to 48-80g of CO2 per kWh. Progress to date – the current level of intensity is 440g.
- Target – phase out public financing for fossil fuels, including subsidies, down to $0 per year. Progress to date – the current level of public financing is $1,100 billion per year – an increase on previous years.
- Target – reach 2 km of high-quality bike lanes per 1,000 inhabitants across urban areas. Progress to date – the current length is 4.4 metres (0.0044km).

We even appear to be increasing, rather than reducing, the intensity of some of the activities that drive climate change. For example, greenhouse gas emissions produced by humans have risen by 50% since 1990.

99.9% of scientists are united in their view that climate change is happening[555]. 80% of people are worried about the impact of climate change on humanity[556]. We know what it will take to address the issue and have clear plans like the one above to do it. So why are we failing so badly to tackle climate change?

This chapter will explore this question, and the next will ask whether there is anything we can do to tackle it more effectively, given what we now know about how human beings think and behave. It will argue that the nature of climate change as a problem is particularly challenging for human beings, as it creates conditions that make it difficult for us to take the steps necessary to resolve it, given the way we think and behave as individuals, groups and nations. Any potential solution to the climate crisis must break this Gordian knot.

What is stopping us from addressing climate change?

There is a wide range of reasons why we struggle to deal with global issues like climate change as a species, from our perception of it as individuals to our ability to gain collective action from our institutions. This chapter will begin by exploring our individual positions and broaden its focus from there.

Individuals and climate change

Our thinking and behaviour as LASID creatures influences how we perceive the issue of climate change, as well as our capacity to react to it in the ways we need to.

Awareness of the scientific consensus – the first question one might ask is how much awareness people have about the weight of evidence suggesting that human-led climate change is taking place. People underestimate how much scientific consensus there is about climate change. Research has shown that 99.9% of scientists agree that human-caused climate change is taking place[557], yet when asked what percentage of scientists has concluded that human-made climate change is happening, people in the UK think it is only 65%. This underestimation is significant, as other research suggests that increased public perceptions of scientific consensus on this issue lead to an increased belief that human-caused climate change is happening and a significant threat. These beliefs are, in turn, predictive of greater support for public action. So, scientists have a role to play in showing their support for the evidence on climate science, as this can help to promote the need for greater action.

Understanding the issue – one might think that a contributor to our failure to solve the climate change crisis is people's lack of knowledge of the topic. A study[558] by psychologist Dan Kahan and colleagues sought to investigate whether deficiencies in public knowledge or thinking capacities led to greater polarisation on disputed political issues like climate change.

They found that people who showed the strongest numeracy and reasoning skills performed better than others in making accurate sense of scientific data when it was presented as results from a study of a new skin rash treatment. But when the same data was presented as results of a study on a more politicised issue – a gun control ban – they actually ended up producing *less* accurate and more polarised results. This suggests that people's ability and willingness to understand scientific evidence is derailed by their need to protect their identity within the cultural groups to which they belong – i.e. when the more politicised issue of gun control was added, this activated people's sense of political identity, and they used their intelligence to double down on their biases and make the facts suit their own position. As a result, on topics such as climate change that are pertinent to people's group identities, the more intelligent a person is, the less accurate and more entrenched their views can become.

This finding is important as it suggests that improving public understanding of science is not in itself an effective solution to alleviating public differences in belief about scientific issues like climate change, even though such education is important in its own right. Instead, we need to remove the temptation for people to process scientific information in ways that protect their identity. Indeed, Kahan and his fellow authors of this study argue passionately that finding ways to protect scientific knowledge from culturally-led biases is the most important thing that psychology can do to assist democratic government. This bold claim may be somewhat exaggerated, but it is an important step, both in tackling climate change and some of the other challenges covered in this book, such as prejudice and truth. The 'solutions' section of this chapter will examine how this might be applied to the issue of climate change.

Motivated perception – as shown in Chapter 9, our beliefs and identities can even influence how we perceive identical information. A study found evidence of a general 'motivated attention framework' in which liberals and conservatives not only perceive climate change evidence differently, but also respond differently to ways this evidence is presented[559]. For example, the researchers presented participants with a graph of annual global temperature changes, and highlighted either stronger or weaker climate evidence in red. They found that liberals were more likely to take action (donating or signing a petition to stop climate change) when the stronger evidence was in red, but conservatives were less likely to act when stronger evidence was in red. The researchers concluded that focusing attention on motivationally consistent information tends to increase the level of action taken by liberals, but discourages conservatives. These findings could help us to tailor communications about climate change more effectively to different groups.

The power and biases of storytelling – our beliefs and world views also influence how we talk to each other about climate change – in particular, the stories we tell. Human beings have used storytelling over millennia as a core way to communicate with each other, pass on knowledge and inspire action. One study[560] found that as people retold stories about climate change these stories became less accurate over time. It also found that when a story was retold to an audience that was known to have a particular world view (for example, a liberal egalitarian view, or an individualistic conservative one), the speaker tended to retune the story to the audience's world view if this was known, as well as connecting the problem to the solution that was favoured by that audience. These findings illustrate how 'echo chambers' can develop between groups of people about the issue of climate change, with people telling each other what they think they want to hear rather than an accurate representation of the facts.

Expanding our radius of care – the last few examples have explored some of the ways in which we process and communicate climate evidence as individuals. Many psychological studies and reports tend to focus on this individual level. Climate change is not just about individual perceptions and actions however, and if we are to address it successfully, we need to do so as a planet of 8 billion people. We will consider this global mobilisation challenge now.

As discussed in Part 1, human beings evolved to live in small tribes. Evidence suggests that the number of neurons in our neocortex limits the amount of information we can process, which in turn limits the number of relationships that we can each keep up with at the same time. The magic number of stable relationships we can maintain at one time is around 150, also known as Dunbar's number, after Robin Dunbar, the author of the research proposing this idea[561]. Dunbar proposed that when a group of humans (or other primates) exceeds this limit, it tends to become unstable, meaning that cohesive social groups consist of 150 or fewer people. If you consider your own group of family members and friends, you may well emerge with a figure below this number.

This limit to tribe sizes has implications for our ability to deal with global issues such as climate change. We care enormously about the people we are closely connected to – those within our tribes. If climate change just affected these people, the chances are we would be incredibly motivated to take almost any action necessary to prevent their suffering, even if it meant us personally having to make major sacrifices. By contrast, it could be argued that we didn't evolve to care for everyone at a global level. We simply don't have the cognitive capacity to compute or feel all the suffering that is going on in the world equally, so we have to prioritise our group. This inhibits our motivation to seek global change as we are more concerned with the people closest to us.

Some people, however, do seem to be prepared to extend their 'radius of concern' way beyond their own tribes to the planet as a whole. These are people with strong 'other-focused values' – those that transcend concern just for themselves. Evidence from an experiment carried out across a diverse set of countries (the Netherlands, China and Columbia) suggests that people with self-focused values were linked with greater levels of climate scepticism than those with other-focused values[562]. A small but significant potential step to help us address climate change may therefore be to inculcate more of these collectivist, self-transcendent values in people, beyond self-focused ones. The authors of the above study suggest that this could be achieved in early adolescence, when people are in the process of developing their values and views on issues such as climate change. So, we can apply our System 2 rational thinking to extend our 'radius of concern' globally, but we need to be brought up with these values to begin with.

On an optimistic note, some evidence suggests that the majority of people are willing to expand their 'radius of care' to other people around the world, as well as future generations, in relation to climate change. In an Ipsos 2023 survey[563] of people's attitudes in a range of countries towards climate change, 63% of responders in Great Britain agreed that their country needs to do more to combat climate change and 66% agreed that if individuals like them don't act immediately on climate change, they will be failing future generations.

Immediacy bias and resistance to change – the problem in tackling this issue is therefore perhaps not people's attitudes but their willingness to take significant action – or to accept it being taken on their behalf – for example, by their government. Despite this shared concern from most people about the problem of climate change and a sense of a need for action, the same survey[564] gave some insights about what people were prepared to do to address climate change:

- 72% of responders in Great Britain agreed that if everyone made small changes that would make a big difference.
- 43% of British respondents agreed that financial incentives/tax cuts for env friendly products/services would help them make changes.
- Only 32% of British respondents agreed they would be willing to pay more tax.

In another survey, the Organisation for Economic Co-operation and Development (OECD) teamed up with Harvard University to explore the attitudes of people across 20 of the world's most carbon-emitting countries about climate change. They found that calls to limit unsustainable behaviours such as eating meat and driving cars did not produce strong support (40% and 37% of respondents respectively) – perhaps in part because they are strong culturally embedded behaviours[565].

Together, these findings suggest that people are willing to make small changes if other people do so too, but are largely unwilling to make bigger sacrifices such as paying more tax, which isn't a massive sacrifice relative to the other lifestyle changes that might be demanded of us. There is also an indication that people need to be incentivised even to make small changes, such as buying environmentally friendly products.

It therefore appears that people are only prepared to make minor changes to their lifestyles, despite their apparent concerns about climate change. Human beings don't like change, and for many people the prospect of having to completely change the way they live in order to address climate change is unthinkable. The popular fear that we will end up 'going back to the stone age' persists when people are told they will have to make changes to their lifestyles. Psychologists Daniel Kahneman and Amos Tversky identified another bias in human thinking that plays a role in these beliefs – *loss aversion*[566]. When we make decisions, we are wired to avoid losses as much as possible. As a result, we would rather avoid potential losses than make similar gains, as the pain of a loss is twice as great as the pleasure of a gain[567].

There are some clear reasons why this might have been evolutionarily beneficial to our ancestors – if we have expended energy on tracking down food, it makes more sense to invest energy in protecting this than spending more energy trying to find more. As with many other traits in human thinking, this has an unfortunate downside when trying to get people to make or accept changes to their lives to avoid climate change. Many people feel that changes to their lifestyles to address climate change will result in losses (less driving, eating less meat, having fewer of the things they like and feel they have a right to), and they feel the pain of a potential loss, and reluctance to change as a result. This sense of potential loss has been exacerbated by many of the messages they have received about climate change from external sources – both those campaigning against change and those seeking it! If we are to get people to support significant changes to their lives to tackle climate change, these must therefore not be presented as losses to people – for example, as sacrifices that they need to make. They can be framed as potential benefits (such as getting more of what really matters to them, building a better, inspiring future etc.) and as ways of avoiding other losses (such as the idea that climate change will threaten the things and people they care about – like their lifestyles and loved ones).

This unwillingness to make significant changes in our lives leads to people seeking more palatable solutions to the crisis, which explains why there is strong support for technical fixes, such as subsidising low-carbon technologies, which is supported by 67% of people in high income countries[568]. Technical fixes like this can contribute to building a better future, but they are not sufficient. Although we will do almost anything to try to avoid this conclusion, the only way we can meet our targets to avoid a climate catastrophe is to change our behaviour to live within the parameters of the planet.

This public fear of lifestyle change can also have an effect on the motivations of politicians, who are unwilling to present and implement the radical policies needed on climate change because they believe the public won't back them. This creates a 'loop of inaction' between politicians and citizens that can be very hard to escape from – particularly in democratic countries in which politicians are increasingly inclined to set policies based on their views of what will be accepted by the electorate so that they can hold on to power. This loop of inaction not only exists at national levels within countries around the world but also internationally, as leaders attempt to build a critical mass of individual countries, countries and other agents to take the necessary action as a species.

It seems it will require a greater sense of urgency to convince people they need to support the stronger measures we need to address climate change. Yet there are a number of traits of human thinking that make it difficult to produce this boost in urgency. First, we are built to prioritise the present over the future – a heuristic known as *hyperbolic discounting* or the *immediacy bias*. As LASID creatures seeking to make most efficient use of our limited cognitive capacity, this trait helped our ancestors to devote their mental resources to respond to immediate threats quickly in order to survive. Unfortunately, it also reduces our ability to address challenges that are slower to develop, more complex or situated in the future, such as the anticipated effects of climate change. A similar point applies to events that are not geographically close to us and affecting our daily lives or those of the people we care about. This lack of physical or temporal proximity reduces our ability to see the urgency of the crisis and therefore take the level of action needed.

Ultimately then, people are concerned with their own immediate day-to-day lives and tribes. This is not a morally condemnable form of selfishness – it is how we are built, and we have been through evolutionary adaptations to be like this.

These factors lead to one of the central challenges for human beings presented by the climate crisis. We respond to immediate, short-term cues. But by the time we have experienced a global disaster of a big enough magnitude to make governments prepared to take the necessary action to address climate change, it may be too late. This is primarily because some of the major changes to our climate will be irreversible[569] so these devastating effects may be here to stay, but also because there is a time lag both between our actions on climate change and the effects we see on the climate as a result (in some cases, of decades) and also between governments deciding to take action and then implementing that action.

A core challenge we have to address if we are to deal with climate change within the timescales needed is to stop this 'loop of inaction' between the public and politicians, and ensure that either one party or the other (or both) begins to take the level action necessary to save us from the worst effects of climate change. The next chapter will explore some options on how this could be achieved.

Our external context

Up this point, this chapter has shown that our ability to act on climate change is hampered by some of our thinking and behavioural traits as individual human beings. This situation cannot be understood fully by simply looking at individuals in isolation however, as being LASID creatures, our context plays a big role in our thinking and behaviour. It is even harder for people to act if most of the systems, structures and values that surround us in society are encouraging us to continue our unsustainable lifestyles as normal, and some of the most powerful actors around us are influencing us against treating climate change with a sense of urgency. These factors will be explored in more detail now.

The power of established norms – a first point to note is that many of us around the world are embedded in a particular lifestyle, culture and set of values and aspirations that represent and promote an unsustainable way of life. WWF estimates that the environmental footprint of the lives we are living in the UK is four times more than our planet can sustain[570].

Most human beings in the West have grown up with these norms surrounding us, and they simply represent 'how life is'. For example, the idea that buying more material goods will make us more effective and happier, and that we need to keep up with other people in the brands and items we have in order to show our status. Or the feeling that we need career or financial success to be seen as successful or to have meaning in life, and that being busy and working long hours helps us to achieve this.

Some of these habits, behaviours and assumptions are unsustainable for our planet, and it can be difficult to extract ourselves from them, even if we are trying to make changes to our lives to address climate change. This can lead to a great deal of contradictory thinking and behaviour – for example, someone might be diligently trying to 'do their bit' by recycling their waste packaging, but at the same time buy an oversized Sports Utility Vehicle (SUV) as their transport. The reasons why they might make these decisions are of course complex, but many are made as a result of the habits, assumptions and expectations we have. As part of any solution to climate change, we therefore need to establish a new set of norms for what a good life looks like, which we can aspire to in our daily lives.

The influence of powerful opposition – these norms and expectations are not simply maintained by us in isolation however, and context is critical to human beings. One of the biggest problems we face in relation to climate change is that a range of powerful actors exist within the world that are seeking the opposite of what we actually need, by either aiming to maintain the unsustainable way we currently live, or taking it to a more extreme level. These actors take a range of forms – from politicians to media owners to companies – but many have significant power and are able to influence our views and values, as well as shaping some of the structures that surround us in our daily lives.

For example, Rupert Murdoch has been accused by scientists of being a 'climate villain', using his media empire (including *The Sun* and Fox News) to sow doubts about the causes and consequences of climate change, and to delay efforts to address it[571]. A 2008 study showed that this had affected people's beliefs: watching Fox News reduced people's acceptance of the fact of climate change compared to other channels, such as CNN[572].

It is not just media barons seeking to derail progress on this issue. An independent report in 2021[573] aimed to identify the world's most obstructive companies holding back policies to address climate change. The top three companies on the list were the petrochemical companies ExxonMobil and Chevron and the car manufacturer Toyota. The report suggests that a company's influence over policy and regulations may have a much greater impact than the emissions produced by its products or operations – a worrying conclusion when one considers these are petrol and car companies. Another independent report[574] found that, in the three years after the Paris climate agreement in 2014, the five biggest publicly-traded oil and gas companies in the US (ExxonMobil, Royal Dutch Shell, Chevron, BP and Total) invested over one billion dollars of their shareholder funds on misleading climate-related branding and lobbying.

It is not just such blatant attempts to influence people about the facts of climate change that have an effect on how we see the issue and our willingness to take action on it. Advertisers use psychological knowledge to manipulate people into buying their products – to build a want or need for a product or service in someone even though they may not have wanted it before. As a result, the entire multibillion dollar industry of advertising helps to maintain the (incorrect) cultural norm that consuming more stuff makes us happy and brings meaning to life. Politicians push the idea of economic growth, productivity and the power of economic markets, so that the business agenda takes clear priority over other goals, such as environmental needs – which are addressed inconsistently and often for political expediency. Influential individuals such as footballers, television stars and social media influencers promote a lifestyle of consumption, air travel, and luxury goods – one that young people and other members of the public aspire to.

Some of the structures and institutions that surround us can also influence us to not see the issue clearly – for example, as Chapter 9 argued, we can easily get sucked into filter bubbles on social media, in which we only hear perspectives that back up our existing views or ways of life, and make it difficult for us to see beyond these.

In summary, an incredibly wide range of influences and structures around us shape how we feel about climate change and our willingness to seek action on it. Many of these promote the continuation of our current unsustainable lifestyles, norms and values, which can prevent us from taking the action needed on climate change. Although concern about the climate emergency has seeped into our culture and is a much more visible priority than it was even ten years ago, it is still largely presented as something that can be solved whilst continuing the lifestyles we already have or as something that threatens these lifestyles but is less important than maintaining them. As a result, we are currently at a bizarre place in our cultures where we still cling to old norms such as consumerism whilst recognising the conflicting priority of environmental concerns. This leads to the confused and inconsistent behaviour and priorities we discussed earlier – both from members of the public and political leaders. Eco-consumerism is a good example of this confusion in action.

Gaining consensus and action from competing global tribes – we also face challenges at a political and international level when seeking to address a global issue such as climate change. There is now basic international consensus that human-made climate change is taking place. The central challenges are to gain global agreement on the actions needed, and to undertake collective action at sufficient speed and depth to meet our targets. A range of psychological and political issues make it hard to gain consensus on these points, and some of these will be explored now.

The first point is simply that there are a lot of separate and often competing tribes that need to balance their interests and work together to address this issue. At the most basic international level, these tribes are the 195 separate countries in the world. At other levels, there are competing businesses, religions and many other varieties of tribe that need to unite on this issue.

At the country level, different nations are at different stages of economic development and some (such as India) argue that other countries have had hundreds of years to burn fossil fuels and build their economies on this as a result. Established industrial nations like the US or European countries argue that we simply need to act now, regardless of the history. Any solution to this particular argument will need to arrive at a fair way to balance the needs of developing countries and subsidise their transition to a non-fossil fuel economy, as well as making clear that the future is based on renewable energy, as are the present and future economic opportunities.

Another challenge exists in the form of countries that stand to benefit from the continued use of fossil fuels – for example, those with plentiful oil reserves like Saudi Arabia (with 21.5% of the world's oil reserves[575]). To meet our climate targets, fossil fuels need to be kept in the ground and production halted. Saudi Arabia however has been accused of various attempts to stifle progress on climate change including lobbying to weaken global climate change legislation[576] and building investment plans to create more demand for its oil and gas in developing countries[577].

National tribes face further challenges as they look to protect their geopolitical interests and avoid ceding power to others during this time of upheaval and transition. Energy use affects many aspects of people's lives and a country's economy and some countries may well do worse from quick action on climate change than others

– for example, those without the natural resources or space to benefit from alternative energy sources such as solar panels, tidal or geothermal energy. These pressures to compete at this time of transition can be exacerbated by existing tribal tensions between countries, especially if these are fuelled further by aggressive and nationalistic political leaders.

The need to reach consensus and cooperation as a species to address the climate crisis therefore presents a range of challenges related to our evolved tendency to live and cooperate in smaller tribes. This extends from the need for people to extend their 'radius of care' about other people beyond their own tribe to such a level that they will change their lives on their behalf, through to the need to balance the claims and needs of different national tribes, each with different circumstances and attitudes of their leadership.

A final issue challenge on the political level relates to the short-term nature of the political system in many democratic countries (such as the US and the UK). The electoral arrangements in these countries mean that governing parties can change every four or five years. This is not to say this short-term political model is wrong in itself, as it gives citizens the chance for reasonably regular reviews of their government, which in democratic terms is a good thing – but it can make it harder to achieve action on big issues like climate change. This is in part because it encourages parties to work within a reasonably short-term window in terms of the policies they will choose – as they need to show the electorate results in the short term so that they will vote for them again at the end of the next electoral cycle. This does not however create strong incentives for bold, long-term political projects from each party.

Another reason why short-term politics can be a hindrance to long-term global issues like climate change is that governing parties may adopt very different policies and values relating to these issues. These policies not only change how much action that country takes to address climate change, but also how its government uses its influence to seek greater, faster action on it at a global scale, and also the cultural and social norms it sets for its own population on this issue. For example, in the US, at the time of writing this book, the Joe Biden administration had made tackling climate change one of its key priorities, and had implemented a raft of policies aimed to meet its target of achieving a net-zero emissions economy by 2050[578]. His predecessor, Donald Trump, however was focused on rolling back actions that aimed to stop climate change[579], including withdrawing from the Paris agreement and lifting bans on oil and gas exploration in parts of Alaska.

Chapter 17
How to tackle climate change more effectively

Despite all these obstacles to us being able to tackle climate change with the depth and speed of action required, evidence suggests there is some hope. Just looking at the US alone, according to a 2021 Pew Research Center report[580] the majority of Americans (across all political tribes) believe not enough is being done about climate change by elected representatives, corporations, the energy industry or the public as a whole, and 64% say efforts to address it need to be prioritised now even if this means deprioritising other issues. Also, although political tribes differ significantly in their attitudes towards climate change, the younger generation of Republicans is much more supportive of action to reduce fossil fuel use than older members. For example, Gen Z Republicans are more than three times as likely as Baby Boomer and older Republicans to support a complete phase out of fossil fuel use (20% vs. 6%). So, what can we do to build on this hope and address some of the behavioural obstacles we face in dealing with the challenge of climate change more effectively?

This chapter is not going to discuss the vast array of measures and policies that are needed to address climate change – these are covered in other places including the WRI State of Climate Action report mentioned earlier. Instead, it will consider the likelihood of getting the change we need and a number of steps – some big, some small – that could help us to address some of the psychological barriers we've identified to achieving this change. Climate change is a collective action problem requiring a global response within a very limited timeframe, and any approach based on psychology needs to focus on both individual and collective factors. The suggestions below aim to integrate both of these elements.

Breaking the loop of inaction

The first question is how we can address the 'loop of inaction' discussed in the previous chapter at both national and global levels that is preventing us from taking the actions needed at the speed needed to avoid the worst effects of climate change. The reality is that we only have a handful of years in which to make these changes – an incredibly short timescale to achieve a global transformation. Based on the progress reports discussed in the last chapter, we are way behind where we need to be to achieve this in the time needed. Something extraordinary and unprecedented therefore needs to happen to accelerate this action.

Regrettably, the most likely outcome for human beings on this issue in the coming decades seems to be that we will fall well short of keeping climate change within the 1.5C limit we have set in the Paris agreement. The likelihood is that we will overshoot this temperature by a significant amount and this will cause enormous climatic changes which will have severe global consequences in countless areas, including food supply, population displacement and geopolitics. Human lives – and the environment – will be transformed in severe and unpredictable ways. We need to face up to this reality – and to do so now. If we don't, our other, less likely, options for solving it will disappear into impossibility.

So, what are these other options? Given the size of the challenge that exists in tackling climate change within the timescales required, history and psychology suggest it is unlikely that human beings can meet this goal without suspending the normal operation of democratic countries, and moving to a state of emergency within them. History suggests that a radical, quick change of lifestyles and behaviour is possible in human societies when it is imposed by governments in emergency situations – for example, our governments banned us from leaving our homes during the Covid-19 lockdown, which would have seemed an unimaginable infringement of our freedom in a democratic society at any other time, yet it was accepted by the majority of people[581]. During World War Two, governments introduced various measures that radically changed people's lives, such as conscription and rationing. It could be argued that we need to invoke a state of emergency similar to a 'war footing' to tackle the climate crisis in an effective way, with significant changes possibly including reduction of meat production, quick phasing out of fossil fuels and significant curbs on aviation. The question is whether politicians have the political will to do this and whether they believe that citizens will accept such strong measures.

The climate emergency differs from these other crises in some significant ways in terms of the public's attitudes towards it. Both the Covid-19 pandemic and World War Two were existential crises that directly affected the population of this country. Although it appears regularly on our news feeds, the climate crisis has not yet affected the British public severely (aside from flooding in some areas), so it is unlikely to be regarded with the same urgency.

A vital question therefore has to be asked – at what point does the climate situation become so bad that the public and politicians are prepared to make the changes needed? Based on history, it appears that the only thing that is likely to break the loop of inaction is that politicians are forced into declaring a state of climate emergency – not because we voted for it or politicians implemented it voluntarily, but because they were forced to do so in the light of an existential crisis at the level of World War Two or Covid-19. Perhaps our most likely hope is therefore to experience a global climate crisis that doesn't cause too much damage but unites the population into demanding immediate, radical action on climate change from politicians. As previously noted though, by the time the crisis becomes this severe, we may already be way past the 1.5C limit, and heading towards grave consequences.

Another possibility is that popular support can be built in certain influential countries that enables the emergence of politicians or parties who are prepared to set a strong approach to the climate crisis as the centrepiece of their platform. This feels like a less likely scenario, because it fails to address the loop of inaction or gain international consensus on action quickly. The leadership of these nations would also need to inspire other countries to cooperate and take action too. These policies may either be enacted through the willing participation of the public within democratic systems or may be delivered through a more authoritarian stance. The latter would challenge the priority we place on freedom and democracy – but it is possible to imagine a party that suggests that climate change is such an important issue that it is worth suspending some freedoms to get it solved.

The possibilities above are either unpalatable or unlikely. But there is another extraordinary and unprecedented way we could address the climate crisis – and its potential depends upon whether the people of the world are ready for it. This alternative is a massive international movement-building campaign that seeks to unite the world population to rise up and force politicians and businesses into global change on the scale and speed we need. This may be our best chance of achieving the changes in a democratic way. Over recent years, there has been a massive number of groups and campaigns seeking to address climate change, from Extinction Rebellion to the United Nations 'Race to Zero' campaign, but none has achieved the level of leverage needed to influence sufficient change. A last-ditch global campaign, funded by wealthy individuals and large companies to achieve an unprecedented level of scale, ambition and funding, and joined by campaign groups around the world, would seek to frame humanity as one in-group battling an external enemy or threat together – that of climate change. Building this sense of a global in-group is not as easy as it may seem due to differing circumstances and power dynamics between smaller groups[582], but evidence suggests this idea of a shared fate – a fight against a common enemy – can bind cooperation between people[583]. Another factor that can do this is building a sense of 'global cosmopolitanism' in which people feel a dual identity, as part of global humanity as well as belonging to sub-groups such as nations within this, and being open about the differences between these sub-groups rather than trying to force humanity into a homogeneous whole[584].

The campaign would argue that this external enemy threatens our livelihoods and children (making use of our tendency for loss aversion), and we have a limited time to defeat it – and a specific deadline would be set. Alongside the fight against a common enemy threatening to inflict massive losses on our in-group, there would be a simple call to action to complete a petition, attend marches or undertake other actions appropriate to each targeted group to tell politicians around the world that we, as the global public, are ready for them to take the radical steps needed to build a better future and address climate change. The campaign would have a simple, definitive title and message – such as 'The time is now' or 'We're ready'.

The campaign would set out a simple road map to show how this issue can be dealt with in a few radical, timed steps. We need to make the solution seem simple, even if it is complex and radical underneath. It will acknowledge how ambitious and radical the plan is – but counterintuitively, this, in combination with its simple presentation, could help to make it seem possible, and build the cultural belief that we can do this. The campaign would aim to counteract people's sense of hopelessness about this issue and show them how we can have power and collective agency when we come together for our mutual survival.

The aim would be to gain the funders and organisational actors needed to produce this campaign at a global scale and depth that has not been achieved before – relentless, repeated communications that reach most individuals around the world. It would therefore aim to gain the participation of powerful non-government actors that influence and control the structures around people, including leading technology and social media companies. It would also use many of the techniques that have been explored in this book to encourage people to join and take action – from building social norms through influence in social media and newspapers, and using advertising techniques. Such a campaign is of course dependent on the participation, generosity and ambition of some of the world's wealthiest and most influential individuals and companies who have benefitted most from our unsustainable way of living to date – but this may be possible, and removes the necessity for a public funding campaign that would be unable to raise the level of funds needed. If successful, the campaign would lead to the global mobilisation project that will be discussed shortly. There is evidence suggesting this approach has potential – for example, the Australian 'Climate 200' project is a crowdfunding initiative to support independent political candidates who will push forward the climate change agenda. It includes donations from wealthy philanthropists such as share trading firm founder Rob Keldoulis, who have contributed millions of dollars to the cause, which has helped to challenge the power and perspectives of the larger parties, including helping pro-climate candidates to win seats in the Australian federal elections in 2022[585].

Steps to seek change

Regardless of the way in which we get to the point of taking substantial action on climate change, the section below sets out some ways this action could be taken most effectively, considering the potential for both action and obstacles to action brought by our makeup as LASID creatures. These can be broadly split into two categories – measures that can be implemented to the structures around people in their lives that they can simply 'slip into' (such as improving public transport) and those that represent changes they will just have to accept (such as reducing meat consumption).

Integrate nature into our priorities, systems and lives – the breakdown in our relationship with nature is at the centre of our problems with climate change. One of the most important stories we need to establish in our global culture is that human beings are part of the natural world, and custodians of it rather than masters of it. This is not only a cultural necessity but also a practical one. Every aspect of our lives, activities and infrastructure as a species needs to take place within the parameters of nature and our planet, as it is the only one we have.

Putting the planet first in this way will demand changes in our fundamental priorities and values, as well as a radical rethinking of our structures and institutions. For example, we need to challenge the idea that material wealth is the sole route to human flourishing, as studies have shown it is not, beyond a basic level of income[586]. We need to adjust structures to reflect this, including much tighter regulation of the industries that promote over-consumption, such as advertising. Restricting the amount of time and physical space we allow for advertising would help us to improve our immediate environments and reduce the continuing pressure to consume more. We could redirect this industry's remarkable skills in influencing people away from destructive ends like over-consumption and towards constructive goals such as influencing cooperative behaviours on climate change and reducing prejudice and violence.

We need to prioritise human flourishing within nature above economic goals and see the latter as a means to an end of the former. These changes in focus will require a change in political and economic systems – not necessarily meaning the end of capitalism, but certainly the end of the neoliberal consensus that has dominated economics since the late 1970s which demands that financial markets should be free to operate in an unfettered way. Our economy needs to work for us, not vice-versa.

As part of these structural changes, we also need to address inequality between human beings – both economic and other forms – as both poverty and extreme wealth are key drivers of human suffering in climate change as well as in people's capacity to make changes on this issue. These are large-scale and complex changes that there is insufficient space to explore in more detail here.

At a simpler level, we need to rebuild our relationship with nature more generally – and there are many reasons why this matters. For example, studies have shown that having a strong sense of connection to nature promotes human well-being and functioning. There is also considerable evidence that greater connection with nature promotes pro-environmental behaviours in people[587]. We therefore need to build nature into our lives and societies more, and a report produced in 2023 by the University of Derbyshire[588] sets out a range of ways we could do this. Steps include integrating nature into our financial system and rewarding actions that protect and promote it, building infrastructure that doesn't encroach on nature and giving everyone the opportunity to have nature present in their daily lives.

Implement the changes as one global programme – many of the most significant changes that will be required to meet our climate targets do not directly relate to individual behaviours, and require larger, structural changes from industry, governments and other institutions such as phasing out the use of fossil fuels in energy production or increasing climate finance flows.

Changes of this nature seem particularly challenging, as they require global industries in competitive marketplaces to transform themselves at a speed that is unprecedented. One way to give this extraordinary effort a chance of success is to portray it as a war-like global mobilisation of industries and governments over a fixed period to make this transformation. This would be a massive global investment project in which countries and companies contributed to the cost of rebuilding our global infrastructure and practices in order to meet our targets on climate change, avoid catastrophe and build a habitable world.

Like the global communication campaign discussed earlier, this project would use a range of psychological principles to maximise its effectiveness, particularly in achieving global cooperation and support across a diverse set of actors (from nations to companies) with differing needs and motivations. These principles include:

- Undertaking the project as a distinct, time-limited exercise, so that many of the steps are taken quickly or simultaneously, and there is a clear end point.
- Bringing every global tribe (nations, industries and other actors) together to address this issue, rather than asking individual tribes to do this on their own.
- Building the sense of a global in-group fighting against an external threat.
- Invoking the idea that 'we all do this together' – it is a collaborative effort requiring a previously unseen sense of solidarity and cooperation as a global group. We take the steps together, and we share the gains and pains that come with it. This includes the rich countries helping the poor – bringing everyone along, as we can't

achieve this if we're divided. Research shows that a majority of people across many nations feel that they need to see others (especially the wealthy) making changes if they are to be willing to change their own lifestyle[589].
- Promoting a sense of confidence that we can achieve these goals – evidence shows that campaigns to promote more sustainable behaviours are more successful when there is a strong rather than weak sense of group efficacy[590].
- Portraying it as an infrastructure project – OECD research suggests that there is general support for infrastructure projects – even transformational ones, and subsidies to help people make changes. The initiative could be seen as a transformative global infrastructure project, similar to the one President Joe Biden tried to build in the US from 2020 – but at an even greater scale and speed.

This global mobilisation project could be one of the steps outlined in the global communication campaign discussed earlier, in order to gain momentum and support from the global public for it.

Reduce the friction of structural changes – if possible, most of the changes to people's lives that will be needed to address climate change should be implemented in a way that changes the infrastructure around us, rather than asking individuals to each take responsibility for making enormous personal changes to their lives. Minimising the 'behavioural friction' like this enables us to make the transition between our old, environmentally unsustainable, lives and our new, planet-friendly ones feel as smooth and effortless as possible, without people feeling that their entire routines have been changed or that they are suffering significant losses or disruption.

For example, increasing the energy efficiency of buildings can be achieved through a national programme to refit people's homes to better energy standards at a greatly subsidised rate or at no cost, so that it is the responsibility of the state to make this happen rather than the individual. Changes like these can be framed as major benefits to people's lives that they don't have to take action on – it will be done for them. Part of the communications strategy around a climate change action plan will be to show people that these things will be done for them – and they just need to support this idea for it to happen. By taking this proactive approach governments show that the effort to implement these changes is being shared, and make it more likely that individuals will be willing to 'do their bit' when they need to.

Another behavioural principle to follow when implementing changes is to emphasise the benefits that they will bring beyond building a sustainable society – for example, showing how having a more energy efficient house will make it warmer.

Incentivise other necessary changes – there will be a range of changes needed to our lifestyles that will be less popular for both individuals and groups, including the suppliers of these 'climate-unfriendly' goods and services. These include reducing both meat consumption and air travel dramatically. Punitive measures such as high taxation of these carbon-heavy goods may be necessary (especially if the revenue is reinvested in climate initiatives), but these don't always eliminate the behaviours they aim to remove (e.g. people still smoke, drink and drive large, carbon-intensive cars, despite higher taxes and costs for these products). We could therefore also try another approach – incentivising climate-friendly behaviours – as evidence suggests that having financial support to change into more sustainable behaviours is important for the majority of people in most countries[591]. For individuals, this might take the form of rewarding people for keeping within a specified 'carbon diet' over the course of a year – an initiative that could be assisted by an app and technology monitoring people's fuel, transport, food and other consumption. It could also include heavily incentivising sustainable alternatives to each choice, so that these become much cheaper and more attractive than the carbon-heavy ones. For example, absurd as it may seem, in the UK air travel is currently subsidised – from airlines paying zero duty on their fuel (unlike motorists) through to passengers having to pay no VAT for their flight tickets[592]. This actively incentivises rather than disincentivises the climate-damaging activity. At the time of writing, it is 50% more expensive to get a return train journey from London to Aberdeen than a return flight. If we turn this on its head and incentivise the sustainable activity (in this case, including using trains and other methods to travel abroad as well), whilst removing subsidies for the unsustainable one (in this case, aviation), it will encourage many more people to change their behaviour. Arrangements will also need to be made with suppliers to compensate them for these changes and smooth the process of transition.

Leverage social identity for climate action – social identity plays a critical but underappreciated role in how we respond to the climate change crisis, both as individuals and as groups, including at an international level[593]. The previous chapter showed how social identity processes can play a role in biasing people against pro-environmental attitudes and behaviours, but they can also provide a powerful push towards them. For example, one study found that seeing the social norms of how other people (in this case, their neighbours) behaved led more people to conserve more energy than any of the other usual appeals used to get people to cut down on energy use – for example, that it would save them money or protect the environment[594].

We should therefore use the insights of social identity theory to develop strategies to promote pro-environmental behaviour, both at small and international group levels. For example, one group of academics in Germany has proposed a Social Identity Model of Pro-Environmental Action (SIMPEA) that identifies three key aspects of social identity that could be leveraged together to provide a powerful drive for pro-environmental behaviours[595]. These are:

- **In-group identification** – each of us belongs to a wide range of in-groups and our attitudes and behaviour towards climate change may be different, depending on which group we activate in our minds. It therefore makes sense to refer to people's membership of in-groups that promote pro-environmental behaviour rather than those that don't – for example, encouraging people to see themselves as citizens of the world rather than a country that relies on the oil industry.

- **Collective efficacy** – making people feel that the challenge of climate change is not theirs alone, and that their in-group is capable of addressing it collectively.
- **In-group norms and goals** – the social norms of the groups we belong to have a significant impact on our behaviour. Messages about climate change that work with, rather than against, these norms tend to be more effective. For example, if a particular group values responsibility as a norm, then taking action on climate change could be framed to them as a way of taking responsibility for the environment.

We can also apply knowledge about the power of social identity to inform how we speak to different groups of people about climate change, including how we make messages more palatable to those who are more sceptical about the issue or are members of groups with this identity. For example, policies and communications on climate change can often seem like contested issues between groups that provoke conflict between them and activate defensive mechanisms within members of those groups to protect their identities. One group (such as Republicans or climate sceptics) might therefore reject information that has come from an out-group (such as Democrats or scientists). Using identity theory, we can help people to lower these barriers that they use to defend their identity, and increase their receptiveness to action on climate change – in this case by making it clear that the messages to take action on climate change come from within their in-group[596].

Academics, policy-makers and campaigners urgently need to develop ideas to apply these models at an international as well as a local level, as the large-scale change that is needed has to date been neglected. Some of the principles from this SIMPEA model have been used in developing the ideas for the international movement building campaign and global implementation program set out earlier, but other ideas resulting from these techniques may be equally or more effective. These insights also highlight the importance of leaders in establishing positive social norms towards tackling climate change. For example, a study showed that when leaders used inclusive language of 'we' and 'us' to promote renewable energy, this gave it a stronger sense of being a norm in their group, and led to greater intention on behalf of in-group members to act in relation to it[597].

Regulate climate change information – applying our knowledge about social identity will help us to address the way people perceive and act on climate change information, but we also need to do more to regulate the information itself and the sources people use to obtain it, so that it is easier and more useful for them to process, as well as being as reliable as possible.

To ensure that the information is as reliable as possible, the steps recommended in Chapter 10 on how to protect the truth can be applied, including 'inoculating' people against climate change misinformation and preventing attempts to seek profit or power by exploiting people's vulnerabilities to manipulation.

Simple labelling of goods and services may also help people to make better decisions on the complex issue of their climate impact. Each individual could be provided with a daily carbon allocation – the amount of carbon they can consume whilst keeping the planet within 1.5C heating limits. This 'carbon diet' measurement helps to anchor a particular figure in people's minds, which acts as their reference point – even if they struggle to meet this. An app could be provided to help people monitor their carbon consumption each day. People have become used to counting calories and understanding recommended daily limits, and similar principles could help them develop their carbon literacy, as well as make less carbon-intensive choices.

Each product or service, from train journeys to cans of baked beans, could carry a mandatory label that tells the potential customer how much carbon it carries overall in its manufacture, consumption and disposal, as well as the contribution this makes to the individual's carbon allocation for the day. High carbon options could be flagged with a black label (for example, travelling by car), and consumers directed to lower carbon alternatives (such as using public transport). Carbon health labels could also be attached to products and services that are particularly high carbon or unnecessary, asking 'Do you really need this?' – for example, air travel. These ratings and labels should be mandatory on any promotional materials such as advertisements that encourage their consumption.

Behaviours could also be measured on the app, with similar labelling principles applied – for example, a car journey would gain a black warning label and suggestions of alternative transport methods.

Tell better stories – the discipline of psychology has learnt a lot about what people do or don't respond to and how to create effective messages. This knowledge needs to be applied consistently to the effort to beat climate change, as messaging is often negative, inconsistent or ineffective at present.

As we have seen, the majority of people are concerned about climate change, but are not affected at a deep enough level to take meaningful action or demand it of their political leaders. The rational, intellectual extension of our 'radius of concern is therefore perhaps not enough to motivate most people to take sufficient action. We therefore need to use communications to awaken the powerful, visceral emotion that comes from our automatic System 1 thinking – such as our care for our own tribe. This leads to a range of communication possibilities, such as framing humanity as one 'in-group' in order to build global cooperation, telling positive stories that fit with the world views of different groups and relate to 'people like me'.

This process of communicating better should start with creating a simple but clear vision of what people's lives would look like in a sustainable future, so that it becomes real to them. Bearing in mind the human tendency to be more concerned by losses than by gains, we also need to challenge the idea that our current lifestyles are worth keeping, and show that we won't be losing but gaining by making changes. We need to challenge the dominant stories of our time, including the fact that the consumerist, rushed and unequal lifestyles that we aspire to actually militate against human flourishing in a variety of ways, and that we have a chance to build a better future when we take action to address the climate emergency.

We should therefore not simply present climate change as a threat we must overcome, and that the future we scrape together as a result of this is all we have to look forward to. We need to build a positive, aspirational vision of the future, showing the tangible benefits of a sustainable future on the things that matter to people so that they feel inspired by it and actually want to move towards it, rather than feeling they will be losing a lot from the lifestyles they have now. The actions taken by governments on people's behalf will need to gradually deliver on these expectations, in order to retain people's commitment and trust to this vision.

Changing the stories we tell like this can help to shift the way people perceive the issue of climate change, alongside the other measures we have discussed in this section.

Conclusions

Climate change is a uniquely difficult problem for human beings to solve, given the LASID creatures we are. It requires us to make substantial changes to our lives in the present – something we do not like doing – in order to avoid negative consequences that are both situated in the future and that do not affect everybody's lives in an immediate way in the present. It is made even harder by the fact that we need to have concern for people beyond our immediate tribes in order to take action – something that demands rational, effortful System 2 thinking, not just automatic System 1 – and are faced with a range of politicians, corporations and other powerful interests that wish to avoid making these changes and that attempt to influence us to avoid taking the action that is necessary. This is in addition to the fact that some of the structures around us, such as information architecture (in the form of social media, newspapers and other sources) make it difficult for us to reach reasoned views without being influenced or driven by aspects of our LASID tendencies, such as tribalism and identity. Overall, this feels like a challenge built by a malevolent games master, which is in theory solvable (we simply need to change our consumption of energy sources), but in practice is as hard as possible for humans to solve, given the creatures we are.

In the light of this, there are no guarantees we will solve the issue of climate change in the way we want to – in other words, to limit global warming to 1.5 degrees C (2.7 degrees F) by 2030[598], in order to avoid the increasingly devastating and irreversible effects that will impact the human population and the way we live.

Perhaps our most likely hope is to experience a global crisis that does not cause too much damage but unites the population into demanding immediate, radical action on climate change from politicians. Even this option demands an unnecessary level of suffering, however. In order to avoid these consequences, human beings are going to have to gather not just our technical knowledge but our understanding of how people think and behave as well as our collective will, and apply them in a way we have not done before – to act quickly and decisively as a global tribe to transform our structures and institutions so that they will enable us to lead good lives within the parameters of the planet.

Part 3

How to build a better future

Chapter 18
Why human beings are struggling

In brief – there are a number of reasons why we are struggling to address some of the challenges of the modern world. These include the difficult nature of the challenges, our unrealistic expectations for solving them and certain negative consequences of how we think. A central reason however is that we evolved to live in a very different world to the one we currently live in, and this 'evolutionary mismatch' also makes it harder for us to deal with our modern challenges.

Up to this point, this book has painted a new, and perhaps surprising, picture of the creatures human beings really are. It has also outlined some of the major challenges and expectations we face in the modern world, and why we are struggling to address them. This chapter will aim to pull together the findings from Part 2 and identify some core reasons why we are struggling with the challenges of the modern world. These will include the limitations of how we think and behave, the changed modern environment we now live in and the unrealistic expectations we currently hold for our behaviour as a species.

Identifying these broader reasons why we are struggling will help to reveal the central problem that human beings face – that the institutions, values and structures we have built in the modern world make it difficult for us to flourish, given the LASID creatures we now know we are in our thinking and behaviour: limited, adapted, simplifying, influenced and deceived. This chapter will consider why this is the case, and will pave the way for the final chapters to tackle the bigger task facing us as human beings – how to build a society, institutions and ideas that are actually suitable for the creatures we really are.

Four reasons why we struggle with our modern challenges

1. Our thinking adaptations can have negative flipsides

The first theme that appears regularly in the challenges discussed in Part 2 is the idea that each of the traits in our thinking and behaviour that have evolved to give us some evolutionary advantage (such as simplifying the world or judging strangers) can also have a negative flipside. For example, the *mere exposure effect* explored in Chapter 3, in which familiarity with something enables us to reduce cognitive energy and let down our guard, can also make us more inclined to support or tolerate destructive political ideas when they are repeated to us and become more familiar.

This 'negative flipside effect' sometimes occurs because the particular thinking trait is a simplification, and there are circumstances where it over-simplifies things and leads us into problems when it is too much of a blunt instrument for other tasks. For example, our capacity for stereotyping is a useful tool in helping us process social information and make decisions quickly, but can lead us to misjudge people on an individual basis. The negative flipside of a trait can also occur when it has a negative side-effect, as in when our tendency to conform to group norms is hijacked by people who wish to manipulate the group to achieve their own, negative ends.

In conclusion, this negative flipside effect is simply due to the compromises, simplifications and choices that have been made to the way we think and behave as we have evolved. It is therefore an impediment that we are stuck with in addressing any challenge as human beings, but one that can be partially addressed through each of us exercising greater awareness of our tendencies as human beings, and greater use of our rational System 2 thinking in situations where the flipside effect could occur. As has already been discussed though, greater use of System 2 thinking requires more cognitive effort, and therefore may be difficult for us to achieve all the time. A more effective way to address this issue will be to change the environment surrounding humans – which will be explored in the next chapter.

2. We have not evolved to live in the modern world

As Part 1 showed, human beings have evolved with particular traits of thinking and behaving. We have evolved these traits to enable us to survive and flourish within a specific environment – the one that our ancestors lived in up to around 12,000 years ago, as hunter-gatherers in mobile, small tribes.

The modern world, however, is very different from the one we evolved to live within, and this issue – described by social psychologist William von Hippel as an 'evolutionary mismatch'[599] –

is a key reason why we struggle to deal with a number of our current challenges.

The time that has elapsed since human beings moved away from hunter-gatherer societies is very short in evolutionary terms. In fact, 12,000 years is a miniscule amount of time compared to the seven million years that have elapsed since our ancestors left the rainforest to live on the savannah. This was a lot of time for their minds and behaviour to evolve and adapt to their new environment. Modern humans, by comparison, have had a mere 12,000 years since our societies changed beyond recognition from hunter-gatherer tribes. But just how much have human lives changed in this time?

Life as a hunter-gatherer would have been a nomadic existence, moving around an area of the country in a tribe that existed off the land. Tribes would have consisted of small groups and their members would know everyone within them. Our ancestors would have been living for day-to-day survival and would have had very little knowledge of the people and lands that existed beyond their immediate vicinity. Encounters with strangers would have either represented a potentially major threat (to safety, resources, or in other ways) or an opportunity (for example, to trade with). Duties would have been split within the group, and each person's role allocated according to their relative capability. People would have sought food with as many calories as possible, and when food was found, it would have been distributed among the group. To its individual members, the tribe was everything – their protection, their sustenance and their meaning. The possibility of being dismissed from one's tribe would have essentially represented a death sentence, so members' loyalty to it and desire to cooperate within it would have been strong.

Now contrast this with your life in the modern world. We live in an almost unrecognisably different environment, which makes completely different demands of us as individuals. Below are just a few areas of our lives that have changed, along with the changing psychological demands they place on human beings:

- **Our tribal bonds have changed** – many human beings no longer live in tight, small, singular tribal groups. Our families often provide a close tribe for us for our childhood, but after this point many children leave the family home, commonly dispersing around the country and the world. At the same time, we are members of numerous tribes throughout our lives, from nations to political parties to workplaces, often simultaneously, for different periods of time and with varying levels of affiliation to each. This increased complexity of our tribal world places many more cognitive and behavioural demands upon us.
- **We exist in greater isolation** – despite the fact that we don't think and behave as individuals in the way that many people assume, modern humans live much more individualistic lives than our ancestors. We can exist without living within our close tribes, as the infrastructures and support systems of our countries and economies enable us to survive as individuals. Yet many people face a sense of social isolation as a result of doing this, which can decrease their sense of wellbeing.
- **Our relationships with other people have changed** – our ancestors would have encountered few strangers on a regular basis, and those they did encounter could have represented a substantial threat to life. In the modern world,

we potentially encounter hundreds of strangers each day, many of whom belong to a range of different tribes from us, whether these are nations, races, organisations or social groups, and most of whom may not represent a threat, although we need to be open to this possibility, whilst upholding the modern value of being friendly and non-judgemental to others who are different from us. This collection of challenges can increase our cognitive load.

- **The world is more complex** – the world has become unimaginably more complex than before, with more information, sources of information and diversity of information for us to manage when trying to make sense of the world. This places greater cognitive demands on our minds.

- **There are more communication channels** – the communication channels available to our hunter-gatherer ancestors would have been restricted to their personal interactions with other members of their tribe, and occasionally those of other tribes. In the relatively recent past, the range of media and communication channels that surround us has exploded as our technological knowledge has developed from printed books and newspapers to broadcast radio and television through to digital channels such as the internet and social media. Each of these new channels presents new complexities and demands on our minds, as well as new ways of influencing us and our thinking. Some, such as digital channels, present an entirely new context beyond the physical world in which we (and our minds) have operated until now. We are only starting to discover the new and different ways in which this new context affects us – for example, evidence[600] suggests that people are more likely to share communications containing content about morality in online rather than offline contexts – especially when it has the potential to provoke moral outrage. This suggests human behaviours may differ between the online and offline worlds, so we need to start understanding these differences quickly – as this may have important consequences. For example, the sharing of moral outrage outlined above has been shown to potentially lead to higher levels of group-think and polarisation[601].

- **There are more influences** – the wider range of people, channels and information around us carry a larger number and wider variety of potential influences on us, from deliberate attempts to persuade and manipulate us, including advertising, politics and social media, through to the existence of a wider range of social norms that differ between the various tribes that we belong to at any one time. This increased set of influences places a set of cognitive and psychological pressures on us that simply didn't exist 12,000 years ago.

- **Food availability has increased** – for most people in the modern Western world, there is no longer a survival imperative to find and consume as many calories as possible every day, as global food production and the economic structures we have built around us enable us to access calories with relative ease. In fact, as explored in Chapter 7, we face the opposite challenge – of too many high-calorie but nutritionally poor foods available to us that can lead to us becoming poorly nourished yet consuming too many calories. This obesogenic environment also gives us fewer opportunities for regular physical exercise, unlike the active lives of our distant ancestors.

- **Institutions and infrastructure have grown** – our hunter-gatherer ancestors had no external groups governing them or institutions surrounding them beyond their own small tribe. We are now surrounded by institutions that govern many parts of our lives, including companies, banks, service providers, local councils and governments. Although these institutions sometimes provide valuable benefits that we wouldn't receive from exclusive membership of small tribes – such as electricity supply and a wider variety of food – they can make it harder for us to gain basic goods we would have obtained from tribal living (such as shelter and human connection) and can be complex and opaque, making us feel we have little power or means of influencing the things that happen to us. Just recall how it feels to wait endlessly on the phone for a call centre to answer your call to your bank!

- **Values, beliefs and norms have changed** – not only has the physical context in which we live changed dramatically since our ancestors, our values and expectations have also transformed. For example, we evolved to cooperate with, and trust, members of our own tribe more than those beyond it or whom we didn't know. We developed a sensitivity to difference in others, a capacity to categorise people and to favour people in our in-group. Yet we now live in a world in which we ask people to look beyond their tribes and cooperate and seek peace with each other. We also condemn prejudice and stereotyping, and urge people to understand the individual before making judgement. In western societies we also value the individual and their freedom, whilst seeing conformity as a potential harm. These modern values, and many others, run counter to some of our deepest evolutionary psychology.

Many other important areas of life could be listed that have changed beyond recognition and presented new challenges to us as creatures, including technology, travel and choices – but you get the idea. The context each of us lives in has changed beyond recognition from that of our hunter-gatherer ancestors.

In the face of all of this external change, how much have we changed as creatures? This is an important question, because if we have been able to adapt our thinking and behaviours over the last 12,000 years to deal with this radical shift in our context, then the changes may not necessarily present us with any problems. In reality though, many of our fundamental traits have remained the same – and this is a key cause of some of the challenges we face as human beings in our modern context.

It helps here to draw a distinction between two different types of adaptation that human beings can go through. One is evolutionary, in which small genetic mutations and adaptations in each generation of people either cause them to thrive more than others – and therefore spread among later generations – or fail to be passed on. These sorts of adaptations typically need long periods of time to affect populations, and research bringing together data from both small and larger evolutionary adaptations suggests that it takes around a million years for a significant change to occur and persist in a population[602]. Remember, it took our ancestors over 6 million years to adapt from the ape-like creatures we were to our hunter-gatherer ancestors living around 12,000 years ago.

It is therefore incredibly unlikely that we could have adapted to such a radical change in our environment as that which has taken place over the last 12,000 years, given the incredibly complex and extensive changes that would be required to change our thinking and behaviour to the levels needed to do this. Indeed, the evidence in Part 1 of this book suggests that we still have the same basic makeup as creatures as our ancestors 12,000 years ago.

Human beings are however highly adaptable creatures, and there are other ways we can adjust to our changing environments beyond genetic evolutionary adaptation, through factors such as the plasticity we have evolved within the human brain, as well as cultural adaptations. We have therefore not remained static during this period – in fact we have adapted with remarkable skill to some of the changes in our environments that have occurred, even within very quick timescales.

One example of how our brains can adapt in remarkable ways is the *Flynn effect*, which refers to the substantial and long-term increase in intelligence test scores that was found across the world during the 20th century. For example, in Britain, children's average scores in the Raven's Progressive Matrices IQ test rose 14 points between 1942 and 2008[603]. An individual's IQ rating is based on their score in relation to the average score of other people of a similar age, with a score of 100 being average performance. This has therefore been a significant rise over time. James Flynn, the academic after whom this phenomenon was named, argued that the key reason for this increase in IQ levels was not the improvements in nutrition people consumed over this period[604], but instead a series of adaptations people's brains made in response to the changes in their environment that occurred over this period, as it became more cognitively challenging, possibly including the increased cognitive complexity of jobs and people's exposure to new technological devices that increased the demands on their cognitive capacities. Essentially our brains adapted to become better at dealing with the new problems and challenges they encountered in the world.

Despite our adaptability, we still think and behave within many of the parameters and biases that we've had for hundreds of thousands of years, the ones we evolved to live a simple, tribal, hunter-gatherer life – such as favouring members of our in-group, and all the other traits discussed in Part 1. Adaptations can be fast, but evolutionary change can be slow. We remain the basic creatures we evolved to be before we left our hunter-gatherer lifestyles 12,000 years ago and began lives based on agriculture, which is where the main changes in our modern environment originated from.

This radical change of environment is one of the reasons why human beings struggle with some of the challenges and expectations we face in the modern world. Essentially the brains we have evolved for one environment and set of challenges are struggling to deal with the radically different challenges, expectations and demands of our comparatively new, modern environment. For example, our tendency to conform with the views of our in-group was evolutionarily adaptive for our ancestors as it aided co-operation and helped to prevent them from being excluded from the small hunter-gatherer tribes they lived in. In certain situations in the modern world however this can cause us problems – for example, when we get trapped in echo chambers on social media, only able to access and tolerate the views of people we agree with, which can lead us to inaccurate views of the world and to greater polarisation and hostility between people.

Evidence suggests that our environment isn't just much more *complex* than the one we evolved to live within – elements of it are also actively *hostile* towards human flourishing. For example, as we saw in Chapter 11, we allow our sources of information in the media to spread inaccurate and biased information, which can lead us to make incorrect judgements or activate aggressive tribal behaviours in us. We have also built structures and ideas that are not focused on human flourishing, but instead seek to exploit our vulnerabilities in thinking and behaviour as LASID creatures for profit, power or other motives. For example, Chapter 7 showed how junk food companies target children with advertising and cartoon characters – this is not to make their lives better, but to make a profit from an audience that is highly influenceable (and therefore vulnerable). This particular structural factor can lead to obesity, suffering and early death for millions of people.

In conclusion, there is a mismatch between our evolved psychology as creatures and the modern world we find ourselves in.

3. The nature of our challenges

Aside from our nature as creatures and its mismatch with our modern environment, there are also factors relating to the challenges human beings currently face that can make them hard for us to address.

First, there is the simple fact that some of them may be very difficult – or even impossible – to solve. Take climate change as an example. Even if there were no evolutionary mismatch between our psychological makeup and this modern challenge, it may still be too big a challenge for human beings to address, as we remain relatively powerless to prevent or influence many major environmental events – whether these are substantial climatic changes, earthquakes or the collision of asteroids into our planet. We have the ability to adapt relatively quickly to the consequences of such events or prepare ourselves for their occurrence – for example, building cities away from tectonic fault lines – but there is little we can currently do to prevent some of these events in the first place.

Another issue is that some of the challenges and expectations we have are arbitrary, and essentially made up by us. For example, the desire to end specific social problems such as conflict, prejudice and inequality is based on a particular view of the world – that these things are wrong and undesirable. People differ in their attitudes to these issues however, and these are influenced by our personal beliefs, political views and other factors. For example, some people (of a right-wing disposition) may feel that economic inequality is not something to be eliminated, but is instead the natural order of things, and that people who work harder should benefit from this, without having to share their assets with those who have less. Others (of a more left wing, redistributionist position) may strongly believe that assets should be shared between people, ranging from the belief that everyone should have the resources to address their most basic needs (such as food, water, shelter and safety) through to the idea that we should share assets more in order to give everyone more equal opportunities to flourish – including education, health care and other benefits. These values exist on a spectrum and there is often no obvious place to draw the line as to what is the 'right' answer. Different groups in society are usually pushing up against each other as they compete to achieve their differing, often conflicting, views of how the world should be. The nature of our challenges is therefore slippery and complex, and the moral foundations to some of them are not always solid.

It is not only the challenges themselves that are sometimes opaque – there also might be many different, and potentially conflicting, ways we might achieve them. For example, even if we agree that economic inequality needs to be addressed, should it be achieved through increasing taxes to redistribute wealth among people, or should we instead reduce taxes and encourage people to build their own wealth?

The lesson from this is not that we should stop having values or seeking the world we want, but we need to recognise the arbitrary nature of even our most cherished values, and the fact that this creates real complications when attempting to seek agreement between large populations of people as to what sort of world we want to work towards. As a result, we need to accept that the process of building a better world and addressing our challenges and expectations can never be complete, or built on entirely solid foundations – instead it is a process of long-term negotiation and adjustment, as our values (and therefore challenges and expectations) can shift and change over time and according to many factors such as social norms and environmental circumstances. The search for a better world therefore needs long-term commitment and a dose of realism from those who are committed to it, whatever version of a 'better world' they are seeking. The next chapter will explore this point in more detail as it tries to build a vision of a 'good society' to steer human beings and our environment towards.

Our challenges and expectations can also change over time, due to a range of factors including the arbitrary nature of the values we are seeking as noted above, changes in technology and changes to our environment. An example of the latter is the challenge of global environmental damage, including climate change. The idea that human beings are having an impact on the global environment and that this is an urgent issue did not become a mainstream topic until the mid-to-late 20th century, even though various industrialised countries had been attempting to tackle the problem of pollution since the middle of the 19th century. Global institutions that could bring countries together to cooperatively tackle global issues like this (such as the United Nations (UN)) simply didn't exist until after the First World War, with the advent of the UN's predecessor, the League of Nations. The Economic and Social Council on 29 May 1968 was the first time the UN paid serious attention to the issue of our global environmental impact[605]. The First Earth Summit was held in 1972, setting out principles for preserving the human environment, and as more attention turned to this issue, more money and technological innovation was invested in monitoring our environment and atmosphere. Pollution and damage to the ozone layer became key concerns in the 1980s, but climate change only became seen as a serious and urgent issue by international organisations like the UN in the late 1980's. This story demonstrates how other factors, in this case changes in globalisation, technology and global events, can also have an impact on the emergence of, and capacity to deal with, a human challenge.

A final aspect of the nature of the challenges we face that can cause us problems is the fact that some can be internally contradictory, and can conflict with each other. For example, humanity can face difficulties in addressing the challenge to reduce or end conflict and violence when it faces an existential threat, such as that presented by Nazi Germany in 1939. Should we engage in conflict and violence in the short term to prevent a greater degree of prejudice, violence and suffering in the longer term? Like the nature of our values on which some of our challenges are based, these questions are complex and abstract, and often without clear, simple answers, which can cause us to struggle more with the challenges themselves.

In conclusion, various aspects of the expectations and challenges we face can make them difficult in their own right for human beings to address.

4. We are confused and inconsistent in our expectations

A final reason why we are struggling to address our challenges and expectations as human beings is that some of these goals can be seen as inconsistent and inaccurate in the first place.

One simple reason for this is a point mentioned at the start of the book – we generally have an inaccurate view of how humans think and behave. We think we are more rational and less limited in our thought and more solidly individualist in our thinking and behaviour than we actually are. Based on this inaccurate view of human beings, we might think that people should be able to cooperate to solve issues such as climate change, or just need to read the right books and absorb the right information in order to avoid falling for conspiracy theories. And, if they fail to achieve these goals, we might be inclined to judge people (individually or as a species) as evil, bad, or just plain stupid.

The 'evolutionary mismatch' we have with the modern world suggests, however, that there is no reason why we *should* be able to resolve some of the challenges we currently face, if we are simply not psychologically equipped to do so within the hostile environment we live in. With a more accurate view of human beings as LASID creatures, we can see that some of our expectations, including ending prejudice completely and tackling climate change quickly enough are incredibly challenging, and may need re-formulating, as some the chapters in Part 2 attempted to do. For example, if we define prejudice as simply the tendency to pre-judge people based on the immediate things we see, hear, smell or know about them, then it could be argued that we can't eliminate prejudice entirely as pre-judging is what human beings are built to do. We can however build values, institutions and societies that help people to limit the effects that these tendencies of thought have on their behaviour, so that we don't behave in a prejudiced way, even if we may instinctively think like this sometimes. A controversial thought perhaps, but this may be 'the best we can do', given the creatures we really are. So, we need to adjust our expectations of ourselves and our challenges, to frame them in a realistic and consistent way that considers the LASID creatures we really are.

As the chapters in Part 2 have shown, to achieve even these revised aims in a consistent way will be a great challenge to human beings and will demand a significant rethink of the values, institutions and societies that surround us.

Summary – why we are struggling in the modern world

There is a range of reasons why we are struggling to meet the challenges and expectations set out in Part 2, including the nature of some of the challenges themselves and the inaccurate expectations we have about our ability to address them. A central reason, however, and one that we have so far failed to adequately understand or address as a society, is that our LASID thinking and behaviour have not evolved to live in the modern world we have created or to address the specific challenges we face. This represents the central problem facing us as human beings, and extends beyond the limited set of specific challenges and expectations set out in this book so far.

Human minds evolved to live in the type of hunter-gatherer societies that people lived in for the majority of the lifespan of our species, up to about 12,000 years ago, when we started to live in agricultural societies – not the modern world we live in, which has changed out of all recognition from that previous world, and in such a short time frame that we have not adapted to deal with it. As a result, we are struggling to adapt to the modern world that we have built and the challenges we face within it.

We are the creators of much of the modern world, so we can change it. Indeed, there is an urgent need to do so, as a significant proportion of human beings are suffering unnecessarily, and our continued existence as a species is under threat. The remainder of this book will explore where we can go from here. It will ask how we can address our central challenge – to build a world fit for the

LASID creatures we actually are. The next chapter will begin by considering what we can do to bridge the gap between LASID human beings and the world we live within.

Chapter 19
Why we need scaffolding

In brief – to address the challenges we face and reduce the level of mismatch between human beings and our modern environment, we need to change the context around us, including our structures, ideas and institutions, as it is currently hostile to human flourishing. To do this, we need to rethink our view of freedom, in order to make it relevant to us as LASID creatures. We also need to build scaffolding around us in various areas of our lives to protect our vulnerabilities as LASID creatures and support us in being the self-determined, co-operative creatures we can be.

To enable human beings to address the challenges we face and flourish more generally, we need to change the world around us to better fit the LASID creatures we are. We cannot, at this point, fundamentally change how human beings think and behave, without waiting for evolution to run its lengthy course over millions of years. In theory, there are several ways we could get people to change their thinking and behaviour in a short time without waiting for evolution to catch up. One is to change the context in which they live – and this could take many forms. In the case of promoting healthy eating, it could include taxing or banning unhealthy foods, educating people about the need to eat healthily and giving everyone the resources to ensure they have access to healthy food.

Other possibilities might not seem to require changing the context human beings live within, such as getting people to do more rational, System 2 thinking. For example, if you regard yourself as a member of the 'Democrat' political tribe and meet someone at a social event who you know to be from a different political tribe, rather than immediately judging them as a particular type of person or preparing yourself to attack their political views (as your System 1 thinking would be automatically leading you to do), you could activate your System 2 thinking and rationally decide to not judge them but get to know them and listen to their opinions. As Part 1 showed, using our System 2 thinking like this can come at a cost of energy and effort, as well as diverting our focus away from other tasks, but it nevertheless has potential as a way of helping us to deal with some of the challenges we face – in this case, prejudice and interpersonal conflict.

Another way to change people's thinking and behaviour could be to delegate or 'outsource' some of their System 1 thinking to other places that could do it in a more reliable and objective way, as philosopher Joseph Heath puts it, in a way that our System 2 thinking would approve of, if it had the time and capacity to think about it[606]. For example, if you are looking to eat healthily and not consume too many calories, you could outsource your food shopping to an app that chooses your menus and snacks for the week within your expenditure budget, cooking time and nutritional and calorie requirements, and delivers only the food you need for these.

Despite initial appearances however, both of these examples of changes in our thinking and behaviour require changes to be made to our context in order for them to happen. The first example requires people to receive the education needed to understand how different aspects of our thinking work and drive our behaviours, as well as to receive the cultural messages that controlling our behaviour like this is desirable, as prejudicial behaviour and conflict is undesirable. The second example requires us to build institutions and technologies to support the delegation of certain forms of System 1 thinking. Changing the context that surrounds us is therefore central to our ability to adapt.

The structures around us

Our context can be described as every aspect of the environment we live within – both immediate factors affecting us, and distant and abstract influences. It includes natural features such as our climate, landscape, predators and availability of resources. It also includes the type and quality of our relationships with others, such as the tribes we are part of, our interpersonal relationships and the power we hold or others hold over us. Less immediate factors can include the norms of the groups and societies we are members of, the institutions that serve us, including education, health care and commercial, and the political, legal and institutional systems we live within.

The latter, less immediate factors can be described as 'structures'. These are things that we don't have total or immediate control over as individuals but which set parameters for our lives when living in large, complex populations. Unlike our hunter-gatherer ancestors, we live in a world in which our relationship with most aspects of our context is mediated by the structures around us. This even applies to some of our natural contextual factors like our availability of resources – which, in hunter-gatherer times would have been under our control and dictated by what food sources we could find in our local environment, but which now is mediated by factors such as property ownership laws, employment contracts, bank agreements and sometimes state benefit policies.

The most effective way of changing the context we live in now is therefore to change these structures around us. Each chapter in Part 2 explored a number of these structures and how they could be changed for particular issues, and below is a small selection of key examples:

- **Social** – the groups we are part of and the norms, expectations and behaviours they have. These might include families, friendship groups, sports clubs and religions.
- **Political** – the political systems that govern us. These include how we are governed (locally, nationally and internationally), how we have a say in how society is run, how we are represented (both locally and internationally), how we are taxed and how this money is spent.
- **Economic** – the economic systems that overarch us. These include how we exchange services and goods and how we distribute wealth.
- **Legal** – the rules and parameters that we live within.
- **Institutional** – the institutions (entities with their own rules containing collections of people) that surround us, including workplaces, education, social security, health care, companies and service providers.
- **Media** – the channels through which we send and receive communications and information. These include television, radio, internet, social media, books and newspapers.
- **Cultural** – the values, ideas, traditions and beliefs that inform our thinking and behaviour.

The structures above are far more complicated than any our hunter-gatherer ancestors had to deal with. They are also fundamentally important to our thinking and behaviour in large groups – partly because they surround and govern our lives, and also because each carries its own rules, assumptions, expectations and values that mould how each of us thinks and behaves as a LASID human being. Yet many of these underlying values and their effects are hidden from those of us at the receiving end of them. Although we can't spend every day of our lives trying to unravel and understand what these underlying ideas and effects are, it pays to be aware of at least some of them and the effects they have on our thinking and behaviour.

Part 2 of this book demonstrated how certain structures play a fundamental role in moulding our thinking and behaviour on particular issues. Below are some further illustrative examples of how structures can carry certain assumptions and effects. In some cases, we are affected simply by the nature of the structures themselves. For example, prejudice and conflict is fuelled among human beings by the fact that our global political landscape is divided into individual nations. Our national boundaries and identities were formed hundreds or thousands of years before we discovered that human beings are LASID creatures, yet, now that we have discovered this, we can see that the splitting of the world into individual nations essentially creates a global tapestry of in-groups, each competing with the other for the world's resources. We are each born into one of these in-groups (i.e. nations), taught its origin story (by the group itself) and raised within the identity and values of that group. For much of the time, the tensions between these in-groups do not result in widespread wars or death, but sometimes they do, and more often cooperation between them can be hampered or conflicts between elements of their populations can be provoked by in-group biases, such as nationalism.

In many cases, we are affected by the assumptions and content of a particular structure. At the simplest level, this can be illustrated by the idea that the assumptions behind a government's education policy influence not only what our children will learn but also the attitudes they may take towards particular issues. Human beings in their childhood and youth are most susceptible to outside influences[607]. Schools in countries that aim to promote racial diversity and understanding in their cultures, their behavioural expectations of pupils and in the topics and approaches they take to teaching them will eventually produce a set of adults with a different set of perspectives and beliefs than those that choose not to do this, or that seek to promote racial division. As an extreme example of this, the Nazis sought to indoctrinate German children with anti-Semitic beliefs through the education system, as well as through the Hitler Youth and wider propaganda that was aimed at the whole population. Studies[608] suggest that this indoctrination programme proved successful – Germans who grew up under the Nazis are significantly more anti-Semitic than those who grew up before or after that period.

To summarise – the very existence of the structures around us has an effect on us as LASID creatures, and they also influence our thinking and behaviour through the assumptions and values that underpin the way they operate – whether we realise this or not.

Our hostile world

Chapter 18 showed how the environment human beings live in has changed immeasurably since our hunter-gatherer ancestors shifted to agricultural societies around 12,000 years ago. This environment has now become hostile to us.

Some of the changes that have occurred in our world over this period have done so in a natural and unplanned way in response to human behaviour – such as the enormous increase in population growth. This could simply be seen as a natural response among a population of creatures to greater availability of food, water and other basic resources due to technological advances and changed living arrangements. Other changes to our world have however taken place as a result of more deliberate decisions and planning from human beings, including the development of the particular economic system that surrounds us, the ways we organise our political systems and the level of regulation we allow in various areas of people's lives in order to keep them safe.

The hostile nature of our environment for human beings is therefore partially one that we have created ourselves, in which some of the structures and ideas that surround us are not actually working to serve us or our needs, but instead are working against us. Two central explanations can be identified for how this has happened, which are compatible and not mutually exclusive. The first is that these ideas and structures were set up with the aim of improving human flourishing but under a faulty idea of how people think and behave, which led to structures being designed or operated in ways that have negative consequences for human beings. It is only in recent decades that we have discovered the inaccuracy of the Enlightenment view of human beings as primarily rational creatures, and very few people even now have a reasonable understanding of our LASID nature as creatures, so it is likely that many structures that surround us will be based on the older, inaccurate view of human beings. For example, we focus the education of children primarily on academic subjects such as language, mathematics and science, without anywhere near enough attention on helping them understand themselves as creatures and develop the skills needed to manage their minds and behaviours throughout life, such as critical thinking and protecting oneself from external social and informational influences.

The second explanation is that some structures simply weren't built with human flourishing in mind in the first place, and instead focused on other aims, such as maximising financial profits in order to build economic growth. For example, the idea of advertising, which seeks to encourage people to consume as much as possible in order to maximise corporate profits, and achieving this by exploiting human cognitive biases and vulnerabilities. This often manipulates people into decisions and behaviours they would not have chosen otherwise, and can result in negative consequences for them, including eating unhealthy foods that cause obesity or leading people to spend more money than they have on a credit card, due to their desire for material goods. Philosophy Professor Joseph Heath argues that innovations like this that exploit people's cognitive biases have a better chance of surviving and being reproduced than those that do not[609] – which is a concerning state of affairs for human beings.

If we are to change the context in which human beings live, we therefore need to challenge and adjust these structures, as well as the things we prioritise in human society. Such changes represent major, transformative and sensitive political decisions so we need to approach them with great care.

How much scaffolding should we build?

As we consider how to use structures to help people in their thinking and behaviour, we start to encounter some difficult political issues, such as how far to go in regulating these structures and moulding human behaviour. It may be the case that human beings are suffering and failing to address key challenges because the world isn't fit for the LASID creatures we are, but why should we have our freedoms taken away to enable this to happen? Should we simply ban things that might be problematic for us as LASID creatures – including unhealthy food, fake news and activities that have a high environmental impact such as flying? Or is there a way we can strike a balance between addressing our challenges in the modern world and protecting our important freedoms as human beings?

Also, which structures do we need to change, and how far should we go within each? Are some issues more important than others? The next couple of chapters will consider some of these questions and start to pull together a picture of what a world fit for LASID creatures might look like.

Defining freedom

Freedom is one of the most emotive and evocative words in Western society. It is at the centre of the constitutions of major liberal democracies, from France to the USA. Millions of people have fought and died for the idea of freedom, and it is frequently used by politicians and influencers to stir crowds and build passions – from the use of the slogan 'Liberté, égalité, fraternité' in the French Revolution through to President Franklin Roosevelt's 'Four Freedoms' speech in 1941 making the case for greater American involvement in the Second World War[610].

But what does it actually mean? What is this thing we are fighting for? The idea of individual freedom as we know it today was born in the Enlightenment. At that time, thinkers such as the French philosopher Voltaire sought to release human beings from the repressive influence of religion, which had dominated Western thought for hundreds of years, and which subjugated human beings as servants of a god. The Enlightenment espoused the ideas of individual freedom, individualism and rationality.

The Enlightenment can be seen as a vital moment of emancipation for human beings, freeing us from the shackles of ignorance, giving us a sense of our enormous potential and sparking 300 years of unprecedented change in the human situation. It can also, however, be seen as a moment that spawned the inaccurate view of human beings as entirely rational creatures that many people still hold today, and that Part 1 of this book sought to replace. This view of human beings led in turn to a particular view of human freedom that is also inaccurate, but that many people still hold today.

In cultures like the UK or US in which freedom is one of the dominant values, challenging our basic definition of it could be something close to heresy, so it needs to be explored with care. The Cambridge English Dictionary broadly defines freedom as the ability to do, say or think what you want, without being controlled or limited by others[611].

Freedom is not one single, definitive idea however. It is a malleable concept, and can be used to influence people towards a particular viewpoint. For example, a right-wing politician might suggest that the freedoms of people in their country are under threat from immigrants. This can trigger a sense of anger, fear and resentment in citizens without them even considering what is meant by this use of the word 'freedom' — essentially it is just a way of stoking underlying prejudices of out-groups. This example also illustrates the idea that there are different types of freedoms and they belong to different people. Looking objectively at this example, we might ask whether the freedoms allegedly being sacrificed by the population of this country to admit immigrants are greater and more important than those that the potential immigrants are losing by not immigrating to this country. Indeed, politics is often a question of evaluating and making a prioritisation between people's competing claims to freedom or the loss of it.

Much of politics over recent centuries in Western democratic societies can be seen as an attempt to find a balance between the need to protect people's freedom (because this matters to us as a principle) and the need to shape people's lives towards specific goals (which can vary depending on who's in charge, from building a fair, equal and sustainable society through to building an Ayrian super race). As far back as 1651, Thomas Hobbes argued in his classic book

Leviathan[612] that people's lives without a state around them would be 'nasty, brutish and short'. Since this point, there has been a jostling for position between those who want minimal state interference and those who see a more collective, less individualistic society as critical for our flourishing as creatures.

So how much should we interfere in people's lives to help them flourish? In reality there is no 'right' answer to this question, and different people will have different positions on a spectrum of possible answers. The levels of freedom we might allow depend on how much we value freedom, how much we care about the other goals, and many other factors, including our political orientation. It is also potentially a very complex question, involving an almost limitless number of variables to consider and the possibility of different goals demanding different levels of sacrifice of freedom. Freedom does seem important to us as individual human beings though, as it enables us to have a degree of control over our lives and be free from unreasonable interference – with the former improving our well-being and the latter sometimes causing us to suffer – sometimes greatly.

In reality, most of us are happy for our freedom to be limited to a certain extent. Most of us are willing to pay taxes to the state so that we have roads that we can drive on, and many people are happy to pay taxes in order to have much more than this – including education, health care and other key services. Many of us are also happy for the state to decide how our children should be educated. Most of us are also happy to have basic laws, including those that stop other people from killing us or stealing our property. So, we don't want total, unfettered freedom – this would be a world without any rules – but we are sensitive about how much of our freedom we want to give up.

We are also willing to give up more freedom on certain issues at certain times as they matter more to us or are more urgent. These can also change over time – for example, during the COVID-19 crisis the citizens of most countries around the world were willing to give up their most basic freedoms, including being able to leave the house. This was in part because they recognised the issue as being important enough to make this sacrifice for, and because they expected this suspension of freedom to only last for a limited period of time.

Our view of humans influences our views on freedom

Our conception of which freedoms matter and what we should do to protect them is heavily dependent on how we see people as creatures – and this is a critical point in this book. If you believe human beings to be rational creatures, this will influence your view of the political, economic and other conditions that are needed to give people the freedoms that matter. Daniel Kahneman[613] argued that a belief in human rationality provides a foundation for a libertarian approach to politics. This runs roughly as follows. If you take the Enlightenment view that people are rational, this may lead you in turn to believe that people have the fundamental ability to be free and think for themselves. What prevents them from achieving this freedom is the interference of external structures (such as the state) in their lives. Under this libertarian viewpoint, the aim of public policy should therefore be to limit these structures as much as possible to their bare bones, so that people can exercise their freedom and choose how they wish to live, as long as it doesn't harm others.

Libertarianism may sound like a reasonably extreme political position, but it is fairly representative of the neoliberal economic ideas that have dominated the Western world since the late 1970s. When this book has discussed the modern world, it has essentially been discussing (to a greater or lesser degree) states that reflect this view. Unfortunately, this libertarian viewpoint is based on a completely incorrect view of human beings as rational creatures. As Part 1 demonstrated, we are not these creatures – we are LASID. As a result, when structures like the economic system around us are set up with a faulty view of humans they are unlikely to make us thrive, and may actually have the opposite effect.

Some examples of this in practice have already been explored in this book. We choose not to extensively regulate social media platforms, which leads to people being pulled into conspiracy theories, extremist politics and political polarisation. We are unwilling to put higher taxes or other disincentives on unhealthy foods, contributing to the growing wave of obesity around the world. This is the case even though when regulation has been carried out at a small level it has been shown to work, such as in the 'sugar tax' announced by the UK government in 2017, which resulted in manufacturers reducing the total sugar sold in soft drinks between 2015 and 2019 by over 35%. So, the evidence has been there in front of our eyes, but we have ignored it. At the same time as all of this, we are willing to allow activities that use behavioural science to *encourage* and influence people to engage in the very activities we want them to stop – such as the continuing role of advertising in influencing people to eat junk food, fly more and consume more.

The incorrect assumption connecting each of these examples is that humans are rational creatures, can make clear, objective decisions and will therefore be able to defend their minds and behaviour against anything that's thrown at them – whether it's the influence of advertising, the power of social media, or the financial incentives of low-cost air travel against more sustainable forms of transport. According to this account, and the views of many people in the modern world, if people don't do this, they're either weak, lazy or evil.

As this book has shown however, this is simply not the case. As LASID creatures, we are not always in control of how we react to these contextual factors, and cannot defend our minds and behaviour against them, or many of the other challenges we are routinely expected to cope with in the modern world. Is it any surprise we are struggling to live in the modern world when it fails to recognize the creatures we are, is geared for creatures with completely different mental and behavioural capabilities than us, and which is often directed at goals (such as economic growth) other than human safety and flourishing within the one natural world we are part of?

An inaccurate view of how human beings think and behave therefore brings an inaccurate view of what freedoms matter to them. This has major consequences when deciding how to build our societies and how to strike the political balance between protecting people's freedom and pursuing other goals. The decision in modern Western societies like the UK and US to follow the libertarian approach, strip back the structures around us and fail to regulate various aspects of our lives – from communications to economic redistribution – is therefore not a neutral one that protects our freedom from outside interference. It may be *aimed* at protecting our freedom, but as we are LASID rather than rational creatures, it mistakes what freedoms we need, and therefore fails to achieve them. Instead, it can have serious negative consequences for us and can actually limit our freedom in important ways, including exposing us to structures that make it difficult for us to exercise rational thought, making us slaves to our System 1 instincts (such as unregulated social media channels that drive us towards identity groups that could polarise us), and allowing our mental vulnerabilities to be exploited by those in power (for example, allowing advertisers to create needs and wants in us that we didn't have before, by using knowledge of how we think and behave). In other words, the absence of regulatory structures and scaffolding around us is not a neutral decision – it is a structure in itself – and one with negative consequences for LASID human beings.

It is therefore clear that we need to regulate human behaviour more than we thought, in order to provide the freedoms that matter to us – even though this will challenge some people's traditional (but mistaken) views of freedom.

A new definition of freedom

We therefore need to use our new, more accurate view of human beings as LASID creatures to help us identify the freedoms that actually matter to us. The points below will briefly explore this, and the next two chapters will start to identify some of the steps we can take to change our context to deliver these freedoms.

The aim of the structural recommendations outlined in the final chapter of this book are largely to prevent harm to human beings rather than to attempt to promote particular details of what a good life consists of, as this is a subjective matter, and one of our most important freedoms may be to build the lives we want, as long as they do not harm others. It can therefore be argued that the approach of this book is to seek minimal regulation of human freedoms where possible, despite the substantial changes to our environment that will be recommended in the final chapter, which are largely due to our reconception of human beings as LASID creatures and the freedoms that matter as a result.

We should also not throw the baby out with the bathwater. Many of the freedoms that we protect today are important and valid – such as our ability to choose the lives we want. We need to identify any additional freedoms that are not currently being considered in the structures that surround us, or freedoms that existing structures are taking away from us, so that we can seek to build them in. These will largely be consequences of the gaps between our current, inaccurate view of humans as rational creatures and our new view of humans as LASID creatures.

These principles lead us to a different definition of freedom from that of the Enlightenment – one that is based on a more realistic view of us as LASID in our thinking and behaviour. This book suggests that the freedom that matters to LASID creatures, and the one we should seek, is *the ability to live lives that are as self-aware, rational and self-determined as possible.* Building a society that gives us this freedom will require us to make changes to the structures around us to ensure they don't manipulate our psychological and behavioural vulnerabilities as LASID creatures, whilst supporting us in promoting our capacity for self-determination, including making better judgements and decisions.

The importance of scaffolding

To promote our freedom as LASID creatures, we therefore need more support from the structures around us, not less. We also need to set up structures that recognise the LASID creatures we really are and change some of the incorrect assumptions that govern our structures – for example, the assumption behind our economic system that human beings are fully rational rather than LASID in their thinking and behaviour.

We can view these supportive structures not as regulation or threats to our freedom, but as 'scaffolding' around human beings that protects us and supports us to use our LASID thinking and behavioural traits more effectively, rather than being surrounded by structures that neglect or exploit them. This is about changing our context – our mental and behavioural environment – to make the most of our potential for self-determination as individual creatures, whilst recognising the fact that we are interdependent. The aim is to set up the conditions for this interdependence to function more effectively, given the LASID creatures we are.

Human beings need this scaffolding (in social, institutional, ideological and other forms) around us in all areas of our lives to protect rather than exploit our vulnerabilities and help us build the peaceful, sustainable lives we want. Essentially, we need it to help us fill the gap between the creatures we are and those we want to be – for example, being better at cooperation outside our immediate in-group if we are to stop climate change, or better at not making biased judgements of others if we are not to reduce prejudice.

Another way of viewing this scaffolding, suggested by Joseph Heath, is that it protects us from our own irrationality[614].

Every political system moves people towards certain default behaviours[615]; as noted earlier, even one with no regulations is not neutral in the behaviours it promotes. We should therefore arrange the systems and scaffolding around us to encourage the positive behavioural goals we want. This does not mean we are trying to get people to repress their 'natural instincts'. As this book has shown, we have lots of different instincts that can take us down different paths of behaviour, and the aim of this scaffolding is to create an environment that lets certain instincts express themselves above others. In other words, it means that we are constructing the choice architecture surrounding us to enable our traits and biases, and all other aspects of our LASID nature, to work for us rather than against us. Environmental fixes like this have been described as 'kluges'[616] – where we can't change something about how human beings think or behave, we can change our environment to enhance our capacities. This could mean something as simple as writing an idea down on paper so we can remember it more effectively, or only serving healthy food in schools in order to ensure children eat healthily.

To see the importance of scaffolding in enhancing human beings and making human life better, one only has to consider its role in human achievement through history. Many contemporary writers on popular psychology rightly celebrate the importance of cooperation among human beings, viewing it as one of, if not the, most important contributors to our growth and technological advancement as a species. This may be a reasonable assertion, but cooperation itself would not be possible without scaffolding around human beings – at least, not beyond the modest scale of the small tribe. As noted earlier, Dunbar's number[617] suggests there is a maximum number of people that one person can maintain social relationships with. This number has been proposed as 150, but regardless of the exact size it suggests that we can build trusting relationships with smaller tribes of people, but that cooperation among greater numbers of people than this requires some form of scaffolding to hold it together. This might take the form of legal rules, political systems or even stories that bind otherwise disparate individuals together. For example, our remarkable peaceful coexistence as creatures is achieved through scaffolding such as laws, institutions and beliefs that tell us how we should behave and provide justice for transgressors. Similarly, the US moon landing in 1969 was a remarkable cooperative venture that demanded scaffolding binding thousands of people, including a common aim, shared beliefs and funding. It also required another critical type of human scaffolding – learning. Our ability to survive as individuals or to make technological advances is largely due to the fact that there is scaffolding in place of previous knowledge that other human beings have gained, as well as places to store it and ways for us to access it. Even our individual creative acts require learning, tradition, culture and equipment – all forms of scaffolding. It therefore does not feel like such an exaggeration to say that almost anything human beings achieve that we value, whether as individuals or groups, is dependent upon having some kind of scaffolding around us.

So scaffolding matters, and if we continue to fail to provide the scaffolding that human beings need, we will continue to struggle as a species to both meet our challenges and cope with life in the modern world, which is only set to become more challenging in the coming decades with the advent of AI, the deepening climate crisis and other factors.

The next chapters will explore what structural changes we should make to build the scaffolding human beings need. We will need many forms of scaffolding, at both large and small scales, and the recommendations in this book will only be able to provide a limited selection of large-scale ideas. There are however many modest, small-scale pieces of scaffolding that can be applied as part of the bigger picture – such as the following example, which could help us circumvent our System 1 tendencies for bias or limited thinking, in order to use this thinking capacity in a more objective way. Many employers now conduct 'blind' shortlisting of interview candidates, in which people's names, ages, ethnic origins and any other information that is irrelevant to their ability to do the job but which might bias a recruiter's view of their ability to do the job is hidden from the recruiter during the shortlisting process of candidates for interviews. This enables the recruiter to focus their thinking capacity on selecting the candidates best suited for the actual role based on relevant variables, rather than irrelevant ones. In this particular example, it also means that human biases are less likely to lead to prejudice and unfair outcomes.

Summary

To conclude this chapter, the structures that surround us, and the assumptions they embody, matter. They have an impact on our thinking and behaviour as LASID creatures, as well as the quality of our experience of life.

In the modern world, the structures that surround us have been built on an incorrect view of human beings as rational calculating machines, and this has resulted in the building of structures that leave us vulnerable to manipulation and unable to exercise our capacities as self-determined creatures. It has also resulted in an incorrect view of what human freedom means, and which freedoms really matter to humans – leading us to be less free.

Given the LASID creatures we are, we need to build scaffolding around us in various areas of our lives to protect our vulnerabilities and support us in being the self-determined, co-operative creatures we can be. The next chapter will explore what a world fit for the LASID creatures we really are might look like.

Chapter 20
What sort of world should we seek?

In brief – we need to develop a new aim for human society, but doing so is fraught with danger as such goals are just arbitrary ideas and can turn into dogmas that cause suffering and death. Our aim should be for 'human flourishing within the natural world we are part of', but we must ensure this goal is subject to ongoing review and challenge rather than hardening into dogma. This aim can be achieved through giving people the basic resources they need, creating a psychologically healthy world that supports people to make best use of their capacities whilst protecting their mental and behavioural vulnerabilities, and ensuring that everything takes place within the natural parameters we live in.

This chapter explores what sort of mental and behavioural environment we should build around us as LASID creatures in order to build a world fit for humans. It will discuss the arbitrary nature of any goals to change the world and why this should give human beings pause for reflection about the goals we're seeking, even when people think they have the most positive and benign aims in mind. It will also consider what overall goal we should set for human society, and the core principles this should include. On the way, it will explore ideas such as what we mean by human flourishing and will challenge human beings to set goals that don't ask too much of humanity and are therefore more difficult to use to harm people later down the line. It will close with a new aim for human society, which will be used in the final chapter to set out some specific, practical ideas as to how to build our environment to give us the scaffolding we need to flourish as a species.

What should we consider when developing our aims?

We have an endless set of choices as to the goals we wish to set for human society. We could choose 'a world in which humans reign supreme', 'a world in which effort is rewarded' or 'a world in which everyone has an equal chance'. Each of these goals is arbitrary and essentially made up. Even the most seemingly sensible and benign aims for how our lives and the world should be – indeed, anything involving the word 'should' – are ultimately arbitrary and open to refutation by anyone who doesn't like them.

Although there is objectively no goal that is the 'right' one, over the years, many philosophers, religious leaders and politicians have tried to convince populations that their particular vision of how society should be *is* the right one. With the help of the machinery of power and the LASID thinking and behaviour of human populations, they have sometimes succeeded in doing this – often with terrible consequences, such as in Stalin's communist Soviet Union or Hitler's Nazi regime. The danger is therefore that goals for society can be turned into dogma by people with power or bad intentions – and this is often because people lose sight of the fact that they are all arbitrary.

Despite the arbitrary nature of any goals, human beings have to set some if we want to improve or change the world in some way. Otherwise, the only choice we have left is to accept the situation we are in, which is not a desirable one, in a mental and behavioural environment that is hostile to LASID human beings.

We therefore need to set some sort of goal. It may be impossible to establish one that can't be leveraged by those in power to harm people, but we can at least attempt to build a reasonable, well-informed one. Recalling some of the reasons we are struggling in the modern world that were mentioned in Chapter 18, we need to build a world that:

- Is based on an accurate picture of the creatures we really are – what Professor William von Hippel calls our 'evolved psychology'[618].
- Addresses the mismatch between our capacities as creatures and the world that we live within now. This includes helping us deal with the negative flipsides of our traits as creatures.
- Sets realistic and consistent expectations for our species, based on an accurate knowledge of how we think and behave.
- Deals with the arbitrary and potentially problematic nature of setting any goals for human society.

What this goal should be will be discussed shortly. To address the final point above – the dangers of setting any goals for human society – we can apply some general principles. First, we should continually be aware of the arbitrary nature of our goals as to how the world should be, as well as the fact that politics, and seeking the world we want, is always a question of grey areas and negotiations between people about what matters and what doesn't. In the end, there never will be a 'perfect' solution and the things we value may not stay static. If we remain vigilant to this, it helps us set realistic expectations of what we can hope for from politics, society and our lives with each other. It also represents an act of intellectual honesty. Second, we should promote ongoing discussion and negotiation in society about these 'grey areas' and disputed goals, in a bid to find arrangements and rules that people generally agree on. This process should be ongoing, because people's views, as well as the circumstances we face, change over time.

People should therefore be encouraged to consider their own visions of a 'good society', and our overall societal goals need to be based on ongoing review and negotiation by the whole of that society, rather than the arbitrary moral viewpoints of a few powerful people.

The aims we should seek – and why we should seek them

Defining the goal for humanity

'Building a world fit for humans' can be seen as a broad principle rather than a specific goal. We need to establish a goal to build society towards that reflects this principle. This goal needs to be clear and we need to establish why this should be more important than any other goals for human beings.

I suggest we need to base our goal on a set of modest intentions that most people would sign up to if they had the knowledge of how human beings think and behave as LASID creatures, and the consequences this has for their capacity to live within the modern world and respond to its challenges. Essentially, we need to base it on the arguments made so far in this book. Overall, this goal should be for human flourishing within the natural world we are part of.

What do we mean by 'flourishing'?

It is important to clarify the definition of flourishing being used above, as it drives the type and level of changes we might make to the structures that surround us.

A starting point is to identify one thing that flourishing does not mean – and that's happiness. As social psychologist William von Hippel notes, human beings did not evolve to be happy – we evolved to be successful at passing on our genes[619]. More importantly, human experience suggests there is much more to life than just happiness, and if we were given the opportunity to take a pill that made us happy all the time, many of us would not take it. So, rather than specifying a vague experiential state that we wish to be in, our definition of flourishing needs to focus on having a set of capacities that are a good fit for our environment and that enable us to live vigorous and healthy lives within it.

When this book refers to flourishing, it is describing the idea of growing and developing successfully as a human being. Another word for it could be 'thriving'. Under this definition, someone would be described as flourishing if they were healthy, happy and in an environment that enables them to express themselves and make full use of their abilities. To use a rather awkward modern phrase, they are being 'the best version of themselves'. This requires human beings to have the freedoms discussed in Chapter 19.

Under this definition, it seems clear that many human beings are not currently flourishing in the modern world, as our capacities are not a good fit for our environment, and vast numbers of people are not living vigorous and healthy lives within it.

What do we need to flourish?

The things we need in order to flourish may seem simple initially. We all need food, drink, warmth and shelter in order to survive. We also need the education to equip us to lead independent, safe lives, and the freedom to be able to live the lives we want, as long as they don't hurt others. This is obviously a very simplified answer, and there are many more things we could add or argue over the importance or level of.

But it is even more complex than this. Our new-found understanding of human beings suggests that we are not the robust, rational individualists that we might have thought we were. We are also creatures that, among other things, have mental blind spots, only deal with approximations of the world and whose behaviour, views and happiness are affected massively by the other people and context around us.

Our ability to flourish is therefore not just dependent on our own individual resources, situation and abilities, but also on the institutions, ideas and other things around us that affect how we see the world and behave towards each other. If we are to flourish, we need an environment that is psychologically healthy for us. As LASID creatures, this is one that supports people to make best use of their capacities whilst protecting their mental and behavioural vulnerabilities. At an individual level, it supports us to be as rational and self-determined as possible, rather than exploiting our psychological vulnerabilities, leaving us in danger of oppression. It also supports us to dial up our capacities for being cooperative members of groups and to dial down our tribal tendencies in a world in which they are often no longer useful. It is therefore about helping people to be effective, both as individuals and as members of groups, as we all occupy both of these roles. When people have this environment, we can say that they are flourishing. They are also better able to deal with the challenges of the modern world, helping them build the healthy, peaceful and sustainable lives they want.

Before the final chapter sets out some specific suggestions as to what a world built for human flourishing within nature might look like, some general guiding principles for this world are outlined below, based on what we know about human beings from Part 1. Our environment would need to:

- **Help people to make more accurate judgements and better decisions** – due to our tendency for cognitive simplification, including our heuristics and biases, we sometimes need help here[620].
- **Steer people's tribal thinking towards cooperation and away from out-group denigration** – our tribal tendencies can steer us towards cooperation with our in-group and negative perceptions of out-groups, leading to a variety of potential negative outcomes. We therefore need to encourage people to see similarities between each other and expand the perceived size of in-groups (such as our global

community) rather than focusing on differences and out-group suspicion.

- **Enhance rather than hamper people's capacity for self-determination** – human beings don't always think as rational individuals, or even as individuals, and we are vulnerable to our System 1 thinking being activated without us knowing it, whether this is with biased information or social contexts that exert pressure on us. We need a mental environment which enhances our ability to think in a rational, self-determined way as individuals, and which does not manipulate us or exploit our irrationality. This principle should be applied consistently across all aspects of our environment, from freeing people from the influence of manipulative advertising through to increasing our awareness of social contexts in which people's thinking and behaviour could be influenced, and from military situations through to workplace meetings. A useful test of this principle in practice would be to ask 'if the person was removed from the particular context they are in and able to think rationally about the same decision or question they are facing, would they reach the same decision or take the same action?' If the answer is 'no', then we change the structures to make it 'yes'.

These principles could be implemented on a formal basis in the structures around us, either on a legal basis or as a set of social norms in our individual behaviours, depending on the importance of the principle. For example, it would become illegal for companies or political parties to undertake manipulative political advertising, but at an individual level, manipulating someone else would simply be socially unacceptable, as it would be too oppressive, heavy-handed and complex to make personal infringements in this area illegal. The expression of racist or hateful views however would be deemed illegal. Like our social goals, these decisions on levels of intervention are arbitrary and would need to be monitored on an ongoing basis.

Our natural parameters

And what of the second part of the sentence expressing our goal – not just of promoting human flourishing, but doing so within the natural world we are part of? If we are taking the bold step to stand back and consider how we could remodel the structures that human beings live in, it seems like a natural and obvious step to insist that this takes place within the natural parameters that we live in. This includes keeping our climate temperature within boundaries that prevent catastrophic changes to our environment, ensuring that we use our natural sources and sinks to a level that our one planet can sustain and protecting the natural world for its own sake.

Living within these parameters is a non-negotiable for human beings if we are to avoid widespread catastrophe, regardless of our wish to promote human flourishing. In the worst-case scenario we need to live within these natural parameters in order to prevent the extinction of our species, but in more positive projections of the future, it is to ensure we flourish, as numerous studies have shown that ongoing access to a healthy natural world is an important ingredient in human flourishing[621]. For example, research suggests that exposure to nature can help to balance our moods[622], and a greater level of connection with nature can increase our sense of well-being[623]. The human relationship with nature is complex, and critical for us. We also need to look beyond the idea of preserving nature on Earth as a means to human ends, and see it as an end in itself – something that is possibly unique and that should be treasured, beyond its role as our life support system.

This part of the overall goal for society has some profound consequences for the society and structures we need to build, and the human behaviours we need to promote. These include the need to:

- **Change our cultural stories and priorities** to acknowledge the fact that human beings are part of nature, not separate or superior to it, as many of our (arbitrary) political and religious stories have incorrectly suggested up to now.
- **Make the preservation of the natural world the key priority of human society**, alongside human flourishing – and build our structures, institutions and ideas to function strictly within its parameters.
- **Promote the human relationship with nature** – not just access to it but awareness of, and connection with, it.

Further steps to address specific challenges

In addition to these steps to achieve our overall goal of human flourishing within the natural world, there is also the option of taking further steps to address some of the specific challenges we face, including those discussed in Part 2 of this book. Taking the steps to meet the overall goal will greatly improve our ability to deal with these challenges, but they may not be sufficient to fully address each challenge.

Rather than add further demands to our list in the final chapter, and at the same time increase the ideological weighting of these steps, making them both less accessible and more open to abuse by an oppressive regime, this can be left as a question for society to resolve – as to how far it is prepared to go to address each challenge.

Why we should choose this goal

Now for the big question – why is the goal for human flourishing within the natural world more important than any other goal to steer human society towards? The arguments for both elements of this goal have been outlined above, but an alternative question to ask is 'what other goal would you set for humanity and society instead of this?'. Chapter 19 showed that a world with no structure or regulation around human beings is not a neutral choice, and as LASID creatures, can lead to consequences for us that we would wish to avoid. It has also been established that human beings are struggling to manage within the hostile environment of the modern world. So, what else is there to build a better society on?

As has been argued, setting a goal on an experiential state, such as happiness, is misplaced, as it is subjective and may not be a state that everyone wishes to achieve all the time. Setting a goal of material wellbeing for people is necessary but not sufficient to promote the goal of flourishing as, for LASID humans, flourishing requires more than simply access to basic resources, as we have mental as well as physical needs that need to be supported by our context. The aim of the recommended goal is to strike a balance between the desire to achieve this goal and the need to protect the human freedom to live the lives we wish, as far as possible. As with many other political decisions, where to draw the line in this balancing act is arbitrary, but this book has aimed to suggest a reasonable place to do so, by focusing its definition of flourishing on having the capacity to avoid harms and exercise greater self-determination, rather than anything more than this.

As creatures with the LASID characteristics that we have explored in this book, there is therefore a convincing argument for setting our goal as human flourishing within the natural world we are part of.

Predicting the criticisms of this model

It is likely that the vision presented in this chapter, and the corresponding recommendations in the next, will attract criticism from those who will argue they are either too much of a shift from the current values and structures that overarch humanity, or that they represent a disproportionate reaction to the challenges we face and involve an unacceptable restriction of our freedoms.

In anticipation of the first point, this book has presented evidence to show that the world we have created for ourselves is proving hostile to human beings in a number of important ways, and to show some of the consequences of this. The current values and structures we have are harming us, so we need a significant change away from them: small changes are not enough. The evidence, as outlined in this book, suggests that the changes proposed to these values and structures will bring many benefits to humanity, including reduced suffering, greater flourishing and a more sustainable future.

In answer to the second criticism, this book has built extensive arguments to show how our modern view of freedom is faulty and based on an incorrect conception of how human beings think and behave, and that we need a new definition of human freedom, which the human goals in this chapter and the recommendations in the next seek to build upon. It is possible that large sections of the population have become inured or blind to the problems and suffering caused by our current human environment, but it must be stated once again that this suffering is real and much of it can be prevented by the steps that have been outlined in this book. The question is whether people are willing to challenge their current structures, ideas and opinions in order to achieve this. As a final point, some of the challenges discussed in this book, such as climate change, are existential and we therefore do not have the luxury of waiting for everyone to come on board with this thinking if we are to resolve them effectively.

A note about the recommendations

The next, and final, chapter will consider what a world fit for the LASID creatures we really are might look like. Before then, it is worth setting out some brief points to give some context to the recommendations:

- **We need to challenge existing assumptions and think differently** – this book has shown that we are stuck in old, inaccurate ways of thinking about human beings and the world, and that these are serving us badly. The recommendations in the final chapter of the book therefore seek to imagine a better, alternative future, and this will not just be within the systems and ideas we have already come to live within. It will include changes to some of our existing structures, ideas and institutions, but will also feature some new ideas that seek to go beyond existing structures, as the time to do it is now.

- **The recommendations will be imperfect** – each of the recommendations in the final chapter and throughout Part 2 has the potential to make a contribution to improving our ability to flourish in the modern world. A principle that must underlie any of these points however is that, given the LASID creatures we are, human beings will not be perfectly adapted to any environment. In day-to-day terms, this means we are not 'perfect' – we are simply the creatures we are – with all the consequences that entails. Our LASID thinking and behaviour evolved to enable us to survive and pass on our genes in the hunter-gather context that our ancestors lived in, but even then, we were not necessarily perfectly adapted to our environment. As Part 1 demonstrated, because of the limited, adapted and simplifying nature of our thinking, there will always be flipsides to some of the traits in our thinking that can potentially be unhelpful to us, even in environments we have adapted to live within. Also, neither our environments nor our thinking are static – the former are constantly changing, and the latter is constantly seeking to adapt to them. We therefore need to accept that human beings may never be perfectly adapted to any environment, and we will always need to adjust to our surroundings as best we can.

- **It's not just about 'nudging'** – the concept of behavioural economics began to have its time in the sun with the publication of *Nudge*, by Richard Thaler and Cass Sunstein, in 2009. The book captured the popular imagination with insights into the biases and irrationalities human beings have in their thinking and behaviour, and how these can be harnessed by policy makers and others to influence people towards better decisions in a way that doesn't significantly diminish their freedom – dubbed 'libertarian paternalism'[624]. It quickly gained influence, inspiring David Cameron's government in the UK to set up a 'Nudge Unit' in the Cabinet Office in 2010 to apply behavioural science to public policy. The phrase 'Nudging' has since entered the common lexicon.

Two things are particularly dispiriting about the use of psychological knowledge in the last 20 years. The first is that it has mainly been used by the commercial sector, with seemingly much slower take up from the not-for-profit and governmental sectors to apply its findings for social good. Behavioural science has been swiftly embraced by the commercial sector, most notably by technology companies such as Google, and by advertisers using it to influence people into buying more stuff, but these effects haven't been balanced out by those seeking to use it to improve the human condition or natural world. Second, there has been a relative lack of scope in the psychological knowledge that has been applied for social good, and the ends to which it has been applied. 'Behavioural economics' largely seems to focus on applying our knowledge of people's heuristics and biases (i.e. the 'Simplification' part of our LASID model), without focusing sufficiently on the other areas, such as our limited perspective, openness to context and influence, and vulnerability to self-deception. This failure to engage with the full picture of our psychology as creatures, or apply it to broader social or political questions, leaves us with a lack of appreciation of the incredible potential this knowledge has to improve human society and individual lives – as well as a lack of ambition to achieve this. This book is an attempt to show the extraordinary possibilities that are open to us if we think bigger and apply this new knowledge about human beings to rebuild the institutions, ideas and societies we live in – to help human beings flourish within the natural world that we are part of. So, in answer to the question 'isn't this book just about nudging?' – no – it's about a great deal more than that.

- **We need consistency in our scaffolding** – the scaffolding we set up to support human beings needs to be consistent between different areas in order to maximise its effectiveness. For example, if steps are being taken in the education system to reduce prejudice, then it also needs to be tackled to the same level in all other settings. If we can build consistent messages and values throughout our structures to respect other people and overcome prejudice, this can greatly increase the likelihood of non-prejudicial attitudes and behaviour.

- **This is a thought experiment – for others to continue –** finally, it is worth stating now, if it wasn't already obvious, that the discussions in Part 3 about how we should structure society for human beings are incredibly broad, and cover a wide range of territory in minimal detail. This is to be expected, and the aim is for this book to be a starting point – to encourage people to think about the creatures we really are, and how we could build better structures and societies around us to help us truly thrive.

Chapter 21
A world fit for humans

*In brief – to achieve the goal of human flourishing within the
natural world we are part of we need to humanise our external
environment to make it favourable rather than hostile to the
LASID creatures we are. Some initial steps to achieve this include
giving every child a good start, extending the content and duration
of education, building a more equal society, promoting our
cooperative capacities and reducing our tribal instincts and
protecting rather than exploiting our mental vulnerabilities. This
task is urgent, and we need to start now.*

This book has explored some of the most severe problems human
beings face and some of the darkest behaviours and episodes in
our history as a species. Sometimes it may feel as if there is little
hope for humanity, but this book has aimed to show that, armed
with more accurate knowledge of how human beings actually
work, we can begin to build a picture of a society in which we can
all flourish within the parameters of the natural world we are part
of.

In summary, we are not the neutral, rational, thinking
machines that many people still think we are. But we have built
the systems, structures and environment around us as if we were
these creatures, as well as to exploit some of our vulnerabilities for
other ends such as profit and power. This has created an

environment that is hostile to human beings, and that fuels many problems for humanity, including obesity, misinformation, violence and inequality. We need to change the environment around us to reflect the creatures we really are – from our LASID thinking and behaviour to our biological traits, such as our preference for calorie rich foods – in order to help us flourish. In other words, we need to 'humanise' our environment to make it favourable rather than hostile to the creatures we are.

Part 2 provided a range of recommendations for empowering human beings and changing our environment in order to address the specific challenges outlined in each chapter. There are many other challenges facing humanity, and each of these requires a similar analysis and set of recommendations. This book aims to inspire others to approach this task. In addition to these specific suggestions, this chapter will set out a number of broader, overarching steps to change the structures, institutions, ideas and other aspects of the environment around us to enable human beings to flourish as part of the natural world. These include some common points shared by more than one of the chapters in Part 2 (such as the need to address economic inequality), as well as other broad principles.

This chapter will set out 10 ways to change our society, culture and institutions to enable us to humanise our mental and behavioural environment. Some of the recommendations will seem like significant changes to our institutions or the way we construct our world, but when we consider how hostile our surroundings can be for LASID creatures at present, it is clear that we need some substantial changes if we are to see human beings flourishing within the parameters of our planet.

It is important to recognise that these are just a limited set of broad suggestions, and there are many other principles that could be added, both from the challenges in Part 2 and wider issues beyond these. The aim is for these steps, although they are limited, to offer some hope and a sense of what might be possible in future human society if we are willing to understand ourselves better and have the courage to use this knowledge to make the world better.

We do not need to start from scratch. Just as some of the freedoms we value today are important and valid even in the light of our new picture of humans as LASID creatures, many of our institutions, structures and ideas are useful, but they just need to be adjusted or strengthened to deal with the reality of the creatures we are. One example is the idea of democracy, which has developed as means of distributing power and freedom among populations, and as Professor Timothy Snyder notes[626], is critical to defend. We just need to strengthen and adapt it as LASID creatures. Other structures, such as our neoliberal economic model, need to be re-imagined – as will be explored below.

10 steps to humanise our environment

1. Start with the human

A core argument of this book has been that if we want to make the world better for human beings or through human intervention, we have to first understand how human beings think and behave. It has also been shown how the majority of people – including those in power and those seeking to change the world – do not have an accurate understanding of human beings as LASID creatures. This principle of 'starting with the human' therefore needs to become a cornerstone of building a better society. We must start by understanding the human, and our policies, structures and behaviours should flow from this.

This principle brings a greater role for psychology in society – a discipline that has been woefully underused in the search to build a better world, but extensively employed by those seeking to exploit people's vulnerabilities for power and profit, such as advertisers, as these actors can see it is the most powerful resource we have available to help us do this. A bridge therefore needs to be built between academic psychology and civil society – including policy makers, practitioners and the general public.

Institutions – both commercial and public – should be established to make the academic knowledge about how human beings think and behave accessible to everyone, and ensure it is applied consistently and thoroughly to public policy. This is a matter for both sides to invest energy and funding in. For example, setting up a global knowledge base that filters the latest findings on key issues (from psychology to medicine) to the general public and that is supported by a strong ongoing publicity programme could help people to keep up with the state of the world and our knowledge – providing another antidote to ignorance, fake news and superstition.

Public awareness campaigns should be run on an ongoing basis to improve everyone's knowledge of how human beings think and behave – both individually and in social contexts. Signage and prompts could be provided in public places, on digital platforms and within institutions to make people aware of their behavioural tendencies and identify situations in which unhelpful or biased thinking traits might be activated, and give people simple strategies to manage the situation. For example, introducing signage on busy roads during the rush hour to remind people that this is when they may feel frustrated and angry towards other drivers, and encourage people to keep the temperature cool in their car, breathe deeply and be patient with other drivers as other people are feeling the same, and we are all human beings. Or introducing a mandatory 'Are you sure you really want this?' prompt button on retail websites at the end of an online purchase to ask people to confirm if they really want to make the purchase then, or whether they want to be reminded in an hour when the dopamine rush of making the purchase with ease has worn off.

Steps have begun to be taken in the last couple of decades to nudge people into positive behaviours (such as binning their litter and reducing their speed on roads) using behavioural science, but there is a vast number of further applications and benefits psychology can have in society, and these should be approached with the aim of educating people of how we think and behave rather than simply 'nudging' them unknowingly into positive behaviours, which is more akin to manipulation and fails to empower people with the self-awareness of their tendencies as creatures.

Overall, we should learn to see ourselves with greater humility and accuracy – as LASID creatures – and ensure that the consequences of this flow into policy making and our daily lives to support human flourishing.

2. Give every child a good start

As has been shown in several chapters in Part 2, the early years of a child's life, including their prenatal period, are critical in shaping their later lives, including their physical and mental health, emotional development and tendency towards aggressive behaviour. Supporting parents and children in this important period of human development therefore represents an essential investment that will pay off many times over in the long term – not just economically, in terms of money saved on treating avoidable chronic illnesses like obesity later in life, or costs of criminal or anti-social behaviour, but also in the quality of life that it provides to individuals and the quality of society it provides to the wider community.

We need to provide every child with the optimal environment for development in their early years. This includes a safe, warm home, nutritious food, nurturing rather than abusive or neglectful parenting and good early years education. Examples of this principle in action could include:

- **Access to basic resources** – every individual should be given the basic material resources they need for a healthy, dignified and self-determined life, including access to nutritious food, a warm home and a basic level of income.

See recommendation 4 below – 'Build a more equal society' – for more details. Additional support beyond this should be provided to parents of children in their early years (up to seven years old) if this is needed.

- **Prenatal and infant health and nutrition** – the health of both parents and infants should be supported, including promoting breastfeeding, maternal nutrition around and after conception and providing a clearer set of guidelines for children's nutrition. Restrictions on marketing and packaging of food will assist this process (see recommendation 6 below) as well as greater availability and lower costs of healthy food. As part of the latter point, healthy foods could be further incentivised and subsidised for parents with young children in order to promote healthy diets for all the family at this critical stage in life.
- **Parenting skills** – not all prospective parents have equal access to the knowledge, life skills and experiences needed to provide positive, nurturing parenting to their children. This is partly an issue of historical inequality in their own childhoods and lives. We therefore need to provide support to all parents to promote better parenting. This could include providing a parenting toolkit and offering parenting classes as soon as prospective parents enter the healthcare system – at the point of pregnancy scans. Attendance of parenting classes could either be mandatory or heavily incentivised through tax breaks or financial rewards during a child's early years for attendance. These classes would include understanding how the early years are so important for a child's later life chances, nutrition, looking after themselves,

modelling good behaviour, and how to nurture a child's emotional development and mental health. Parental support groups should be offered and incentivised throughout early life, in order to help children build healthy, happy and flourishing lives.
- **Supporting parents** – parents need support to balance their work lives and wellbeing with their parental roles. This includes access to free early years child care, and nursery education.

3. Extend the content and duration of education

This book has shown how our context plays a massive role in shaping our thinking and behaviour as LASID creatures. There may therefore be no more important area of scaffolding in our lives than the education we receive. As a society, this is the only formal opportunity we have to teach people the range of skills, ideas, values and behaviour we believe are important. Our new picture of human beings as LASID creatures should therefore make us reflect on what role we need education to play in our lives. By limiting our educational focus to primarily academic subjects we are failing to help our young people develop the other critical capacities and areas of knowledge they need to flourish in life as LASID creatures. We therefore need to expand the role of education to help us flourish as LASID creatures. Formal education also ends within the first quarter of most people's lives, yet there are many critical skills and capabilities people can learn throughout life, as well as benefiting from the nurturing and supportive role of this institution around them. We should therefore give people access to lifelong educational opportunities, to help them flourish as LASID creatures.

In terms of its breadth, education needs to be about nurturing the whole LASID human, and not simply confined to academic topics, although these should continue to be a core area of the syllabus as they remain a critical piece of scaffolding. The chapters in Part 2 of this book set out a range of additional educational topics needed to help address the limited set of human challenges discussed within them, and there may be more relating to other challenges. Below is a summary of some of these, in order to illustrate the breadth of education we need as LASID creatures.

- **Thinking training** – to help us understand how we think and behave as LASID creatures, the impact this has on our thinking and behaviour and how to manage our minds better. Essentially, equip everyone with the 'species self-awareness to understand, and make the best of, themselves as a LASID creature. See Chapter 12 for details.
- **Individuals and society** – to explore the different ways we can build societies and how these affect humans as LASID creatures. Educate people about our human 'superpower' of cooperation, the values of a cooperative society and the need for structures to make this happen. Also make students aware of the assumptions behind their society, values and daily lives (such as these stories and aims we set for a 'good society') so that they live in an informed way about them, and are in a position to continually challenge them, while accepting that they play an important role.
- **Health literacy** – give people the skills and knowledge to enable them to look after their health, including nutrition,

food literacy, managing our relationship with food and how to find physical activity that they enjoy (see Chapter 8 for details).

- **Critical thinking** – help people to understand how external sources can influence them and how to exercise 'intellectual self-defence' against manipulation (see Chapter 8 for details). This includes the skill of information literacy to enable students to assess the veracity of the information they encounter and find trusted sources, as well as techniques to inoculate people against misinformation – both of which were discussed in Chapter 10.
- **Skills to overcome negative tribal tendencies** – Chapter 12 explored a range of skills that could be taught to reduce hostility and suspicion of out-groups, including non-stereotypical thinking, perspective taking and intergroup contact. Chapter 15 set out further educational steps to reduce violence, including how to identify situational cues that could lead to aggression and violence, and how to navigate these situations successfully.

Aside from providing taught learning opportunities, the education system also needs to provide a safe, healthy and nurturing environment for our children. It therefore needs to focus its duty of care on some key areas including:

- **Nutrition** – schools need to provide nutritious, healthy food to students, and help to model and set the eating behaviours they establish for later in life. Only nutritious food should be available in these institutions, both in meals and in any snack machines or cafés on site. Unhealthy food, and any

- associations with it, including advertising or corporate partnerships, should be removed from schools.
- **Physical activity** – students need to be given a physically active environment at school, including more PE lessons and opportunities to find the exercise they enjoy (see Chapter 8 for details)
- **Provide emotional support and growth** – the expansion of emotional support services to children and young people could greatly benefit their mental health and general development, both at school and later in life. In particular, the provision of regular (for example, monthly) 1-1 support sessions for every pupil with a qualified pastoral care teacher could help every child to feel safe and heard at school, and make an invaluable contribution to both their experience of education and their emotional growth, particularly during teenage years.

Educational opportunities should also be available to everyone throughout their lives. This lifelong education should not be mandatory, as people should be free to live their own lives as adults, but access to formal learning and support should be available throughout life on the skills set out above, as well as traditional academic topics. The opportunity for a certain amount of paid 'education top up' time each year (for example, two weeks) could be established as a mandatory principle for employers to offer their employees – in a similar manner to jury duty. The role of adult education centres should also be expanded to accommodate this increased demand, and make this education available at rates that are affordable to all.

4. Build a more equal society

Inequality was identified as a key driver of several of the human challenges explored in Part 2, including health, prejudice and violence; not simply economic inequality, but also inequality of opportunity, access to safe environments, healthy food and physical exercise. In each of these chapters, a common recommendation was to give every human being access to the basic resources they need for a healthy, dignified and self-determined life. This may appear to be a radical suggestion, but it is one of the big actions that could make a fundamental improvement to the human situation on a practical basis. It would also represent a moral milestone for humanity, and evidence of our ability to take action on this.

The resources for a healthy, dignified and self-determined life for a LASID creature are more extensive than most policymakers have conceived or allowed to date. They include access to nutritious food, an adequate and warm home, a safe local environment, a breadth of education and good early years development. To deliver these resources will require a wide range of steps, including the provision of genuinely affordable quality housing for all (and a highly regulated property rental market that protects tenants), lower priced or subsidised healthy food, legislation to bring more supermarkets and fewer fast food outlets to poorer areas, and investment in local infrastructure, such as better and cheaper public transport, safer streets and public spaces. It would also include the provision of a Universal Basic Income to all (explored in Chapter 8), which would give people the financial foundation that can help them pursue the lives they want, within the parameters of the planet.

Aside from the basic resources for a healthy, dignified and self-determined life, human beings also need equal access to opportunities, services and environments, including local sports facilities, university education and jobs, as well as opportunities for a greater say in politics. To provide these things, there needs to be a re-balancing of institutions (both state and private) to ensure that people with less income have good access to them, and that barriers for disadvantaged groups to access them are removed. This will also require policymakers to act upon research that identifies the less obvious psychological barriers that poorer people and minority groups face to access these opportunities and services – for example, how greater economic inequality is linked to lower political participation[627].

Inequality has a wide variety of serious consequences for human wellbeing and society. Some of these were demonstrated in Part 2 of the book, including reduced physical and mental health, increased levels of prejudice and violence and reduced social cohesion[628]. At the most extreme level of consequences, psychologist Donald Dutton and colleagues argue that the evolution of evil in a society, in the form of extreme human destructiveness, begins with people's basic human needs being frustrated, including security, control over essentials and access to information[629]. A more equal society would therefore provide a powerful antidote to human suffering and the foundation for human flourishing.

Taking this step will require nations to spend more on the welfare of their citizens, and would need to be largely financed by a more redistributive tax system, of both individuals and companies. Public approval of these measures could be achieved through the adoption of some of the new cultural values outlined later in recommendation 10 below, including an understanding of the importance of a more equal society to the LASID creatures we are, and a recognition of our interdependence as creatures, resulting in the more cooperative idea that a flourishing society is dependent on everyone flourishing – not just a few.

Political scientist Professor Robert Inglehart has built a set of evidence that suggests societies with high levels of existential security for their populations tend to be more tolerant, trusting and open to more progressive ideas, such as the emancipation of minority groups and promotion of environmental sustainability[630]. When people feel threatened, they resort to greater tribalism and self-protection. Although our societies in the modern western world could be described as affluent, this affluence is increasingly restricted to a small proportion of the population, and this economic inequality creates insecurity for the rest of the population, therefore driving people towards more insular, self-serving political ideas, with Brexit in the UK and the rise of Trump in the US good examples of this. In other words, addressing inequality can set the political temperature and the potential for positive change – so it is a starting point for some of the principles in this book.

5. Make information useful for humans

Human beings rely on information to make choices that guide their behaviour. These choices can have important consequences – for example, knowing whether a political party delivered on its promises could influence people's voting behaviour in future elections, or knowing whether particular foods are healthy or not could lead to food choices that promote or reduce chronic diseases.

Several chapters in Part 2 also showed how, as LASID creatures, human beings are highly sensitive to the way information is presented. We can be easily manipulated by information being framed in a particular way, or by social information such as seeing that other people approve of a particular product or viewpoint. Information is therefore power.

Together, these two points mean that we need to be extremely careful in how we allow information to be presented and distributed within human society. We need to move it away from being used as a device to manipulate people in order to gain profit or power, and towards making it accessible and useful for individuals to help them make better decisions and lead better lives.

This can be achieved through a range of steps, including:

- **Reassert the primacy of the truth** – following Chapter 10, we need to prioritise the upholding of truth as a key value in modern society, as it represents a form of glue that binds us together and enables us to trust, and cooperate with, each other. We also need to put institutions and measures in place to back this principle up – see the recommendations in Chapter 10 for more details of possible steps in this area, including making it harder for people to share misinformation on social media.
- **Manage information more effectively** – Chapter 10 introduced a number of steps to achieve this, including labelling information sources such as newspapers and social media accounts, extending the reach of fact checking and making it harder to share misinformation.
- **Make information clearer** – we need to make information easier for humans to understand and remove opportunities

for it to mislead people, especially in contexts where they have to make important decisions. The former can be achieved through more human-focused design of information, particularly in relation to figures and financial information. The latter, of removing opportunities to mislead people, can be achieved through establishing strong and consistent regulation of communications in all industries and areas of life, including the regulation of food packaging and labelling, as set out in Chapter 8, and the reshaping of how social media companies work, as set out in Chapter 10.

- **Provide easy access to independent sources of information** – we need a series of independent, verified and easy-to access sources of information for people to use on any issue, including current affairs, so that every individual has access to the same objective information.

- **Establish a global information charter and governing body** – as set out in Chapter 10, we need to establish a set of global principles and standards as to how information should be used by institutions around the world, from governments to mass media to companies. This information charter could be monitored and enforced by a new, independent global body free from national biases, which is responsible for ensuring human beings have access to reliable information, wherever they live in the world. It could also oversee the provision of some key global sources of information, as set out in Chapter 10.

6. Adjust our environment to protect rather than exploit our mental vulnerabilities

This book has set out a range of examples of how our thinking can be influenced by the structures and ideas in our environment in ways that have negative consequences for us. For example, the way media channels 'spin' a particular political angle on a set of statistics, or choose to emphasise or omit particular details from a news story can influence our view of it, and our consequent voting behaviour. Sometimes, external agents also actively seek to exploit our cognitive vulnerabilities as LASID creatures in order to gain profit or power – such as advertisers seeking to influence us to want products that we would not otherwise be interested in, or social media companies prioritising posts that sow moral outrage and spread misinformation among users. These are examples of an environment that is hostile to human beings, our freedom to think for ourselves and our flourishing more generally.

We therefore need to reduce the power of external influences to manipulate us and exploit our mental vulnerabilities, and repurpose our environment to support us and protect these vulnerabilities. To achieve this, a variety of steps will need to be taken to adjust our institutions, structures and ideas. Below are a few brief examples.

- **Set structural defaults to positive behaviours** – the environments and institutions we build around us are rarely neutral in the behaviours they promote, and sometimes we have to make a choice of which behaviours to promote when we set up an environment. We should therefore adopt the principle of choosing default environmental settings that protect people's capacity for self-determination as LASID creatures and promote their flourishing, rather than the alternatives. For example, regulate supermarkets to ensure that their layout promotes healthy eating and saves consumers the most money, rather than exploiting their biases to spend more and eat junk food. We should also ensure that our defaults promote environmentally sustainable behaviours – for example, ensuring the most sustainable forms of travel are cheaper and more convenient than the least, such as public transport rather than car use.

- **Restrict the role of marketing** – advertising and marketing exploit human psychological vulnerabilities in order to seek profit and power, and often at considerable cost to people's well-being – for example, driving obesity, alcohol consumption and consumerism. They also restrict our mental freedom – our capacity to think for ourselves. As a result, we should remove or weaken the capacity of marketing to influence us, including:
    o Banning all manipulative advertising, advertising to children under 16, and advertising of unhealthy products, including junk food and alcohol. See page 153 of Chapter 8 for details.
    o Regulating product packaging and labelling – apply the recommendations set out on page 156 of Chapter 8 to all commercial sectors to remove the ability for companies to make any claims about their products or provide any extraneous contextual information that could be used to manipulate people's LASID traits. For example, showing a group of friends sharing a pack of crisps, activating the positive idea

of friendship in the consumer's mind and potentially manipulating their choice.
- **Media** – Chapter 10 explored a range of steps we can take to improve the media landscape and make it less hostile to us as LASID creatures. These include creating a better media landscape in which information is seen as a social asset, featuring non-commercial media channels. Another step is to reshape how social media companies work, moving them away from a model that incentivises audience engagement for profit, as well as holding media responsible for the information that is spread on their platforms. More detailed scaffolding could be applied within social media environments to help people engage their rational thought rather than being swept away by their instinctive System 1 reactions – for example, making people 'pause before they post' to give them time to reflect with System 2 thinking before they post or retweet something using System 1.
- **Political communications** – the power of political communications to manipulate people should also be reduced. As Chapter 10 noted, there has been a drop in the levels of truth in politics in recent years, and both political communications and politicians themselves should be subject to the principles of a global information charter that monitors and prevents the spread of misinformation or biased information. Politicians should also be made to follow these principles, and made personally accountable when they attempt to manipulate the public or communicate mistruths. See the recommendations in Chapter 10 for more details. Our democratic structures could also be adjusted to promote

more political involvement and agency on behalf of the public – for example making voting mandatory could help to combat the voter suppression techniques used to create apathy and reduce political participation among the public – to the benefit of one of the parties[631].

Alongside these steps we can set up tools and processes within everyday life to help people identify situations in which they could be vulnerable to being influenced by the way information is presented, and also help them to manage their thinking and behaviour in such situations. For example, including signage at an entrance to a shop to remind people that the way the shop is laid out could influence their buying decisions, and providing a guide to help them become less influenced as a shopper. These skills would be taught as part of the 'thinking skills' noted in recommendation 1 earlier, but could be topped up throughout life by being placed in situations where influence could occur, such as in workplaces, meetings and when consuming media such as newspapers or television.

As a final point in this section, we could also help people to develop a greater sensitivity to the way we communicate with each other interpersonally in daily life, and to be aware of how we can manipulate and mislead others through the ways we communicate. A social norm could be established to encourage people to practice clear communication – to try not to exploit or mislead others through the things we say and how we say them.

7. Adjust our environment to promote our cooperative capacities and reduce our tribal instincts

This book has shown how, as LASID creatures, our tribal instincts can be powerful drivers of both our thinking and behaviour, and can be activated by external factors such as situations or communications – often without us realising it. These tribal instincts take a variety of forms, including negative judgements towards out-group members, conformity, the influence of social identity and the capacity for cooperation. Negative consequences of our tribal tendencies can include prejudice, violence and killing, whereas positive consequences can include cooperation.

We need to build scaffolding around human beings that helps us to avoid the activation of negative tribal thinking and behaviour, and that helps to promote cooperation. Below are some ways we can achieve this:

- **Promote cooperative values** – as noted on page 270 of Chapter 12, we need a significant cultural shift to establish the principle of cooperation as a driving force that shapes the way we build our societies and institutions. This not only will help to reduce prejudice, suffering and violence but will improve the quality of all our lives.
- **Widen our moral circle** – as noted on page 327 of Chapter 15, we need to encourage human beings to see themselves as part of bigger groups that transcend their own smaller tribes, and to see commonalities with each other. This extends to the idea of seeing all human beings as part of one global in-group. This widening of our moral circle can be promoted through a range of methods. One is to establish

more global institutions to oversee and regulate particular issues, thereby strengthening the sense of a global community. These would be global non-governmental bodies funded by national governments, operating independently of politics within individual countries. They could include an institution to promote the global sense of an in-group, reduce prejudice and facilitate cooperation between people, using insights from psychology and other disciplines (including sociology, history and philosophy) to inform its work. Other global institutions could include those already mentioned in this book, such as those addressing climate change, education standards, violence prevention and implementing the global information charter.

- **Reform our institutions** – we should take this step in order to make them less biased and violent, and also to promote more cooperative models of living and working. In some cases, this will require a complete review of the workings and culture of particular institutions, such as the police in the UK and US (see Chapter 15). In other cases, reducing bias could include introducing processes that overcome our tendency for biased thinking, such as the 'blind' interview techniques discussed on page 275, or those that identify situations in which we might be most prone to contextually-influenced biases, such as when we are online and feeling annoyed by an opinion someone has expressed. More cooperative models of working and living could include those such as the 'jigsaw classrooms' described in Chapter 12, that engage children in cooperative rather than competitive working.

- **Promote positive representations of people** – particularly minority groups, across all institutions and areas of society, including the media and politics. At the same time, we should closely monitor and penalise negative or stereotypical representations of people, including 'dog-whistle' messages in newspapers or from politicians stirring up negativity towards other groups or people, or promoting stereotypical judgements of people. For example, banning politicians from using the language of nationalism, superiority or hate against any out-group – from refugees to entire nations. This could be achieved through the 'global information charter' discussed in point 5 above and in Chapter 10.
- **Promote intergroup contact** – we should provide opportunities for all people to have contact with those in other groups, whether these are based on race, sex, age, religion or other key variables. As discussed on page 267, these opportunities can be provided in a range of institutions, from education to workplaces, and can still have benefits even if the contact takes place online rather than in-person.
- **Minimise aggressive cues** – an important step in reducing violence is to remove factors in society that stimulate aggression and violence. One example of this is to tightly restrict the availability of weapons, including banning guns in the US. Another is to provide stronger regulation of, and penalties for, hateful, prejudiced or violent speech in any media channels, including on public social media platforms. Media channels should also be encouraged to take greater

responsibility for their representation of violence and aggression, in the light of its effects on the public.

- **Defuse the power of the situation to promote violence** – this book has demonstrated the enormous influence that situational factors can have on human behaviour – including leading us to become killers. Situations can be identified that place strong social pressures on human beings to activate negative tribal behaviours, such as military operations, football crowds or even group situations under the influence of alcohol. Steps can be taken to avoid these situations escalating, such as banning alcohol at football games, and warnings and guidance can also be given to people before and during these situations about the dangers within the situation and how to overcome them.

- **Build safer political conditions** – our democratic political systems are barriers against the rise of hate and violence, but they need to be strengthened and nurtured. A range of steps can be taken to achieve this, including decentralising politics to give people more power locally, changing voting systems to proportional representation to ensure every vote counts and lowering the voting age to expand the electorate and involve younger people. Alongside steps like these to increase the power of people, the public need to be better informed about the responsibilities this places on their shoulders to use this power and to make well-informed decisions.

- **Take stronger international action to prevent and stop conflict and mass killing** –this step includes establishing a permanent UN violence prevention force, strengthening the International Criminal Court and expanding peacebuilding activities between countries. See page 336 of Chapter 15 for more details.

8. Adjust our environment to support our cognitive capacities and save time and energy

In this new vision of a humanised world presented in this chapter, we will need to encourage and prompt human beings to use their System 2 rational thinking more sometimes, which may increase people's cognitive loads. This can however be balanced by setting up scaffolding around people to support and protect some of their System 1 thinking traits so they are not wasting cognitive effort on trying to defend their minds. We can also introduce other initiatives to reduce people's cognitive load and make our use of cognitive energy more effective, thus increasing our cognitive ease and promoting our flourishing, as well as giving us time and energy to do more of the things we want.

We can reduce the load on our brains by outsourcing some of our mental tasks to technologies around us such as computers or apps – for example when faced with a task in which our System 1 thinking could be biased or distracted, or one that requires cognitively draining System 2 thinking. A range of possible tasks could be externalised in this way, and below are some examples within particular categories.

- **Choice** – a variety of decision-making tasks could be outsourced to computer algorithms, enabling us to make better calculations, avoid temptation and overall make the best choices. For example, a personally-tailored food shopping and nutrition app to help people choose the meals they can eat each day in order to meet their nutritional, calorific and budgetary needs and not go beyond them. The app could also order the food for them, and include prompts when they are about to buy something that doesn't fit into their plan, to support their System 2 thinking in trying to deter them from this behaviour or nudge them into healthier options. A similar principle could apply to buying clothing, cars or most other items, in order to reduce the effort of doing so.

- **Calculation** – we could use algorithms to help us understand how much time we have available each day for different tasks (such as sleep, work, travel and shopping), and to help us assess what we can realistically do on each day and the toll this will take on our health and stress levels. This could help us save cognitive effort and enable us to make informed decisions that reduce the stress in our lives, such as saying 'no' to activities and giving us enough time for sleep and relaxation.
- **Politics** – in the process of voting for political candidates, we are inclined towards many biases, including recency bias that leads us towards greater recall of the most recent things a politician has said or done rather than their record over time, voting in line with our identity rather than the values we adhere to and being too influenced by a candidate's personality rather than their party's policies. Using a computer algorithm to analyse each candidate's policies and track record over the longer term could help to inform our individual decisions as voters by reducing our biases and basing our votes on the policies that we most agree with rather than extraneous factors.

It is important to note that in these cases, we are not relinquishing control to an external agent – we are simply devising an interface and set of processes that make it easier for us to state our basic preferences and let someone or something else do the cognitive processing needed to enact them on our behalf. In areas in which a personal decision is essential (such as voting) or more nuanced (such as morality) the algorithm wouldn't make the decision for us – it would simply inform our own decision. But in other cases, such as planning our meals, the decision itself could be automated, as well as the actions that follow it – in this case, ordering the food. This outsourcing principle could apply to a wide range of areas of life, from shopping to ethical decisions, and therefore represents a potential marketplace for 'social mind entrepreneurs' – people who want to help to build the scaffolding to support people in flourishing, both at a day-to-day level and in broader ways – from apps to help people eat better, through to social media platforms that help people to move out of their funnels.

Artificial Intelligence (AI) has a role to play in these processes. Interestingly, AI and machine learning use similar principles to the human mind in order to function, such as the use of rules and heuristics, and therefore need to be treated with caution, as they can also possess the potential for error[632]. They do however also have the potential to support decision making by human beings, particularly in situations where our own thinking is likely to be clouded by emotion or other biases. As with any other new technology, AI could represent either a threat (for example, being used by those in power to consolidate power and exploit weaknesses in our LASID thinking) or a benefit (for example, providing us with a way to outsource some of our mental tasks). By taking the other steps outlined in this chapter to improve society, such as limiting the power of companies, and having a society focused on human flourishing, we will be able to reduce the risk of AI representing a threat and maximise its potential to be a benefit to humanity.

9. Repurpose the economy as a means to our ends

As this book has argued, human flourishing can be derailed by dogmas – beliefs and lines of thought as to how the world should be that seem attractive to us but are actually arbitrary and can lead us towards harmful situations. The neoliberal economic model that has overarched our lives in recent decades is an example of such a dogma, and one that has resulted in tragic consequences for many human beings, including increased inequality, less investment in the social services we all depend on and the degradation of our environment.

Our economic system is not just about how we build and distribute resources. It is one of the most influential structures surrounding us, as it plays a fundamental role in how we each see and experience the world. It influences our health and wellbeing (through our access to basic resources), the way we treat other people (such as the value of competition or cooperation), the way we see ourselves (in terms of wealth and other factors) and our goals in life (such as seeking material success). Our current economic thinking is based on the mistaken idea that we are not LASID creatures but the Enlightenment model of completely rational, consistent and logical creatures, always seeking to maximise the benefits we get, or 'econs' to borrow economist Richard Thaler's phrase[633]. This leads to a number of incorrect assumptions and negative consequences.

First, LASID human beings need more in their lives than just wealth and material goods. Among other things, we need meaning, dignity and a feeling of being a valued part of a wider community. Under the current economic system, however, countries and their citizens around the world are engaged in the relentless task of achieving greater productivity and economic growth. This aim is a central influence on how the majority of people in the world use their time in their lives – with economically productive work being the central priority for how we use our time, and other elements of our lives fit around this, if there is time.

The values of our economic system also influence our political choices and cultural values. For example, in Western countries like the UK there remains a strong sense that a life of economically productive work is the only valuable one, so hard, economically productive, work and wealth accumulation are seen as desirable traits, and our benefits systems are geared up to provide only minimal benefits for people who aren't currently working in this way. Our neoliberal approach to economics also follows the mistaken Enlightenment idea that freedom comes from providing as little scaffolding and regulation around people as possible. It also assumes that economic growth will 'trickle down' from the richest to the poorest people, and brings a reluctance to redistribute wealth, even if, as a consequence, some people do not have access to the most basic resources such as food and shelter. As has been demonstrated throughout this book, these values are not consistent with the evidence as to what LASID people need in their lives in order to flourish. We need more scaffolding around us, not less. We need less inequality, not more. We need greater redistribution of wealth and the basic resources needed to live a healthy, dignified and self-determined life.

On top of all this, by prioritising continual economic growth above other aims, our economic system also fails to enable us to live within the limits of the natural world around us – another key aspect of the new goal we have set out.

One of the most fundamental recommendations in this chapter is therefore that we need a new economic model if we are going to meet our goal of flourishing within the natural world we are part of. As an example, one attractive model that aims to meet this goal is Doughnut Economics[634], developed by economist Kate Raworth, which suggests that our economy needs to function within two sets of parameters that can be seen as concentric rings: first, social parameters, to ensure everyone gets the basic things they need to survive, and second, ecological parameters, to ensure that we operate within the environmental limits of our one planet. There is a doughnut-shaped space between these two sets of parameters in which human beings can thrive. This type of model not only provides a sympathetic economic environment to start addressing some of the key challenges we discussed in Part 2, such as inequality and climate change, but also refocuses our values away from conflict and competition, and towards cooperation, as well as re-defining the idea of what a useful human life should include – something that could improve the well-being of many people, as they are given the freedom to pursue the lives they want.

This book is not necessarily calling for an end to capitalism, as it is an idea that has brought many benefits to humanity, improving global living conditions by distributing food, goods and services and powering extraordinary developments in technology. Nor is this book necessarily opposed to economic growth. Strong economies can help countries become wealthy enough to enable them to distribute their resources around the population so that everyone gets the basic resources they need for a good life (see earlier point), as well as to deliver the social structures we have outlined in this book that will help us lead flourishing lives – from good public transport to broader, life-long education. We do however need to move away from the current extreme finance-led version of capitalism, which is based on a faulty, Enlightenment view of human beings as rational creatures, and suggests that economic growth is all that is needed for human flourishing, and therefore is essentially the same thing. The evidence from this book suggests that, for the LASID creatures we actually are, we need the economy to be human-led; the servant of human beings rather than the master, and one of several means we use to reach the end of human flourishing, rather than prioritised above everything else as an end in itself.

The economy also needs to sit within the parameters of the scaffolding that LASID human beings need around them in order to flourish, which have been discussed in Part 3, as well as the parameters of the natural world. The latter parameters include not just living within the environmental limits of our planet or the preservation of the natural world but its promotion and re-expansion, due to the valuing of nature in its own right, and the recognition that nature is critical to human flourishing – not just as a resource but because it is the environment we have evolved to thrive within.

Viewing the economy in this way – as subordinate to other priorities for human beings, including human flourishing and living within the parameters of nature – is a key lesson for us to learn as a species and one that will have profoundly positive consequences when we learn it.

Examples of this principle in action:

- **Reduce the lobbying power of companies** – to influence any issue, including food nutrition labelling regulations.
- **Regulate corporate activities to fit within the parameters of human flourishing and nature** – including changing the business model of social media companies away from the 'attention economy' (see page 219 of Chapter 10) and penalising negative representations of human groups (see page 269 of Chapter 12).
- **Tax global companies fairly** – large global companies are currently able to pay proportionately far less tax than other companies or individuals by exploiting international loopholes. Global taxation structures should be tightened and policed with greater consistency and strength in order to ensure all companies pay their fair share. Proceeds from this tax revenue can be invested in building better societies for human flourishing.
- **Rethink the role of work** – based on the role it can play in human flourishing, rather than its capacity to build economic growth. For example, studies show that working over 40 hours a week is associated with negative consequences for human wellbeing, including emotional exhaustion and a reduced sense of accomplishment[635]. Recent trials have found that reducing working hours to a 4-day week increases productivity, reduces burnout and leads to a greater sense of wellbeing[636].

- **Reintegrate human beings into the natural environment** – fund a global re-expansion of the natural environment and explore how human beings can integrate it more into their lives in order to promote greater flourishing.
- **Rethink our relationship with wealth and property** – the idea of property and its ownership emerged around 12,000 years ago, at the time our hunter-gatherer ancestors were making the transition to agriculture. Some social psychologists have argued that the advent of property was a key driver of the entry of inequality and its negative consequences into human society, even though it has also brought a lot of positive outcomes. We could therefore consider how to make the idea of property work better for LASID creatures, as well as how to adjust it to help us reintegrate into the natural environment, such as giving people more access to nature, expanding the right to roam, and giving rights to land rather than people so that common land exists but to be enjoyed rather than exploited by human beings.

10. Apply new political priorities and cultural ideas

Ideas are critically important in human society. They help us to understand the world, find meaning, work out who we are and gain a sense of how we should think and behave. As a result, they are one of the most important pieces of scaffolding we have. To return to the words of social psychologist Professor Joe Forgas, human beings use 'consensual delusions'[637] to give our lives and societies meaning and drive our behaviour towards particular goals. From these shared ideas we build our societies, and form the stories we tell each other – simple but powerful ways of transmitting complex information, traditions and beliefs.

This book has shown how ideas can lead to mistaken beliefs, biases or dogmas that can be used to exercise power over people, and how they have brought great suffering over human history, from the race theory of the Nazis to the intolerance of some religious creeds. It has also shown, however, that we need to establish some new ways of thinking about ourselves as a species, as well as the conditions we should live in and the values we should hold. Like every conception of what a good society and a good life consist of, these new ideas are arbitrary. We should not adopt them as dogmas, but as guiding principles that we continually challenge and review, so that they adjust to fit our circumstances and needs, and do not become 'baked in', as unchallengeable laws.

These ideas should not only become principles that everyone understands, but should also guide the societies, structures and institutions human beings set up around them. We need to build inspirational stories and pictures of a future based on these principles. Over the course of this book a number of principles have emerged that could be central to building a world fit for human beings as LASID creatures. Below is a selection of these potentially transformative ideas:

- **Start with the human** – this point has already been discussed in recommendation 1 above, but represents an important idea to establish. We must start by understanding human beings, and our policies, actions and behaviours should flow from this. Our new understanding is of human beings as LASID creatures, which has significant consequences for how we should build society.

- **We need a new view of freedom** – as LASID creatures, meaningful human freedom does not come from a society with minimal regulation and structures around people, as this brings substantial negative consequences for human beings. Instead, freedom for LASID human beings comes when we have support to protect our mental and behavioural vulnerabilities and to live self-determined lives as far as possible. See Chapter 19 for more details of this argument.
- **We need scaffolding** – human beings, as LASID creatures, need external scaffolding around them (in the form of institutions, structures and ideas) in order to protect their mental and behavioural vulnerabilities and help them to live self-determined lives. See Chapter 19 for further discussion of this point.
- **We should seek human flourishing within nature** – this is the central principle on which we should build our structures and institutions, with all other factors in human society, including the economic system, acting as means to this end. See Chapter 20 for more details. It includes living within the natural limits of our planet, requiring us to take immediate and extensive action to tackle climate change – see Chapter 17. It also includes fundamentally rethinking our place within, and relationship with, the natural world. Human beings are not only custodians of nature but are part of it, and need to protect it as an end in itself. Living within the parameters of nature as part of it will demand a number of major structural, institutional and societal changes that

are beyond the remit of this book – but as an example, will require include a change in the world's food production and supply system to shift from meat and dairy to plant-based foods – a move that is deemed essential to build a sustainable future for our growing global population[638].

- **We need a shared conception of the truth** – as explored in Chapter 10, we need to reinforce the idea of the truth as a priority for human beings, as well as the importance of a shared conception of the truth, in order to promote global cooperation and communication.
- **We are one in-group** – as discussed in recommendation 7 above and Chapter 15, we need to broaden our moral circle wherever possible and see ourselves as part of larger in-groups, ultimately seeing human beings as one in-group and recognising the commonalities between us.
- **We are interdependent** – following from the point above, the evidence surveyed in this book suggests that human beings are not only one in-group but are dependent on each other for their flourishing. See Chapter 12 for details. We therefore need to build societies, structures and ideas that promote and enable this, as this book is aiming to do.
- **We need a culture of cooperation** – in order to establish structures around LASID human beings that promote the cooperative aspects of their tribal tendencies, we need to build our societies, institutions and practices on a principle of cooperation rather than competition. See Chapter 12 for more details.

Conclusions

For many years, politicians and thinkers have been trying to respond to the major challenges that human beings face and the question of how to build a better, more sustainable world in which human beings flourish. They have largely failed to address these challenges, and this book argues that our best hope of doing so successfully is to build our society and institutions around the creatures we really are – not the fantasy creatures that we would like to be.

As noted earlier in the book, the idea of human moral progress is a myth, based on an out-of-date view of how human beings think and behave. It can lull us into a false sense of security in the belief that the world is automatically getting better without any effort from us. As LASID creatures, our thinking and behaviour are dependent on our context, and therefore gaining any improvement in our behaviour towards a particular goal (such as those discussed in this book) requires us to put continual effort into building and maintaining the contextual structures around us – from institutions to social norms – that will promote the progressive behaviours we want to see.

Thanks to the insights of psychology and other disciplines, we now know (or at least have a pretty good idea) as a species how to maximise our chances of meeting some of our key challenges, including improving health, reducing violence and addressing climate change, as well as how to build a global society in which human beings flourish within the natural world we are part of. The big question is whether we are prepared to take the steps necessary to do these things, including challenging our existing dogmas, structures and ways of doing things. If we really want to achieve this, we need to build a movement to humanise the world, demand it from our politicians and take action to make it happen. We know what we need to do – it's up to us now.

The suggestions outlined in this book are simply initial ideas for moving forward, but they provide a direction of travel for others to join and contribute more detailed work and ideas to, as we seek to humanise our global society to enable human flourishing within the parameters of the natural world we are part of.

Finally, it bears repeating that this book can be seen as a thought experiment and just the start of a process of humanising our world. There is much to do now to take this forward. If you are inspired by the ideas in the book, spread the word about it and the need to humanise society based on what we know about human beings from psychology and other sciences. For academics, there is a need to find ways of building closer ties with politics, civil society and the public in order to ensure their work is applied to make the world better, and to apply this psychological thinking to other human challenges. For politicians and practitioners, there is the need to take these ideas seriously and start taking action to humanise our world – right now. Because humanity and the planet can't wait any longer.

Acknowledgements

This book would not exist without the help of a number of people who have given me their support, time, and wisdom. Massive thanks to everyone who has helped, in any way.

Particular thanks go to the academics and experts from social psychology and other disciplines who patiently and generously answered my questions and guided me around a number of topics, as well as those who contributed to my podcast series 'Humans & Hope', which helped to seed the idea for this book. These include Dr Sue Churchill, Nick Davies, Professor Kelly Fielding, Professor Joe Forgas, Professor Peter Harris, Professor Jolanda Jetten, Assistant Professor Daniel Jolley, Dr Jonathan Leader Maynard, Professor Stephen Reicher, Professor Rhiannon Turner and Professor Vivian Vignoles. I am responsible for any errors in interpreting their wise counsel!

I'm also very grateful to the readers who took the time to review the first draft of the book and send me their feedback. The final product was made inordinately better by the insights and suggestions offered by Andrew Copson, Gail Dampney, John Good, Elizabeth Holmes, Neal Lawson, Dave Mateer, David Murray, Eleanor Reeves, Jeremy Singer, Richard Slade and Adrian Worrall. Elly Donovan provided generous and wise advice on how to most effectively promote the book, which I very much appreciated.

Thanks also to my family – Inga, Izzy, Adie, Bridget and George – for their patience while I was grumpily immersed in the writing process, and everything else they bring.

Finally, special thanks to three people who provided invaluable ongoing encouragement, support and ideas throughout the process of developing and writing this book – Professor Peter Harris, Elizabeth Holmes and Matthew Chambers.

References

1. SUVs - United Kingdom. *Statistica.* <https://www.statista.com/outlook/mmo/passenger-cars/suvs/united-kingdom#analyst-opinion>.
2. MacKay, T. Can psychology change the world? *British Psychological Society* (2008). < https://www.bps.org.uk/psychologist/can-psychology-change-world>.
3. Gazzaniga, M. S., Heatherton, T. F. & Halpern, D. F. *Psychological science.* (WW Norton New York, 2006).
4. Ebbage, A. Thinking outside the box: How does the brain work? It is the most complex computer in the known universe yet its secrets have remained elusive and fascinating. Now techniques are being developed that are helping us to unravel its mysteries. *Engineering & Technology* **15**, 68-71 (2020).
5. Vopson, M. M. Estimation of the information contained in the visible matter of the universe. *AIP Advances* **11** (2021).
6. There are 6×10^80 Bits of Information in the Observable Universe. *Universe Today* (2021). <https://www.universetoday.com/153035/there-are-6x1080-bits-of-information-in-the-observable-universe/>.
7. Kahneman, D. *Thinking, fast and slow.* 138 (Farrar, Straus and Giroux, 2011).
8. Hood, B. *The Self Illusion: Why there is no 'you' inside your head.* (Hachette UK, 2012).
9. Kahneman, D. *Thinking, fast and slow.* 71 (Farrar, Straus and Giroux, 2011a).
10. Gazzaniga, M. S., Heatherton, T. F. & Halpern, D. F. *Psychological science.* 291 (WW Norton New York, 2006a).
11. Goldin, C. & Rouse, C. Orchestrating impartiality: The impact of "blind" auditions on female musicians. *American economic review* **90**, 715-741 (2000).
12. Bian, L., Leslie, S.-J. & Cimpian, A. Gender stereotypes about intellectual ability emerge early and influence children's interests. *Science* **355**, 389-391 (2017).
13. Kahneman, D. *Thinking, fast and slow.* 21 (Farrar, Straus and Giroux, 2011b).
14. Kahneman, D. *Thinking, fast and slow.* 90 (Farrar, Straus and Giroux, 2011c).
15. Kahneman, D. *Thinking, fast and slow.* 21 (Farrar, Straus and Giroux, 2011d).
16. Haidt, J. *The happiness hypothesis: Putting ancient wisdom and philosophy to the test of modern science.* (Random House, 2006).
17. Kahneman, D. *Thinking, fast and slow.* 45 (Farrar, Straus and Giroux, 2011e).
18. Kahneman, D. *Thinking, fast and slow.* 73-74 (Farrar, Straus and Giroux, 2011f).
19. Kahneman, D. *Thinking, fast and slow.* 74 (Farrar, Straus and Giroux, 2011g).
20. Kahneman, D. *Thinking, fast and slow.* 52-58 (Farrar, Straus and Giroux, 2011h).

21 Bargh, J. A., Chen, M. & Burrows, L. Automaticity of social behavior: Direct effects of trait construct and stereotype activation on action. *Journal of personality and social psychology* **71**, 230 (1996).
22 Kahneman, D. *Thinking, fast and slow.* 85 (Farrar, Straus and Giroux, 2011i).
23 Kahneman, D. *Thinking, fast and slow.* 86 (Farrar, Straus and Giroux, 2011j).
24 Kahneman, D. *Thinking, fast and slow.* 75-77 (Farrar, Straus and Giroux, 2011k).
25 Gazzaniga, M. S., Heatherton, T. F. & Halpern, D. F. *Psychological science.* 300 (WW Norton New York, 2006b).
26 Gilbert, D. T. & Wilson, T. D. Prospection: Experiencing the future. *Science* **317**, 1351-1354 (2007).
27 Wilson, T. D. & Gilbert, D. T. Affective forecasting. *Advances in experimental social psychology* **35**, 345-411 (2003).
28 Gilbert, D. T., Morewedge, C. K., Risen, J. L. & Wilson, T. D. Looking forward to looking backward: The misprediction of regret. *Psychological Science* **15**, 346-350 (2004).
29 Epley, N. & Gilovich, T. Putting adjustment back in the anchoring and adjustment heuristic: Differential processing of self-generated and experimenter-provided anchors. *Psychological science* **12**, 391-396 (2001).
30 Serenko, A. & Bontis, N. What's familiar is excellent: The impact of exposure effect on perceived journal quality. *Journal of Informetrics* **5**, 219-223 (2011).
31 Kahneman, D. *Thinking, fast and slow.* 66 (Farrar, Straus and Giroux, 2011l).
32 Tversky, A. & Kahneman, D. The Framing of Decisions and the Psychology of Choice. *Science (American Association for the Advancement of Science)* **211**, 453-458 (1981). https://doi.org/10.1126/science.7455683
33 Kahneman, D. *Thinking, fast and slow.* 44 (Farrar, Straus and Giroux, 2011m).
34 Gazzaniga, M. S., Heatherton, T. F. & Halpern, D. F. *Psychological science.* 252 (WW Norton New York, 2006c).
35 von Hippel, W. *The Social Leap: The New Evolutionary Science of Who We Are, Where We Come From, and What Makes Us Happy.* 19 (HarperCollins Publishers, 2022).
36 Haidt, J. *The righteous mind: Why good people are divided by politics and religion.* (Vintage, 2012).
37 von Hippel, W. *The Social Leap: The New Evolutionary Science of Who We Are, Where We Come From, and What Makes Us Happy.* 27 (HarperCollins Publishers, 2022a).
38 Holt-Lunstad, J., Smith, T. B. & Layton, J. B. Social relationships and mortality risk: a meta-analytic review. *PLoS medicine* **7**, e1000316 (2010).
39 Holt-Lunstad, J., Smith, T. B. & Layton, J. B. Social relationships and mortality risk: a meta-analytic review. *PLoS medicine* **7**, e1000316 (2010a).
40 Greene, J. *Moral tribes: Emotion, reason, and the gap between us and them.* (Penguin, 2014).
41 Pinker, S. *The better angels of our nature: The decline of violence in history and its causes.* (Penguin uk, 2011).
42 Kahneman, D. *Thinking, fast and slow.* 90-91 (Farrar, Straus and Giroux, 2011n).
43 Kahneman, D. *Thinking, fast and slow.* 90 (Farrar, Straus and Giroux, 2011o).

44	Gazzaniga, M. S., Heatherton, T. F. & Halpern, D. F. *Psychological science.* 497 (WW Norton New York, 2006d).
45	Vaughan, G. M. & Hogg, M. A. *Social psychology.* 55 (Pearson Higher Education AU, 2013).
46	Tajfel, H. Quantitative judgement in social perception. *British journal of psychology* **50**, 16-29 (1959).
47	Criminal Victimization report. (2002). < https://bjs.ojp.gov/library/publications/criminal-victimization-2022 >.
48	Payne, B. K. Prejudice and perception: the role of automatic and controlled processes in misperceiving a weapon. *Journal of personality and social psychology* **81**, 181 (2001).
49	Greenwald, A. G., Oakes, M. A. & Hoffman, H. G. Targets of discrimination: Effects of race on responses to weapons holders. *Journal of Experimental Social Psychology* **39**, 399-405 (2003).
50	Gazzaniga, M. S., Heatherton, T. F. & Halpern, D. F. *Psychological science.* 498 (WW Norton New York, 2006e).
51	Dovidio, J. F., Kawakami, K., Johnson, C., Johnson, B. & Howard, A. On the nature of prejudice: Automatic and controlled processes. *Journal of experimental social psychology* **33**, 510-540 (1997).
52	Dovidio, J. F., Kawakami, K., Johnson, C., Johnson, B. & Howard, A. On the nature of prejudice: Automatic and controlled processes. *Journal of experimental social psychology* **33**, 510-540 (1997a).
53	Tajfel, H., Billig, M. G., Bundy, R. P. & Flament, C. Social categorization and intergroup behaviour. *European journal of social psychology* **1**, 149-178 (1971). https://doi.org:10.1002/ejsp.2420010202
54	Guassi Moreira, J. F., Van Bavel, J. J. & Telzer, E. H. The neural development of 'us and them'. *Social cognitive and affective neuroscience* **12**, 184-196 (2017).
55	Hogg, M. A. *Social identity theory.* (Springer, 2016).
56	Crocker, J. & Major, B. in *The psychology of prejudice* 289-314 (Psychology Press, 2013).
57	Social Norms. *Stanford Encyclopedia of Philosophy* (2023). < https://plato.stanford.edu/entries/social-norms/>.
58	Vaughan, G. M. & Hogg, M. A. *Social psychology.* 127 (Pearson Higher Education AU, 2013a).
59	Vaughan, G. M. & Hogg, M. A. *Social psychology.* 121 (Pearson Higher Education AU, 2013b).
60	von Hippel, W. *The Social Leap: The New Evolutionary Science of Who We Are, Where We Come From, and What Makes Us Happy.* 27 (HarperCollins Publishers, 2022b).
61	Bauer, C. & Ferwerda, B. in *Extended Abstracts of the 2020 CHI Conference on Human Factors in Computing Systems.* 1-10.
62	Arzheimer, K. Angus Campbell/Philip E. Converse/Warren E. Miller/Donald E. Stokes, The American Voter, New York 1960. *Schlüsselwerke der Politikwissenschaft*, 67-72 (2007).
63	Berelson, B. R., Lazarsfeld, P. F. & McPhee, W. N. *Voting: A study of opinion formation in a presidential campaign.* (University of Chicago Press, 1986).
64	Kelly, M., Ngo, L., Chituc, V., Huettel, S. & Sinnott-Armstrong, W. Moral conformity in online interactions: Rational justifications increase influence of peer opinions on moral judgments. *Social Influence* **12**, 57-68 (2017).
65	Hogg, M. A. & Turner, J. C. Social identity and conformity: A theory of referent informational influence. *Current issues in European social psychology* **2**, 139-182 (1987).

66   Deutsch, M. & Gerard, H. B. A study of normative and informational social influences upon individual judgment. *The journal of abnormal and social psychology* **51**, 629 (1955).
67   Suhay, E. Explaining group influence: The role of identity and emotion in political conformity and polarization. *Political Behavior* **37**, 221-251 (2015).
68   Chituc, V. & Sinnott-Armstrong, W. Moral conformity and its philosophical lessons. *Philosophical psychology* **33**, 262-282 (2020). https://doi.org:10.1080/09515089.2020.1719395
69   Cialdini, R. B. & Goldstein, N. J. Social influence: Compliance and conformity. *Annu. Rev. Psychol.* **55**, 591-621 (2004).
70   Vaughan, G. M. & Hogg, M. A. *Social psychology*. 240 (Pearson Higher Education AU, 2013c).
71   Gazzaniga, M. S., Heatherton, T. F. & Halpern, D. F. *Psychological science*. 481 (WW Norton New York, 2006f).
72   Lesar, T. S., Briceland, L. & Stein, D. S. Factors related to errors in medication prescribing. *Jama* **277**, 312-317 (1997).
73   Hovland, C. I., Janis, I. L. & Kelley, H. H. Communication and persuasion. (1953).
74   Ma, H. & Miller, C. "I felt completely turned off by the message": The effects of controlling language, fear, and disgust appeals on responses to COVID-19 vaccination messages. *Journal of Health Communication* **27**, 427-438 (2022).
75   Krosnick, J. A. & Alwin, D. F. Aging and susceptibility to attitude change. *Journal of personality and social psychology* **57**, 416 (1989).
76   Etzioni, A. COVID-19 Tests Communitarian Values. *The Diplomat* (2020).
77   Haney, C., Banks, C., Zimbardo, P. & Aronson, E. *A study of prisoners and guards in a simulated prison.* (1973).
78   Docwra, R. *Life - and how to think about it.* (Big Idea publishing, 2021).
79   Hood, B. *The Self Illusion: Why there is no 'you' inside your head.* 214 (Hachette UK, 2012a).
80   Kahneman, D. *Thinking, fast and slow*. 14 (Farrar, Straus and Giroux, 2011p).
81   Kahneman, D. *Thinking, fast and slow*. 199 (Farrar, Straus and Giroux, 2011q).
82   Ditto, P. H. & Lopez, D. F. Motivated skepticism: Use of differential decision criteria for preferred and nonpreferred conclusions. *Journal of personality and social psychology* **63**, 568 (1992).
83   Kahneman, D. *Thinking, fast and slow*. 215 (Farrar, Straus and Giroux, 2011r).
84   Kahneman, D. *Thinking, fast and slow*. 204 (Farrar, Straus and Giroux, 2011s).
85   Leary, M. R., Tambor, E. S., Terdal, S. K. & Downs, D. L. Self-esteem as an interpersonal monitor: The sociometer hypothesis. *Journal of personality and social psychology* **68**, 518 (1995).
86   Alicke, M. D., Klotz, M. L., Breitenbecher, D. L., Yurak, T. J. & Vredenburg, D. S. Personal contact, individuation, and the better-than-average effect. *Journal of personality and social psychology* **68**, 804 (1995).
87   Gazzaniga, M. S., Heatherton, T. F. & Halpern, D. F. *Psychological science*. 553 (WW Norton New York, 2006g).
88   Taylor, S. E. & Brown, J. D. Illusion and well-being: a social psychological perspective on mental health. *Psychological bulletin* **103**, 193 (1988).
89   DePaulo, B. M. & Kashy, D. A. Everyday lies in close and casual relationships. *Journal of personality and social psychology* **74**, 63 (1998).

90	Twain, M. *Following the Equator-A Journey around the world*. (Read Books Ltd, 2020).
91	Bloom, D. E. The shape of global health: the world has come a long way, but still has a long way to go. *Finance & Development* **51**, 6-12 (2014).
92	World Population Prospects: The 2022 Revision (2022). <https://population.un.org/wpp/>.
93	Bloom, D. E. The shape of global health: the world has come a long way, but still has a long way to go. *Finance & Development* **51**, 6-12 (2014a).
94	Obesity fact sheet. *World Health Organisation* (2024). <https://www.who.int/en/news-room/fact-sheets/detail/obesity-and-overweight>.
95	Obesity fact sheet. *World Health Organisation* (2024a). <https://www.who.int/en/news-room/fact-sheets/detail/obesity-and-overweight>.
96	Brownell, K. D. & Horgen, K. B. *Food fight: The inside story of the food industry, America's obesity crisis, and what we can do about it*. 44 (Contemporary books Chicago, 2004).
97	World Health Statistics 2023. *World Health Organisation* (2023). <https://www.who.int/publications/i/item/9789240074323>.
98	Noncommunicable diseases factsheet *World Health Organisation* (2023). <https://www.who.int/news-room/fact-sheets/detail/noncommunicable-diseases>.
99	Sturm, R. The effects of obesity, smoking, and drinking on medical problems and costs. *Health affairs* **21**, 245-253 (2002).
100	WHO Acceleration plan to stop obesity. *World Health Organisation* (2022). <https://www.who.int/publications/i/item/9789240075634>.
101	Obesity fact sheet. *World Health Organisation* (2024b). <https://www.who.int/en/news-room/fact-sheets/detail/obesity-and-overweight>.
102	World Bank dataset (2024). <https://data.worldbank.org/indicator/NY.GDP.MKTP.CD?locations=GB>.
103	Obesity fact sheet. *World Health Organisation* (2024c). <https://www.who.int/en/news-room/fact-sheets/detail/obesity-and-overweight>.
104	World Health Statistics 2023. *World Health Organisation* (2023a). <https://www.who.int/publications/i/item/9789240074323>.
105	Gluckman, P. & Hanson, M. *Mismatch: Why our world no longer fits our bodies*. (Oxford University Press, USA, 2006).
106	Obesity fact sheet. *World Health Organisation* (2024d). <https://www.who.int/en/news-room/fact-sheets/detail/obesity-and-overweight>.
107	Brownell, K. D. & Horgen, K. B. *Food fight: The inside story of the food industry, America's obesity crisis, and what we can do about it*. 12 (Contemporary books Chicago, 2004a).
108	Buckling up to save lives: UN celebrates five decades of seat belt laws. (2023). <https://news.un.org/en/story/2023/06/1137412>.
109	Dovey, T. *Eating behaviour*. (McGraw-Hill Education (UK), 2010).
110	Brownell, K. D. & Horgen, K. B. *Food fight: The inside story of the food industry, America's obesity crisis, and what we can do about it*. 13 (Contemporary books Chicago, 2004b).
111	Dovey, T. *Eating behaviour*. 116 (McGraw-Hill Education (UK), 2010a).
112	Gluckman, P. & Hanson, M. *Mismatch: Why our world no longer fits our bodies*. 160 (Oxford University Press, USA, 2006a).

113	Andre, P., Boneva, T., Chopra, F. & Falk, A. Globally representative evidence on the actual and perceived support for climate action. *Nature Climate Change* **14**, 253-259 (2024).
114	Gluckman, P. & Hanson, M. *Mismatch: Why our world no longer fits our bodies*. 120 (Oxford University Press, USA, 2006b).
115	Gluckman, P. & Hanson, M. *Mismatch: Why our world no longer fits our bodies*. 161 (Oxford University Press, USA, 2006c).
116	Media Nations Report 6. (2023). <https://www.ofcom.org.uk/research-and-data/tv-radio-and-on-demand/media-nations-reports/media-nations-2023 >.
117	Brownell, K. D. & Horgen, K. B. *Food fight: The inside story of the food industry, America's obesity crisis, and what we can do about it*. 72 (Contemporary books Chicago, 2004c).
118	Cregan-Reid, V. *Primate Change: How the world we made is remaking us*. 221 (Hachette UK, 2018).
119	Curioni, C. C. & Lourenço, P. M. Long-term weight loss after diet and exercise: a systematic review. *International journal of obesity* **29**, 1168-1174 (2005).
120	Pavlou, K. N., Krey, S. & Steffee, W. P. Exercise as an adjunct to weight loss and maintenance in moderately obese subjects. *The American journal of clinical nutrition* **49**, 1115-1123 (1989).
121	Opdenacker, J., Boen, F., De Bourdeaudhuij, I. & Auweele, Y. V. Explaining the psychological effects of a sustainable lifestyle physical activity intervention among rural women. *Mental Health and Physical Activity* **1**, 74-81 (2008).
122	Brownell, K. D. & Horgen, K. B. *Food fight: The inside story of the food industry, America's obesity crisis, and what we can do about it*. 72 (Contemporary books Chicago, 2004d).
123	Brownell, K. D. & Horgen, K. B. *Food fight: The inside story of the food industry, America's obesity crisis, and what we can do about it*. 72 (Contemporary books Chicago, 2004e).
124	Brownell, K. D. & Horgen, K. B. *Food fight: The inside story of the food industry, America's obesity crisis, and what we can do about it*. 73 (Contemporary books Chicago, 2004f).
125	Dovey, T. *Eating behaviour*. 64 (McGraw-Hill Education (UK), 2010b).
126	Gluckman, P. & Hanson, M. *Mismatch: Why our world no longer fits our bodies*. 160 (Oxford University Press, USA, 2006d).
127	Cregan-Reid, V. *Primate Change: How the world we made is remaking us*. 223 (Hachette UK, 2018a).
128	Gardner, C. D. et al. Effect of low-fat vs low-carbohydrate diet on 12-month weight loss in overweight adults and the association with genotype pattern or insulin secretion: the DIETFITS randomized clinical trial. *Jama* **319**, 667-679 (2018).
129	Gluckman, P. & Hanson, M. *Mismatch: Why our world no longer fits our bodies*. 162 (Oxford University Press, USA, 2006e).
130	Gluckman, P. & Hanson, M. *Mismatch: Why our world no longer fits our bodies*. 162 (Oxford University Press, USA, 2006f).
131	Neel, J. V. Diabetes mellitus: a "thrifty" genotype rendered detrimental by "progress"? *American journal of human genetics* **14**, 353 (1962).
132	Gluckman, P. & Hanson, M. *Mismatch: Why our world no longer fits our bodies*. 162 (Oxford University Press, USA, 2006g).
133	Gluckman, P. & Hanson, M. *Mismatch: Why our world no longer fits our bodies*. 173 (Oxford University Press, USA, 2006h).
134	Gluckman, P. & Hanson, M. *Mismatch: Why our world no longer fits our bodies*. 163 (Oxford University Press, USA, 2006i).

135 Gluckman, P. & Hanson, M. *Mismatch: Why our world no longer fits our bodies*. 171 (Oxford University Press, USA, 2006j).
136 Gluckman, P. & Hanson, M. *Mismatch: Why our world no longer fits our bodies*. 166 (Oxford University Press, USA, 2006k).
137 Robinson, S. et al. Impact of educational attainment on the quality of young women's diets. *European journal of clinical nutrition* **58**, 1174-1180 (2004).
138 Dovey, T. *Eating behaviour*. 99 (McGraw-Hill Education (UK), 2010c).
139 Dovey, T. *Eating behaviour*. 105 (McGraw-Hill Education (UK), 2010d).
140 Dovey, T. *Eating behaviour*. 100 (McGraw-Hill Education (UK), 2010e).
141 Alblas, M. C. *Consuming media, consuming food?: Reactivity to palatable food cues in television content*. (2021).
142 Haynes, C., Lee, M. D. & Yeomans, M. R. Interactive effects of stress, dietary restraint, and disinhibition on appetite. *Eating behaviors* **4**, 369-383 (2003).
143 Dovey, T. *Eating behaviour*. 53 (McGraw-Hill Education (UK), 2010f).
144 Dovey, T. *Eating behaviour*. 54 (McGraw-Hill Education (UK), 2010g).
145 Cullen, K. W. et al. Child-reported family and peer influences on fruit, juice and vegetable consumption: reliability and validity of measures. *Health education research* **16**, 187-200 (2001).
146 Dovey, T. *Eating behaviour*. 79 (McGraw-Hill Education (UK), 2010h).
147 Salvy, S.-J., Jarrin, D., Paluch, R., Irfan, N. & Pliner, P. Effects of social influence on eating in couples, friends and strangers. *Appetite* **49**, 92-99 (2007).
148 Salvy, S.-J., Jarrin, D., Paluch, R., Irfan, N. & Pliner, P. Effects of social influence on eating in couples, friends and strangers. *Appetite* **49**, 92-99 (2007a).
149 Baumeister, R. F. & Sommer, K. L. What do men want? Gender differences and two spheres of belongingness: comment on Cross and Madson (1997). (1997).
150 Brownell, K. D. & Horgen, K. B. *Food fight: The inside story of the food industry, America's obesity crisis, and what we can do about it*. 23 (Contemporary books Chicago, 2004g).
151 Genes are not destiny. < https://www.hsph.harvard.edu/obesity-prevention-source/obesity-causes/genes-and-obesity/>.
152 Brownell, K. D. & Horgen, K. B. *Food fight: The inside story of the food industry, America's obesity crisis, and what we can do about it*. 22 (Contemporary books Chicago, 2004h).
153 Brownell, K. D. & Horgen, K. B. *Food fight: The inside story of the food industry, America's obesity crisis, and what we can do about it*. 22 (Contemporary books Chicago, 2004i).
154 De Ridder, D., Adriaanse, M., Evers, C. & Verhoeven, A. Who diets? Most people and especially when they worry about food. *Appetite* **80**, 103-108 (2014).
155 Van Gestel, L. C., Kroese, F. M. & De Ridder, D. T. Nudging at the checkout counter–A longitudinal study of the effect of a food repositioning nudge on healthy food choice. *Psychology & health* **33**, 800-809 (2018).
156 Gluckman, P. & Hanson, M. *Mismatch: Why our world no longer fits our bodies*. 172 (Oxford University Press, USA, 2006l).
157 Gluckman, P. & Hanson, M. *Mismatch: Why our world no longer fits our bodies*. 172 (Oxford University Press, USA, 2006m).
158 Brownell, K. D. & Horgen, K. B. *Food fight: The inside story of the food industry, America's obesity crisis, and what we can do about it*. 50 (Contemporary books Chicago, 2004j).

159 Convenience food - United Kingdom. *Statista Market Insights* (2024). <https://www.statista.com/outlook/cmo/food/convenience-food/united-kingdom>.
160 *McDonald's Newsroom*, <https://www.mcdonalds.com/gb/en-gb/newsroom.html> (
161 How many McDonald's restaurants are there in the U.K. and the world? (2018).
162 Brownell, K. D. & Horgen, K. B. *Food fight: The inside story of the food industry, America's obesity crisis, and what we can do about it*. 37 (Contemporary books Chicago, 2004k).
163 Zhang, Y. *et al.* Correlation between frequency of eating out of home and dietary intake, sleep, and physical activity: A survey of young CDC employees in China. *International Journal of Environmental Research and Public Health* **19**, 3209 (2022).
164 Brownell, K. D. & Horgen, K. B. *Food fight: The inside story of the food industry, America's obesity crisis, and what we can do about it*. 37 (Contemporary books Chicago, 2004l).
165 Goodhart. Television through the ages. (2020). <https://www.museumofthehome.org.uk/explore/stories-of-home/television-through-the-ages/>.
166 Certain, L. K. & Kahn, R. S. Prevalence, correlates, and trajectory of television viewing among infants and toddlers. *Pediatrics* **109**, 634-642 (2002).
167 How Much Time Do US Adults Spend Watching TV? (2023). <https://www.marketingcharts.com/television/tv-audiences-and-consumption-229018>.
168 Brownell, K. D. & Horgen, K. B. *Food fight: The inside story of the food industry, America's obesity crisis, and what we can do about it*. 36 (Contemporary books Chicago, 2004m).
169 Koplan, J. P. & Dietz, W. H. Caloric imbalance and public health policy. *Jama* **282**, 1579-1581 (1999).
170 Brownell, K. D. & Horgen, K. B. *Food fight: The inside story of the food industry, America's obesity crisis, and what we can do about it*. 208 (Contemporary books Chicago, 2004n).
171 Reidpath, D. D., Burns, C., Garrard, J., Mahoney, M. & Townsend, M. An ecological study of the relationship between social and environmental determinants of obesity. *Health & place* **8**, 141-145 (2002).
172 Powell, L. M., Auld, M. C., Chaloupka, F. J., O'Malley, P. M. & Johnston, L. D. Associations between access to food stores and adolescent body mass index. *American journal of preventive medicine* **33**, S301-S307 (2007).
173 Parks, S. E., Housemann, R. A. & Brownson, R. C. Differential correlates of physical activity in urban and rural adults of various socioeconomic backgrounds in the United States. *Journal of Epidemiology & Community Health* **57**, 29-35 (2003).
174 Parnham, J. C. *et al.* The ultra-processed food content of school meals and packed lunches in the United Kingdom. *Nutrients* **14**, 2961 (2022).
175 Head. Ultra-processed foods make up almost two-thirds of Britain's school meals.
176 Brownell, K. D. & Horgen, K. B. *Food fight: The inside story of the food industry, America's obesity crisis, and what we can do about it*. 137 (Contemporary books Chicago, 2004o).
177 Walking and cycling statistics -England (2023).

178	Simons-Morton, B. G., Taylor, W. C., Snider, S. A. & Huang, I. W. The physical activity of fifth-grade students during physical education classes. *American Journal of Public Health* **83**, 262-264 (1993).
179	Brownell, K. D. & Horgen, K. B. *Food fight: The inside story of the food industry, America's obesity crisis, and what we can do about it*. 78 (Contemporary books Chicago, 2004p).
180	Physical activity guidelines for children and young people. (2021). < https://www.nhs.uk/live-well/exercise/physical-activity-guidelines-children-and-young-people/>.
181	Sahud, H. B., Binns, H. J., Meadow, W. L. & Tanz, R. R. Marketing fast food: impact of fast food restaurants in children's hospitals. *Pediatrics* **118**, 2290-2297 (2006).
182	Gluckman, P. & Hanson, M. *Mismatch: Why our world no longer fits our bodies*. 192 (Oxford University Press, USA, 2006n).
183	Gluckman, P. & Hanson, M. *Mismatch: Why our world no longer fits our bodies*. 198 (Oxford University Press, USA, 2006o).
184	Brownell, K. D. & Horgen, K. B. *Food fight: The inside story of the food industry, America's obesity crisis, and what we can do about it*. 8 (Contemporary books Chicago, 2004q).
185	Poti, J. M. & Popkin, B. M. Trends in energy intake among US children by eating location and food source, 1977-2006. *Journal of the American Dietetic Association* **111**, 1156-1164 (2011).
186	Cancer: Carcinogenicity of the consumption of red meat and processed meat. (2015). < https://www.who.int/news-room/questions-and-answers/item/cancer-carcinogenicity-of-the-consumption-of-red-meat-and-processed-meat>.
187	Piernas, C. & Popkin, B. M. Snacking increased among US adults between 1977 and 2006. *The Journal of nutrition* **140**, 325-332 (2010).
188	Piernas, C. & Popkin, B. M. Snacking increased among US adults between 1977 and 2006. *The Journal of nutrition* **140**, 325-332 (2010a).
189	Darmon, N. & Drewnowski, A. Does social class predict diet quality? *The American journal of clinical nutrition* **87**, 1107-1117 (2008).
190	Darmon, N. & Drewnowski, A. Does social class predict diet quality? *The American journal of clinical nutrition* **87**, 1107-1117 (2008a).
191	Nielsen, S. J. & Popkin, B. M. Patterns and trends in food portion sizes, 1977-1998. *Jama* **289**, 450-453 (2003).
192	Nielsen, S. J. & Popkin, B. M. Patterns and trends in food portion sizes, 1977-1998. *Jama* **289**, 450-453 (2003a).
193	Food and Diet. <https://www.hsph.harvard.edu/obesity-prevention-source/obesity-causes/diet-and-weight/ >.
194	Dovey, T. *Eating behaviour*. 77 (McGraw-Hill Education (UK), 2010i).
195	Advertising to children: UK the worst in Europe. *Food Magazine* (1997).
196	<https://www.eatnatural.com/> (
197	Campbell, J. Some cereal bars for children contain over 40% sugar, watchdog finds. (2015). <https://www.independent.co.uk/life-style/food-and-drink/news/some-cereal-bars-for-children-contain-up-to-over-40-fat-watchdog-finds-a134231.html >.
198	*Traffic Light Labelling: A Guide For Food Businesses*, <https://ashbury.global/blog/traffic-light-labelling/ > (2024).
199	*Traffic Light Labelling: A Guide For Food Businesses*, <https://ashbury.global/blog/traffic-light-labelling/ > (2024a).
200	*Understanding Food Labels*, <https://www.nutrition.org.uk/creating-a-healthy-diet/food-labelling/> (

201	Poulter, S. Breakfast cereal boxes 'mislead' shoppers over how much sugar, fat and salt they contain, says Which? (2018). <https://www.dailymail.co.uk/news/article-5863231/Breakfast-cereal-boxes-mislead-shoppers-sugar-fat-salt-contain-Which.html>.
202	*Which? calls on government to fix food labelling 'chaos'*, <https://www.bbc.co.uk/news/business-44533752 > (2018).
203	*Which? calls on government to fix food labelling 'chaos'*, <https://www.bbc.co.uk/news/business-44533752 > (2018a).
204	Consoli. Television: Clutter climbs higher. *MediaWeek* (1999).
205	Brownell, K. D. & Horgen, K. B. *Food fight: The inside story of the food industry, America's obesity crisis, and what we can do about it.* 106 (Contemporary books Chicago, 2004r).
206	Brownell, K. D. & Horgen, K. B. *Food fight: The inside story of the food industry, America's obesity crisis, and what we can do about it.* 104 (Contemporary books Chicago, 2004s).
207	Brownell, K. D. & Horgen, K. B. *Food fight: The inside story of the food industry, America's obesity crisis, and what we can do about it.* 105 (Contemporary books Chicago, 2004t).
208	Davis. Call to tighten junk food advert rules after obesity link shown (2018).
209	Dovey, T. *Eating behaviour*. 93 (McGraw-Hill Education (UK), 2010j).
210	Dovey, T. *Eating behaviour*. 94 (McGraw-Hill Education (UK), 2010k).
211	Dovey, T. *Eating behaviour*. 95 (McGraw-Hill Education (UK), 2010l).
212	Faria, J. Food advertising in the United States – statistics & facts. (2023). < https://www.statista.com/topics/2223/food-advertising/#topicOverview>.
213	Brownell, K. D. & Horgen, K. B. *Food fight: The inside story of the food industry, America's obesity crisis, and what we can do about it.* 110 (Contemporary books Chicago, 2004u).
214	Brownell, K. D. & Horgen, K. B. *Food fight: The inside story of the food industry, America's obesity crisis, and what we can do about it.* 108 (Contemporary books Chicago, 2004v).
215	Skopeliti, C. Four in five billboard ads in England and Wales in poorer areas. (2024). <https://www.theguardian.com/media/2024/mar/04/four-in-five-billboard-ads-in-england-and-wales-in-poorer-areas >.
216	2021-23 Out of Home Advertising Spend Analysis
217	"Check it out!" – Families bombarded with 'supermarket sweep' of sugary promotions during their weekly shop. (2018). <https://www.actiononsugar.org/news-centre/sugar-in-the-news/2018/2018-stories/check-it-out--families-bombarded-with-supermarket-sweep-of-sugary-promotions-during-their-weekly-shop.html>.
218	Market Insights - Food worldwide. (2024). < https://www.statista.com/outlook/cmo/food/worldwide#revenue>.
219	Brownell, K. D. & Horgen, K. B. *Food fight: The inside story of the food industry, America's obesity crisis, and what we can do about it.* 10 (Contemporary books Chicago, 2004w).
220	Nestle, M. Food politics. *Omega* (2011).
221	*About us*, <https://www.actiononsalt.org.uk/about/index.html > (
222	Brownell, K. D. & Horgen, K. B. *Food fight: The inside story of the food industry, America's obesity crisis, and what we can do about it.* 7 (Contemporary books Chicago, 2004x).
223	Prime Minister to create 'smokefree generation' by ending cigarette sales to those born on or after 1 January 2009 (2023). <https://www.gov.uk/government/news/prime-minister-to-create-smokefree-generation-by-ending-cigarette-sales-to-those-born-on-or-after-1-january-2009>.

224 WHO Acceleration plan to stop obesity. *World Health Organisation* (2022a). <https://www.who.int/publications/i/item/9789240075634>.
225 Fielden, A. L., Sillence, E., Little, L. & Harris, P. R. Online self-affirmation increases fruit and vegetable consumption in groups at high risk of low intake. *Applied Psychology: Health and Well-Being* **8**, 3-18 (2016).
226 Fielden, A. L., Sillence, E., Little, L. & Harris, P. R. Online self-affirmation increases fruit and vegetable consumption in groups at high risk of low intake. *Applied Psychology: Health and Well-Being* **8**, 3-18 (2016a).
227 Gluckman, P. & Hanson, M. *Mismatch: Why our world no longer fits our bodies*. 198 (Oxford University Press, USA, 2006p).
228 Brownell, K. D. & Horgen, K. B. *Food fight: The inside story of the food industry, America's obesity crisis, and what we can do about it*. 299 (Contemporary books Chicago, 2004y).
229 Breastfeeding Report Card. *US Centers for Disease Control and Prevention* (2022).
230 Brownell, K. D. & Horgen, K. B. *Food fight: The inside story of the food industry, America's obesity crisis, and what we can do about it*. 264 (Contemporary books Chicago, 2004z).
231 Asnicar, F. *et al.* Microbiome connections with host metabolism and habitual diet from 1,098 deeply phenotyped individuals. *Nature medicine* **27**, 321-332 (2021).
232 Gluckman, P. & Hanson, M. *Mismatch: Why our world no longer fits our bodies*. 173 (Oxford University Press, USA, 2006q).
233 Brownell, K. D. & Horgen, K. B. *Food fight: The inside story of the food industry, America's obesity crisis, and what we can do about it*. 264 (Contemporary books Chicago, 2004a1).
234 Patel, S. B. & Kariel, J. Vol. 372 (British Medical Journal Publishing Group, 2021).
235 Improving food in the neighbourhood <https://www.hsph.harvard.edu/obesity-prevention-source/obesity-prevention/food-environment/supermarkets-food-retail-farmers-markets/>.
236 Safe, Affordable, and Accessible Physical Activity <https://www.hsph.harvard.edu/obesity-prevention-source/obesity-prevention/physical-activity-environment/safe-affordable-and-accessible-physical-activity-and-obesity-prevention/#ref3>.
237 Florence. Diet Quality and Academic Performance. *Journal of School Health*, **78** (2008).
238 Mozaffarian, D., Angell, S. Y., Lang, T. & Rivera, J. A. Role of government policy in nutrition—barriers to and opportunities for healthier eating. *Bmj* **361** (2018).
239 Brownell, K. D. & Horgen, K. B. *Food fight: The inside story of the food industry, America's obesity crisis, and what we can do about it*. 264 (Contemporary books Chicago, 2004a2).
240 Mozaffarian, D., Angell, S. Y., Lang, T. & Rivera, J. A. Role of government policy in nutrition—barriers to and opportunities for healthier eating. *Bmj* **361** (2018a).
241 Mozaffarian, D., Angell, S. Y., Lang, T. & Rivera, J. A. Role of government policy in nutrition—barriers to and opportunities for healthier eating. *Bmj* **361** (2018b).
242 Mozaffarian, D., Angell, S. Y., Lang, T. & Rivera, J. A. Role of government policy in nutrition—barriers to and opportunities for healthier eating. *Bmj* **361** (2018c).
243 Baicker, K., Cutler, D. & Song, Z. Workplace wellness programs can generate savings. *Health affairs* **29**, 304-311 (2010).

244 Schulte, P. A. *et al.* Work, obesity, and occupational safety and health. *American journal of public health* **97**, 428-436 (2007).
245 Schulte, P., Wagner, G., Downes, A. & Miller, D. A framework for the concurrent consideration of occupational hazards and obesity. *Annals of occupational hygiene* **52**, 555-566 (2008).
246 Van Gestel, L. C., Kroese, F. M. & De Ridder, D. T. Nudging at the checkout counter–A longitudinal study of the effect of a food repositioning nudge on healthy food choice. *Psychology & health* **33**, 800-809 (2018a).
247 WHO Acceleration plan to stop obesity. *World Health Organisation* (2022b). <https://www.who.int/publications/i/item/9789240075634>.
248 Metcalfe, S. Sugar tax explainer (2022). <https://www.instituteforgovernment.org.uk/explainer/sugar-tax>.
249 Mozaffarian, D., Angell, S. Y., Lang, T. & Rivera, J. A. Role of government policy in nutrition—barriers to and opportunities for healthier eating. *Bmj* **361** (2018d).
250 Mozaffarian, D., Angell, S. Y., Lang, T. & Rivera, J. A. Role of government policy in nutrition—barriers to and opportunities for healthier eating. *Bmj* **361** (2018e).
251 Nirajan. Healthier ready-to-eat meals would have 'huge' EU climate benefits – report (2024). <https://www.theguardian.com/environment/2024/apr/17/healthier-ready-to-eat-meals-would-have-huge-eu-climate-benefits-report>.
252 Mozaffarian, D., Angell, S. Y., Lang, T. & Rivera, J. A. Role of government policy in nutrition—barriers to and opportunities for healthier eating. *Bmj* **361** (2018f).
253 Food Pricing, Taxes, and Agricultural Policy. <https://www.hsph.harvard.edu/obesity-prevention-source/obesity-prevention/food-environment/food-pricing-and-agricultural-policy-and-obesity-prevention/>.
254 Clem, J. & Barthel, B. A look at plant-based diets. *Missouri medicine* **118**, 233 (2021b).
255 Clem, J. & Barthel, B. A look at plant-based diets. *Missouri medicine* **118**, 233 (2021).
256 Clem, J. & Barthel, B. A look at plant-based diets. *Missouri medicine* **118**, 233 (2021a).
257 Mass Media and Technology to Encourage Activity.
258 Bloom, D. E. The shape of global health: the world has come a long way, but still has a long way to go. *Finance & Development* **51**, 6-12 (2014b).
259 Mencken, H. L. *Minority Report: H.L. Mencken's Notebooks.* (A.A. Knopf, 1956).
260 Islam, M. S. *et al.* COVID-19–Related Infodemic and Its Impact on Public Health: A Global Social Media Analysis. *The American Journal of Tropical Medicine and Hygiene* **103**, 1621-1629 (2020). https://doi.org:10.4269/ajtmh.20-0812
261 Ashurst. Methanol Toxicity. (2023). <https://www.ncbi.nlm.nih.gov/books/NBK482121/>.
262 Amin. COVID-19 mortality preventable by vaccines. (2022). <https://www.healthsystemtracker.org/brief/covid19-and-other-leading-causes-of-death-in-the-us/#Share%20of%20adult%20population%20and%20adult%20COVID-19%20deaths%20by%20vaccination%20status,%2025%20jurisdictions%20in%20the%20U.S.,%20June%202021%20to%20February%202022>.

263 Evolution, Climate Change and Other Issues. (2009). <https://www.pewresearch.org/politics/2009/07/09/section-5-evolution-climate-change-and-other-issues/>.
264 Lewandowsky, S., Ecker, U. K. & Cook, J. Beyond misinformation: Understanding and coping with the "post-truth" era. *Journal of applied research in memory and cognition* **6**, 353-369 (2017).
265 Lewandowsky, S., Ecker, U. K. & Cook, J. Beyond misinformation: Understanding and coping with the "post-truth" era. *Journal of applied research in memory and cognition* **6**, 353-369 (2017a).
266 Lasser, J. et al. From alternative conceptions of honesty to alternative facts in communications by US politicians. *Nature human behaviour* **7**, 2140-2151 (2023).
267 In four years, President Trump made 30,573 false or misleading claims. *Washington Post* (2021).
268 Van der Linden, S. *Foolproof: Why misinformation infects our minds and how to build immunity*. (WW Norton & Company, 2023).
269 Van der Linden, S. *Foolproof: Why misinformation infects our minds and how to build immunity*. 197 (WW Norton & Company, 2023a).
270 Lasser, J. et al. From alternative conceptions of honesty to alternative facts in communications by US politicians. *Nature human behaviour* **7**, 2140-2151 (2023a).
271 Tan, A. S. & Bigman, C. A. Misinformation about commercial tobacco products on social media—implications and research opportunities for reducing tobacco-related health disparities. *American Journal of Public Health* **110**, S281-S283 (2020).
272 Natoli, E. E. & Marques, M. D. The antidepressant hoax: Conspiracy theories decrease health-seeking intentions. *British Journal of Social Psychology* **60**, 902-923 (2021).
273 Jolley, D., Marques, M. D. & Cookson, D. Shining a spotlight on the dangerous consequences of conspiracy theories. *Current Opinion in Psychology* **47**, 101363 (2022).
274 Richards, L., Molinaro, P., Wyman, J. & Craun, S. *Lone offender: a study of lone offender terrorism in the United States (1972-2015)*. (National Center for the Analysis of Violent Crime, Federal Bureau of ..., 2019).
275 Jolley, D., Meleady, R. & Douglas, K. M. Exposure to intergroup conspiracy theories promotes prejudice which spreads across groups. *British Journal of Psychology* **111**, 17-35 (2020).
276 Snyder, T. *On Tyranny: Twenty Lessons from the Twentieth Century*. 65 (Random House, 2017).
277 Van der Linden, S. *Foolproof: Why misinformation infects our minds and how to build immunity*. 201 (WW Norton & Company, 2023b).
278 Lewandowsky, S. In conversation with Richard Docwra. (12th February 2024).
279 Luo, Y. & Zhao, J. Motivated attention in climate change perception and action. *Frontiers in psychology* **10**, 1541 (2019).
280 Kahneman, D. *Thinking, fast and slow*. 62 (Farrar, Straus and Giroux, 2011t).
281 Kahneman, D. *Thinking, fast and slow*. 81 (Farrar, Straus and Giroux, 2011u).
282 Kahneman, D. *Thinking, fast and slow*. (Farrar, Straus and Giroux, 2011v).
283 Kahneman, D. *Thinking, fast and slow*. 199 (Farrar, Straus and Giroux, 2011w).
284 Kahan, D. M. in *Culture, politics and climate change*   203-220 (Routledge, 2014).

285 Klein, E. *Why we're polarized.* (Simon and Schuster, 2020).
286 Douglas, K. M., Sutton, R. M. & Cichocka, A. The psychology of conspiracy theories. *Current directions in psychological science* **26**, 538-542 (2017).
287 Hills, T. T., Noguchi, T. & Gibbert, M. Information overload or search-amplified risk? Set size and order effects on decisions from experience. *Psychonomic Bulletin & Review* **20**, 1023-1031 (2013).
288 Bawden, D. & Robinson, L. The dark side of information: overload, anxiety and other paradoxes and pathologies. *Journal of information science* **35**, 180-191 (2009).
289 Van der Linden, S. *Foolproof: Why misinformation infects our minds and how to build immunity.* 141 (WW Norton & Company, 2023c).
290 Lewandowsky, S. & Pomerantsev, P. Technology and democracy: A paradox wrapped in a contradiction inside an irony. *Memory, mind & media* **1**, e5 (2022).
291 Soroka, S., Fournier, P. & Nir, L. Cross-national evidence of a negativity bias in psychophysiological reactions to news. *Proceedings of the National Academy of Sciences* **116**, 18888-18892 (2019).
292 Brady, W. J., Wills, J. A., Jost, J. T., Tucker, J. A. & Van Bavel, J. J. Emotion shapes the diffusion of moralized content in social networks. *Proceedings of the National Academy of Sciences* **114**, 7313-7318 (2017).
293 Van der Linden, S. *Foolproof: Why misinformation infects our minds and how to build immunity.* 130 (WW Norton & Company, 2023d).
294 Lewandowsky, S. & Pomerantsev, P. Technology and democracy: A paradox wrapped in a contradiction inside an irony. *Memory, mind & media* **1**, e5 (2022a).
295 Davies, N. *Flat earth news: An award-winning reporter exposes falsehood, distortion and propaganda in the global media.* (Random House, 2011).
296 Lewandowsky, S., Ecker, U. K. & Cook, J. Beyond misinformation: Understanding and coping with the "post-truth" era. *Journal of applied research in memory and cognition* **6**, 353-369 (2017b).
297 Nick Davies: 'Churnalism has taken the place of what we should be doing: Telling the truth'. (2008). <https://pressgazette.co.uk/publishers/nationals/nick-davies-churnalism-has-taken-the-place-of-what-we-should-be-doing-telling-the-truth-40117/>.
298 Broockman, D. & Kalla, J. The manifold effects of partisan media on viewers' beliefs and attitudes: A field experiment with Fox News viewers. *OSF Preprints* **1**, 1-42 (2022).
299 Kull, S., Ramsay, C. & Lewis, E. Misperceptions, the media, and the Iraq war. *Pol. Sci. Q.* **118**, 569 (2003).
300 Lewandowsky, S., Ecker, U. K. & Cook, J. Beyond misinformation: Understanding and coping with the "post-truth" era. *Journal of applied research in memory and cognition* **6**, 353-369 (2017c).
301 Lewandowsky, S. & Pomerantsev, P. Technology and democracy: A paradox wrapped in a contradiction inside an irony. *Memory, mind & media* **1**, e5 (2022b).
302 Sommeiller. Income inequality in the U.S. by state, metropolitan area, and county. (2016).
303 Lewandowsky, S. & Pomerantsev, P. Technology and democracy: A paradox wrapped in a contradiction inside an irony. *Memory, mind & media* **1**, e5 (2022c).
304 Casara, B. G. S., Suitner, C. & Jetten, J. The impact of economic inequality on conspiracy beliefs. *Journal of Experimental Social Psychology* **98**, 104245 (2022).
305 Wilkinson, R., Pickett, K. & Cato, M. S. (Penguin, London, 2009).

306 Garand, J. C. Income inequality, party polarization, and roll-call voting in the US Senate. *The Journal of Politics* **72**, 1109-1128 (2010).
307 Van der Linden, S. *Foolproof: Why misinformation infects our minds and how to build immunity*. 157 (WW Norton & Company, 2023e).
308 Lewandowsky, S. & Pomerantsev, P. Technology and democracy: A paradox wrapped in a contradiction inside an irony. *Memory, mind & media* **1**, e5 (2022d).
309 Lewandowsky, S. & Pomerantsev, P. Technology and democracy: A paradox wrapped in a contradiction inside an irony. *Memory, mind & media* **1**, e5 (2022e).
310 Van der Linden, S. *Foolproof: Why misinformation infects our minds and how to build immunity*. 162 (WW Norton & Company, 2023f).
311 Lasser, J. et al. From alternative conceptions of honesty to alternative facts in communications by US politicians. *Nature human behaviour* **7**, 2140-2151 (2023b).
312 Lewandowsky, S., Ecker, U. K. & Cook, J. Beyond misinformation: Understanding and coping with the "post-truth" era. *Journal of applied research in memory and cognition* **6**, 353-369 (2017d).
313 Kozyreva, A., Wineburg, S., Lewandowsky, S. & Hertwig, R. Critical ignoring as a core competence for digital citizens. *Current Directions in Psychological Science* **32**, 81-88 (2023).
314 Kozyreva, A., Wineburg, S., Lewandowsky, S. & Hertwig, R. Critical ignoring as a core competence for digital citizens. *Current Directions in Psychological Science* **32**, 81-88 (2023a).
315 Lewandowsky, S. et al. Technology and democracy: Understanding the influence of online technologies on political behaviour and decision-making. (2020).
316 Van der Linden, S. *Foolproof: Why misinformation infects our minds and how to build immunity*. 186 (WW Norton & Company, 2023g).
317 Van der Linden, S. *Foolproof: Why misinformation infects our minds and how to build immunity*. 219 (WW Norton & Company, 2023h).
318 Van der Linden, S. *Foolproof: Why misinformation infects our minds and how to build immunity*. 277 (WW Norton & Company, 2023i).
319 Kozyreva, A. et al. Resolving content moderation dilemmas between free speech and harmful misinformation. *Proceedings of the National Academy of Sciences* **120**, e2210666120 (2023).
320 Kozyreva, A., Lewandowsky, S. & Hertwig, R. Citizens versus the internet: Confronting digital challenges with cognitive tools. *Psychological Science in the Public Interest* **21**, 103-156 (2020).
321 Lewandowsky, S. & Pomerantsev, P. Technology and democracy: A paradox wrapped in a contradiction inside an irony. *Memory, mind & media* **1**, e5 (2022f).
322 Van der Linden, S. *Foolproof: Why misinformation infects our minds and how to build immunity*. 199 (WW Norton & Company, 2023j).
323 Kozyreva, A., Lewandowsky, S. & Hertwig, R. Citizens versus the internet: Confronting digital challenges with cognitive tools. *Psychological Science in the Public Interest* **21**, 103-156 (2020b).
324 Fazio, L. Pausing to consider why a headline is true or false can help reduce the sharing of false news. *Harvard Kennedy School Misinformation Review* **1** (2020).
325 Kozyreva, A., Lewandowsky, S. & Hertwig, R. Citizens versus the internet: Confronting digital challenges with cognitive tools. *Psychological Science in the Public Interest* **21**, 103-156 (2020a).

326   Van der Linden, S. *Foolproof: Why misinformation infects our minds and how to build immunity.* 253 (WW Norton & Company, 2023k).
327   Van der Linden, S. *Foolproof: Why misinformation infects our minds and how to build immunity.* 131 (WW Norton & Company, 2023l).
328   Lewandowsky, S., Ecker, U. K. & Cook, J. Beyond misinformation: Understanding and coping with the "post-truth" era. *Journal of applied research in memory and cognition* **6**, 353-369 (2017e).
329   Van der Linden, S. *Foolproof: Why misinformation infects our minds and how to build immunity.* 131 (WW Norton & Company, 2023m).
330   Luther, M. *Letter from a Birmingham Jail.* (HARPER ONE, 2025).
331   Flynn, S. Woman awarded $1m after gas station worker told her: 'I don't serve Black people'. (2023). <https://www.independent.co.uk/news/world/americas/oregon-lawsuit-gas-station-serve-black-people-b2271544.html >.
332   Mackie, D. M., Hamilton, D. L., Susskind, J. & Rosselli, F. Social psychological foundations of stereotype formation. *Stereotypes and stereotyping*, 41-78 (1996).
333   Vaughan, G. M. & Hogg, M. A. *Social psychology.* 365 (Pearson Higher Education AU, 2013d).
334   Bartol, K. M. & Butterfield, D. A. Sex effects in evaluating leaders. *Journal of applied psychology* **61**, 446 (1976).
335   Izraeli, D. N. Sex effects in evaluating leaders: A replication study. *Journal of Applied Psychology* **70**, 540 (1985).
336   Mastari, L., Spruyt, B. & Siongers, J. Benevolent and hostile sexism in social spheres: The impact of parents, school and romance on Belgian adolescents' sexist attitudes. *Frontiers in Sociology* **4**, 47 (2019).
337   Glick, P. & Fiske, S. T. in *Social cognition*   116-160 (Routledge, 2018).
338   Vaughan, G. M. & Hogg, M. A. *Social psychology.* 365 (Pearson Higher Education AU, 2013e).
339   Crosby, F., Bromley, S. & Saxe, L. Recent unobtrusive studies of Black and White discrimination and prejudice: A literature review. *Psychological bulletin* **87**, 546 (1980).
340   Crosby, F., Bromley, S. & Saxe, L. Recent unobtrusive studies of Black and White discrimination and prejudice: A literature review. *Psychological bulletin* **87**, 546 (1980a).
341   Dovidio, J. F., Gaertner, S. L. & Pearson, A. R. On the Nature of Prejudice: The Psychological Foundations of Hate. (2005).
342   Crosby, F., Bromley, S. & Saxe, L. Recent unobtrusive studies of Black and White discrimination and prejudice: A literature review. *Psychological bulletin* **87**, 546 (1980b).
343   Van Dijk, T. A. Stories and racism. *Narrative and social control: Critical perspectives* **21**, 121-142 (1993).
344   Duncan, B. L. Differential social perception and attribution of intergroup violence: Testing the lower limits of stereotyping of Blacks. *Journal of personality and social psychology* **34**, 590 (1976).
345   Allport, G. W. *The Nature of Prejudice.* (Doubleday, 1958).
346   Sternberg, R. J. A duplex theory of hate: Development and application to terrorism, massacres, and genocide. *Review of general psychology* **7**, 299-328 (2003).
347   Rai, T. S., Valdesolo, P. & Graham, J. Dehumanization increases instrumental violence, but not moral violence. *Proceedings of the National Academy of Sciences* **114**, 8511-8516 (2017).
348   Vaughan, G. M. & Hogg, M. A. *Social psychology.* 365 (Pearson Higher Education AU, 2013f).

349 The Gallup Poll Social Audit on Black/White Relations in the United States. (1997).
350 Universities criticised for 'tokenistic' support for Black Lives Matter. (2020). <https://www.theguardian.com/education/2020/jul/06/universities-criticised-for-tokenistic-support-for-black-lives-matter>.
351 Fajardo, D. M. Author race, essay quality, and reverse discrimination. *Journal of Applied Social Psychology* **15**, 255-268 (1985).
352 Antisemitic incidents 2023. (2024). <https://cst.org.uk/news/blog/2024/02/15/antisemitic-incidents-report-2023>.
353 Vaughan, G. M. & Hogg, M. A. *Social psychology*. (Pearson Higher Education AU, 2013g).
354 Schiller, B. R. The economics of poverty and discrimination. *(No Title)* (1995).
355 Harris-Britt, A., Valrie, C. R., Kurtz-Costes, B. & Rowley, S. J. Perceived racial discrimination and self-esteem in African American youth: Racial socialization as a protective factor. *Journal of Research on Adolescence* **17**, 669-682 (2007).
356 Harris-Britt, A., Valrie, C. R., Kurtz-Costes, B. & Rowley, S. J. Perceived racial discrimination and self-esteem in African American youth: Racial socialization as a protective factor. *Journal of Research on Adolescence* **17**, 669-682 (2007a).
357 Rosenberg, M. *Conceiving The Self*. (Basic Books, 1979).
358 Easterbrook, M. J. & Hadden, I. R. Tackling educational inequalities with social psychology: Identities, contexts, and interventions. *Social Issues and Policy Review* **15**, 180-236 (2021).
359 Easterbrook, M. J. & Hadden, I. R. Tackling educational inequalities with social psychology: Identities, contexts, and interventions. *Social Issues and Policy Review* **15**, 180-236 (2021a).
360 Rosenthal, R. & Jacobson, L. Pygmalion in the classroom. *The urban review* **3**, 16-20 (1968).
361 Aronson, E. The Social Animal (7th edn) (1996).
362 Aronson, E. *The Social Animal (7th edn)*. 305 (WH Freeman, 1996a).
363 Snyder, M. & Swann, W. B. Hypothesis-testing processes in social interaction. *Journal of personality and social psychology* **36**, 1202 (1978).
364 Adorno, T. *The authoritarian personality*. (Verso Books, 2019).
365 Aronson, E. *The Social Animal (7th edn)*. 305 (WH Freeman, 1996b).
366 Ritzer, G. & Ryan, J. M. *The Concise Encyclopedia of Sociology*. 21 (Wiley, 2011).
367 Aronson, E. *The Social Animal (7th edn)*. 305 (WH Freeman, 1996c).
368 Sibley, C. G. & Duckitt, J. Personality and prejudice: A meta-analysis and theoretical review. *Personality and Social Psychology Review* **12**, 248-279 (2008).
369 Duckitt, J. Differential effects of right wing authoritarianism and social dominance orientation on outgroup attitudes and their mediation by threat from and competitiveness to outgroups. *Personality and Social Psychology Bulletin* **32**, 684-696 (2006).
370 Ostrom, T. M. & Sedikides, C. Out-group homogeneity effects in natural and minimal groups. *Psychological bulletin* **112**, 536 (1992).
371 Hackel, L. M., Looser, C. E. & Van Bavel, J. J. Group membership alters the threshold for mind perception: The role of social identity, collective identification, and intergroup threat. *Journal of Experimental Social Psychology* **52**, 15-23 (2014).

372   Van Dijk, T. A. Stories and racism. *Narrative and social control: Critical perspectives* **21**, 121-142 (1993a).
373   Pettigrew, T. F. Regional differences in anti-Negro prejudice. *The Journal of Abnormal and Social Psychology* **59**, 28 (1959).
374   Watson, J. Some social and psychological situations related to change in attitude. *Human Relations* **3**, 15-56 (1950).
375   Pettigrew, T. F. Personality and sociocultural factors in intergroup attitudes: A cross-national comparison. *Journal of conflict resolution* **2**, 29-42 (1958).
376   Kirkland, S. L., Greenberg, J. & Pyszczynski, T. Further evidence of the deleterious effects of overheard derogatory ethnic labels: Derogation beyond the target. *Personality and Social Psychology Bulletin* **13**, 216-227 (1987).
377   Hodson, G., Dovidio, J. F. & Gaertner, S. L. The aversive form of racism. *The psychology of prejudice and discrimination* **1**, 119-135 (2004).
378   Corenblum, B. & Stephan, W. G. White fears and native apprehensions: An integrated threat theory approach to intergroup attitudes. *Canadian Journal of Behavioural Science/Revue canadienne des sciences du comportement* **33**, 251 (2001).
379   Stephan, W. G. & Stephan, C. W. Intergroup anxiety. *Journal of social issues* **41**, 157-175 (1985).
380   Aronson, E. *The Social Animal (7th edn)*. 325 (WH Freeman, 1996d).
381   Jacobs, P., Landau, S. & Pell, E. To Serve the Devil, Vol. 2: Colonials and Sojourners. *New York: Vintage* (1971).
382   Hovland, C. I. & Sears, R. R. Minor studies of aggression: VI. Correlation of lynchings with economic indices. *The Journal of Psychology* **9**, 301-310 (1940).
383   Corenblum, B. & Stephan, W. G. White fears and native apprehensions: An integrated threat theory approach to intergroup attitudes. *Canadian Journal of Behavioural Science/Revue canadienne des sciences du comportement* **33**, 251 (2001a).
384   Bissell, K. & Parrott, S. Prejudice: The role of the media in the development of social bias. *Journalism & Communication Monographs* **15**, 219-270 (2013).
385   Bissell, K. & Parrott, S. Prejudice: The role of the media in the development of social bias. *Journalism & Communication Monographs* **15**, 219-270 (2013a).
386   Wahl, O. F. News media portrayal of mental illness: Implications for public policy. *American Behavioral Scientist* **46**, 1594-1600 (2003).
387   Mastro, D. E. & Greenberg, B. S. The portrayal of racial minorities on prime time television. *Journal of Broadcasting & Electronic Media* **44**, 690-703 (2000).
388   Harry to marry into gangster royalty? *Daily Star* (3rd November 2016). <https://www.dailystar.co.uk/news/latest-news/prince-harry-meghan-markle-gangster-17055768>.
389   Harry's girl is (almost) straight outta Compton. *Mail Online* (2nd November 2016). <https://www.dailymail.co.uk/news/article-3896180/Prince-Harry-s-girlfriend-actress-Meghan-Markles.html>.
390   Turvill, W. IPSO rejects accuracy complaint over Katie Hopkins' Sun 'cockroaches' column. (2015). <https://pressgazette.co.uk/publishers/nationals/ipso-rejects-accuracy-complaint-over-katie-hopkins-sun-cockroaches-column/ >.
391   UN Human Rights Chief urges U.K. to tackle tabloid hate speech, after migrants called "cockroaches". (2015). <https://www.ohchr.org/en/press-

	releases/2015/04/un-human-rights-chief-urges-uk-tackle-tabloid-hate-speech-after-migrants >.
392	Ford, T. E. Effects of stereotypical television portrayals of African-Americans on person perception. *Social psychology quarterly*, 266-275 (1997).
393	Rudman, L. A. & Borgida, E. The afterglow of construct accessibility: The behavioral consequences of priming men to view women as sexual objects. *Journal of Experimental Social Psychology* **31**, 493-517 (1995).
394	Van der Linden, S. *Foolproof: Why misinformation infects our minds and how to build immunity*. 131 (WW Norton & Company, 2023n).
395	Soral, W., Liu, J. & Bilewicz, M. Media of contempt: Social media consumption predicts normative acceptance of anti-Muslim hate speech and islamoprejudice. *International Journal of Conflict and Violence (IJCV)* **14**, 1-13 (2020).
396	Van der Linden, S. *Foolproof: Why misinformation infects our minds and how to build immunity*. 131 (WW Norton & Company, 2023o).
397	Faddoul, M., Chaslot, G. & Farid, H. A longitudinal analysis of YouTube's promotion of conspiracy videos. *arXiv preprint arXiv:2003.03318* (2020).
398	Brady, W. J., McLoughlin, K., Doan, T. N. & Crockett, M. J. How social learning amplifies moral outrage expression in online social networks. *Science Advances* **7**, eabe5641 (2021).
399	Kahn, K. B., Spencer, K. & Glaser, J. Online prejudice and discrimination: From dating to hating. *The social net: Understanding our online behavior* **2**, 201-219 (2013a).
400	Kahn, K. B., Spencer, K. & Glaser, J. Online prejudice and discrimination: From dating to hating. *The social net: Understanding our online behavior* **2**, 201-219 (2013b).
401	Cooban, A. EU stops advertising on X over hate speech. Fines could follow next year (2023). <https://edition.cnn.com/2023/11/22/tech/eu-advertising-x-hate-speech/index.html>.
402	O'Donoghue, D. Priti Patel's UK immigration proposals branded 'ugly, dog whistle politics'. (March 24 2021). <https://www.pressandjournal.co.uk/fp/politics/uk-politics/2999689/priti-patel-immigration/ >.
403	Valentino, N. A., Neuner, F. G. & Vandenbroek, L. M. The changing norms of racial political rhetoric and the end of racial priming. *The Journal of Politics* **80**, 757-771 (2018).
404	Valentino, N. A., Neuner, F. G. & Vandenbroek, L. M. The changing norms of racial political rhetoric and the end of racial priming. *The Journal of Politics* **80**, 757-771 (2018a).
405	Jardina, A. & Piston, S. Trickle-down racism: Trump's effect on whites' racist dehumanizing attitudes. *Current Research in Ecological and Social Psychology* **5**, 100158 (2023).
406	Jardina, A. & Piston, S. Trickle-down racism: Trump's effect on whites' racist dehumanizing attitudes. *Current Research in Ecological and Social Psychology* **5**, 100158 (2023a).
407	Jardina, A. & Piston, S. Trickle-down racism: Trump's effect on whites' racist dehumanizing attitudes. *Current Research in Ecological and Social Psychology* **5**, 100158 (2023b).
408	Jardina, A. & Piston, S. Trickle-down racism: Trump's effect on whites' racist dehumanizing attitudes. *Current Research in Ecological and Social Psychology* **5**, 100158 (2023c).
409	YouGov poll. (8th June 2020). < https://yougov.co.uk/topics/society/survey-results/daily/2020/06/08/1ab21/1>.

410 Racism is still a huge problem in UK's workplaces, finds report *Manchester University* (15th April 2019). <https://www.manchester.ac.uk/discover/news/racism-is-still-a-huge-problem/>.
411 Ashe, S., Borkowska, M. & Nazroo, J. (2020).
412 Police Race Action Plan. (2022).
413 Head of Britain's police chiefs says force 'institutionally racist'. (5th January 2024). < https://www.theguardian.com/uk-news/2024/jan/05/head-of-britains-police-chiefs-says-force-is-institutionally-racist-gavin-stephens>.
414 Hamed, S., Bradby, H., Ahlberg, B. M. & Thapar-Björkert, S. Racism in healthcare: a scoping review. *BMC Public Health* **22**, 988 (2022).
415 Birtel, M. D., Wood, L. & Kempa, N. J. Stigma and social support in substance abuse: Implications for mental health and well-being. *Psychiatry research* **252**, 1-8 (2017).
416 Gazzaniga, M. S., Heatherton, T. F. & Halpern, D. F. *Psychological science.* 502 (WW Norton New York, 2006h).
417 Kawakami, K., Dovidio, J. F. & van Kamp, S. Kicking the habit: Effects of nonstereotypic association training and correction processes on hiring decisions. *Journal of experimental social psychology* **41**, 68-75 (2005).
418 Blair, I. V. The malleability of automatic stereotypes and prejudice. *Personality and social psychology review* **6**, 242-261 (2002).
419 Monteith, M. J., Ashburn-Nardo, L., Voils, C. I. & Czopp, A. M. Putting the brakes on prejudice: on the development and operation of cues for control. *Journal of personality and social psychology* **83**, 1029 (2002).
420 Vaughan, G. M. & Hogg, M. A. *Social psychology.* 437 (Pearson Higher Education AU, 2013h).
421 Broockman, D. & Kalla, J. Durably reducing transphobia: A field experiment on door-to-door canvassing. *Science* **352**, 220-224 (2016).
422 Bruneau, E. G. & Saxe, R. The power of being heard: The benefits of 'perspective-giving'in the context of intergroup conflict. *Journal of experimental social psychology* **48**, 855-866 (2012).
423 vanden Heuvel, K. How did we avoid a Cuban Missile 'Armageddon'? Strategic empathy. (2022). <https://responsiblestatecraft.org/2022/10/12/what-the-cuban-missile-crisis-can-teach-us-about-the-war-in-ukraine/>.
424 Stephan, W. G. & Stephan, C. W. The role of ignorance in intergroup relations. *Groups in contact: The psychology of desegregation*, 229-255 (1984).
425 Stephan, W. G. & Stephan, C. W. The role of ignorance in intergroup relations. *Groups in contact: The psychology of desegregation*, 229-255 (1984a).
426 Turner, R. N. in *Oxford Research Encyclopedia of Psychology*   (2020).
427 Dovidio, J. F. *et al.* Perspective and prejudice: Antecedents and mediating mechanisms. *Personality and Social Psychology Bulletin* **30**, 1537-1549 (2004).
428 Turner, R. N. Conversation with Richard Docwra. (29th January 2024).
429 Turner, R. N. Conversation with Richard Docwra. (29th January 2024a).
430 Pettigrew, T. F. & Tropp, L. R. A meta-analytic test of intergroup contact theory. *Journal of personality and social psychology* **90**, 751 (2006).
431 Turner, R. N. in *Oxford Research Encyclopedia of Psychology*   (2020a).
432 White, F. A., Turner, R. N., Verrelli, S., Harvey, L. J. & Hanna, J. R. Improving intergroup relations between Catholics and Protestants in Northern Ireland via E-contact. *European Journal of Social Psychology* **49**, 429-438 (2019).

433 Turner, R. N. & Cameron, L. Confidence in contact: A new perspective on promoting cross-group friendship among children and adolescents. *Social issues and policy review* **10**, 212-246 (2016).
434 AJC. <https://www.ajc.org/translatehate/Soros>.
435 Dasgupta, N. & Greenwald, A. G. On the malleability of automatic attitudes: combating automatic prejudice with images of admired and disliked individuals. *Journal of personality and social psychology* **81**, 800 (2001).
436 Aronson, E. *The Social Animal (7th edn).* 344 (WH Freeman, 1996e).
437 Aronson, E. *The Social Animal (7th edn).* 347 (WH Freeman, 1996f).
438 Turner, R. N. Conversation with Richard Docwra. (29th January 2024b).
439 FTSE Women Leaders Review 2024. (2024). < https://ftsewomenleaders.com/ >.
440 Andrews, J. UK diversity in business statistics 2023. (2023). <https://www.money.co.uk/business/business-statistics/diversity-in-business-statistics>.
441 McCarthy, M. *On the Contrary.* (Creative Media Partners, LLC, 2023).
442 <https://www.oed.com/viewdictionaryentry/Entry/139215 >.
443 Global study on homicide 2023. *United Nations* (2023).
444 von Hippel, W. *The Social Leap: The New Evolutionary Science of Who We Are, Where We Come From, and What Makes Us Happy.* 27 (HarperCollins Publishers, 2022c).
445 Global study on homicide 2023. *United Nations* (2023a).
446 Waller, J. Perpetrators of genocide: An explanatory model of extraordinary human evil. *J. Hate Stud.* **1**, 5 (2001).
447 Dutton, D. G., Boyanowsky, E. O. & Bond, M. H. Extreme mass homicide: From military massacre to genocide. *Aggression and Violent Behavior* **10**, 437-473 (2005).
448 Dutton, D. G., Boyanowsky, E. O. & Bond, M. H. Extreme mass homicide: From military massacre to genocide. *Aggression and Violent Behavior* **10**, 437-473 (2005a).
449 Smith, R. Human destructiveness and politics: the twentieth century as an age of genocide. *Genocide and the modern age: Etiology and case studies of mass death* **2**, 21 (1987).
450 Dutton, D. G., Boyanowsky, E. O. & Bond, M. H. Extreme mass homicide: From military massacre to genocide. *Aggression and Violent Behavior* **10**, 437-473 (2005b).
451 Waller, J. Perpetrators of genocide: An explanatory model of extraordinary human evil. *J. Hate Stud.* **1**, 5 (2001a).
452 Dutton, D. G., Boyanowsky, E. O. & Bond, M. H. Extreme mass homicide: From military massacre to genocide. *Aggression and Violent Behavior* **10**, 437-473 (2005c).
453 Waller, J. Perpetrators of genocide: An explanatory model of extraordinary human evil. *J. Hate Stud.* **1**, 6 (2001b).
454 Estimated total populations, fatalities, and injuries during the atomic bombings of Hiroshima and Nagasaki from August 6-9, 1945 <https://www.statista.com/statistics/1369672/hiroshima-nagasaki-casualties/>.
455 Browne, M. 100 years of Maxim's 'Killing machine'. (26th November 1985). <https://www.nytimes.com/1985/11/26/science/100-years-of-maxim-s-killing-machine.html>.
456 Browne, M. 100 years of Maxim's 'Killing machine'. (26th November 1985a). <https://www.nytimes.com/1985/11/26/science/100-years-of-maxim-s-killing-machine.html>.

457 Vaughan, G. M. & Hogg, M. A. *Social psychology.* 466 (Pearson Higher Education AU, 2013i).
458 Carver, C. S. & Glass, D. C. Coronary-prone behavior pattern and interpersonal aggression. *Journal of personality and social psychology* **36**, 361 (1978).
459 Vaughan, G. M. & Hogg, M. A. *Social psychology.* 465 (Pearson Higher Education AU, 2013j).
460 Caramaschi, D., de Boer, S. F. & Koolhaas, J. M. Differential role of the 5-HT1A receptor in aggressive and non-aggressive mice: an across-strain comparison. *Physiology & behavior* **90**, 590-601 (2007).
461 Gazzaniga, M. S., Heatherton, T. F. & Halpern, D. F. *Psychological science.* 483 (WW Norton New York, 2006i).
462 Women in the justice system. (2022). <https://www.gov.scot/publications/women-justice-system/pages/5/>.
463 Gazzaniga, M. S., Heatherton, T. F. & Halpern, D. F. *Psychological science.* 483 (WW Norton New York, 2006j).
464 Mazur, A., Booth, A. & Dabbs Jr, J. M. Testosterone and chess competition. *Social Psychology Quarterly*, 70-77 (1992).
465 Vaughan, G. M. & Hogg, M. A. *Social psychology.* 452 (Pearson Higher Education AU, 2013k).
466 Geen, R. G. Aggression and antisocial behavior. (1998).
467 Vaughan, G. M. & Hogg, M. A. *Social psychology.* 459 (Pearson Higher Education AU, 2013l).
468 Bandura, A., Ross, D. & Ross, S. A. Imitation of film-mediated aggressive models. *The Journal of Abnormal and Social Psychology* **66**, 3 (1963).
469 Huesmann, L. R., Eron, L. D., Lefkowitz, M. M. & Walder, L. O. Stability of aggression over time and generations. *Developmental psychology* **20**, 1120 (1984).
470 Huesmann, L. R., Eron, L. D., Lefkowitz, M. M. & Walder, L. O. Stability of aggression over time and generations. *Developmental psychology* **20**, 1120 (1984a).
471 Huesmann, L. R., Eron, L. D., Lefkowitz, M. M. & Walder, L. O. Stability of aggression over time and generations. *Developmental psychology* **20**, 1120 (1984b).
472 Zillmann, D. (Erlbaum Associates, 1979).
473 Giancola, P. R. Individual difference and contextual factors contributing to the alcohol-aggression relation: Diverse populations, diverse methodologies: An introduction to the special issue. *Aggressive Behavior* **29**, 285-287 (2003). https://doi.org:10.1002/ab.10070
474 Gustafson, R. Alcohol and aggression: A replication study controlling for potential confounding variables. *Aggressive Behavior* **18**, 21-28 (1992).
475 Taylor, S. P. & Sears, J. D. The effects of alcohol and persuasive social pressure on human physical aggression. *Aggressive Behavior* **14**, 237-243 (1988).
476 Vaughan, G. M. & Hogg, M. A. *Social psychology.* 429 (Pearson Higher Education AU, 2013m).
477 Zimbardo, P. G. in *Nebraska symposium on motivation.* (University of Nebraska press).
478 Vaughan, G. M. & Hogg, M. A. *Social psychology.* 383 (Pearson Higher Education AU, 2013n).
479 Ndahiro, K. In Rwanda, we know all about dehumanizing language. *The Atlantic* **13** (2019).

480 Bandura, A., Underwood, B. & Fromson, M. E. Disinhibition of aggression through diffusion of responsibility and dehumanization of victims. *Journal of research in personality* **9**, 253-269 (1975).
481 Leyens, J. P., Demoulin, S., Vaes, J., Gaunt, R. & Paladino, M. P. Infrahumanization: The wall of group differences. *Social Issues and Policy Review* **1**, 139-172 (2007).
482 Aronson, E. *The Social Animal (7th edn).* 323 (WH Freeman, 1996g).
483 Bandura, A. in *Social referencing and the social construction of reality in infancy*   175-208 (Springer, 1992).
484 Cohen, D., Nisbett, R. E., Bowdle, B. F. & Schwarz, N. Insult, aggression, and the southern culture of honor: An" experimental ethnography.". *Journal of personality and social psychology* **70**, 945 (1996).
485 Gazzaniga, M. S., Heatherton, T. F. & Halpern, D. F. *Psychological science.* 482 (WW Norton New York, 2006k).
486 Winchester, N. Trends in Violent Crime. (2023). <https://lordslibrary.parliament.uk/trends-in-violent-crime/#heading-7>.
487 Tolan, P. H. & GORMAN–SMITH, D. What violence prevention research can tell us about developmental psychopathology. *Development and psychopathology* **14**, 713-729 (2002).
488 Vaughan, G. M. & Hogg, M. A. *Social psychology.* 475 (Pearson Higher Education AU, 2013o).
489 Dutton, D. G., Boyanowsky, E. O. & Bond, M. H. Extreme mass homicide: From military massacre to genocide. *Aggression and Violent Behavior* **10**, 437-473 (2005d).
490 Global study on homicide 2023. *United Nations* (2023b).
491 Ng, B., Kumar, S., Ranclaud, M. & Robinson, E. Ward crowding and incidents of violence on an acute psychiatric inpatient unit. *Psychiatric Services* **52**, 521-525 (2001).
492 Tinson, A. Overcrowding is highest for those with low incomes. (2020). <https://www.health.org.uk/news-and-comment/charts-and-infographics/overcrowding-is-highest-for-those-with-low-incomes>.
493 Harries, K. D. & Stadler, S. J. Determinism revisited: Assault and heat stress in Dallas, 1980. *Environment and Behavior* **15**, 235-256 (1983).
494 Carlsmith, J. M. & Anderson, C. A. Ambient temperature and the occurrence of collective violence: a new analysis. *Journal of personality and social psychology* **37**, 337 (1979).
495 Cohn, E. G. The prediction of police calls for service: The influence of weather and temporal variables on rape and domestic violence. *Journal of environmental psychology* **13**, 71-83 (1993).
496 Maes, M., De Meyer, F., Thompson, P., Peeters, D. & Cosyns, P. Synchronized annual rhythms in violent suicide rate, ambient temperature and the light-dark span. *Acta Psychiatrica Scandinavica* **90**, 391-396 (1994).
497 Collaborators, G. P. V. U. S. Fatal police violence by race and state in the USA, 1980–2019: a network meta-regression. *The Lancet* **398**, 1239-1255 (2021).
498 How George Floyd Died, and What Happened Next (July 29, 2022). <https://www.nytimes.com/article/george-floyd.html>.
499 Hughes, C. Addressing violence in education: From policy to practice. *Prospects* **48**, 23-38 (2020).
500 Modecki, K. L., Minchin, J., Harbaugh, A. G., Guerra, N. G. & Runions, K. C. Bullying prevalence across contexts: A meta-analysis measuring cyber and traditional bullying. *Journal of Adolescent Health* **55**, 602-611 (2014).
501 Wolke, D. & Lereya, S. T. Long-term effects of bullying. *Archives of disease in childhood* **100**, 879-885 (2015).

502 Janowski, K. UN Says Russia Continues to Torture, Execute Ukrainian POWs. *United Nations* (26th March 2024). < https://ukraine.un.org/en/264368-un-says-russia-continues-torture-execute-ukrainian-pows>.
503 Global study on homicide 2023. *United Nations* (2023c).
504 Dutton, D. G., Boyanowsky, E. O. & Bond, M. H. Extreme mass homicide: From military massacre to genocide. *Aggression and Violent Behavior* **10**, 437-473 (2005e).
505 Browne, K. D. & Hamilton-Giachritsis, C. The influence of violent media on children and adolescents: a public-health approach. *The Lancet* **365**, 702-710 (2005a).
506 Federman, J. *National television violence study: Executive summary*. (University of California. Center for Communication and Social Policy, 1995).
507 Patton, D. U. et al. Social media as a vector for youth violence: A review of the literature. *Computers in Human Behavior* **35**, 548-553 (2014).
508 Patchin, J. & Hinduja, S.   (2013).
509 Patton, D. U. et al. Social media as a vector for youth violence: A review of the literature. *Computers in Human Behavior* **35**, 548-553 (2014a).
510 Kiilakoski, T. & Oksanen, A. Cultural and peer influences on homicidal violence: A Finnish perspective. *New Directions for Youth Development* **2011**, 31-42 (2011).
511 Kiilakoski, T. & Oksanen, A. Cultural and peer influences on homicidal violence: A Finnish perspective. *New Directions for Youth Development* **2011**, 31-42 (2011a).
512 Patton, D. U. et al. Social media as a vector for youth violence: A review of the literature. *Computers in Human Behavior* **35**, 548-553 (2014c).
513 Transcript of Trump's speech at January 6th rally. (2021). < https://www.npr.org/2021/02/10/966396848/read-trumps-jan-6-speech-a-key-part-of-impeachment-trial>.
514 Dutton, D. G., Boyanowsky, E. O. & Bond, M. H. Extreme mass homicide: From military massacre to genocide. *Aggression and Violent Behavior* **10**, 437-473 (2005f).
515 Dutton, D. G., Boyanowsky, E. O. & Bond, M. H. Extreme mass homicide: From military massacre to genocide. *Aggression and Violent Behavior* **10**, 437-473 (2005g).
516 Browning, C. R. *Ordinary Men: Reserve Police Battalion 101 and the Final Solution in Poland*. The story of Battalion 101 has been taken from the book 'Ordinary Men: Reserve Police Battalion 101 and the Final Solution in Poland' by Robert Browning, and the accompanying 2023 Netflix TV series of the same name. The book is highly recommended for a deeper understanding of the story of the unit and the factors influencing the behaviour of its members. (HarperCollins, 2017).
517 Waller, J. E. *Becoming evil: How ordinary people commit genocide and mass killing*. (Oxford University Press, 2007).
518 Browning, C. R. *Ordinary Men: Reserve Police Battalion 101 and the Final Solution in Poland*. (HarperCollins, 2017a).
519 Waller, J. Perpetrators of genocide: An explanatory model of extraordinary human evil. *J. Hate Stud.* **1**, 13 (2001c).
520 Waller, J. E. *Becoming evil: How ordinary people commit genocide and mass killing*. (Oxford University Press, 2007a).
521 Buss, D. *Evolutionary psychology: The new science of the mind.* (Routledge, 2019).

522 Leader Maynard, J. Rethinking the role of ideology in mass atrocities. *Terrorism and Political Violence* **26**, 821-841 (2014).
523 Waller, J. E. *Becoming evil: How ordinary people commit genocide and mass killing*. (Oxford University Press, 2007b).
524 Dutton, D. G., Boyanowsky, E. O. & Bond, M. H. Extreme mass homicide: From military massacre to genocide. *Aggression and Violent Behavior* **10**, 437-473 (2005h).
525 Browning, C. R. *Ordinary Men: Reserve Police Battalion 101 and the Final Solution in Poland*. 172 (HarperCollins, 2017b).
526 Browning, C. R. *Ordinary Men: Reserve Police Battalion 101 and the Final Solution in Poland*. 173 (HarperCollins, 2017c).
527 Waller, J. E. *Becoming evil: How ordinary people commit genocide and mass killing*. 213 (Oxford University Press, 2007d).
528 Browning, C. R. *Ordinary Men: Reserve Police Battalion 101 and the Final Solution in Poland*. 77 (HarperCollins, 2017d).
529 Waller, J. E. *Becoming evil: How ordinary people commit genocide and mass killing*. 234 (Oxford University Press, 2007f).
530 Haney, C., Banks, C., Zimbardo, P. & Aronson, E. *A study of prisoners and guards in a simulated prison*. (1973a).
531 Waller, J. E. *Becoming evil: How ordinary people commit genocide and mass killing*. 257 (Oxford University Press, 2007g).
532 Browning, C. R. *Ordinary Men: Reserve Police Battalion 101 and the Final Solution in Poland*. 72 (HarperCollins, 2017e).
533 Waller, J. Perpetrators of genocide: An explanatory model of extraordinary human evil. *J. Hate Stud.* **1**, 21 (2001d).
534 Waller, J. Perpetrators of genocide: An explanatory model of extraordinary human evil. *J. Hate Stud.* **1**, 7 (2001e).
535 Choosing cruelty: The psychology of perpetrators (2015). <https://www.facinghistory.org/resource-library/choosing-cruelty-psychology-perpetrators>.
536 Brown, R. & Wade, G. Superordinate goals and intergroup behaviour: The effect of role ambiguity and status on intergroup attitudes and task performance. *European Journal of Social Psychology* **17**, 131-142 (1987).
537 Vaughan, G. M. & Hogg, M. A. *Social psychology*. 443 (Pearson Higher Education AU, 2013p).
538 Waller, J. E. *Becoming evil: How ordinary people commit genocide and mass killing*. 292 (Oxford University Press, 2007h).
539 Relations, U. o. O. I. o. G. & Sherif, M. *Intergroup conflict and cooperation: The Robbers Cave experiment*. Vol. 10 (University Book Exchange Norman, OK, 1961).
540 Blake, R. R. & Mouton, J. S. From theory to practice in interface problem solving. *Psychology of intergroup relations* **2**, 67-87 (1986).
541 Loftin, C., McDowall, D., Wiersema, B. & Cottey, T. J. Effects of restrictive licensing of handguns on homicide and suicide in the District of Columbia. *New England Journal of Medicine* **325**, 1615-1620 (1991).
542 Dodd, V. Met police found to be institutionally racist, misogynistic and homophobic. *The guardian [Internet]* (2023).
543 Frequentlly Asked Questions <https://dangerousspeech.org/faq/?faq=578 >.
544 Connolly, K. Panel rethinks death toll from Dresden raids. (3rd October 2008). <https://www.theguardian.com/world/2008/oct/03/secondworldwar.germany>.
545 Regan, D. T. Effects of a favor and liking on compliance. *Journal of experimental social psychology* **7**, 627-639 (1971).

546 Klein, E. *Why we're polarized.* 253-257 (Simon and Schuster, 2020a).
547 Dutton, D. G., Boyanowsky, E. O. & Bond, M. H. Extreme mass homicide: From military massacre to genocide. *Aggression and Violent Behavior* **10**, 437-473 (2005i).
548 Power, S. *"A problem from hell": America and the age of genocide.* (Basic Books, 2013).
549 Waller, J. E. *Becoming evil: How ordinary people commit genocide and mass killing.* 257 (Oxford University Press, 2007i).
550 Ferragamo, K. The role of the international Criminal Court. (2023). <https://www.cfr.org/backgrounder/role-international-criminal-court>.
551 Ferragamo, K. The role of the international Criminal Court. (2023a). <https://www.cfr.org/backgrounder/role-international-criminal-court>.
552 The State of the Global Climate 2020. (2021). <library.wmo.int>.
553 Tracking Climate Action: How the World Can Still Limit Warming to 1.5 Degrees C. (2023). <https://www.wri.org/insights/climate-action-progress-1-5-degrees-c >.
554 Tracking Climate Action: How the World Can Still Limit Warming to 1.5 Degrees C. (2023a). <https://www.wri.org/insights/climate-action-progress-1-5-degrees-c >.
555 Lynas, M., Houlton, B. Z. & Perry, S. Greater than 99% consensus on human caused climate change in the peer-reviewed scientific literature. *Environmental Research Letters* **16**, 114005 (2021).
556 Public perceptions on climate change report *Pertitia* (2022).
557 Lynas, M., Houlton, B. Z. & Perry, S. Greater than 99% consensus on human caused climate change in the peer-reviewed scientific literature. *Environmental Research Letters* **16**, 114005 (2021a).
558 Kahan, D. M., Peters, E., Dawson, E. C. & Slovic, P. Motivated numeracy and enlightened self-government. *Behavioural public policy* **1**, 54-86 (2017a).
559 Luo, Y. & Zhao, J. Motivated attention in climate change perception and action. *Frontiers in psychology* **10**, 1541 (2019a).
560 Böhm, G., Pfister, H.-R., Salway, A. & Fløttum, K. Remembering and communicating climate change narratives–The influence of world views on selective recollection. *Frontiers in Psychology* **10**, 1026 (2019).
561 Dunbar, R. I. Neocortex size as a constraint on group size in primates. *Journal of human evolution* **22**, 469-493 (1992).
562 Grapsas, S., Becht, A. I. & Thomaes, S. Self-focused value profiles relate to climate change skepticism in young adolescents. *Journal of Environmental Psychology* **87**, 101978 (2023).
563 Earth Day 2023 Public opinion on climate change report. *Ipsos Global Advisor* (2023).
564 Earth Day 2023 Public opinion on climate change report. *Ipsos Global Advisor* (2023a).
565 Designing Socially Acceptable and Effective Climate Policies. *OECD* (2022).
566 Kahneman, D. & Tversky, A. in *Handbook of the fundamentals of financial decision making: Part I*   99-127 (World Scientific, 2013).
567 Why do we buy insurance? <https://thedecisionlab.com/biases/loss-aversion>.
568 Designing Socially Acceptable and Effective Climate Policies. *OECD* (2022a).
569 Climate Change 2021: The Physical Science Basis (2021). <https://www.ipcc.ch/report/sixth-assessment-report-working-group-i/>.
570 Thriving within our planetary means report. (2021). <https://www.wwf.org.uk/what-we-do/uk-global-footprint>.

571 'Climate villain': scientists say Rupert Murdoch wielded his media empire to sow confusion and doubt (23rd September 2023). <https://www.theguardian.com/media/2023/sep/23/rupert-murdoch-climate-change-denial#:~:text=Murdoch%20described%20himself%20in%202015,Independent%20bodies%20have%20challenged%20this>.

572 Feldman, L., Maibach, E. W., Roser-Renouf, C. & Leiserowitz, A. Climate on cable: The nature and impact of global warming coverage on Fox News, CNN, and MSNBC. *The International Journal of Press/Politics* **17**, 3-31 (2012).

573 The Carbon Policy Footprint Report 2021. (2021). <https://influencemap.org/report/The-Carbon-Policy-Footprint-Report-2021-670f36863e7859e1ad7848ec601dda97>.

574 How the oil majors have spent $1Bn since Paris on narrative capture and lobbying on climate. (2019). <https://influencemap.org/report/How-Big-Oil-Continues-to-Oppose-the-Paris-Agreement-38212275958aa21196dae3b76220bddc>.

575 OPEC Share of Crude Oil Reserves. (2023). <https://www.opec.org/opec_web/en/data_graphs/330.htm>.

576 Dowler, C. a. Leaked documents reveal the fossil fuel and meat producing countries lobbying against climate action (2021). <https://unearthed.greenpeace.org/2021/10/21/leaked-climate-lobbying-ipcc-glasgow/>.

577 Revealed: Saudi Arabia's grand plan to 'hook' poor countries on oil. (27th November 2023). <https://www.theguardian.com/environment/2023/nov/27/revealed-saudi-arabia-plan-poor-countries-oil>.

578 President Biden's Historic Climate Agenda. *The White House* (2021). <https://www.whitehouse.gov/climate/>.

579 Gross, S. What is the Trump administration's track record on the environment? (2020). <https://www.brookings.edu/articles/what-is-the-trump-administrations-track-record-on-the-environment/>.

580 Gen Z, Millennials Stand Out for Climate Change Activism, Social Media Engagement With Issue. (2021). <https://www.pewresearch.org/science/2021/05/26/gen-z-millennials-stand-out-for-climate-change-activism-social-media-engagement-with-issue/>.

581 Collignon, S., Makropoulos, I. & Rüdig, W. Consensus secured? Elite and public attitudes to "lockdown" measures to combat Covid-19 in England. *Journal of Elections, Public Opinion and Parties* **31**, 109-121 (2021).

582 Rosenmann, A., Reese, G. & Cameron, J. E. Social identities in a globalized world: Challenges and opportunities for collective action. *Perspectives on psychological science* **11**, 202-221 (2016).

583 von Hippel, W. *The Social Leap: The New Evolutionary Science of Who We Are, Where We Come From, and What Makes Us Happy*. 197 (HarperCollins Publishers, 2022d).

584 Rosenmann, A., Reese, G. & Cameron, J. E. Social identities in a globalized world: Challenges and opportunities for collective action. *Perspectives on psychological science* **11**, 202-221 (2016a).

585 Bonyhady, N. The big money behind the teals' big victory. (November 7, 2022). <https://www.smh.com.au/politics/federal/the-big-money-behind-the-teals-big-victory-20221106-p5bvxb.html>.

586 Kahneman, D. & Deaton, A. High income improves evaluation of life but not emotional well-being. *Proceedings of the national academy of sciences* **107**, 16489-16493 (2010).

587	The Silk Mill Vision of a Nature Connected Society. (2023). <https://findingnature.org.uk/2023/09/18/the-silk-mill-vision/>.
588	The Silk Mill Vision of a Nature Connected Society. (2023a). <https://findingnature.org.uk/2023/09/18/the-silk-mill-vision/>.
589	Designing Socially Acceptable and Effective Climate Policies. *OECD* (2022b).
590	Chen, M.-F. in *Social and Environmental Issues in Advertising* 84-102 (Routledge, 2018).
591	Designing Socially Acceptable and Effective Climate Policies. *OECD* (2022c).
592	Price of aviation. *Transport & Environment*
593	Fritsche, I., Barth, M., Jugert, P., Masson, T. & Reese, G. A social identity model of pro-environmental action (SIMPEA). *Psychological review* **125**, 245 (2018).
594	Nolan, J. M., Schultz, P. W., Cialdini, R. B., Goldstein, N. J. & Griskevicius, V. Normative social influence is underdetected. *Personality and social psychology bulletin* **34**, 913-923 (2008).
595	Fritsche, I., Barth, M., Jugert, P., Masson, T. & Reese, G. A social identity model of pro-environmental action (SIMPEA). *Psychological review* **125**, 245 (2018a).
596	Schultz, T. & Fielding, K. The common in-group identity model enhances communication about recycled water. *Journal of Environmental Psychology* **40**, 296-305 (2014).
597	Fielding, K. S. & Hornsey, M. J. A Social Identity Analysis of Climate Change and Environmental Attitudes and Behaviors: Insights and Opportunities. *Frontiers in Psychology* **7** (2016). https://doi.org/10.3389/fpsyg.2016.00121
598	Tracking Climate Action: How the World Can Still Limit Warming to 1.5 Degrees C. (2023b). <https://www.wri.org/insights/climate-action-progress-1-5-degrees-c >.
599	von Hippel, W. *The Social Leap: The New Evolutionary Science of Who We Are, Where We Come From, and What Makes Us Happy.* 185 (HarperCollins Publishers, 2022e).
600	Brady, W. J., McLoughlin, K., Doan, T. N. & Crockett, M. J. How social learning amplifies moral outrage expression in online social networks. *Science Advances* **7**, eabe5641 (2021a).
601	Brady, W. J., McLoughlin, K., Doan, T. N. & Crockett, M. J. How social learning amplifies moral outrage expression in online social networks. *Science Advances* **7**, eabe5641 (2021b).
602	Uyeda, J. C., Hansen, T. F., Arnold, S. J. & Pienaar, J. The million-year wait for macroevolutionary bursts. *Proceedings of the National Academy of Sciences* **108**, 15908-15913 (2011).
603	Flynn, J. R. Requiem for nutrition as the cause of IQ gains: Raven's gains in Britain 1938–2008. *Economics & Human Biology* **7**, 18-27 (2009).
604	Flynn, J. R. Requiem for nutrition as the cause of IQ gains: Raven's gains in Britain 1938–2008. *Economics & Human Biology* **7**, 18-27 (2009a).
605	Jackson, P. From Stockholm to Kyoto: A brief history of climate change. *UN Chronicle* **44** (2007).
606	Heath, J. *Enlightenment 2.0.* (HarperCollins Canada, 2014d).
607	Voigtländer, N. & Voth, H.-J. Nazi indoctrination and anti-Semitic beliefs in Germany. *Proceedings of the National Academy of Sciences* **112**, 7931-7936 (2015).

608 Voigtländer, N. & Voth, H.-J. Nazi indoctrination and anti-Semitic beliefs in Germany. *Proceedings of the National Academy of Sciences* **112**, 7931-7936 (2015a).
609 Heath, J. *Enlightenment 2.0.* 209 (HarperCollins Canada, 2014).
610 FDR and the Four Freedoms Speech. *Franklin D. Roosevelt Presidential Library and Museum* (1941).
611 'Freedom' definition. *Cambridge Dictionary.* <https://dictionary.cambridge.org/dictionary/english/freedom>.
612 Hobbes, T. *Leviathan.* (Dover Publications, 2012).
613 Kahneman, D. *Thinking, fast and slow.* 411 (Farrar, Straus and Giroux, 2011x).
614 Heath, J. *Enlightenment 2.0.* 324 (HarperCollins Canada, 2014a).
615 Thaler, R. H. & Sunstein, C. R. *Nudge: The Final Edition.* (Penguin Books Limited, 2012).
616 Heath, J. *Enlightenment 2.0.* 97 (HarperCollins Canada, 2014b).
617 Dunbar, R. I. Neocortex size as a constraint on group size in primates. *Journal of human evolution* **22**, 469-493 (1992a).
618 von Hippel, W. *The Social Leap: The New Evolutionary Science of Who We Are, Where We Come From, and What Makes Us Happy.* 208 (HarperCollins Publishers, 2022f).
619 von Hippel, W. *The Social Leap: The New Evolutionary Science of Who We Are, Where We Come From, and What Makes Us Happy.* 126 (HarperCollins Publishers, 2022g).
620 Kahneman, D. *Thinking, fast and slow.* 411 (Farrar, Straus and Giroux, 2011y).
621 How connecting with nature benefits our mental health. (2021).
622 Richardson, M., McEwan, K., Maratos, F. & Sheffield, D. Joy and calm: How an evolutionary functional model of affect regulation informs positive emotions in nature. *Evolutionary Psychological Science* **2**, 308-320 (2016).
623 How connecting with nature benefits our mental health. (2021a).
624 Kahneman, D. *Thinking, fast and slow.* 413 (Farrar, Straus and Giroux, 2011z).
625 Einstein, A. *The World As I See It.* (Book Tree, 2007).
626 Snyder, T. *On Tyranny: Twenty Lessons from the Twentieth Century.* (Random House, 2017a).
627 Solt, F. Economic inequality and democratic political engagement. *American journal of political science* **52**, 48-60 (2008).
628 Jetten, J. et al. Consequences of economic inequality for the social and political vitality of society: A social identity analysis. *Political Psychology* **42**, 241-266 (2021).
629 Dutton, D. G., Boyanowsky, E. O. & Bond, M. H. Extreme mass homicide: From military massacre to genocide. *Aggression and Violent Behavior* **10**, 455 (2005j).
630 Inglehart, R. *Cultural Evolution: People's Motivations are Changing, and Reshaping the World.* 214 (Cambridge University Press, 2018).
631 Heath, J. *Enlightenment 2.0.* 346 (HarperCollins Canada, 2014c).
632 Why do we take mental shortcuts? *Decision Lab.* <https://thedecisionlab.com/biases/heuristics#:~:text=In%20their%20paper%20%E2%80%9CJudgment%20Under,well%20as%20anchoring%20and%20adjustment>.
633 Thaler, R. H. *Misbehaving: The Making of Behavioural Economics.* (Penguin Books Limited, 2015).
634 Raworth, K. *Doughnut Economics: The must-read book that redefines economics for a world in crisis.* (Random House, 2017).

635 Maslach, C. & Leiter, M. P. Understanding the burnout experience: recent research and its implications for psychiatry. *World psychiatry* **15**, 103-111 (2016).
636 Kelly, O. *et al.* The Four Day Week: Assessing global trials of reduced work time with no reduction in pay: Evidence from Ireland. Report No. 1910963658, (University College Dublin, 2022).
637 Forgas, J. in *Humans and Hope* (ed R Docwra) (Docwra, R, 2021).
638 Monbiot, G. *Regenesis: Feeding the World without Devouring the Planet.* (Penguin Books Limited, 2022).

Milton Keynes UK
Ingram Content Group UK Ltd.
UKHW020733210924
448561UK00010B/152